Ivan Van Laningham

SAMS Teach Yourself

Python in 24 Hours

SAMS
A Division of Macmillan USA
201 West 103rd St., Indianapolis, Indiana, 46290 USA

Sams Teach Yourself Python in 24 Hours

International Standard Book Number: 0-672-31735-4

Library of Congress Catalog Card Number: 99-65588

Printed in the United States of America

First Printing: April 2000

02 01 00 4 3 2 1

Trademarks

All terms mentioned in this book that are known to be trademarks or service marks have been appropriately capitalized. Sams Publishing cannot attest to the accuracy of this information. Use of a term in this book should not be regarded as affecting the validity of any trademark or service mark.

Warning and Disclaimer

Every effort has been made to make this book as complete and as accurate as possible, but no warranty or fitness is implied. The information provided is on an "as is" basis.

Aquisitions Editor
Scott D. Meyers

Development Editor
Scott D. Meyers

Managing Editor
Charlotte Clapp

Project Editor
George E. Nedeff

Copy Editor
Barbara Hacha

Indexer
Heather McNeill

Technical Editor
Aahz Maruch

Team Coordinator
Amy Patton

Media Specialist
Craig Atkins

Interior Design
Gary Adair

Cover Design
Aren Howell

Copywriter
Eric Borgert

Layout Technicians
Ayanna Lacey
Heather Hiatt Miller
Stacey Richwine-DeRome

Contents at a Glance

Contents

About the Author

When there was a priesthood of computer operators, **Ivan Van Laningham** was a member; he helped create the Y2K problem. In college, he was an anthropology major, acquiring a continuing interest in archaeology and archaeoastronomy. He is now a software engineer for a voicemail company, but has also served in the Vietnam War, worked for the U.S. Postal Service, been a joat for a mobile home park, obtained his forklift operator's license, lost his shirt as a luthier, and clerked in a bookstore where he worked for his future wife. Since meeting UNIX in 1983 when hired as a hardware technician for a company later purchased by Motorola, he has been programming in C and C++ for a living (currently on Windows platforms). His other computer languages include 1401 Autocoder, COBOL, RPG, Sinclair Basic, PostScript, and Lisp. He has been programming in X Windows since X11R2. His heart has been with Python since encountering *Programming Python* at the University of British Columbia bookstore. Each year in March, he attends the Maya Meetings (`http://copan.bioz.unibas.ch/meso/infotexasmeet98.html`) in Austin, Texas, a ten-day international conference and workshop on Mayan hieroglyphic writing. Ivan works as a software engineer for Callware Technologies, Inc. (`http://www.callware.com`), a voicemail company in Salt LakeCity.

Dedication

To my parents, Naomi and George, and their parents, Sarah, Leslie, Florence, and Leon, all of whom taught me that it is sometimes necessary to feed your hand to a tiger if you want to find out how the teeth work.

Acknowledgments

Some years ago, the artist Christo Javacheff (`http://www.artcyclopedia.com/artists/christo.html`) built a work of art called "Running Fence," a fence that ran from coast to coast across the United States. Books are like this fence: connections among widely separated points in time and space.

This is why any attempt to thank everyone who contributed to this book is doomed to failure. In some sense, this book was written by all the people I have ever known. All I can do is to single out a very few people for special mention. Some who have been forgotten will know who they are, and are invited to email me so that I may set the record straight online. Others may have no idea that they had anything to do with this book, even though the absence of their contributions would have meant the absence of this book.

I would like to thank Fred Segovich and Peter Ahlsberg who in 1983 invited me to join a community of passionate eccentrics because they thought I would fit in. They were right, and even though I left that community in 1990, the community has never left me.

I would like to thank Patrick E. Kane and William Bradford Smith. Pat said "sure" at exactly the right time and changed my life. Bill helped me through my early, panic-stricken, encounters with UNIX with his cheerful attitude and plain conviction that "it's just a bunch of bits, Ivan." I would also like to thank Bill, and the other members of the "Chanute Mafia," for his (and their) service to our country in a time of great trouble. Keep 'em flying, Bill.

More directly, Pat helped by testing many of the programs in this book to make sure that they would run on his bizarre collection of hardware.

For stimulating conversation and dialogue about a wide range of subjects more or less related to this book, including Python, Mayan epigraphy, Zen Buddhism, Chinese snakes, split ergativity, and Vietnam, I would like to thank (in no particular order): Gordon McMillan, Tim Peters, Andrew M. Kuchling, Guido van Rossum, Fredrik Lundh, David Ascher, Mark Minaga, Charles E. Reed, Dan Bammes, Ellen Emerson White, Amy

Sedivy, Xuhua (Howard) Lin, Ying Wang, Duncan Steele, Simon Cassidy, Paul Hill, John Justeson, Lloyd B. Anderson, Nicholas Hopkins, J. Kathryn Josserand, Dave Beazley, Andy Robinson, Marilyn Knapp Litt (hi, LG!), Karen Offutt, Bobbie Keith, and the Fred formerly known as Fred.

I would also like to thank Xuhua (Howard) Lin, for the wonderful calligraphy, "Python Mind, Beginner's Mind," which appears at the end of Hour 24.

I would like to thank the author who anonymously posted the Klingon programming aphorisms to the Web. I have adapted some of these aphorisms for use in Hour 7.

I would like to thank John Esser and Mike Hess for making Callware a better place to work than it has ever been before.

Aahz Maruch deserves special mention for serving as the technical editor for this book; without his astute and sharp-eyed commentary, there would have been many more errors here for the readers to find. Thanks, Aahz: I knew you'd keep me honest. Scott Meyers, my editor for this book, should be nominated for boddhisatva-hood (if there isn't any such word, there ought to be), due to the mass quantities of patience and forbearance he was required to bring to bear on this project. Other members of the team at Sams deserve mention: Katie Robinson, Barbara Hacha, Gene Redding, Heather Mcneill, Amy Patton, George Nedeff, and all the others listed on the credits page. Thank you all.

Despite their careful attentions, however, I am sure that errors remain. A thousand years ago, the Mayans who built a great civilization in the jungles of Central America believed that mistakes in calendrical calculations were the fault not of the scribes or the astronomers, but were the result of direct intervention by the gods. I believe this too. If you find any errors in this book, please notify gods **A** through **Z** of the Mayan pantheon (`http://www.pauahtun.org/driveletter.html`).

I would like to thank Harley, Teddy Bear, and Trillin for reminding me of my real place in the scheme of things, and that cats come before Pythons, always. It's hard to be depressed when someone short is patting your nose with a paw.

I would like to thank my wife, Audrey Thompson, for the love, interest, humor, charm, and insight she brings to my life. I am every day more and more delighted to be part of the greatest conversation of all.

Tell Us What You Think!

As the reader of this book, *you* are our most important critic and commentator. We value your opinion and want to know what we're doing right, what we could do better, what areas you'd like to see us publish in, and any other words of wisdom you're willing to pass our way.

You can email or write me directly to let me know what you did or didn't like about this book—as well as what we can do to make our books stronger.

Please note that I cannot help you with technical problems related to the topic of this book, and that due to the high volume of mail I receive, I might not be able to reply to every message.

When you write, please be sure to include this book's title and author as well as your name and phone or fax number. I will carefully review your comments and share them with the author and editors who worked on the book.

Email: `webdev_sams@mcp.com`

Mail: Mark Taber
Associate Publisher
Sams Publishing
201 West 103rd Street
Indianapolis, IN 46290 USA

Introduction

This book's primary aim is to teach you how to program. Only secondarily does it aim to teach you Python, perhaps the coolest programming language on the planet. You don't need to know any programming before you begin; all you need is the desire to learn. If you have a computer and a connection to the internet, you can get Python for free: see Hour 1 for details on how to obtain and install it. Python runs on more different kinds of operating systems than any other programming language, so you should be able to find a version to fit yours; Windows, Unix, Amiga, and Macintosh will all run Python just fine.

If you have never programmed before, you have a distinct advantage. Many people come to Python only after having spent years learning the arcane complexities of other, more difficult, programming languages, and they must begin by forgetting as much as they can about those other languages. You, on the other hand, don't have any preconceptions to overcome, and thus you have what is called, in Zen, "Beginner's Mind." People who have studied Zen for years purposely cultivate this state. In essence, every time they come to practice, or meditate, they strive to refrain from bringing what they already know to their practice. For they know that nothing prevents the learning of new things more than the knowledge of what has been learned. The aim of practice is to learn new things, or to see old things in a new way. Writers know this too. Just because you wrote a book once doesn't mean you know how to write a book; every book is different, every book, and every program, demands new thoughts, sometimes new approaches. If you have no approaches to discard, there are no approaches to block your learning. And sometimes you need approaches at right angles to every other approach you've ever tried.

Don't let the Zen scare you off, though. While Zen attitudes inform the book, you won't have to sit on funny cushions and endure painful cross-legged meditation sessions in order to learn how to program; what it does mean is that you should strive to forget your ordinary, day-to-day cares. Concentrate on practicing Python, not on understanding it, and simply aim as best you can to hit each day's target. Don't think about tomorrow's lesson or lessons, think about today's. This may seem like very elementary advice, so elementary that it doesn't need to be said; but you would be surprised at how many people attempt programming, and fail because they're too busy thinking about what they're going to do with programming once they learn it, how much money they're going to make, or what big problems they're going to solve.

You're not qualified to think about those things until you know how to program. If you spend time thinking about them, you won't have time to learn programming, and you will probably give up. If you give up, you will not be a very good programmer. If you pay attention to the lessons, and you practice, you can be a good programmer. If you practice until you can think in Python, and cultivate "Python Mind, Beginner's Mind," it is possible to become a great programmer. It's all in the mind, and all in the practice.

Python is an ideal first programming language; its syntax is simple, clear, and powerful, and it encourages you to write and think clearly. Unlike other programming languages you may have tried, or have heard of, there are few tricks, few gotchas, few complicated rules that you need to remember at all times in order to prevent your program from going wild. Programming in Python means that you will write more readable, more maintainable programs, and you will be grateful for this in the future. Some languages emphasize clever tricks, or the ability to perform highly complex tasks with just one line of code, at the expense of readability; if you can't read a program three weeks after you write it, then that means that you will have a hard time fixing problems in it later. And every program has problems that surface sometime during its lifetime; you already know, I'm sure, that these problems are called bugs. Python won't exterminate your bugs for you, but it does make it harder to put them in, in the first place. It makes it very easy to think about the problem you want to solve and not about the precise syntax of every punctuation mark.

All you need to succeed in programming Python is the ability to think clearly and the motivation to do so. Practice clarity of thought as you practice Python, and success at both will come to you, as will understanding.

How to Use This Book

This book is divided into 24 lessons, arranged in three groups of eight. Each lesson should take about an hour to complete; if you take more or less time, then that is what it takes for you. The three parts of the book, and their aims, are inspired by a famous Zen book by Shunryu Suzuki, *Zen Mind, Beginner's Mind*, which you do not have to read (it won't hurt you, though). The three parts of Suzuki's book are, in order, *Right Practice*, *Right Attitude*, and *Right Understanding*. The three parts of this book will teach you, in order, the basic elements of Python, the object model used in Python, and the graphical user interface many people use with Python. I will leave it as an exercise for you to determine how my three parts relate to Suzuki's.

Q&A, Quiz, and Exercises

At the end of each hour's lesson, you'll find three final sections.

- Q&A—a couple of questions with answers for common questions about the topic
- Quiz—some questions to test your knowledge
- Exercises—optional (but helpful) ways to increase your skills in Python

Practice each lesson, think about what you've done, and understand where the hour's activities fit into your overall programming plan. Before beginning the next hour, clear your mind and think only about the practice before you, not about the practice behind you. At the end of the book, if you have worked and understood all the examples and completed all the exercises, you should have a rock-solid foundation for further work in Python. There will be a great deal more to do, but what you will have learned in this book will take you a long way.

This Book's Web Site

Python is a language that is slow to change; this is by design. The creator of Python, Guido van Rossum, describes himself as a very conservative programmer. Changes to the language are undertaken only after a great deal of discussion between Guido and the proponents of the change, so it is very unlikely that programs written in earlier versions of Python will fail. However, that does occasionally happen. To keep posted of the latest news about Python, you should visit the language's official Web site: `http://www.python.org/`. There is a wealth of information there. For other valuable Python resources, visit *The Vaults of Parnassus* at `http://www.vex.net/parnassus/`.

You can download all the examples from this book at `http://www.pauahtun.org/TYPython/`, where the author maintains the code, a FAQ ("Frequently Asked Questions") for this book, and an errata sheet. Poking around the Web site will reveal why it is called "pauahtun.org." Comments about the book and error reports should be mailed to `ivanlan@callware.com`; if you can't get one of the programs to work, check the FAQ first to see if others have had the same problem: "the student must teach himself." If the FAQ doesn't answer your question the author will.

PART I

Python Mind, Beginner's Mind

Hour

Hour 1

What Is Python?

Beautiful is better than ugly.

—Tim Peters

The first hour of this book introduces Python: what it is, its history, and what it is and isn't good for. You won't even need a computer for this part unless you do the exercises that call for reading a paper on a Web site.

Why Program? Why Program in Python?

If all you want to do with a computer is balance your checkbook, you do not need to know how to program. Better tools are available—such as pencil, paper, and calculator. And if all you use your computer for is word processing and page layout, again, you don't need to learn programming; lots of programs are available that do what you want extremely well.

But if no software is available that does what you need, or if what exists is unsatisfactory, the only answer is to roll your own. This simple principle has probably led to more programming breakthroughs, and better software, than any other. Linux is the perfect example; Linus Torvalds, unhappy with existing implementations of UNIX for PCs, decided to write his own version. Today, Linux is popular enough to worry Bill Gates and Microsoft.

UNIX was developed at AT&T's laboratory in Murray Hill, New Jersey, in the early '70s. A powerful multiuser operating system, it was the brainchild of Dennis Ritchie, Brian Kernighan, and Ken Thompson, who had spare time and a spare computer that no one else wanted to use. Even this unwanted computer was much too expensive for home hobbyists until the late '80s. Those of us who used UNIX in our everyday jobs looked at the feeble operating systems available for PCs and just laughed. We were spoiled by our "big iron." In 1987, however, Andrew Tannenbaum developed a very small UNIX-like operating system that would run on home PCs; he called it *Minix*. Linus Torvalds later developed a more portable and more useful version of it called Linux, which has become at least as capable as commercial versions and runs even on very inexpensive home PCs. The major difference between Minix and Linux, in the early days, was that the licensing for Minix was more restrictive than that for Linux. The difference today is that thousands of Linux hobbyists are out there, and nearly everything that you could want to do has at least been started by someone else.

Scientists, especially, often have needs for software that doesn't exist and frequently write their own to further their own research agendas. Although I'm not a scientist, I do have a research agenda; I find the Mayan calendar fascinating, and I spent years writing C programs to help me pursue this interest. When I found Python, I rapidly abandoned the code I'd already written and reimplemented everything using Python. The programs and libraries I ended up with are cleaner, simpler, smaller, and much more powerful, and I was able to build everything I needed in far less time than the original code took.

Many other people find themselves in the position of having to learn at least some programming in order to automate repetitive, boring tasks. An example would be some small programs that collect a team's weekly reports from a special directory or folder, checks that everyone has updated their report, performs some simple processing to combine the individual reports into one, and prints the result or emails it to the team leader. I had to do something like this early in my programming career, and I succeeded, but with a great deal of hackery, using several different scripting languages. If Python had been available at the time, I could have done it in less time, with fewer lines of code, and in a single programming language.

Here is a list of several such repetitive tasks that I've had to deal with over the years; many of them can now be done satisfactorily in Python:

- Collecting reports, processing them into a larger one
- Checking URLs in a Web document for connectedness
- Periodically making backups of important files and directories
- Sending an automatic report by email to fool your boss into thinking you're really accomplishing something
- Automatically drawing PERT charts from much simpler input
- Making a list of every file in a particular directory tree, and doing different things with each file based on its suffix, or extension
- Making lists of files in a particular order, which can be used in other programs
- Keeping track of your video collection

In the past, writing your own software for special purposes meant learning a great deal of complicated and arcane syntax before even the simplest programs could be written. FORTRAN, an early but still popular language, is well suited to scientific programming because it has many useful mathematical features, but its syntax is—well, non-obvious. C, another language you've probably heard of, has many adherents because of the power it gives to the programmer, but it is not at all difficult to write tricky, almost unreadable programs with it. C programmers admit that the language encourages bad programming habits, but "FORTRAN enforces them." Python, in contrast, enforces—or at least encourages—good programming habits, and it attempts to shorten the learning curve so that the time spent learning details of the language is reduced as much as possible.

The following are some small working programs in FORTRAN, C, and Python; they don't do much, but the traditional beginner's program in any language merely prints the phrase "Hello, World" so that you can see it.

FORTRAN:

```
PROGRAM
    PRINT *, "Hello World"
END PROGRAM
```

C:

```
#include <stdio.h>
main() {
        printf("Hello World\n");
}
```

Python:

```
print "Hello World"
```

I believe that Python is very nearly the perfect first computer language; the syntax is relatively simple and unadorned, and instead of "many ways to do a thing," usually one obvious best way exists—or only a few good ways. Important features, some of them extremely useful for scientific programming, are built into the standard Python distribution instead of being add-on packages that must be tracked down, requiring considerable expertise to install. For fancier programming tasks, you do need to add an extension package called Tcl/Tk, but the Windows installation package will automatically add this for you. Despite the language's basic simplicity, it allows complex and sophisticated ideas to be expressed in an intuitive way because it applies, systematically and rigorously, a concept called *object-oriented programming* (OOP).

In the hours that follow, I will try to give you a solid understanding of the basics of Python programming. The first third of the book covers the most basic elements of Python. The middle third covers objects from the ground up because objects are of fundamental importance in using the full power of the language. The final third of the book covers Python's portable graphical user interface, *tkinter*. Also in the final third, we'll cover a bit of Web *common gateway interface* (CGI) programming, just to give you a hint of how useful such skills can be.

In this book, I assume you know nothing about programming. Without the preconceptions and unnecessary information acquired from other programming languages, you will have a distinct advantage, and I hope that it will become evident that programming computers is very often much easier that it is made out to be. I do, however, assume that you can use computers and have a basic knowledge of programs such as word processors, text editors and the command-line interface for your particular platform (DOS or your favorite shell such as *ksh*, *csh,* or *bash* on UNIX).

Although I've talked about many rational reasons to program, the final point I want to make is that building programs that work is fun. There's nothing quite like the thrill of being able to put together some basic instructions and seeing the result run exactly the way you imagined it on a computer—a machine that some people see as obstreperous and frustrating. Programming in Python, for me, has never been just a job. I hope that after you finish this book, you will be able to have just as much fun as I do in programming.

The History of Python

Python was developed in late 1989 by Guido van Rossum over a Christmas vacation when his research lab was closed and he had nowhere to go. He drew features from many other languages, such as *ABC*, *Modula-3*, *C* (at least the less controversial features), and several others. He was fond of watching *Monty Python's Flying Circus* on television, and when it came time to name the language, he chose Python. After use and experimentation among a small group of friends and colleagues, Python was released into the public domain in 1991. Unlike some other languages, Python is not only completely free, it has no restrictions whatsoever on its use. Programs developed in the language are not required to be released into the public domain, programmers are not required to submit changes back to Guido, and programs written in Python can be sold to and by anyone without licensing fees.

In addition to the language syntax itself, the decision to place Python in the public domain has been a major factor in its adoption worldwide. Other languages may have more users, but few languages can boast such a passionate user community as Python. Python may be a young programming language, but these passionate users gather for international conferences at least once a year, and sometimes more often.

The user community has created an informal organization dedicated to supporting and expanding the use of Python: the *Python Software Activity* (PSA), which has about 300 individual and 30 corporate members. Individual members pay good money to support Python; corporate members pay more. Membership is not required, it is strictly voluntary; no one ever has to pay a penny to use Python for any reason, so it is remarkable that so many have contributed to the language's growth.

In the early years, one question frequently asked was, "What if Guido gets hit by a bus?" The community worried that if Guido died, so would Python. In 1998, the *Python Consortium* was founded as a means for ensuring the survival and growth of Python. Corporate members of the consortium pay a substantial sum of money to Guido to work on Python (and nothing else), provide other useful services to the Python community, and appoint a successor for the time he might be unwilling or unable to direct the future course of Python.

It seems certain that Python will not just survive but will move into the twenty-first century with vigor. Guido describes himself as a "conservative programmer" who is determined that Python will change at his direction and only in directions that he thinks are necessary. A primary advantage of this outlook is that programs written in early versions of Python will continue to run unchanged, for the most part, in future versions. I began using Python when the version was 1.3, and it is now at 1.5.2; all the code I wrote still runs, without change, on the latest version. Version 1.5.2 is the basis for the examples and code snippets in this book; the next version, 1.6, is due out later in 1999 or early 2000, and should run, without change, all code given in this book. Sometime in late 2000 or early 2001, version 2.0 should go into beta, and almost all the code in this book should still run perfectly. Although the code here was written using 1.5.2, it has been tested on earlier versions, where possible. If you encounter any problems due to version differences, check the book's Web site for any corrections already noted. If you don't find a correction or revision at the Web site, write to the author with a full description of the problem.

`goto` Considered Harmful

In 1968, Edsger W. Dijkstra, one of the greats of programming, wrote a letter to the editor of *Communications of the ACM* in which he argued that the `goto` statement, a feature of virtually all programming languages at the time, had an adverse effect on programmers' thinking.

A `goto` is an instruction in computer language that tells the computer to go to another place in the program and execute the instructions found there. When those instructions are finished, the programmer must remember where the computer must be told to `goto` next. Programming without `goto`s is called *structured programming,* because it is usually quite clear to the programmer and readers what the program is doing at any one time. The use of `goto` in a program means that the actions of the program must be painstakingly traced, usually with a larger possibility of error.

In 1968, the vast majority of programs were written in what is now known as *spaghetti code*, a style marked by lots of `goto`s, no modularization, and few subroutines. We'll discuss subroutines, or procedures and functions, in later lessons, as well as modularization.

I was writing COBOL programs in 1968. Like everyone else, I wrote spaghetti code; that stuff was darn hard to read, even for the author, and nearly impossible to read unless you wrote it. The only structured programming constructs were of limited utility; they were hard to use, and documentation was hard to get. Often, the only way to determine the logic of a program was by referring to something called a *flowchart*, a specialized diagram with particular symbols for input, output, and decisions. If the author of the program didn't draw a flowchart, the only way to get one was to feed the program to another program that read the first one and drew the diagram automatically. Few programs were written from flowcharts drawn beforehand—which was supposed to be the correct way to write a program. Speaking from personal experience, I can truthfully say that `goto` does, indeed, encourage you to make a mess of your program.

> COBOL is one of the earliest programming languages; it helped popularize the use of computers back in the era of large mainframe machines, such as the IBM 360. It was invented by Admiral Grace Hopper and colleagues. Admiral Hopper is known for the saying, "It is easier to obtain forgiveness than permission." COBOL was notable for being written in human-readable, understandable words, not specialized numbers meaningful only to computers. Today, it is considered hopelessly wordy. I considered including a "Hello, World" program to demonstrate just how wordy, but it was too long.

Both Benjamin Whorf and Noam Chomsky believe that language structures thinking; you can think only the thoughts that you have words to express. Very simply, if your language contains no future tense, you find it difficult (if not impossible) to think about events not in the past or present. Computer programming languages are good evidence for this viewpoint; if no "words" or methods exist in a computer language to express something you want to do, it is hard to think about the things you're not allowed to do. Initial programming languages were monolithic constructs, perpetrated (rather than created) to further the proprietary aims of the companies that invented them. It was almost impossible to add new features to the languages because you didn't have access to the source of the language or to the creators of the language. In addition, no provision had been made to allow programmers to add anything to the language that hadn't been thought of by the designers.

Extensibility became a goal for language designers; when Guido designed and built Python, he made it very easy to add features and modules to the language. He also left out the `goto` statement, providing instead many useful structured programming techniques, and he designed the language around a new set of principles: *object-oriented design*. Early software engineering theorists maintained that the data on which a program operated was paramount; define how your data was structured, they said, and the methods you used to manipulate it would be self-evident. Later, *objects*, software entities that combined both the structured data and the manipulative methods, would become even more important in programming. Guido made it easy to use objects in Python, much easier than most other languages. Some languages grafted objects into a primarily linear core, but Python was designed from the outset to have an object orientation. You can *think* about objects in Python, and we'll spend several hours on mastering the skills and techniques of object-oriented programming in the second third of the book. You'll find that when you can think about objects, it is extremely simple to implement them in Python.

What Python Is and Is Not Good At

Python is an excellent language for many purposes. Python programs can take the place of shell scripts, sometimes reducing significantly the number of lines required to perform a job. Quite a few C++ programmers out there use Python for *prototyping*, which means that instead of writing out in laborious detail the specifications for a program, they build a prototype in Python that could include a *graphical user interface* (GUI). Because Python is so well designed, prototyping with it takes less time than writing or drawing a full specification (sometimes dramatically less time). Programmers who do this sort of thing also say that they end up with a better end product because Python encourages clear and elegant thinking. Even when the final shipping version of a product must be written in C++, they say that using Python first results in a much smaller, much better-designed result.

However, a few areas exist where Python does not shine. Operating on very large text files using complicated *regular expressions* (RE) with Python generally takes much longer than it would with Perl, for example. Although the differences between the two languages in RE handling can often be minimized by using some simple optimization techniques, it's often true that Perl is better suited for a few tasks than Python. In general, however, the speed at which a programmer can build a tool or prototype more than makes up for the difference in execution speed. The time between idea and implementation in most languages accounts for a great deal of the high cost of programs, but with Python this expensive gap can be shortened so much that, according to Frank Stajano, programmers can have "executable ideas." Writing down your ideas in Python clarifies them and will often give you a production-quality program in a very short time.

Programs that must act in real-time are probably not suitable for complete implementation in Python. Interpreted languages, in general, are too slow for the sort of instant response expected from such server programs. For example, Python would be a poor choice for a voice mail engine that was required to serve several hundred telephone lines at once. However, you can choose several options to improve the reaction time of such an engine. First, some crucial areas of the code can be written in a low-level language such as C, and the Python engine can treat the sections in C the same way that it treats built-ins. The string module is written in C; therefore, operations on strings in Python are extremely quick. This means that Python is *extensible*, making the speed of low-level languages available to Python. Second, low-level languages can *embed* Python, making it easy to call Python functions from C (or similar languages). This embeddability makes the power of Python available to the low-level language. These two properties make Python an extremely practical *glue* language, one that enables existing parts to work together as a unified whole.

Summary

In this first hour, you've learned what programming is, why you might want to know how to program, and why Python is a good choice for your first programming language. You've learned some of the history of the language and a bit of the history of programming languages in general, and you've been exposed to one of the most influential ideas of computer science: the language you choose to program in affects what you can program and how it is structured. Finally, we covered some areas where Python is not necessarily the best choice and some ways to make up for Python's weaknesses in those areas.

Workshop

Q&A

Q Is Python portable?

A Python can be made to run on nearly every platform; pre-compiled binaries are available for most operating systems. The only major operating system that doesn't support it is NetWare, and, at least one person has admitted publicly that he's working on the port.

Q Can I use Python as a CGI language?

A Yes. All that is required is that the machine running the Web server must both support and allow Python programs. You may run into resistance from Web server administrators, however, who might not want to add another CGI language to their systems.

Q Is Python secure for CGI programming?

A It's a safer language for this purpose than Perl, but not as safe as Java.

Q Will Python pave the way to fame and fortune?

A Not necessarily, but it sure won't hurt you to learn it.

Q Are any major companies using it for production programs?

A Yes, indeed. Companies that rely on it include NASA, Yahoo, Red Hat, Infoseek, and Industrial Light and Magic. We also know that some other big players in the computer industry use it but are reluctant to admit it because they feel that Python gives them a real competitive edge. Building things faster than other companies makes them very responsive to customers and very likely to get repeat business.

Quiz

1. Good reasons to pick Python as your first programming language are
   a. Power, speed, monolithic
   b. Flexible, extensible, embeddable
   c. Elegance, clarity, simplicity
   d. Real-time, powerful regular expressions, similarity to C
2. Who first proposed that using `goto` in programs led to unstructured programs?
   a. Nicklaus Wirth
   b. Edsger Dijkstra
   c. Benjamin Whorf
   d. Benjamin Charles E. Thompson, Jr.
3. Who invented Python?
   a. Tim Peters
   b. Ivan Van Laningham
   c. Guido van Rossum
   d. Edsger Dijkstra

Answers

1. Good reasons to pick Python are b and c; it's flexible, extensible, embeddable, elegant, clear, and simple.
2. Edsger Dijkstra considered the `goto` statement harmful because it allowed programmers to "make a mess of their programs."
3. Guido van Rossum is the creator of Python, despite what Tim Peters may claim and what I would wish. However, Tim has contributed greatly to the development of Python (in addition to being a very funny guy), whereas I consider myself lucky to use it.

Exercises

Visit `http://www.python.org/`, the home base for all things Python. As this book was being written, another extremely valuable on-line resource appeared, The Vaults of Parnassus, which can be found at `http://www.vex.net/parnassus/`. This is a rich site with full searching capability, and is full of links to software written in Python all over the world.

Join either the Python mailing list or the Python-tutor mailing list. You can find out more and can join at `http://www.python.org/psa/MailingLists.html`.

Read Edsger Dijkstra's short letter about `goto`, which can be found on the ACM Web site at

`http://www.acm.org/classics/oct95/`

It's tough going; for a little relief, try Edward Hall's excellent book based on Whorf's theories, *The Silent Language*.

Make your own list of repetitive tasks that you hate to do that you think you might want to have a computer do for you. As you go through this book, refer back to the list to see if you can think of solutions. Try to build at least one of these timesavers before you get to the end. If you only write one program and manage to save yourself even a few minutes of time per week, you've paid for this book.

If you are the determined, completist sort, you could read Shunryu Suzuki's *Zen Mind, Beginner's Mind*. Another fun read (well, I think it's fun!) is Richard Wexelblat's *History of Programming Languages*. Complete bibliographic information for all books mentioned in the text is in Appendix A, "References." Of course, if you *are* a determined completist, you should consider writing a book.

HOUR 2

The Python Interpreter

Explicit is better than implicit.

—Tim Peters

During this second hour, we're going to learn what the Python interpreter is, what the difference is between compiled and interpreted languages, what IDLE is and how to run it, and write and run our very first Python program.

The Interpreter: A Minimalist Guide

Two major categories of programming languages exist: compiled and interpreted. The first type is ordinarily a great deal faster than the second, but interpreted languages are usually easier to use and debug. *Compiled languages* are those where the programmer enters meaningful commands and statements into an editor and saves the result as a file; after this is done, the programmer runs a special program called a compiler on the saved file. The compiler reads the source code (source code is what you type into an editor and save in a file) and translates the instructions that programmers can read and write into machine language, which is meant to be understandable only to the computer. After the compiler is finished with the translation, the machine instructions are put into a special file. On DOS and Windows machines, the name of the special file must end in `.exe`, which tells the operating system that the file is available for execution. On UNIX systems, the operating system provides a way for the programmer to mark the machine language file as executable. On both kinds of systems, the programmer or user can simply type the name of the program (leaving out the `.exe` suffix, if the file has one, on DOS and Windows) into a command-line window or interface to run it. Most large programs, such as word processors, Web browsers, and database applications are built in this way.

An editor is a program that lets you type statements, or lines of text, into a window and save the text into a file. Examples of editors include vi on UNIX and Notepad on Windows.

The second variety, interpreted languages, eliminates the compiler. *Interpreted language* programs can usually be run in one of two ways: interactively or in batch mode. Running programs interactively is often not particularly convenient because the programmer starts a program called the *interpreter* (for Python, this program is called `python` or `python.exe`) and types commands into its user interface area. The disadvantage with this method is that programs typed in this way cease to exist when the interpreter stops running. In *batch mode*, the programmer enters the program into a file (the same as for compiled languages) and then tells the interpreter to run the file. An example for either UNIX or DOS is `python hello.py`; this command line first tells the operating system to run the `python` program, and when Python runs, it reads `hello.py` into memory and executes the instructions.

Interpreters read a file, and instead of translating the entire file into machine language, they execute each line in the file as it is read. This not only gets rid of compilation, but when an error is found, the interpreter tells the programmer right away; the programmer can then fix it immediately and resume execution. This is an advantage because the compilation and execution ordinarily take much longer than the interpreted execution does, and when an error is found, corrections can be applied immediately.

The interactive mode is most useful when you're trying out a new technique or a new trick you've learned, or when telling the interpreter to do a few simple things so that you can learn how the language works. In these first few hours, you will be dealing primarily with interactive mode because you need to concentrate on the low-level basics of the Python language. You will be practicing, learning the foundations upon which you will later build useful programs. Most of this practice won't result in things you'll want to keep.

Before you can run the interpreter for Python, however, you need to obtain and install it, unless your computer already has it installed for you. Red Hat Linux, for example, installs Python for you when the Linux Operating System is installed, so you can just run it. On Windows and other Linux or UNIX distributions, you must download it; you should refer to Appendix A for complete instructions, which include compilation instructions if you should need them. If your vendor has installed Python for you, make sure that IDLE is also installed. IDLE is a special editing program written by Guido van Rossum entirely in Python; we will use IDLE to edit and run programs throughout this book. If you don't have it installed, refer to Appendix A. The Windows installer includes it for you, so you don't have to worry.

> If you are installing the Windows version of Python, one change I would strongly recommend that you make is to tell the installation program to put Python into a folder called Python. The installation default is a folder called `c:\Program Files\Python`, but I think it should be `c:\Python`. Spaces in directory names can cause problems with some other programs, including Python programs, if they aren't expecting spaces in folder names. However, if you choose to use the default location, no great harm will befall you, and other useful packages will already know where they need to live when you run the installer.

Whether you're running Windows, Macintosh, or UNIX/Linux, you should be sure to install the Tcl/Tk package. With Windows, this is easy; answer Yes when the installation program asks if you want to install the Tcl/Tk package. You'll need to do more work on UNIX systems, but then UNIX users are generally expected (or required) to know more about their computers than Windows or Macintosh users are; you may have to track down a guru and ask her. Links to places to download Tcl/Tk for UNIX can be found at `http://www.python.org/download/`, and you can find binary installation packages for Linux at `http://www.andrich.net/python/`. You will need at least the Tcl/Tk package to complete this book because the last third requires it.

Python 1.5.2 requires Tcl/Tk 8.0and will not run (at least not without a lot of work that you don't want to do) With Tcl/Tk 8.1 The Windows installer will install the correct version if you tell it to install Tcl/Tk, but on UNIX you may have to build and install it yourself. This is a topic which is beyond the scope of this book.

I recommend downloading and installing two additional packages for Windows. You won't need them for this book, but they will come in very handy for further work as you find more applications and more tasks for your Python skills. These are the Win32Api Extensions and the PythonWin packages. The Win32Api lets you access the same parts of the Windows operating systems that programmers in compiled languages, such as C, can. The PythonWin package gives you an alternate editor and execution environment from the one used and described in this book. Some people prefer it to IDLE, but I don't cover it here.

Interactivity and Environment

After Python is installed on your machine, you need to do very few other things to get it running. Most installation procedures take care of these automatically for you. The Windows installation, for example, modifies the registry to add settings Python needs to find libraries of methods and functions for you. If your Python came preinstalled on Linux, the information that Python needs to run and to find the libraries is added to a special file called `site.py`; therefore, you need to make no changes yourself.

In earlier versions of Python, you would probably have had to set the `PYTHONPATH` environment variable, but beginning with Python 1.5.2, this is no longer necessary. A correctly installed Python knows where it is supposed to look for modules (which you'll learn about later) and will load them without complaint. You would need to set `PYTHONPATH` only if you have special needs, such as loading modules you don't want anyone else on your computer to know about. The most work you should have to do on any operating system is on Windows NT. You might have to add the Python and Tcl locations to your path, which you can do by selecting Start, Settings, Control Panel, and then double-clicking the System icon. After you have the System panel up, click the Environment tab, and the property page you should see ought to look somewhat like the one shown in Figure 2.1 (which is on my home NT system).

Notice that in the Value box, I have typed the locations of the Python interpreter and the Tcl libraries as `Tcl\bin`. When you add these folders to the environment page and click the Apply button, you should be able to run Python without any problems. You will have to close and then reopen any running command windows before these changes will take effect.

If you type **`python`** and your operating system complains that there isn't any such thing, you need to modify your `PATH` environment variable. First, you must find your copy of Python, and for this you either need to be knowledgeable enough already to find it (or remember where you put it), or you need to ask your system or network administrator. After you have succeeded in finding it, suppose that it's in a location such as `/usr/local/bin`; check your `PATH` variable again to make sure this location isn't there (if it is, something else is wrong, and you'll need assistance finding out what)

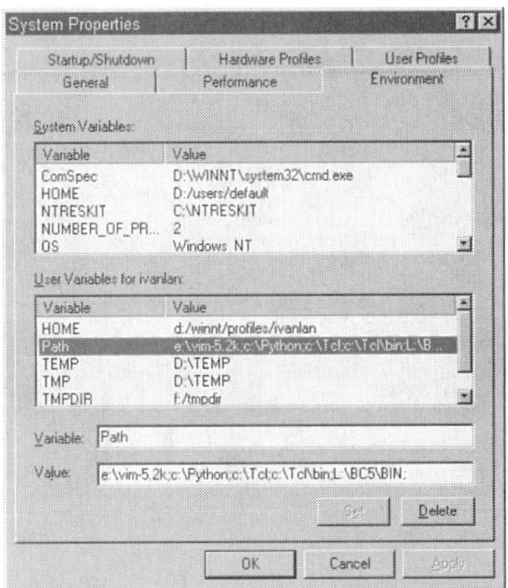

FIGURE 2.1
The Environment property page (tab) on NT.

To add this to your path on UNIX/Linux systems, you'll need to type something like **`PATH=$PATH:/usr/local/bin; export PATH`** at your shell prompt; or even better, add it to your shell startup file. This file should be called something like `.profile`, `.bashrc`, or `.cshrc`, and should be found in your home directory. Just edit this startup file and add the appropriate locations to the line where your PATH variable is already being set. If you can't figure this out, you may need to get some help, but it's not really hard; read the statements that are already in your startup file, and the context should make it clear what you need to change.

If Python is someplace like `c:\python\python.exe`, you need to type **`PATH PATH%;c:\python;c:\Tcl;c:\Tcl\bin`** into a DOS box (command prompt). If you're running Windows 95/98, add the preceding line near the end of your `AUTOEXEC.BAT` file and restart your system. When it's restarted, it will know where Python lives. Figure 2.2 shows a Notepad session with a correctly modified `AUTOEXEC.BAT`.

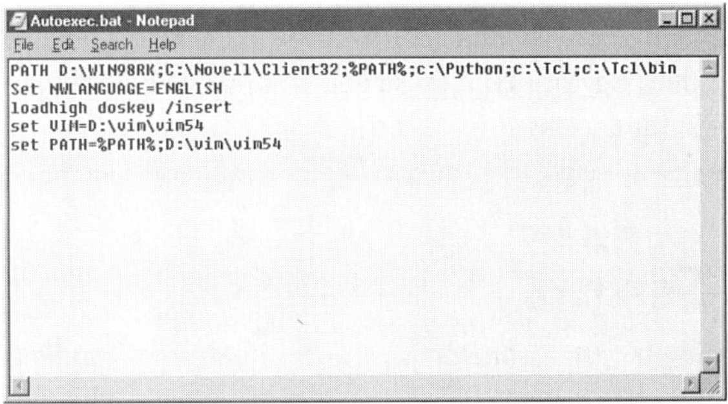

FIGURE 2.2
Modifying your `AUTOEXEC.BAT` file.

Finally, you should be able to type **`python`** on your Windows or UNIX box and see something similar to Figure 2.3.

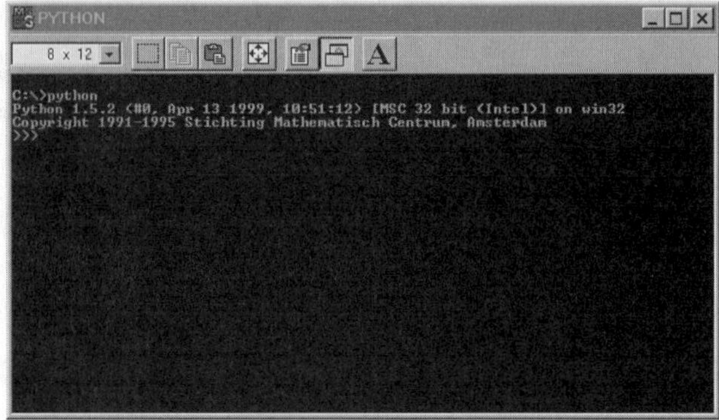

FIGURE 2.3
What happens when you type **`python`**.

The `>>>` is called the *Python prompt*—a set of characters that lets you know that the Python interpreter is ready to respond to a command from you. If you like, you could see what happens when you type commands; try typing **`"Hello, World"`** (make sure that you enter the quotation marks, too), and hit Enter. Figure 2.4 shows you some things to try.

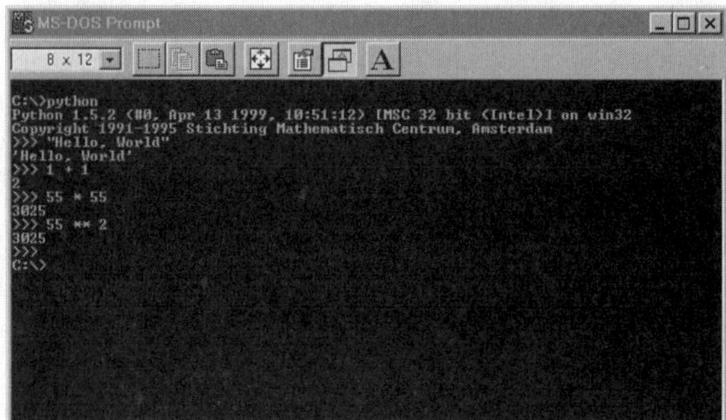

FIGURE 2.4
Typing things into the interpreter.

To exit the interpreter, use Ctrl+Z on Windows. On UNIX and in IDLE, the command is Ctrl+D. In both cases, you type these exit commands by holding down the Control (or Ctrl) key at the same time you press the ***Z*** or ***D*** key on your keyboard. It's always a good idea to learn how to exit any program before you learn much else.

Running Scripts

Although typing program statements into the interpreter can be fun, easy, and educational, it's not all that rewarding when you want to save what you've done. In the normal interpreter, which is run from a command prompt (a DOS box on PCs, a terminal emulator window on UNIX, and so on), there is no way to save your work. Entering commands interactively is like tossing money into a well: you may feel good afterward, but you can't get it back.

You can either use a text editor (as mentioned previously, you can always use Notepad on Windows; if you've got a favorite text editor, though, use that), type programs into the editor, and save the text into a file that ends with the suffix, or extension, `.py`. Python doesn't require that you use the `.py` suffix, but I strongly recommend that you do so, especially if you are running Windows. Life will be easier; I promise.

Regardless of the platform you are on, the way to run these scripts is the same; you just need to type

```
python script.py
```

into your command prompt (whatever it is). In the next section, we'll actually do this.

Hello, Python!

Although I like to use vi to write my Python programs, you should use whatever you're comfortable with. The Notepad program that comes with Windows is perfectly adequate for a while, but later you will appreciate other useful features, such as automatic indentation, that are available in more sophisticated editors.

NEW TERM *Code* are lines of human-readable instructions in a particular programming language.

Open your editor and type in the following code:

```
print "Hello, World!"
print "Goodbye, World!"
```

(Make sure that the two lines start at the left margin of your text document; no whitespace should come before the `print` keyword.) Save these lines into a text file called `helloworld.py`, start up a DOS box (or whatever you use) in the same directory where you saved it, and you're now ready to run your first real Python program.

NEW TERM *Whitespace* includes tabs, spaces, and carriage returns (also known as *end of line* markers). It's important to know about whitespace in Python because the spaces or tabs at the beginning of a line indicate the indentation level of the line. Everything with matching indentation goes together. Other languages use special characters or special keywords to mark lines that go together, but matching levels of spaces or tabs is more readable. Other languages also use special characters to mark the end of a meaningful line of code, but Python uses the normal end-of-line marker.

A *keyword* is a word in a programming language that tells the language to do something; `print` is a keyword in Python. You may not use keywords as variable names or function names in your programs (you'll learn about variables and functions later in this book).

Type

```
python helloworld.py
```

into your command window and see what happens.

You should see something that looks like Figure 2.5.

FIGURE 2.5
Hello, Python!

You've just run your very first Python program—the traditional "Hello, World" program. That is, however, the last program you're going to run for a while; in the next chapter, we'll concentrate on understanding basic mathematics with Python, and we'll use the interactive capabilities of the interpreter to do so. We're not going to use the command window as we have been, however; there's something better, called IDLE.

IDLE stands for Integrated DeveLopment Environment, and it was written by Python's creator, Guido van Rossum, completely in Python, using Python's graphical user-interface component, *tkinter*. We'll learn more about tkinter in the final third of this book, but using IDLE will give you a foretaste of the kinds of projects you can tackle with tkinter.

If you have modified your path so that both the Python and Tcl directories are found in it, the easiest way to ensure that IDLE is always available is to make a desktop shortcut to it. This is pretty easy on Windows and not too difficult on Red Hat Linux 6.0, but it is not really possible on other flavors of UNIX. I'll describe how to make the shortcut under Windows, but for Linux and UNIX, I suggest you refer to your documentation to find out how to make one for your platform (if it's possible at all). Otherwise, you must type **`idle`** into a terminal emulator window to run it.

The first thing you need to do is to find where IDLE lives, and to do that, you need to know where Python lives; this should be simple because the Python directory should be in your path. On all my Windows systems, Python is in `c:\Python`, and you should open a Windows Explorer Window in the Python directory. Within the Python directory, you should find several folders, one of which is named Tools; enter that directory, and it should contain another folder called IDLE. Inside the IDLE folder you should see an icon for `idle.py`, and right next to it should be `idle.pyw`, which is the one we're looking for. Right-click the `idle.pyw` icon and select Create Shortcut on the pop-up menu; Windows should create a whole new icon for you, called Shortcut to `idle.pyw`. Grab that icon and drop it on your desktop; you can change the name if you wish, and you can even change the icon (although I happen to like the cute little green python icon, as shown in Figure 2.6) to whatever you want. Another way to create the desktop shortcut is to click your Start menu, click Settings, and select Taskbar & Start Menu. Click the Start Menu Programs tab and push the Advanced button. Under the Programs tree, you should see an entry for Python 1.5; select (or double-click) that, and the right side of the Explorer window should contain four icons, one of which is labeled IDLE (Python GUI). Right-click that icon and pick Create Shortcut. Drag the created shortcut to your desktop and rename/customize it to your satisfaction. After you're satisfied with the desktop location and appearance of your IDLE shortcut, double-click it to start it running. The main window should appear, and it should look like Figure 2.6.

FIGURE 2.6
The IDLE main window.

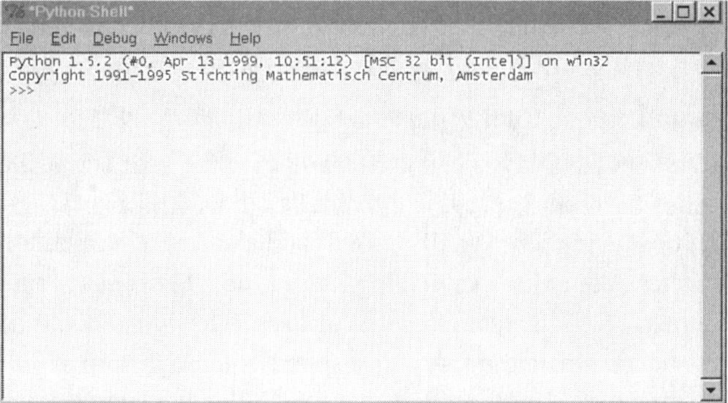

You can exit from IDLE in three ways: select File, Exit from the menu bar, type **Ctrl+D** into the main window, or type **Ctrl+Q** into any IDLE window that has the focus. Try exiting in one of these ways and then start IDLE up again to try the other ways. Use the method you like best. Now we're ready to go on to more advanced topics; in the next chapter, we'll start learning how to do basic mathematics in Python using IDLE.

Summary

In this second hour, you've learned the difference between compiled and interpreted programming languages, how to install Python and Tcl, how to set your path so that Python can be found and easily started in a DOS box or terminal emulator window, and how to exit from the interpreter. You've learned how to run simple scripts, how to make a shortcut to IDLE, and how to start it up. And of course, you've learned how to exit from IDLE—always a good thing.

Workshop

Q&A

Q What platforms support IDLE?

A UNIX, Windows, and Macintosh, because those are the only platforms that support tkinter.

Q What do I do if IDLE won't run?

A This problem has many causes, so it's hard to say. Try to get help from someone you know who knows more about computers than you do. If you can't get help there, the best thing to do is to visit the Python home page at `http://www.python.org`. Look for links to the mailing lists and sign up for the Python Tutor mailing list; this list is specifically designed to help beginners such as yourself get over the first hurdles in programming Python.

Q Can I run Python programs without having to type `python` *`script.py`*?

A Yes. On UNIX, you can use *chmod* to make your script file executable. Type **`chmod +x`** ***`script.py`***, and that tells UNIX (or Linux) to treat the file the same way it treats programs. You'll have to add a special first line to your program, however, which should look something like **`#!/usr/bin/env python`**. To find the correct syntax, read the manual page for `exec`. Then you should be able to type **`script.py`** at the command line. A way also exists to do this on Windows NT, but it's substantially more complicated; if you search the documents at the Python home page, `http://www.python.org`, you can find a clear tutorial on how to do this.

Quiz

1. What is IDLE?
    a. A South Indian dumpling.
    b. An integrated interpreter environment written entirely in Python.

   c. What you become on Saturday morning.
   d. What your cats are all the time.

2. What's going on if you type **`python`** and you receive a message that says, "`The name specified is not recognized as an internal or external command, operable program, or batch file`"?
   a. You haven't set your path correctly.
   b. Someone stole Python.
   c. The computer is just being stubborn; keep retrying the command.
   d. You're on Windows, and Bill Gates doesn't want you to run Python.

3. What is the >>> called?
   a. Voodoo.
   b. The "triple spit" sign.
   c. The Python prompt, which tells you that Python is eagerly awaiting your commands.
   d. Hash.

4. What happens if you type a command to the Python interpreter that it doesn't recognize?
   a. Nothing.
   b. It reboots your computer.
   c. It prints a special Traceback message that reads `NameError:`, followed by the word you typed that it didn't recognize. If you type two or more words, it gives you a `SyntaxError:`.
   d. It makes you type your command correctly 500 times.

Answers

1. IDLE is an integrated interpreter environment written entirely in Python.
2. You haven't set your path correctly if the DOS command prompt complains that it doesn't recognize the name you typed.
3. The >>> is called the Python prompt; be sure to distinguish this from a command prompt window, which is the technical name for a DOS box.
4. If you type a command to the Python interpreter that it doesn't recognize, it gives you the Traceback message. These messages are usually, but not always, fairly informative. Luckily, Python doesn't reboot your machine, and it doesn't stop running. I once worked on a machine that required regular runs of special diagnostic

programs, and to enter the special diagnostic mode, you had to type about 15 commands exactly right. After you did that, all the diagnostic programs had extremely picky syntax, which involved what seemed like 30 command-line parameters separated by commas. If a parameter wasn't used, you had to enter the comma anyway, just to let the machine know that the parameter wasn't used. Most of the parameters weren't used. If you typed one too many or one too few commas, diagnostic mode was exited, and the machine hung, forcing a reboot. This was not a popular machine.

Exercises

Play with the interpreter by running it in a DOS box; play with IDLE. See if you can find differences in the way each behaves.

Visit the Python home page, `http://www.python.org`, and find the mailing list page. Sign up for the Tutor mailing list. I'm on it, and many more knowledgeable people are, too. We're all there just to answer your questions and help you get over the speed bumps of learning Python. When you can snatch the pebble from our hands, it will be time for you to leave, Grasshopper. Or at least take your place among the teachers.

HOUR 3

Basic Arithmetic with Python

Simple is better than complex.

—Tim Peters

In this hour, we're going to study basic arithmetic using Python and IDLE. These are very simple ideas, but they provide the foundation for the many, more complex concepts that follow. Although it is not at all necessary to be a math whiz to program, you do need to know some basic high school math; if you've had an introductory course in algebra, you're all set. Even if you haven't had such a course, you will have no difficulty if you know how to work simple formulas.

Those of you who didn't do well in math, take note: I took high school algebra and nearly flunked it (I had a bad teacher, but even more important, I wasn't paying attention). I caught up with some of the basic techniques much later, in an Army introductory electronics course. Two years after taking that course, I was teaching it.

Addition and Subtraction

Everyone starts with addition and subtraction because these are the foundation stones of all mathematics. I'm sure you know the rules, and no real differences exist between the rules you know and the rules of mathematics in Python (or in any programming language, for that matter).

We'll try some adding and subtracting. Start the Python interpreter by typing **`python`** at the command prompt, and then type in **`1 + 1`** at the prompt. If Python doesn't respond with `2`, you've got a real problem! Now try some more complicated problems, such as adding some large numbers and adding positive and negative ones. It helps if you think of all the whole numbers (integers) as existing on an infinite line, with zero in dead center and the numbers as expressions representing points you can reach by traveling forward or backward using addition and subtraction. For instance, suppose you are at position 0 and you want to go to position -45. Obviously, you need to travel backward 45, but you can get there by two methods: you can add a negative number or you can subtract a positive one. Try it. You should see the following in your interpreter window (see Figure 3.1).

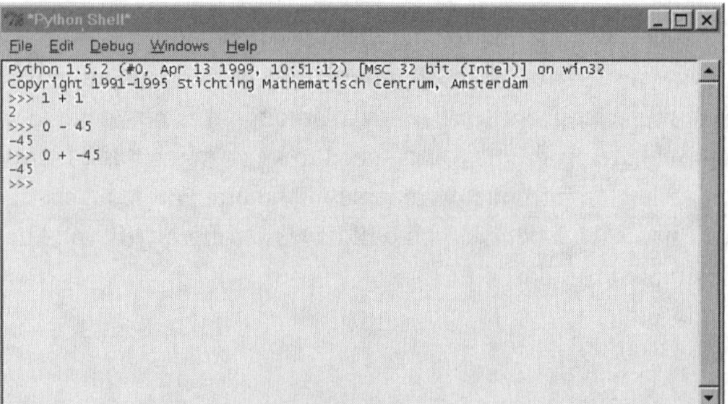

FIGURE 3.1
1 + 1.

That all seems pretty clear, but what happens when you start adding and subtracting really large numbers? With pencil and paper, it's no problem. No matter how big the numbers are that you work with, simple patience will eventually get you a correct answer. But if you have a modern scientific calculator, or an ancient Chinese or Japanese abacus (see Figure 3.2), you will run out of "places" when you add larger and larger numbers.

FIGURE 3.2
A (computerized) Japanese abacus.

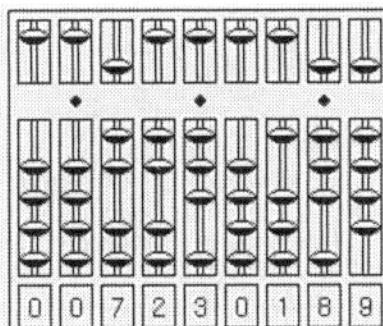

Note that "places" are pretty easy to see on an abacus. They're a little harder to see on a computer because there's not a one-to-one correspondence between the internal representation of numbers that computers use and the printed form computers use to show you those numbers. Most computers use 32 "bits" to represent numbers internally, and one of those bits is usually used to hold the sign—the plus or minus indicating a positive or negative number—leaving only 31 bits for the numeric value. What this means is that the largest possible signed integer in Python is 2,147,483,647 (two billion plus change).

> You've heard the term before, but we'll review just to be sure. A *bit* is a single on-off number; it can represent either the number 0 or the number 1. Nothing else. To represent bigger numbers, you need to string these bits together, and that's what modern computers do. They string their bits together into *bytes* (8 bits) and *words* (usually 32 bits) to make it easier to use and easier to comprehend.

Figure 3.3 shows what happens when you try to print numbers near this 32-bit boundary.

In the preceding figure, you can see that the only way to effectively use all 32 bits of a normal integer is to print the values in *hexadecimal*; the rules for printing hex numbers establish quite firmly that such representation is *unsigned* so that all bits can be seen. Note also that Python has a special name for the largest signed value: *maxint*. This value lives in a special module called `sys`, and the way you gain access to maxint in your programs is to import the `sys` module. You'll learn more about *import* later, but for right now, you can think of it as pulling in everything that lives in the module you import.

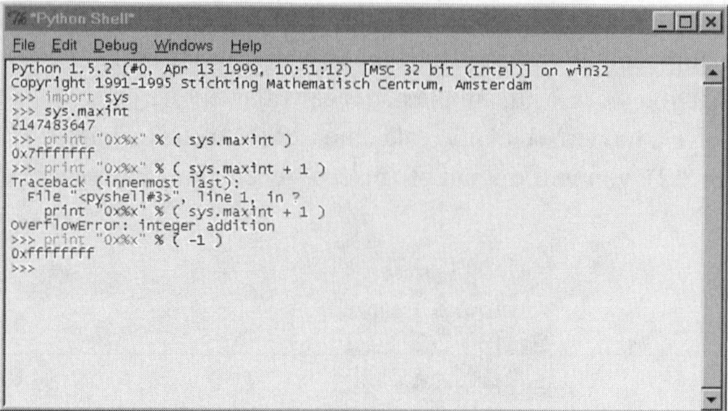

FIGURE 3.3
32-bit numbers.

Hexadecimal is a way of grouping bits to make it easier for humans to visualize them. The binary number 1111 displays four bits, but programmers usually write this as "F" instead. Hexadecimal means "base 16," so individual hex digits go from 0 through F—0-15 in decimal. If you want to appear to your friends and spouse as the ultimate computer geek, number your video tapes in hex, starting with tape 0.

OK, let's see what happens in Python when you add a really big number to a small one. If we add 9999999999 to 1, for instance, Figure 3.4 shows what Python does.

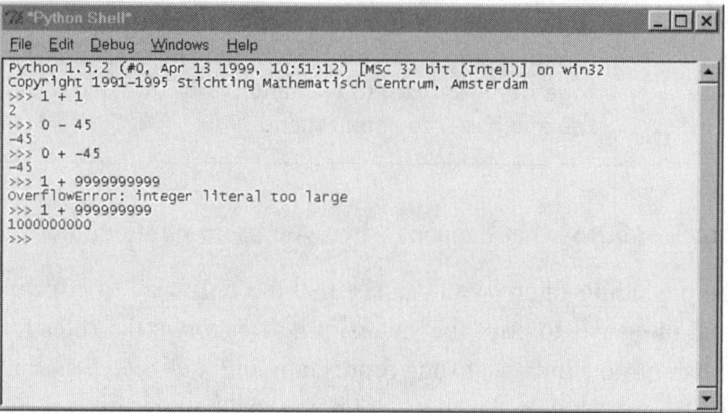

FIGURE 3.4
1 + a lot.

Hmmm. What does this mean? Just what it says: the number we added was too big for Python to handle. That is, Python tried to convert 9999999999 into its internal representation, and it ran out of bits. We get the same thing if we try to subtract a large number, too. So what do we do? Well, it turns out that there's a very simple way around it: all we have to do is tell Python that it should treat a big number like a big number. We do that by giving Python a hint: just tack on an *L* after any large numbers if you think they're going to overflow (which is what running out of bits means). Figure 3.5 shows an example.

```
*Python Shell*
File Edit Debug Windows Help
Python 1.5.2 (#0, Apr 13 1999, 10:51:12) [MSC 32 bit (Intel)] on win32
Copyright 1991-1995 Stichting Mathematisch Centrum, Amsterdam
>>> 1 + 1
2
>>> 0 - 45
-45
>>> 0 + -45
-45
>>> 1 + 9999999999
OverflowError: integer literal too large
>>> 1 + 999999999
1000000000
>>> 1 + 9999999999L
10000000000L
>>>
```

FIGURE 3.5
1 + a lot, again.

3

Tacking on an *L* after any large numbers tells Python "this number is a *long*." A *long* number can be any length it needs to be; the places, or rods on that abacus, are limited only by the amount of memory in your computer and your patience. We'll try a really big number now: copy the next line, and then paste it into the IDLE main window (visit `ftp://www.pauahtun.org/pub/googol.txt` to download a text file containing the number, or just type in a `1` followed by 100 zeros):

```
1000000000000000000000000000000000000000000000000000000000000000000000000000000
0000000000000000000000L
```

Add a plus sign (+) after it and then paste the same number again. Press Return. What you end up with is shown in Figure 3.6.

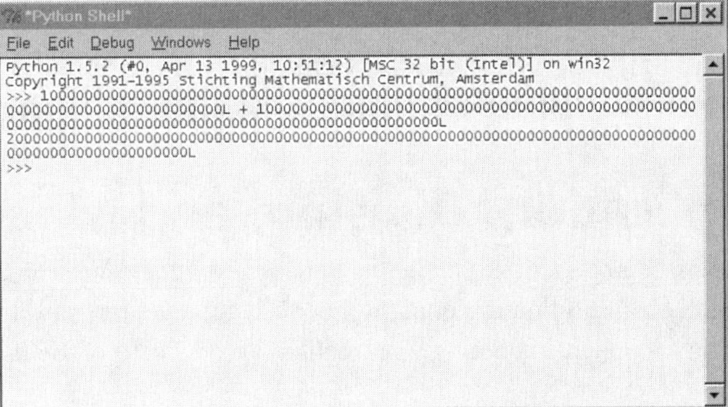

FIGURE 3.6
Adding two really large numbers.

One followed by 100 zeros is called a *googol*. It was invented by the U.S. mathematician Edward Kasner and named by his nine-year-old nephew, Milton Sirotta.

You can add regular integers and long integers without trouble. Python's rules state that whenever you perform arithmetic functions with any two operands, the smaller operand is "widened" to the type of the larger. Thus, if you add 1 + 1000000000000000000000000L, Python automatically turns 1 into 1L for you.

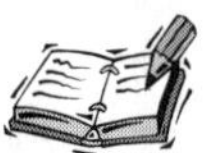

Operators such as + and - operate on *operands*. For example, the expression "1 + 4" means "apply the plus operator to the operands 1 and 4."

You will also need to be concerned with a third type of number: *floating point numbers*. These are numbers that have a decimal point, such as 1.1 and 3.14159265359. Adding and subtracting these numbers often gives you results that you might not expect; in Figure 3.7, for example, the answer you might guess you would see is 0.00001.

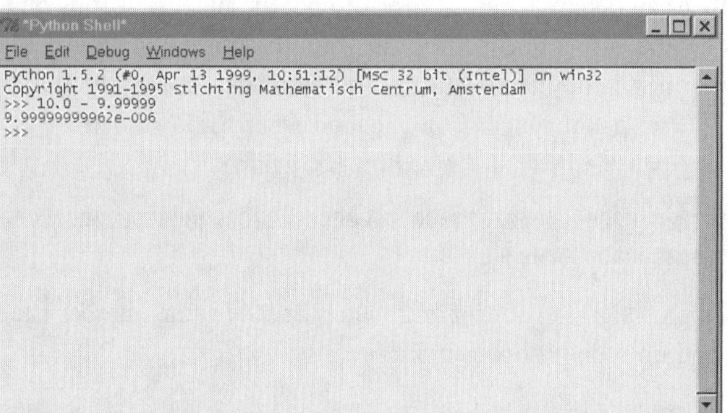

FIGURE 3.7
Subtracting floating point numbers.

What you get instead is something called "scientific notation," which we'll talk more about in a later section of this chapter. In the meantime, it's time to go on to other topics.

Multiplication, Division, and *Modulo*

In the preceding section, you learned about adding and subtracting using normal integers, long integers, and floating point numbers. In this section, you'll learn about multiplication, division, and something you might not have heard of—*modulo*, using the same types of numbers.

Again, the rules for these operations in Python aren't very different from what you already know, but you do need to be aware that the type of operand very much determines how Python treats a number. For example, 10 divided by 4.0, as shown in Figure 3.8, gives the expected 2.5.

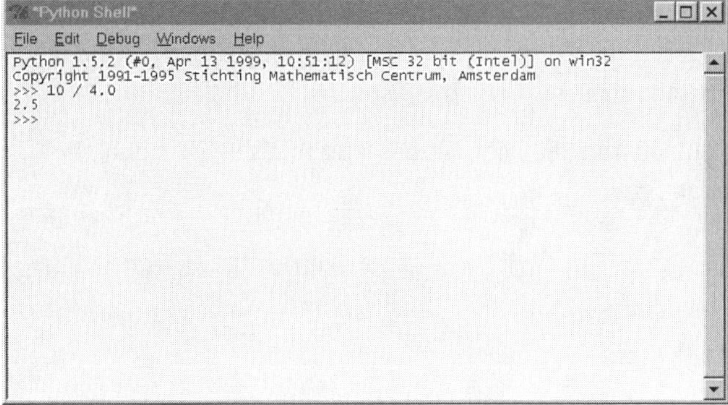

FIGURE 3.8
Division.

But in Figure 3.9, we get something different.

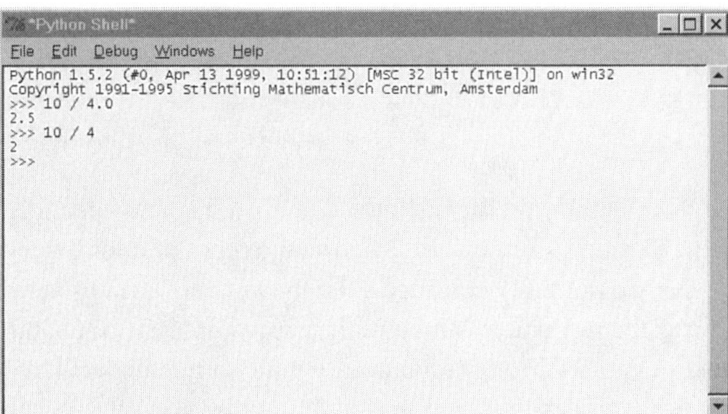

FIGURE 3.9
More division.

The difference is that in the first case, by putting the decimal point into the 4.0 operand, we told Python that we cared about decimal point information. In the second case, by leaving out the decimal point, we explicitly told Python that we *didn't* care. And Python obligingly dropped off the .5 that we told it we didn't need. Thus, as in addition and subtraction, Python figures out the right thing to do based on the information you give it about the operands. It also means that we have to be careful regarding the types of the operands; it is easy to leave out a decimal point when you really mean to put one in, but you will obtain unexpected results.

The ease by which you can obtain unexpected, or unintended, results when dividing has been an ongoing topic of debate on the Python mailing list. Some have advocated a special operator distinct from the `/` now used by division that would indicate to Python that it should always use pure integer division (shown in Figure 3.9) or should always use pure floating point division (Figure 3.8). These suggestions have included a `/.` for pure floating point and `//` for pure integer division. None of the suggestions, and I'm leaving out a great many others, have gained any credibility with Guido, but he says that he's keeping an open mind about Python 2.0.

As with addition and subtraction, long integers are easily multiplied and divided, as shown in Figure 3.10.

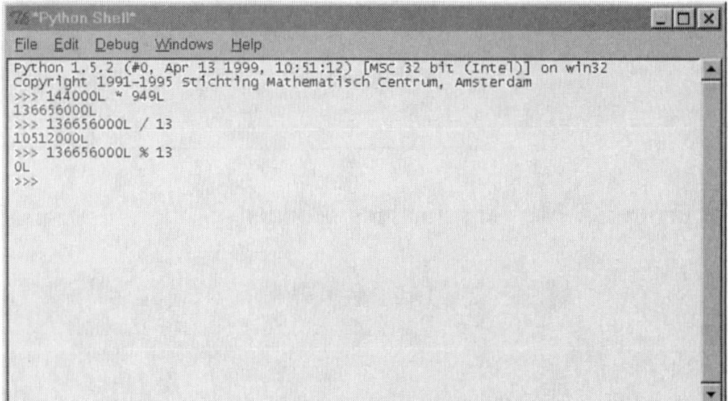

FIGURE 3.10
Long division and multiplication.

Notice that the third problem shown above used a new operator: the `%` sign, or *modulo* operator. This operator performs a normal integer or a long integer division and throws away what we normally consider to be the answer. The answer returned by the modulo operator is the remainder, which in the preceding case, 136656000L % 13, was zero because 13 divides 136,656,000 evenly with no remainder. The modulo operator comes in very handy, especially in calendrical calculations; leap-year rules exist in virtually every calendar, and those that have no leap years usually rely even more heavily on modular arithmetic. The Mayan calendar is a prime example of the latter, but our own Gregorian calendar, of course, does have leap-year rules. The Julian calendar, from which the Gregorian is derived, has a very simple leap-year rule: any year evenly divisible by 4 is leap. The Gregorian rule modifies this by stating that century years (1700, 1900, and so on) are leap *only* if they are also evenly divisible by 400. Figure 3.11 shows how to determine whether the year 2000 is a leap year.

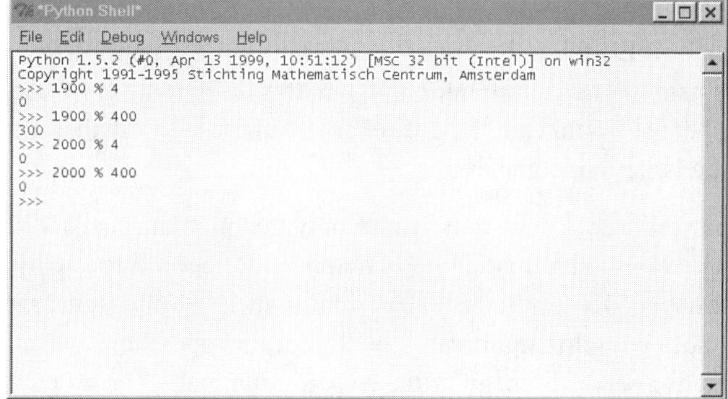

FIGURE 3.11
Leap years and century years.

2000 is a leap year; 1900 was not. I know of at least one detective story that was solved when the investigator broke the suspect's alibi when he realized that 1900 was not a leap year. Naturally, I can't remember the story or the author, but calendar freaks often have rather selective memories.

A special function exists that you can use if you need both the answer and the remainder from a division: `divmod(x,y)` returns both `x / y` *and* `x % y`. You can try this in an IDLE window by typing **`print divmod(53,13)`** and seeing what the result is. The `(4, 1)` notation is a special one for groups that we will learn about later in the first part of the book.

Rounding, `floor()`, and `ceil()`

The topics we talk about in this section deal exclusively with floating point numbers. Whenever you perform any mathematical operation on floating point numbers, you need to be aware of the limitations of the underlying computer representation of those numbers. Computers keep track of numbers only in *binary*, or base 2. In base 2 only two digits are present: 0 and 1. This is an ideal number system for computers because 0 and 1 can be represented by a simple on-off device: light bulbs, toggle switches, vacuum tubes, and transistors are all examples. Converting whole numbers, or integers, from one base into another is easy, and computers have been doing it for years. They're very good at it, too. When integers are converted from one base to another, you don't lose any information. That is, a one-to-one mapping always occurs from numbers in one base to numbers in another base; no guessing is involved. For example, the digits in base 16 (hexadecimal) are 0 through F, and these map directly to the numbers 0 through 15 in base 10, decimal. Computer scientists say that no loss of *precision* occurs when operating on integers.

Everything changes when you toss in decimal points, however. The ways that floating point numbers are represented on computers have, historically, been diverse, complex, and contorted. Only in the last few years has there been the emergence of anything like a standard for the representation of these kinds of numbers, and many people find even this standard, IEEE-64, to be full of pitfalls and shortcomings. Regrettably, not nearly enough space exists in this entire book to cover this fascinating topic. And probably only about three people would care if I did cover it. Suffice it to say that the problems are multitude and the issues are complex.

In this section, we need to be aware only that problems exist with the loss of precision when working with floating point numbers. Rather unexpectedly, it turns out that multiplication and division under such circumstances involve some measure of error, but the error does not grow significantly with repeated operations, whereas repeated addition and subtraction serves to magnify the error substantially. The moral is to use floating point addition and subtraction carefully, perhaps attempting to balance such operations with multiplication and division whenever possible.

When you need to do floating point math, sooner or later you'll want to convert at least some floating point results into integers, sometimes into long integers. In Python, an easy way to do this is to use the built-in *type conversion* functions. A few examples are shown in Figure 3.12.

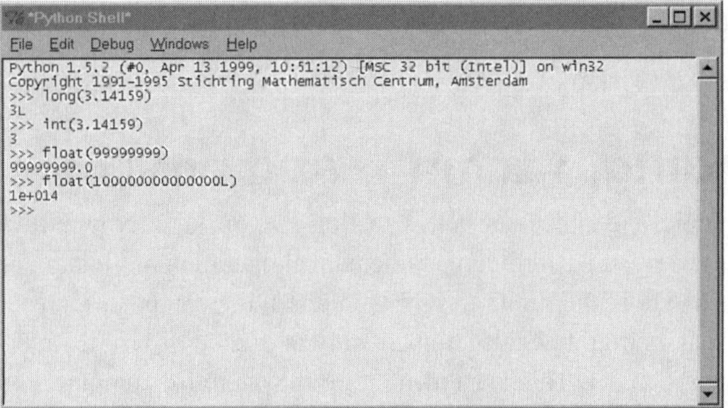

FIGURE 3.12
Some type conversions.

Sooner or later, however, you're going to run into situations where you need these conversions to go in a particular direction; that is, sometimes you need answers rounded up and sometimes rounded down. The proper way to ensure that answers get rounded the way you need them is to use the math functions `floor()` and `ceil()`. Remember earlier when we imported the sys module? That's what must be done whenever you need to use specialized math functions; you import the `math` module. In this case, we're going to use a different form of the import statement, as you can see in Figure 3.13.

FIGURE 3.13
floor() and ceil().

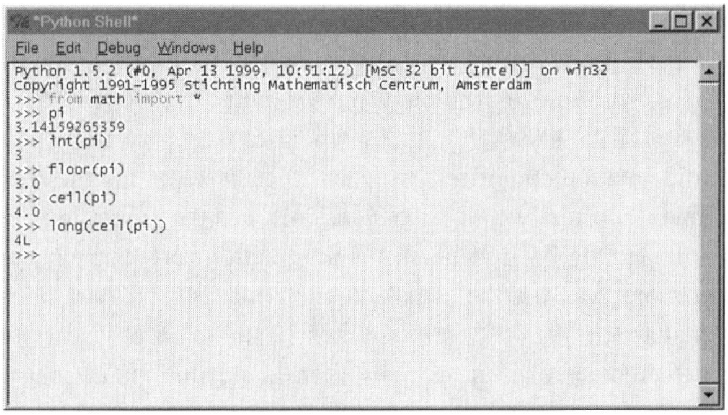

```
Python 1.5.2 (#0, Apr 13 1999, 10:51:12) [MSC 32 bit (Intel)] on win32
Copyright 1991-1995 Stichting Mathematisch Centrum, Amsterdam
>>> from math import *
>>> pi
3.14159265359
>>> int(pi)
3
>>> floor(pi)
3.0
>>> ceil(pi)
4.0
>>> long(ceil(pi))
4L
>>>
```


If we didn't use this special form, then the way we would have to access the value of *pi* would be to write **`math.pi`**; similarly, the only way to get to `floor()` and `ceil()` would be **`math.floor()`** and **`math.ceil()`**. Many people prefer not to use this `from x import *` form, maintaining that it's not always safe. It is possible for names in an imported module to conflict with those that programmers might want to use in their programs, but the possibility is slight, and usually you will know if a problem occurs. However, if I haven't read the code from the module that I'm going to import, I will almost never use the `import *` form. Well-documented (or at least well-known) modules, such as tkinter, are the exception.

You can see from the preceding figure most all of what you need to know to use these math functions properly; just make sure that your parentheses match. Another thing you can see is that one function, `long()`, can take as input the output value of another function, `ceil()`. This is an important point to remember; instead of using numbers as input values to functions, you can use functions that work out some other value as input.

Another area to be concerned with when rounding off floating point numbers is, "What happens when my values are negative?" We'll put off talking about those until somewhat later in this hour.

Exponentiation

Exponentiation, or raising to a power, is something that you might remember from high school math. Simply, it means to take a number and multiply it by itself a certain number of times. For instance, 2^2, means to multiply two times two, or *square* it, giving the result of 4. Similarly, 2^3 means to multiply two times two times two, or *cube* it, giving the result of 8.

Scientific notation, or as it is more properly termed, *floating point notation*, uses exponents to keep from writing very large numbers with many repetitive zeros. Earlier, in Figure 3.7, you saw an example when we subtracted 10.0 - 9.99999 and got the surprising answer of 9.99999999962e-006 when we might have expected the answer 0.00001. Scientific notation comprises two parts: the *exponent* and the *fraction part* (which is sometimes incorrectly called the *mantissa*). For our surprising answer, the e-006 is the exponent, and the 9.99999999962 is the fraction part. The *e* stands for exponent and the -006 portion gives you the actual exponent that is used. Numbers written like this are usually stated as "9.99999999962 times 10 to the negative (or minus) sixth"—if you bother to pronounce all those nines after the decimal point. Negative exponents tell you that our base, 10, should be divided by itself a certain number of times. 10^{-1}, for example, is the same as the fraction 1/10, or 0.1. Our minus 6 exponent here means to divide 10 by itself 6 times, or 1/1000000. This is a small number, and its decimal equivalent is 0.000001. Figure 3.14 demonstrates this.

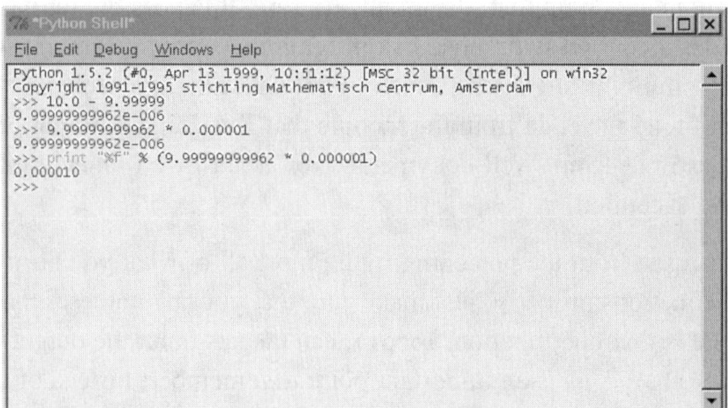

FIGURE 3.14
Negative exponents.

Notice that the printed answer is 0.00001, or extremely close to what we expected in the first place. Remember what I said earlier about rounding errors in addition and subtraction tending to magnify substantially? When you're working with very small numbers, such as 10^{-6}, these errors add up (pun intended).

Scientific notation is used very widely in programming and scientific circles; it's a good idea to become at least somewhat familiar with it. Some of the more common references you might encounter are 10^{3}, 1000; 10^{6}, a million; 10^{9}, a billion; and 10^{12}, a trillion. (These are the U.S. English terms for amounts greater than 1,000, by the way; each has a different meaning in Great Britain and Canada.) And remember the 1 followed by 100 zeros that we used above—the googol? Well, two ways exist to write googol in scientific notation: 10^{100} is one way and $10^{10^{10}}$ is another; both mean the same thing, however. After Kasner invented the googol, another mathematician invented what's called the *googolplex*, which is defined as 10^{googol}, and which I won't attempt to write out in full. For the curious, at the Web page for this book, you will find a Python program for printing googols and googolplexes. It will run until you run out of patience, computer memory, computer hard disk space, or the heat death of the universe, whichever comes first. Figure 3.15 shows a quick way to print a googol in Python.

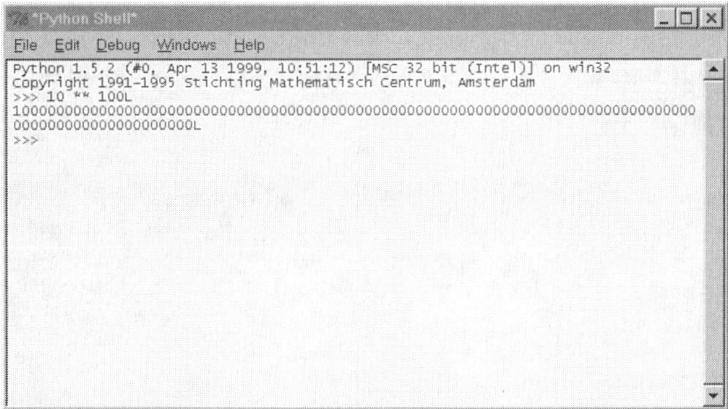

FIGURE 3.15
A googol.

3

Parenthesization

After you get comfortable with scientific notation, you will probably discover that a lot of really useful information is locked up in mathematical formulas all over the Net (and sometimes in real books, too). Such formulas, at least all but the most trivial, have two symbols in common: parentheses. There's a reason for that. Parentheses are there to indicate *the order of operations*. That is, you can look at a formula and know exactly where to start working on it, even if you don't understand what work needs to be done or what the formula is supposed to do.

Python, in common with many other programming languages, has an elaborate system of rules, called *precedence* rules, which allow the programmer to leave out many parentheses to enhance readability. All you have to do is memorize 20 or 30 complex rules, rewrite your equations to satisfy these rules, and you, too, can write unreadable code even in that most readable of languages—Python.

I'm not a fan of operator precedence rules, as you can probably tell. I like things laid out explicitly, and I prefer to tell computers what I want them to do, not have them tell me. Thus, I have my own rules, which are a great deal simpler:

Rule 1: If all mathematical operations are additions or subtractions, forget parentheses.

Rule 2: If you use any other kind of operator, parenthesize everything.

When I was first learning how to program, I got bitten several times by precedence rules. They differ from what I expected. If a formula is written like this: "400 + 1 / 3," then I expected it to divide 401 by 3. That's not what happens, as Figure 3.16 shows.

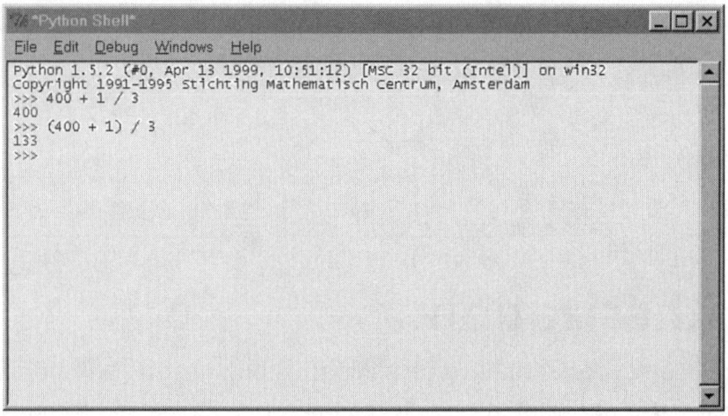

FIGURE 3.16
The dangers of precedence rules.

```
Python 1.5.2 (#0, Apr 13 1999, 10:51:12) [MSC 32 bit (Intel)] on win32
Copyright 1991-1995 Stichting Mathematisch Centrum, Amsterdam
>>> 400 + 1 / 3
400
>>> (400 + 1) / 3
133
>>>
```

If, when you follow my rules and parenthesize everything, and your code starts to look too cluttered with parentheses to live, then you are trying to cram too much on one line. Break it up into more lines. This enhances readability, which is a very good thing. Remember that someone is going to have to maintain your code; sometimes that someone will be you and sometimes not. Look critically at each line and ask yourself, "In six weeks will I remember what this line does?" If the answer is no, consider rewriting the line.

"Gotchas" and Other Miscellaneous Topics

The most important "gotcha" to remember about Python when dealing with numbers of any sort is the way that Python applies `floor()` and `ceil()` to negative numbers. Python differs from C and C++ in the way it does this, so if you have had experience with either of those languages, you need to be alert to the possibility of error. Figure 3.17 demonstrates the problem.

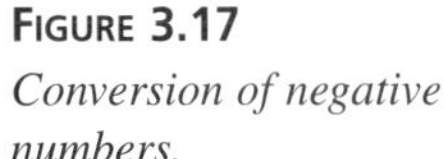

FIGURE 3.17
Conversion of negative numbers.

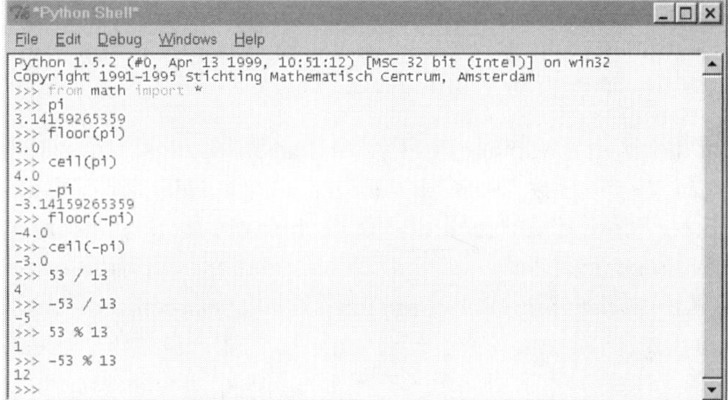

In C, applying `floor()` to pi gives you 3, but applying it to -pi gives you -3, not -4 as Python does. When you use `ceil()` gives you 4 and -4, respectively. Why is this? Furthermore, `floor()` is defined as "rounding downward"; shouldn't this mean that both languages behave the same way? Well, no. The reason for the difference is that, in the case of Python, downward is taken to mean smaller, in the same way that 0.0001 < 0 < 10000, and 0.0000000000001 is smaller than 0.0001. But in C, smaller means closer to zero. Thus, in Python, -4 is downward from -3.14159265359; integer division behaves the same way as `floor()` and `ceil()` do, truncating toward the smaller number rather than closer to zero.

This can cause problems when you're not expecting them. For example, I had a function in C that calculated the difference, in days, of the Gregorian calendar from the Julian; this value is termed the *deviation*, and it is constant over a period of 100 or 200 years. I transferred the function to Python and quickly tested it; it seemed to work, but two or three days later I had occasion to try it on negative dates. It claimed that before 0 (I use the astronomer's notation here, in which there was a year 0 and years before 0 are labeled with a minus sign instead of BC), there was no deviation. This was plainly wrong, and I tracked it down, finally, to a line of code that read `devn = 2 - leaper + ( leaper / 4 )`. Both `devn` and `leaper` are *variables*, which just means "a place to store a value." (You'll learn about variables in the next chapter.) Because `leaper` stores the century, when it was negative, the division `leaper / 4` returned a smaller value rather than the closer to zero value I was expecting.

Now, it turns out that for a great many calendrical calculations, the Python way is the preferred way; those of you reading this who do not know other programming languages won't have a problem with this because you won't already know how it works. I "knew" how it was supposed to work, and I was upset when it didn't work that way. To compound matters, I was taking code that worked in C, porting it to Python, and not testing the Python functions adequately.

The moral here is clear: learn your tools, test your code thoroughly, and don't always assume you know all there is to know about your tools. You can be unpleasantly surprised.

One of the great advantages of Python that I was most attracted to was the built-in support for long integers. Working with the Mayan calendar in C and C++ can be extremely frustrating, since if you require support for very large numbers, you must write it yourself. Python made Mayan calendrical calculations easy, but some areas would have been made even easier if no real difference existed between ordinary and long integers, or if Python detected a long integer and automatically used the appropriate size as required.

The distinction between ordinary integers and long integers seems to be largely arbitrary. Guido has said that he might do away with it in Python 2.0, but that's a long way off. In the meantime, you just have to be careful when doing arithmetic that might overflow signed 32-bit integers; if you happen to be dealing with the Mayan calendar, for example, it's not hard at all to exceed the two-billion-plus-change limit.

Ways exist to automatically change numbers from 32-bit to long as required, but you won't learn about these methods until later. Even then, the boundary between the two types of whole numbers can't be made completely transparent, and it is often easier to simply perform all math on longs to start with, although you do pay a speed penalty for doing so. You wouldn't want to use all longs, of course, if you weren't working with a problem that required them. For most ordinary programs, normal 32-bit integers are fine.

Summary

In this hour, we've covered all the basic arithmetic operators in Python, and you've used the interpreter to explore how the interpreter behaves. You should be getting a feel for Python, so that when we start talking about variables and flow control in the next chapter, you should be fairly comfortable. We've also discussed rounding, some floating point functions, scientific notation, parenthesization, and a difference in philosophy between Python and some other languages.

For your convenience and review, I've included a table of the math operators used in Python. Some of these operators mean different things when they're applied to objects other than numbers, but we'll cover those as they come up. I'll provide tables like this one in the summaries for any chapter where special symbols are used. Later in the book, I'll also give a detailed description of why operators behave differently when used with different objects.

TABLE 3.1 Math Operators in Python

Symbol	*Meaning*
+	Addition/Identity
-	Subtraction/Negation
*	Multiplication
/	Division
%	Modulo Operator
**	Exponentiation
divmod(x,y)	Function to return both x / y and x % y

3

Workshop

Q&A

Q Which is better? A computer or an abacus?

A That depends. If you're waiting on customers in a store and ringing up purchases, an abacus is clearly the right tool—unless you want automatically printed receipts. If you want to write programs, abaci have notoriously long download times.

Q When was scientific notation invented?

A At least two early uses of it occurred before 1890, but those may have been artifacts of translation. One genuine early reference to it was in Jeans' *Theoretical Mechanics*, a 1907 text, where he cites the earth's mass as 6×10^{27} grams. (Thanks to John Harper of Victoria University, Wellington, New Zealand, for this citation.)

Quiz

How do you tell the Python interpreter that a number is a long integer?

1. long("10000000000000000000000000000000000000")
2. 10000000000000000000000000000000000L
3. string.atol("10000000000000000000000000000000")
4. *any integer* / 1L

What happens when you multiply a floating point number times a really big long integer?

1. You get an OverflowError.
2. Python transforms the answer into a complex number.

3. Python tells you that you wouldn't understand the answer anyway.
4. When the really big number has 300 or so digits, Python starts to respond with `1.#INF` (or `inf` on Linux) instead of a numeric answer; otherwise, it reports an answer using scientific notation.

If *binary* is base 2 and *hexadecimal* is base 16, what is *octal* and who uses it?

1. Base 32; used by Macintosh programmers.
2. It has nothing to do with numbers; *octal* is the name of the # symbol.
3. Base 8; used by UNIX programmers who wear suspenders and smoke pipes.
4. Base 8; but no one uses it.

Answers

All the given methods will work.

The last. The limits of floating point arithmetic on Windows and Linux top out at an exponent of plus or minus 308, which is a pretty good sized (or very small) number. Outside those limits, the floating point libraries start returning a conventional symbol for infinity.

Octal is indeed base 8; and it's used mostly by UNIX programmers and programs—not all of us wear suspenders. The most visible usage is by the *chmod* program on UNIX, which lets users change permissions on their files. And the fancy name for the # symbol is *octothorpe*.

Exercises

If you do happen to discover that you care about such things as floating point accuracy and the loss of precision caused by computer representation of floating point numbers, by all means check out Donald Knuth's *The Art of Computer Programming*, particularly Volume 2, *Seminumerical Algorithms*, Chapter 4, which includes much history.

If the topic of large numbers such as the googol interests you, the following are a few Web sites to investigate. Some of the algorithms given are amenable to implementation in Python, and you can find some of these implementations at this book's Web site.

1. Large Finite and Infinite Numbers:
   `http://www.sci.wsu.edu/math/faculty/hudelson/moser.html`
2. How Much is a Gazillion?:
   `http://www.straightdope.com/mailbag/mgazilli.html`

3. How to Get a Googolplex: `http://www.informatik.uni-frankfurt.de/~fp/Tools/GetAGoogol.html`
4. Names of Small and Large Numbers: `http://studwww.rug.ac.be/~hvernaev/FAQ/node26.html`
5. Googolplex: `http://www.informatik.uni-frankfurt.de/~fp/Tools/Googool.html` (best)
6. Pi and Its Friends: `http://www.go2net.com/internet/useless/useless/pi.html`
7. Mayan Time Periods and Period Glyphs: `http://www.pauahtun.org/calglyph.html`

Find out how big a number it takes to crash Python. How big must a number be to crash your computer? (Back up all your files first.)

HOUR 4

Variables and Control Flow

Complex is better than complicated.

—Tim Peters

This hour, we'll learn what variables are and how to use them. We'll learn how to tell Python how to make decisions and what to do after it makes them. Doing the same thing over and over until some condition is true or false is what computers are good at, so we'll learn how to do this in Python. After you learn these ideas, we'll use some of them to write a small, but useful, program.

Variables

You might remember what variables are: all those *x*'s and *y*'s from high school algebra—the ones that plagued you when you were trying to sleep in study hall. Any formula has variables. A formula gives you the framework for working out a problem, but to actually work out the answer, you have to plug real values into the variables and do the math. Of course, those of us who *were* trying to sleep in study hall shuddered at the thought of "doing the math."

Variables in formulas and computer programming function the same way; they're just places to put actual values. In algebra, however, variables are placeholders for numeric values only; whereas in computer programs variables can hold *any* type of information. They can hold them for as long as your program is running or for only milliseconds, if that's all you need. You can also use variables as "scratch paper"—someplace to write down an intermediate value so it's not forgotten while you work on a different part of the formula or problem. If it will help to think of variables as "Post-It" notes, by all means do so.

Variables in Python can be named anything you want—as long as you don't call one by the same name as a Python reserved word and as long as they start with a letter or an underscore (_). Allowed names are names such as `i`, `z1` and `_old`, but names that won't work are `123abc` and `if`. Like anything else, however, that's not all there is to it. Some names for variables are better than others, and some names are better in some contexts than others. I'll explain some of this later in the chapter, but a good general guideline is to give your variables names that mean something. Sometimes that means that they should have long names, sometimes short ones.

Also called *keywords*, reserved words are words that Python reserves the right to use and that it won't let you use in any way but the right way. These words include `if`, `for`, and so on. A complete table showing all these words is included at the end of this chapter.

Fire up the interpreter and we'll try using some variables (see Figure 4.1).

Notice that when you're running IDLE or Python in a command window, you can just type the name of a variable and press Enter to see the value. When you use Python to run programs, however, you can't do that; you need to use another statement, the `print` statement. The `print` statement can be used several ways, and I'll describe them all later; right now, just remember that in interactive mode (IDLE) `print` *`variablename`* and *`variablename`* behave identically.

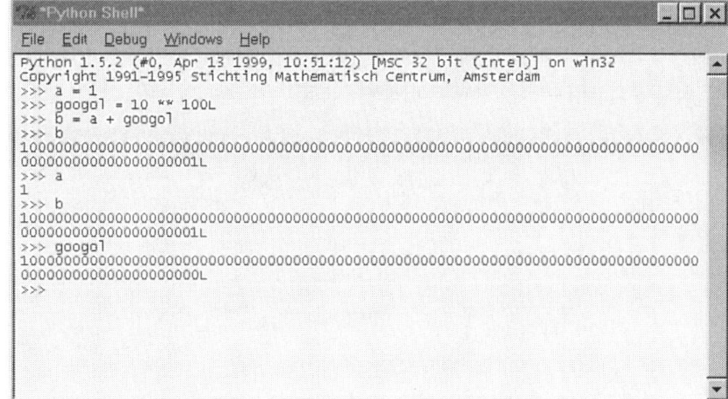

FIGURE 4.1
Some variables.

Figure 4.1 shows another important concept—*assignment*. The `=` sign means to take the value on the right side and store it in the variable found on the left side. This is different from the double equals (==) sign that you will see later, when we discuss the `if` statement; the single equals sign is an assignment statement, and not an algebraic operator. The double equals sign is a comparison operator. The two signs are very different in meaning. The line that says `googol = 10 ** 100L` also shows you that you can put an expression on the right side; an *expression* is just a piece of code that does some work. In this case, `10 ** 100L` calculates the value 10^{100}; the `=` sign stuffs the calculated value into the variable named `googol`. From now on until you exit Python, googol contains the same value, unless you change it.

You can do that, of course. Variables act the same way in equations or calculations as actual numbers do. Exactly. And that means, as Figure 4.2 shows, that after you have created a variable (by assigning a value to it), you can use it as if it were a number.

FIGURE 4.2
Calculating with and assigning to variables.

```
Python 1.5.2 (#0, Apr 13 1999, 10:51:12) [MSC 32 bit (Intel)] on win32
Copyright 1991-1995 Stichting Mathematisch Centrum, Amsterdam
>>> googol = 10 ** 100L
>>> googol
10000000000000000000000000000000000000000000000000000000000000000000000000000000
000000000000000000000L
>>> from math import *
>>> x = pi ** 2
>>> x
9.86960440109
>>> print x
9.86960440109
>>> print googol
10000000000000000000000000000000000000000000000000000000000000000000000000000000
000000000000000000000L
>>> anothervariable = googol + long(x)
>>> print anothervariable
10000000000000000000000000000000000000000000000000000000000000000000000000000000
000000000000000000009L
>>> print anothervariable, x, googol, pi
10000000000000000000000000000000000000000000000000000000000000000000000000000000
000000000000000000009L 9.86960440109 1000000000000000000000000000000000000000000
0000000000000000000000000000000000000000000000000000000000L 3.14159265359
>>>
```

4

You can also see one of the other ways to use `print`: not only can you print several variables at a time by separating them with commas, you can substitute actual numbers (which are called *constants*) and even strings (see Figure 4.3).

FIGURE 4.3
More fun with `print`.

```
*Python Shell*
File Edit Debug Windows Help
Python 1.5.2 (#0, Apr 13 1999, 10:51:12) [MSC 32 bit (Intel)] on win32
Copyright 1991-1995 Stichting Mathematisch Centrum, Amsterdam
>>> year = 1999
>>> l = 1999 % 4
>>> c = 1999 % 400
>>> label = "Hello, year"
>>> print label, year
Hello, year 1999
>>> print l, c
3 399
>>> print year, "is not a leap year."
1999 is not a leap year.
>>>
```

Variables provide an important tool in your programming kit, but to really do useful things, you need more. You need to know how to tell the computer to make a decision, and based on the outcome of the decision, what to do next. Decisions are the topic of the remainder of this chapter. When you tell Python what decisions to make, you're controlling the logic of the program. This is normally called *control flow*, and a number of basic decision-making special words in Python help you direct the flow of program logic. We'll begin with the most important (and certainly the earliest created) unit: `if`.

`if`, `elif`, and `else`

The `if` statement is the most basic control-flow statement in programming. Its syntax in Python is very simple:

```
if test:

    do something
```

The `test` portion includes, almost always, a *comparison operator*. A table of all Python's comparison operators is included in the summary at the end of this chapter, but the first one you should learn is the one for equality: ==. A common use is to test that a variable has a certain value, as shown in the following example:

```
if i == 1:

    do something
```

You can translate the test above into English like this: "If the variable i *is equal to* the value 1, then *do something*." The *do something* part can be any number of program statements, including other `if` statements. Other programming languages allow `test` to be an *expression* so that the `if` statement can do two or more kinds of work at once, but Guido decided not to allow that. For example, allowing programmers to use `if` as a variable name means that techniques such as this are legal:

```
if i = 1:

    do something
```

That is, you could assign the value `1` to the variable `i`, and then test to see whether the result is true. However, this could easily be a mistake. You could have meant to test for equality but forgotten to add the second = sign; here, the test is always going to be true because `i` is *always* going to have the value `1`. C programmers spend an inordinate amount of time chasing bugs such as this one, and Guido felt there were more rewarding ways to spend your debugging time.

The *do something* part of the `if` must be indented; in most other programming languages, the indentation is optional. In Python it is not. Other languages, for the most part, use special markers to indicate the beginning and the end of the *do something* part, which is called a *block*. Pascal, for example, uses THEN and END, so that an `if` construct would look like this:


```
if b < 0
then
    result := result + pi ;
end ;
```

The < symbol means *less than*, whereas the > symbol means *greater than*. The same code in C would look like this:

```
if ( b < 0 )
{
    result = result + pi ;
}
```

or, optionally, like this:

```
if ( b < 0 ) result = result + pi ;
```

The required indentation in Python is one of the more discussed features of the language; programmers seem, for the most part, to either love it or hate it. A few people like the language but don't care for the indentation (the technical editor for this book is one); and on the whole, the feature most likely to start a language war is this required indentation. I happen to think that indentation as a way to mark sections of code that go together is very attractive and helps make Python one of the most readable languages around. It's also the feature that Guido is least likely to change, so my advice is to learn to like it if you don't already.

When I was learning how to program, the term *iff* kept turning up in commentary on programs or in newsgroup postings. It mystified me for a long time because it obviously wasn't part of any programming languages; then I finally ran into an obscure comment in an obscure program that said, "iff: if and only if." Now you don't need to be mystified for years.

The complete syntax for the `if` statement allows for more control over the logical flow of your programs:

```
if test :
        do something
elif test :
        do something
elif test :
        do something
           ...
else :
        do something
```

The *do something* blocks can be any length and can include any legal Python program statements. We'll see how this all works by trying it out on IDLE. Remember the Gregorian and Julian leap-year rules we talked about in the last chapter? Start up IDLE; Figure 4.4 shows a complete `if` construct for determining whether any year is a leap year in the Gregorian calendar.

FIGURE 4.4
The `if` *for the Gregorian calendar.*

```
*Python Shell*
File Edit Debug Windows Help
Python 1.5.2 (#0, Apr 13 1999, 10:51:12) [MSC 32 bit (Intel)] on win32
Copyright 1991-1995 Stichting Mathematisch Centrum, Amsterdam
>>> y = 1900
>>> leap = "no"
>>> if y % 400 == 0:
        leap = "yes"
elif y % 100 == 0:
        leap = "no"
elif y % 4 == 0:
        leap = "yes"
else:
        leap = "no"


>>> print y, "leap:", leap, "in the Gregorian calendar"
1900 leap: no in the Gregorian calendar
>>>
```

> Notice, in Figure 4.4, that the way to tell IDLE you are finished with an indented block of code is to insert a blank line at the end of the block. Simply hit the Enter key an extra time. This works the same way in the command-line interpreter, but it doesn't indent lines for you the same way IDLE does.

For the Julian calendar, of course, you only have to test for divisibility by four; this means that the year 1900 was a leap year in the Julian calendar.

You can combine more than one test on a line, if you want, by using the special logical operators `and`, `or`, and `not`. If you put two tests into one `if`, using `and` means that both conditions must evaluate to true, but if the first test is false, the second one will not be checked. For `or`, either one can be true. If the first test is true, the second is not checked because there's no point. Figure 4.5 shows how they work.

FIGURE 4.5
The `if` and `and` statements.

```
*Python Shell*
File Edit Debug Windows Help
Python 1.5.2 (#0, Apr 13 1999, 10:51:12) [MSC 32 bit (Intel)] on win32
Copyright 1991-1995 Stichting Mathematisch Centrum, Amsterdam
>>> y = 1900
>>> leap = "no"
>>> if y % 400 == 0 and y % 100 == 0:
        leap = "yes"


>>> leap
'no'
>>>
```

The first test—for divisibility by 400—failed; therefore, the test for divisibility by 100 was never run.

`for` and `range()`

Although `if` is extremely useful, it's not always the easiest way to do things, especially if you want to do something over and over, merely changing the value of a variable each time you do that thing. Python's `for` statement is ideally suited for this task. In other languages, you must calculate how many times you want to do something, set beginning variables, and perform many other hard-to-remember details. Python's `for` statement is deceptively simple: it basically means, "Here's a list of things; `for` every item in this list, *do something*":

```
for target in list :
        do something
else:
        do something if no break statement was encountered.
```

The *target* just means a variable name; the *do something* part is formally termed the *body* of the `for` statement. During the execution of the body, you can, optionally, issue a `break` statement, which does exactly what it sounds like; it breaks out of the body part. If you didn't issue a `break`, then (and only then) the `else` body is executed. You actually won't see `else` clauses used very much because they aren't often called for; when they are, though, they're usually godsends. We'll see more of `break` when we talk about `while`, but in the meantime, see Figure 4.6 for an example of `for`.

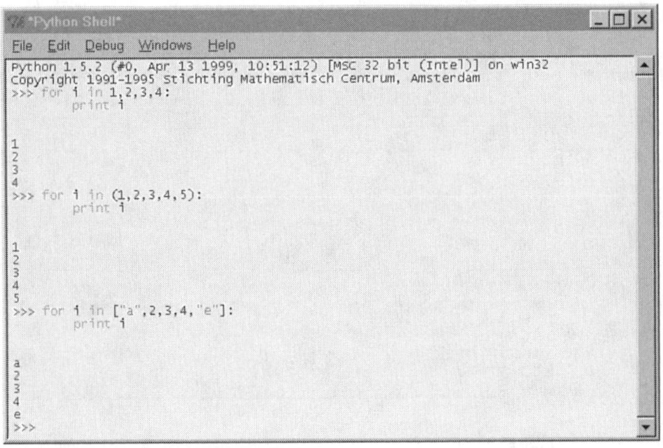

FIGURE 4.6
The `for` statement.

```
*Python Shell*
File Edit Debug Windows Help
Python 1.5.2 (#0, Apr 13 1999, 10:51:12) [MSC 32 bit (Intel)] on win32
Copyright 1991-1995 Stichting Mathematisch Centrum, Amsterdam
>>> for i in 1,2,3,4:
        print i

1
2
3
4
>>> for i in (1,2,3,4,5):
        print i

1
2
3
4
5
>>> for i in ["a",2,3,4,"e"]:
        print i

a
2
3
4
e
>>>
```

In the preceding figure, *list* is replaced by `1,2,3,4`, `(1,2,3,4,5)` and `["a",2,3,4,"e"]`; `for` sees four, five, and again five items, respectively, in the lists, and inserts, in order, the values it finds in *list* into the variable `i`. You can see this happening as the current value of `i` is printed on each iteration. Notice also that *list* is not required to contain only numbers; strings work just fine.

NEW TERM To iterate means to do something over and over; each single time you do a thing is an iteration. Hammering a nail could be described as an iterative process, in which each blow of the hammer is an iteration. When the loop is completed, you've got a completed nail. And sore fingers.

The `for` statement would obviously be more useful if we could escape from having to type into the program a list of all possible values for `list`, and that is just what `range()` does for us. The `range()` function is a nifty built-in function (*built in* means that Python always knows about it; you don't have to do anything special to use it) that produces ordered lists of numbers on demand. You can use it in four ways. The first, and simplest, is shown in the first line of Figure 4.7.

FIGURE 4.7

The `range()` *function.*

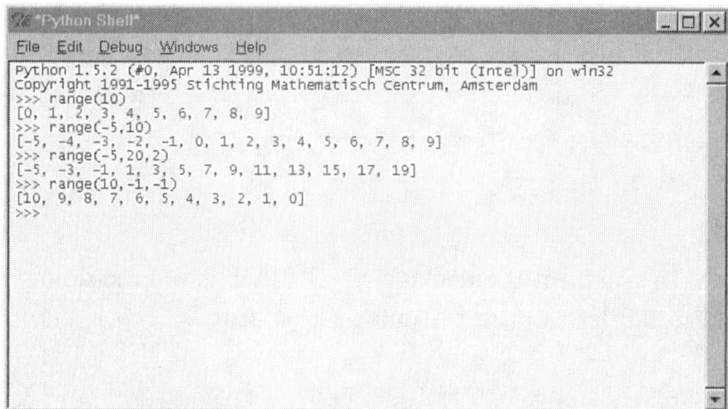

```
Python 1.5.2 (#0, Apr 13 1999, 10:51:12) [MSC 32 bit (Intel)] on win32
Copyright 1991-1995 Stichting Mathematisch Centrum, Amsterdam
>>> range(10)
[0, 1, 2, 3, 4, 5, 6, 7, 8, 9]
>>> range(-5,10)
[-5, -4, -3, -2, -1, 0, 1, 2, 3, 4, 5, 6, 7, 8, 9]
>>> range(-5,20,2)
[-5, -3, -1, 1, 3, 5, 7, 9, 11, 13, 15, 17, 19]
>>> range(10,-1,-1)
[10, 9, 8, 7, 6, 5, 4, 3, 2, 1, 0]
>>>
```

This first syntax, `range(10)`, just tells the function to make a list containing digits from 0 through 9; the single argument is not the size of the list but the ending digit of the list, and the default starting digit is always 0. Like C, numeric sequences start at 0 and stop (when going positive) at a digit one less than the limit; that is, if the limit is 10, stop at 9. What happens when you make a number negative? What happens when you try `range(0)`?

The second form shown in the figure, `range(-5,10)`, tells `range()` to make a list that stops before it gets to 10, as before, but to start at -5. This is how to get a list that starts with a negative number.

The third, `range(-5,20,2)`, shows that three possible arguments exist to the function: an option start, a required stop, and an optional step. You can see that this form starts at -5, jumps by two each time, and ends at 19.

Finally, the fourth demonstrates that `range()` does not always have to proceed in a positive direction. If start is greater than stop and step is negative, `range()` counts backward.

Combining `for`, `range()`, and `if` is very common; Figure 4.8 shows an example.

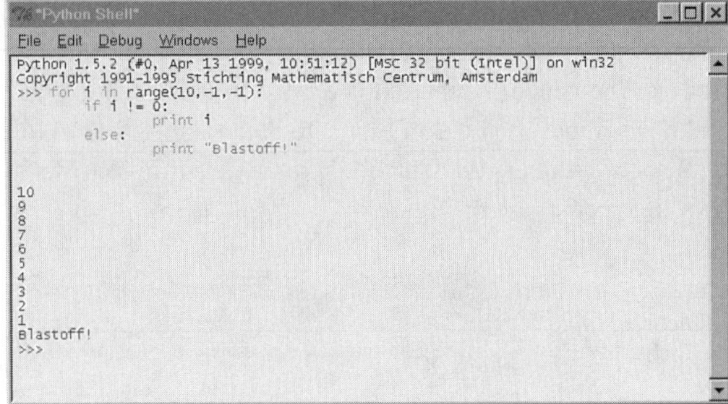
```
Python 1.5.2 (#0, Apr 13 1999, 10:51:12) [MSC 32 bit (Intel)] on win32
Copyright 1991-1995 Stichting Mathematisch Centrum, Amsterdam
>>> for i in range(10,-1,-1):
        if i != 0:
                print i
        else:
                print "Blastoff!"


10
9
8
7
6
5
4
3
2
1
Blastoff!
>>>
```

FIGURE 4.8
The `for`, `range()`, and `if` statements.

while

The `while` statement is one that also tells Python to keep doing something over and over, but it has a different syntax than the `for` statement. This syntax is shown in Figure 4.9.

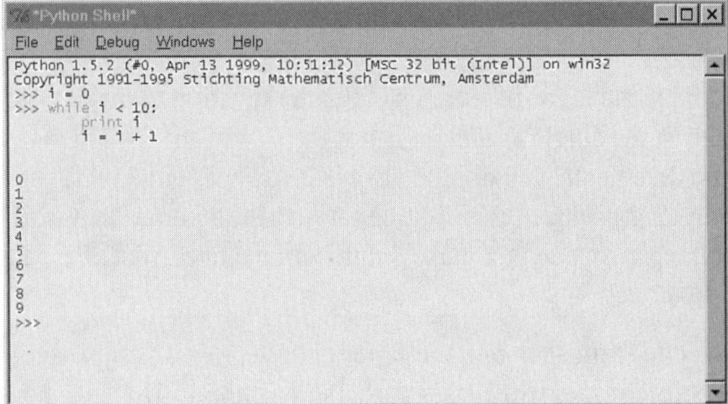
```
Python 1.5.2 (#0, Apr 13 1999, 10:51:12) [MSC 32 bit (Intel)] on win32
Copyright 1991-1995 Stichting Mathematisch Centrum, Amsterdam
>>> i = 0
>>> while i < 10:
        print i
        i = i + 1


0
1
2
3
4
5
6
7
8
9
>>>
```

FIGURE 4.9
The `while` statement with a test.

Of course, counting from 0 to 9 isn't very interesting. But `while` isn't only for counting; it's also for looking for a particular item in a sequence or for checking to see if something has happened. Figure 4.10 shows the first of these situations.

Notice that `while 1` is always true; this means that unless you, the programmer, intervene, `while 1` will keep on going forever. This is called an *infinite loop*; infinite loops that do go on forever are to be avoided, but infinite loops are quite useful as long as you make sure that they are *terminated*. Here, we're looking through some numbers; because, like the `if` statement, we can't assign values in the *test* part of the `while` (see Figure 4.11 to see what happens when we try), we have to modify the value of `i` ourselves. That's why the `i = i - 1` statement exists. Finally, notice what happens when we see the value we're looking for: we use the `break` statement to (appropriately enough) break out of, or terminate, the infinite `while` loop.

FIGURE 4.10
The `while 1` *statement.*

```
*Python Shell*
File  Edit  Debug  Windows  Help
Python 1.5.2 (#0, Apr 13 1999, 10:51:12) [MSC 32 bit (Intel)] on win32
Copyright 1991-1995 Stichting Mathematisch Centrum, Amsterdam
>>> i = 10
>>> msg = "Hey, the rocket left without me!"
>>> while 1:
        if i < 0:
                print msg
                break
        else:
                print i
        i = i - 1


10
9
8
7
6
5
4
3
2
1
0
Hey, the rocket left without me!
>>>
```

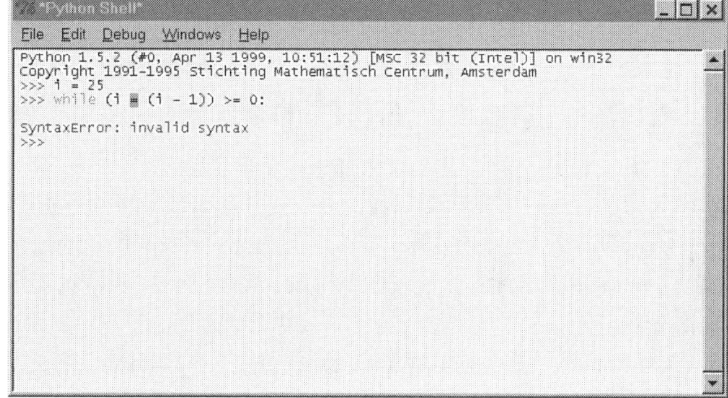

FIGURE 4.11
An invalid `while` *statement.*

The full syntax for `while`, like `for`, contains an `else` clause:

```
while test:
    do something
else:
    do something if no break statement was encountered.
```

Again, the `else` clause is not used much but can occasionally be quite valuable.

The second sort of `while`, in which you are just spinning your wheels until something else happens, is demonstrated in Figure 4.12.

True, this is a fairly artificial example, but later on we'll find uses for this style of `while` loop that are less so.

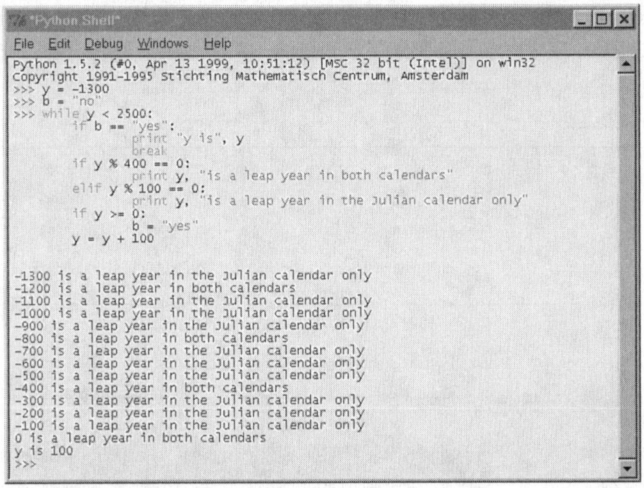

FIGURE 4.12
The `while` and `if` statements combined.

```
*Python Shell*
File Edit Debug Windows Help
Python 1.5.2 (#0, Apr 13 1999, 10:51:12) [MSC 32 bit (Intel)] on win32
Copyright 1991-1995 Stichting Mathematisch Centrum, Amsterdam
>>> y = -1300
>>> b = "no"
>>> while y < 2500:
        if b == "yes":
                print "y is", y
                break
        if y % 400 == 0:
                print y, "is a leap year in both calendars"
        elif y % 100 == 0:
                print y, "is a leap year in the Julian calendar only"
        if y >= 0:
                b = "yes"
        y = y + 100


-1300 is a leap year in the Julian calendar only
-1200 is a leap year in both calendars
-1100 is a leap year in the Julian calendar only
-1000 is a leap year in the Julian calendar only
-900 is a leap year in the Julian calendar only
-800 is a leap year in both calendars
-700 is a leap year in the Julian calendar only
-600 is a leap year in the Julian calendar only
-500 is a leap year in the Julian calendar only
-400 is a leap year in both calendars
-300 is a leap year in the Julian calendar only
-200 is a leap year in the Julian calendar only
-100 is a leap year in the Julian calendar only
0 is a leap year in both calendars
y is 100
>>>
```

`break`, `continue`, and `pass`

As you've seen earlier, the `break` statement is used to break out of a containing `for` or `while` loop. In other situations, you may find it necessary to not break out of but to start the loop over again from the top. This is exactly what the `continue` statement does; when it's encountered, it immediately goes right to the top of the containing `for` or `while` loop, skipping whatever code is left in the block. Python performs whatever test is indicated in the `for` or `while`. As an example, we can add a `continue` to the code in Figure 4.12; you can see this in Figure 4.13.

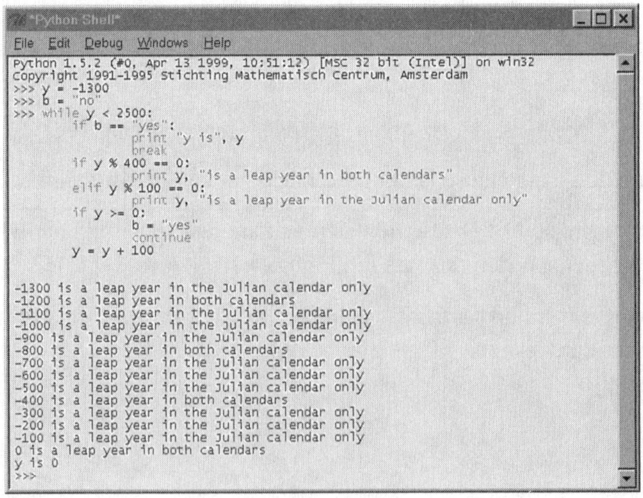

FIGURE 4.13
The `while`, `break`, and `continue` statements.

```
*Python Shell*
File Edit Debug Windows Help
Python 1.5.2 (#0, Apr 13 1999, 10:51:12) [MSC 32 bit (Intel)] on win32
Copyright 1991-1995 Stichting Mathematisch Centrum, Amsterdam
>>> y = -1300
>>> b = "no"
>>> while y < 2500:
        if b == "yes":
                print "y is", y
                break
        if y % 400 == 0:
                print y, "is a leap year in both calendars"
        elif y % 100 == 0:
                print y, "is a leap year in the Julian calendar only"
        if y >= 0:
                b = "yes"
                continue
        y = y + 100


-1300 is a leap year in the Julian calendar only
-1200 is a leap year in both calendars
-1100 is a leap year in the Julian calendar only
-1000 is a leap year in the Julian calendar only
-900 is a leap year in the Julian calendar only
-800 is a leap year in both calendars
-700 is a leap year in the Julian calendar only
-600 is a leap year in the Julian calendar only
-500 is a leap year in the Julian calendar only
-400 is a leap year in both calendars
-300 is a leap year in the Julian calendar only
-200 is a leap year in the Julian calendar only
-100 is a leap year in the Julian calendar only
0 is a leap year in both calendars
y is 0
>>>
```

The only difference between this example and the previous one is that because the `continue` is encountered, *100* will not be added to *y*. The final value here is *0*, whereas in the previous example it was *100*.

One more important statement, `pass`, is not much used in `for` and `while` loops; it's mostly seen in `class` statements, which will be covered in the second part of this book. The `pass` statement is used to indicate to Python that it should do nothing, not something; the official terminology for a statement like this is a *no-op*, short for *no operation*. It may seem quite strange that computers would need a special instruction because they only do things that they are explicitly told (that's the myth, anyway). In the early days of computer game software, though, no-ops were often used to build something called *timers*; even though a no-op does nothing, it still takes time. Therefore, to make certain events happen at the right time, programmers would use `for` loops that did nothing for a set number of times, thus giving the proper delay so that some event could be started correctly. No-ops, such as `pass`, are not as important as they once were, but now and then you do need them. Figure 4.14 shows the correct usage for `pass` with an `if` statement. If you try to get by without a body for the `if` statement, you will get a syntax error.

```
if test:
else:
    do something
```

The preceding is not legal Python syntax. The following is the correct syntax.

FIGURE 4.14
The `if` *and* `pass` *statements.*

```
Python 1.5.2 (#0, Apr 13 1999, 10:51:12) [MSC 32 bit (Intel)] on win32
Copyright 1991-1995 Stichting Mathematisch Centrum, Amsterdam
>>> i = 20
>>> if i > 50:
        pass
else:
        print i, "is too small"


20 is too small
>>>
```

A Complete Program

As promised, the following is a listing for a complete program using some of the concepts discussed in this chapter.

LISTING 4.1 Complete Program Using Control Flow

```
#!/usr/bin/env python
import sys
import string
if len (sys.argv) < 2:
    print "Usage: leap.py year, year, year..."
    sys.exit (0)
for i in sys.argv[1:]:
    try:
        y = string.atoi (i)
    except:
        print i, "is not a year."
        continue
    leap = "no"
    if y % 400 == 0:
        leap = "yes"
    elif y % 100 == 0:
        leap = "no"
    elif y % 4 == 0:
        leap = "yes"
    else:
        leap = "no"

    print y, "leap:", leap, "in the Gregorian calendar"

    if y % 4 == 0:
        leap = "yes"
    else:
        leap = "no"

    print y, "leap:", leap, "in the Julian calendar"

print "Calculated leapness for", len ( sys.argv ) - 1, "years"
```

You can either type it into an editor and save it as a file named **`leap.py`**, or you can download it from this book's Web page. Run it by typing **`python leap.py 1900 1904 2000`** into a DOS box or a UNIX shell. Then try it with bogus parameters, such as **`abcde 1900 2000`** and see what happens. You'll learn about that funny-looking `[1:]` later, along with the `len()` function and the other statements you haven't seen before.

Summary

As part of the discussion on variables, you learned that certain words in Python are reserved for special purposes. Table 4.1 lists all of Python's reserved words.

TABLE 4.1 Reserved Words in Python

and	elif	global	or
assert	else	if	pass
break	except	import	print
class	exec	in	raise
continue	finally	is	return
def	for	lambda	try
del	from	not	while

Be aware that you can use names of functions as variable names in Python; that is, it is entirely possible to use `int` as a variable name, even though that is the name of a function, written as `int()`. Figure 4.15 shows what happens when you do this.

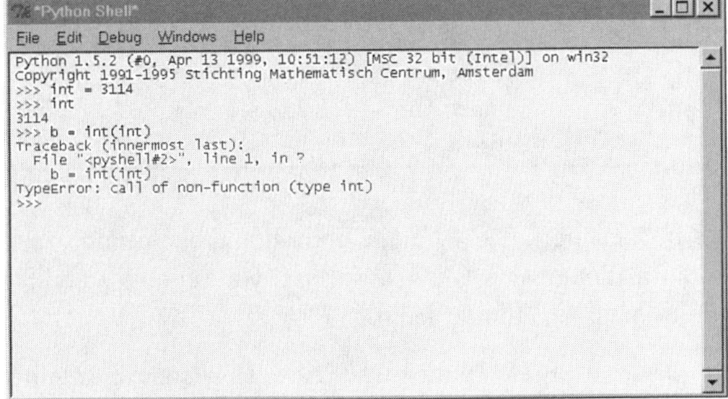

FIGURE 4.15
Python is too nice for its own good.

Function names in Python are only variables with a special type; they are not protected against misuse.

You also learned how to use the `if` statement that uses the *comparison* operators, which are all shown in Table 4.2.

TABLE 4.2 Comparison Operators in Python

a < b	True if a is less than b	a <= b	True if a is less than or equal to b
a > b	True if a is greater than b	a >= b	True if a is greater than or equal to b

continues

TABLE 4.2 continued

a == b	True if a is exactly equal to b	a != b	True if a is not equal to b
a is b	True if a is the same object as b	a is not b	True if a is not the same object as b
a < b < c	True if a is less than b AND b is less than c		Also works for >
not a	True if a is 0 or None (a special non-value value)	a or b	If a is 0 or None, use b; otherwise, use a
a and b	If a is 0 or None, use a; otherwise, use b		

The term "same object" used in the preceding table means a variable that contains the same information; that is, `a is b` is true if you set both `a` and `b` to `hello`, or if you assign the value `1` to both of them.

In this chapter, you also learned other basic flow control statements: `for`, `while`, `break`, `continue` and `pass`. You also learned about `range()`, which is a helper function for `for`. Finally, many of these concepts were used in a complete program.

Workshop

Q&A

Q How many control, or logic, flow operators are there?

A Very few—only six, with the notable absence of `goto`. You really don't need any others.

Q What's with these colons?

A They provide a distinct marker for the end of `if` and other statements; it's perfectly acceptable to code an `if` statement like the following, for example:

```
if a < b < c:  print a, b, c
else:  print c, b, a
```

Using the colon is the only way to separate the `if` and the body. Although I think the style I have used so far (and will continue to use) is more readable, it's a matter of personal preference.

Q It's obviously not good programming practice to use function names as names for variables because Python doesn't cooperate very well; are there languages that are smart enough to figure out the right thing to do when the programmer uses, for example, `int` or `range` as a variable name?

A It's a matter of opinion whether such behavior is smart, but yes, there are. A reason exists for not using them.

Q What if you want your program to go off someplace and never return? Couldn't you use `goto` in such a case?

A Yes, you could, but you wouldn't remember where you came from. The problem with `goto`s is not so much where you go, but that you have no idea how you got there.

Quiz

What are variables?

1. *x*'s and *y*'s.
2. Numbers that change randomly when you're not looking.
3. Names that stand for values that you can change.
4. Stars that change brightness.

What is the technical term for the *do something* part of an `if`, `for`, or `while`?

1. body.
2. block.
3. body block.
4. caltrop.

What does "$a > b < c$" mean?

1. It's not a legal Python statement, so it's meaningless.
2. Combine the values of *a* and *c* and put the result in *b*.
3. Compare the three values and if *b* is smaller than the other two, the statement is true.
4. Print *b* only if *a* and *c* are bigger.

Answers

Variables are names that stand for values that you can change.

The right term for *do something* is the body; a *block* of code shares the same level of indentation.

Compare the three values and if *b* is smaller than the other two, the statement is true. You're not limited to two comparisons, either. You can say, perfectly legally, `if a < b < c < d < ...` and continue the comparison chain as long as you want.

Exercises

Try to re-think the complete leap-year program given in Listing 4.1 to see whether you could come up with a better way to write it that would use `while` instead of `for`. There's no point in rewriting code, however, if you don't see an improvement.

Search on the Net for references to the very earliest computers and see whether any information about programming languages is available for them. See what logic-control statements were available for these early languages and computers.

Hour 5

Basic Data Types I: The Numeric Data Types

Flat is better than nested.

—Tim Peters

During the previous four hours, you've covered some basic ground and you've learned about variables. But what about the things you store in those variables? You've noticed that you can put pretty much anything you want into a variable: numbers, strings, and even functions. Surely there must be some rules? Yes, indeed there are, and the types of data and the rules governing how Python treats those types is the subject we cover in this hour and the next. In this hour, we will discuss the following numeric data types:

- Integer
- Long integer
- Floating point
- Complex

Data Types

Computers have a hard time determining what programmers mean unless they have some clues. Data typing is one of the ways that Python reacts to a programmer's clues. All it means is that what you put in a variable has a type. The categories that data items fall into are called *data types*, and, in Python, they include: numeric, sequence, function, and user-defined. The user-defined types will be covered in the middle third of this book. Numeric types are covered in this chapter, and the others in the next.

Data types, in Python (and in most programming languages), are divided into two broad categories: basic (or primitive) and user-defined. This second category is often called an object, but again, we will learn more about objects later in the book. Objects are a very important idea in programming, but the distinction between objects and basic types is not always clear, especially in the case of functions, and it is also true that not every object is a user-defined data type.

In this hour and the next, we will deal only with the basic data types, which are *numeric*, *sequence*, and *dictionary*. Functions are dealt with in the next chapter, and other user-defined types, or objects, are covered in Part II of this book. The first two of the basic types are subdivided further, and we'll talk about the subdivisions next.

Numeric Types

Computers aren't smart. Most computer languages need to be told explicitly just what sort of number a number is when you use one. Compiled languages must be told in advance; that is, you need to declare what type a variable is before you can assign a value to it, and after you do that, attempting to assign a value that is not of the correct type will result in some sort of compiler error. For example, suppose that in C you declare a variable like this:

```
int n;
```

That means that the variable *n* is going to contain integers—positive or negative whole numbers. Later in your code, if you try this:

```
    n = 3.14159;
```

The C compiler will complain, and you won't be allowed to do it. Python, however, will happily let you change the type of a variable without complaint. This is because Python is *dynamically typed*, whereas C is *statically typed*. That means, in simple terms, that after you declare a variable as a certain type in C, it can't ever be changed. In Python, you don't declare a type when you create a variable by assigning to it, so you can change a variable's type as often as you want. You can do that, in fact, so often that you can render a program unreadable. Few people do this; Python is such a readable language that no one really wants to work at making a program opaque.

If it's not a good idea to change a variable's type all the time, why allow it? What is dynamic typing good for? Why not make programmers declare up front what a thing is, and then make them stick to it? That is, after all, what most other computer languages do.

Python, however, operates on the assumption that you, the programmer, know what you are doing. Static types in other languages are an example of the opposite assumption—that you need protection from yourself. Dynamic typing, when not abused, can be a major keystroke saver, and it is extremely convenient. For example, suppose you're reading strings typed in by a user; you want to convert those strings into numbers and use them as inputs to your program. If the user is allowed to type in integers, floats, and longs, in a conventional programming language you would have to provide at least three different variables of the three different types. But in Python, you need only one variable, which can hold any of the three allowed types; this is easy because any variable can hold any type.

We begin our discussion with a type that you're already familiar with: *integers*.

Integer

Integers, as you recall from earlier chapters, are simply whole numbers: positive, negative, and zero. Like other programming languages, integers in Python suffer from size limitations; most languages implement integers as 32-bit quantities, which means that as far as Python is concerned, integers outside of the range `-maxint` to `+maxint` simply do not exist. You can see what this range is by starting Python on the command line or in IDLE, whichever you prefer, importing the `sys` module, and doing things with `maxint`. Listing 5.1 shows what you can expect on your usual PC; I get the same behavior on my Linux system.

LISTING 5.1 Adding 1 to *maxint*

```
Python 1.5.2 (#0, Apr 13 1999, 10:51:12) [MSC 32 bit (Intel)] on win32
Copyright 1991-1995 Stichting Mathematisch Centrum, Amsterdam
>>> from sys import *
>>> maxint
2147483647
>>> -maxint
-2147483647
>>> maxint + 1
```

continues

LISTING 5.1 continued

```
Traceback (innermost last):
   File "<pyshell#3>", line 1, in ?
     maxint + 1
 OverflowError: integer addition
 >>>
```

Some systems out there have 64-bit integers, and I believe Crays have 128-bit integers. The error you see in the listing, `OverflowError`, would still happen on these systems, but the range `-maxint` to `+maxint` would be much larger. I don't have access to machines with these large integers, but by using Python's long integer data type, it is a simple matter to find out what these ranges would be on such machines. Listing 5.2, `inttest.py`, is one that you should save in a file and run with Python. As with all the code in this book, you can download it from this book's Web site instead of typing it in.

LISTING 5.2 Code for Handling Large *maxints*

```
from sys import *
z = long ( maxint )
z1 = -z
print "32-bit machine:"
print "maxint:", z, "-maxint:", -z, "(2 ** 31L) -1:", (2 ** 31L) -1
print "-----------------------------------------------------------------"
y = (2 ** 63L) - 1
print "64-bit machine:"
print "maxint:", y, "-maxint:", -y
 print "-----------------------------------------------------------------"
 z = (2 ** 127L) - 1
 print "128-bit machine:"
 print "maxint:", z, "-maxint:", -z
```

Figure 5.1 shows what happens when you run `inttest.py`.

Notice that on a 32-bit machine, the largest integer you can use is (2 ** 31L) - 1; this is because one bit must be used for the sign of the number, either positive or negative. On most machines, this is called the *high-order bit*, but it's just as effective and perhaps more accurate to call it the *sign bit*. The reason you can't have a number that is exactly 2 ** 31L (that is, 2147483648) is complex and too intricate to go into here, but it has to do with the way that numbers are represented by the underlying machine bits—that is, in binary. Interested readers should check the exercises section of this chapter for a reference to a discussion of positional number systems, where computer representations of numbers are placed in context. Other computer languages allow integers to be stored without a sign, and such numbers are called, understandably, *unsigned numbers*. Unsigned numbers allow you to use all 32 bits to represent positive integers only.

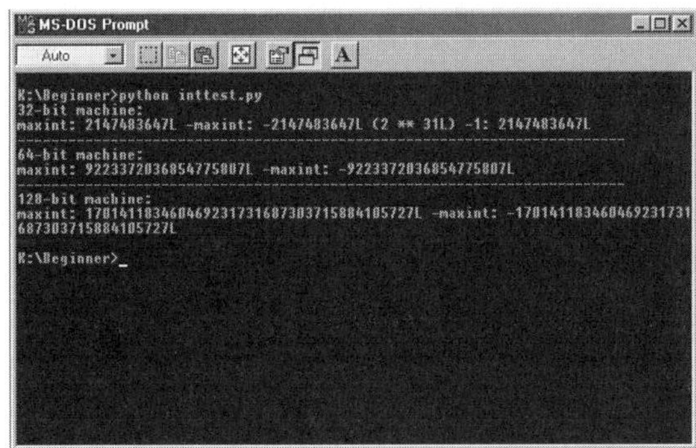

FIGURE 5.1
Output from Python `inttest.py`.

Similarly, on a 64-bit machine, the largest integer you can use is (2 ** 63) - 1, and on a 128-bit machine it is (2 ** 127) - 1. Unless you are doing research into the workings of calendars, you will not ordinarily bump up against the `maxint` limit even on 32-bit machines. The limits on 64-bit and 128-bit are very large; only large-scale scientific research and research on the Mayan calendar will push them. Long integers are Python's way around these limits, and we discuss them next.

Long Integer

Long integers, casually known as *long*s, or *bigints*, have been in Python since the very beginning. Essentially, they behave just like normal integers without limits. The conversion of integers to longs and vice versa is, unfortunately, not transparent to programmers; there is hope that Guido will erase the distinction between the two types in Python 2.0. With a little care, though, you can write algorithms that will perform these conversions when you need them to be transparent to users of your programs.

What do we mean by no limits? It really doesn't mean that you can use numbers of infinite size, only that the ordinary limits on numbers are abolished. What it means in practice is that the size of any given long is subject to the practical constraints of your machine; you can't, for instance, use a number in your program that takes up more space than you have memory for. For example, on my machine at home, a Windows NT 4.0 server, I have 256 megabytes of main memory. Disregarding the trivial overhead of the operating system and the even more trivial restraints imposed on programs run by the operating system, the largest long I could theoretically use is something like 2,013,265,920 digits long. This is a pretty good-sized number, but of course, because it can be calculated, it is not infinite. Internally, longs are stored as base 32768 numbers, with each digit occupying 16 bits; because 32768 is 2 ** 15, you can see that the 16th bit is used for something else. That 16th bit is used to implement an "overflow flag," used to track carries, borrows, and so forth, much like you do when working problems on paper. You can find out more about how bigints are built by doing some of the exercises at the end of this chapter.

Large numbers are, in practice, also limited by your patience; no one wants to wait the five years or so required right now to print out a googolplex, for instance. Nonetheless, longs can be very useful. Suppose you want to know the number of miles in a light year. With Python, this is a trivial calculation, providing that you know the speed of light (*c*) is approximately 300,000 kilometers per second or 186,000 miles per second. If the accuracy of this number leaves you unsatisfied, you can find out how to measure it yourself at `http://www.ph.unimelb.edu.au/~mbailes/P140/lecture22/index.htm`. Listing 5.3 shows a simple procedure to calculate the length, in space, of a light year (even though you won't learn about functions until the next chapter, I've gone ahead and implemented this as a function so that after you provide a better measurement of the speed of light you can reuse this procedure to refine your calculations).

LISTING 5.3 *c.py*

```
def c( p ) :
    spy = 60 * 60 * 24 * 365.2422
    n = long ( spy ) * long ( p )
    return n
if __name__ == "__main__" :
    n = c ( 186000 )
    print n
```

The 365.2422 is the usual approximation, in days, for the length of the year; the Gregorian calendar uses the approximation 365.2425, which, although not very close, is still closer than the figure used for the Julian calendar: 365.25 days. However, you should know that astronomers who use light years use Julian years because they think that so many variables are involved that the accuracy will always be substantially less than perfect. Duncan Steel, an astronomer, has written a short note describing several good reasons for preferring the simplicity of calculation provided by Julian years in astronomical distance measurements. This note can be found at `http://www.pauahtun.org/TYPython/steel.html`.

Running the short program, `c.py`, will produce the following output:

```
5869588236000L
```

This is, indeed, about 6 trillion miles, just as you were told in school but refused to believe. I know I spent days calculating this figure out by hand; didn't everyone? As noted previously, a better measurement of the speed of light will increase your accuracy, as will a better measurement of the length of the year. (This latter is problematic, of course; Simon Cassidy, a noted calendrical scholar, has much to say on this subject. A good place to start reviewing what Simon has to say is his home page, at `http://hermetic.nofadz.com/cal_stud/cassidy/`.)

Floating point

We talked about floating point numbers and scientific notation in earlier chapters, so I won't spend too much time on them. Python always stores floating point numbers in what are called *doubles* in C (from *double-precision* floating point numbers), which usually means 64 bits of memory; because some of those bits are used for other purposes, the largest real number you can represent is about 1.79769e+308, and the smallest is around 2.22507e-308, at least on most computers. Naturally, floating point numbers outside this range don't exist as far as Python is concerned. If you refer to floating point numbers outside of the range that Python understands, you will get odd results. See what your machine does when you assign a variable to the maximum floating point value of 1.79769e+308, and then double it. On my NT machine, I get the value `1.#INF`. There are ways to persuade Python to let you know that an error condition exists, and we cover those in a later chapter.

On some machines, usually the same ones that have 64-bit and 128-bit integers, Python's floating point numbers use more bits, which increases the range of real numbers you can represent. Python stores its basic data types in terms of the underlying hardware; therefore, as machines get faster and more capable in the future, so too will Python.

If you are curious about how floating point numbers are represented on your machine, a C program is available at this book's Web site which, when you run it, tells you the maximum and minimum limits of floating point arithmetic, along with lots of other informative details: `http://www.pauahtun.org/TYPython/machar.zip`. I've made it available in source and in binary form for Linux and DOS; users of other machines will have to find a way to get it compiled from the supplied source code.

Complex

Complex numbers, like longs, have been part of Python for a while. Very few other languages include built-in support for complex numbers; FORTRAN is the only one that I know of. It helps, of course, if you know what complex numbers are and what they're good for.

To address the latter first, complex numbers are extremely useful in electrical engineering, where they describe the behavior of complicated electrical circuits with an admirable simplicity. They're useful in celestial mechanics, equation systems that help astronomers plot the orbits of planets, asteroids, and moons. And recently, they've achieved a bit of fame in the computer graphics field, popularized (if that's the word) by Benoit Mandelbrot, the IBM Fellow who discovered the mathematical set that bears his name. In a later chapter, I'll show you how to use complex numbers in drawing the Mandelbrot set.

As to what they are, remember earlier chapters where you thought of all the whole numbers as appearing on a single line with 0 at the center and extending infinitely in both directions, negative and positive. These whole numbers, ...-3, -2, -1, 0, 1, 2, 3..., are called the integers. Python's long integers are on the same number line because they're just bigger integers. Floating point numbers, too, appear on the number line; if you subdivide the line into infinitely many points between each whole number, those subdivisions are the floating point numbers. Together, the integers and the floating point numbers are called the *real numbers*, and an infinite number of them exist.

What we think of when we talk about numbers and the number line is actually a conflation of four *number systems*, or numerical contexts.

1. Natural numbers, or counting numbers: 1, 2, 3, and so on
2. Integers: -3, -2, -1, 0, 1, 2, 3, and so on
3. Rational numbers: 3/4, 5/8, 1/10, and so on
4. Real numbers: 3.14159, 1.001, and so on, including irrational numbers

You may have heard of *irrational numbers*, of which *pi* (the ratio of the circumference of a circle to its diameter) is the best-known example. These are numbers which cannot be expressed as a ratio of whole numbers (*a/b*). When you attempt to determine their actual values, not only do they not work out to a simple value, such as 1.5/0.5 = 3.0, nor to a repeating decimal, such as 10.0/3.0 = 3.33333333333333…, but they repeat infinitely without any semblance of a pattern. Carl Sagan's science fiction novel *Contact* describes a message hidden in pi, somewhere out in the vicinity of the 100 billionth decimal place. If this were true, we would indeed have a message from the gods, not just from space aliens, but such a possibility is so unlikely that it can be rejected out-of-hand. Mathematics simply does not work that way. At this book's' Web site, you'll find Python code to print out pi to however many places you desire so that you, too, can join the search for messages from aliens.

Despite being called irrational, these numbers still appear on the number line; as with any other type of number on that line, an infinite number exist. Numbers that are not irrational are, naturally enough, called *rational.*

Numbers exist, however, that are not part of the number line that we have been talking about; these are the *imaginary* numbers. Early in mathematical history, even negative numbers were considered nonsensical—an attitude that is perhaps most pronounced in Mayan mathematics, where negative numbers were used but never named. Later, when the first inklings of what are now called imaginary numbers appeared, mathematicians were culturally disposed to ignore their findings.

The classic example of an imaginary number is the square root of -1. As we know, a square is the result of multiplying a number times itself; this number is called the *root.* For example, 5 is the square root of 25. If we remember our basic algebra, we know that in situations where the signs of the multiplicands are the same, the result is always positive. The rules for square roots, however, dictate that the sign must be the same; therefore, no way exists to calculate a square root for a negative number. At the same time, because negative numbers exist, such numbers must have squares, and therefore, square roots. We're in the same position as Mayan mathematicians here; we can point to the results that make us believe that such numbers exist, but as far as actually calculating the precise value of one of them in real number terms, we are at a loss.

5

Although we cannot directly use imaginary numbers, we can work with them quite easily in the form of *complex* numbers. Modern mathematicians place the imaginary numbers on a line perpendicular to the number line of real numbers, and complex numbers have both a real component and an imaginary component. Complex numbers have rules for addition, subtraction, multiplication—in fact, every operation that can be performed on real numbers can be performed on complex numbers. By following those rules, we can find the square root of -1. The real part of a complex number is simply written as is, whereas the imaginary part is written as a real number followed by a suffix of *i* or *j*. Because Python uses *j*, I will also use *j* throughout this book. The square root of -1 is written (0,1j); multiplication of complex numbers follows this rule:

```
(a,b)(c,d) = (ac-bd, ad+bc)
```

Working it out, then, gives us the following:

```
(0,1j)(0,1j)
(0 * 0) - (1 * 1), (0 * 1) + (1 * 0)
(0 - 1), (0 + 0)
(-1, 0j)
```

And the *0j* part drops out when mapping to a real number, giving us -1.

The equivalent operation in Python is quite simple because complex numbers are built in. In Python, all we need to do is define a number as complex, which is very easy. The following shows how to tell Python that the variable *a* is a complex number:

```
a = 0 + 1j
```

To square that complex number is equally simple:

```
s = a * a
```

Because Python keeps track of what kind of number a variable contains, it knows that *a* is complex and that the square, *s*, should also be complex. Applying normal math operators to complex numbers will do the correct thing, as you can see when you multiply two complex numbers. In fact, any operation that you can perform on floating point numbers can be performed on complex numbers, and so it should be no surprise to find that complex math functions have their own module. Remember that in earlier chapters, we often obtained direct access to math functions, such as `sqrt()`, by doing this:

```
from math import *
```

This line tells Python to find the `math` module and pull in all the functions it finds there; that way, you can say, for example:

```
i = sqrt(1.0)
```

If we try the same trick with complex numbers, Python complains, as seen in Figure 5.2.

FIGURE 5.2
Math functions.

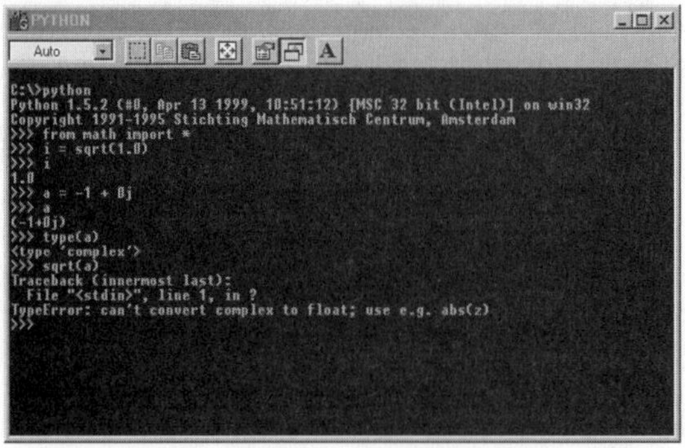

Because we want complex math functions, we can instead import the *complex math* (`cmath`) module with

```
from cmath import *
```

which will take care of the error we saw previously, as shown in Figure 5.3 for the same conditions.

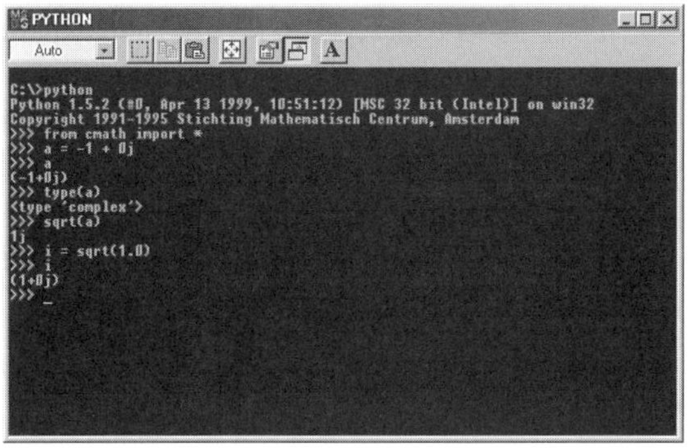

FIGURE 5.3
Complex math functions.

```
C:\>python
Python 1.5.2 (#0, Apr 13 1999, 10:51:12) [MSC 32 bit (Intel)] on win32
Copyright 1991-1995 Stichting Mathematisch Centrum, Amsterdam
>>> from cmath import *
>>> a = -1 + 0j
>>> a
(-1+0j)
>>> type(a)
<type 'complex'>
>>> sqrt(a)
1j
>>> i = sqrt(1.0)
>>> i
(1+0j)
>>> _
```

Of course, that leads to another problem, as you can see by examining the last few lines in the preceding figure: All the functions in the `math` and `cmath` modules have the same names. If `cmath` is imported last, all the floating point functions get replaced with their complex equivalents, and thus all floating point numbers are treated as complex numbers. But what if we need to use functions in both modules? This clearly points up one of the dangers of using the `from` *`module`* `import *` format—sooner or later, you're bound to lose something you need! The solution is to use what's called *qualification*. You just need to specify exactly which module should provide which function, as shown in Figure 5.4.

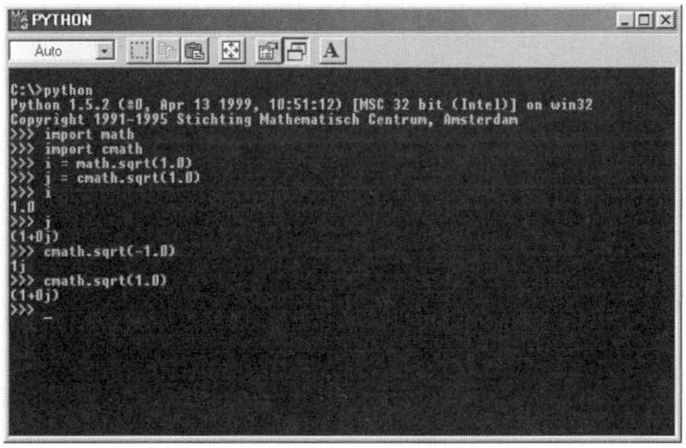

FIGURE 5.4
Complex and floating point math functions.

```
C:\>python
Python 1.5.2 (#0, Apr 13 1999, 10:51:12) [MSC 32 bit (Intel)] on win32
Copyright 1991-1995 Stichting Mathematisch Centrum, Amsterdam
>>> import math
>>> import cmath
>>> i = math.sqrt(1.0)
>>> j = cmath.sqrt(1.0)
>>> i
1.0
>>> j
(1+0j)
>>> cmath.sqrt(-1.0)
1j
>>> cmath.sqrt(1.0)
(1+0j)
>>> _
```

The `.` is the qualification operator; we use it to specify a module, as a prefix, in which to find a particular function—the same as we did previously to call the correct `sqrt()` function. The `.` has other uses, which we discuss in the object section of this book, but for now it will be most useful in helping Python figure out where to get a function from.

Summary

In this hour, we've talked about data types in general and numeric types in particular. You've seen integer, long integer, floating point, and complex numeric types and how they are implemented in Python. We talked about complex numbers—relating them to real numbers—and the functions available that use them. You've learned a bit about number systems and have also seen how to make sure you're getting the right math functions when you need them. In the next hour, we'll cover more advanced ground and talk about the remaining data types: sequence and dictionary.

Workshop

Q&A

Q What is an example of complex numbers that is used in the real world?

A The strength of an electromagnetic field is the most direct example; because such a field has an electric component and a magnetic component, you can use complex numbers as a measure of that strength.

Q I ran `machar.exe` on my machine, and it shows that it's only using 53 bits out of 64 for my floating point numbers. What's going on?

A The 53 bits are used only for the *mantissa*, or fractional part, but another 11 bits are used for the exponent. You have a total of 64 bits in which to store floating point numbers.

Quiz

1. What are the two components of complex numbers?
    a. Real and unreal
    b. Imaginary and nightmare
    c. Imaginary and real
    d. Scary and posh

2. What five number systems did we talk about?
   a. Natural, unnatural, imaginary, rational, and irrational
   b. Natural, integer, rational, real, and complex
   c. Ordovician, Silurian, Devonian, Jurassic, and Triassic
   d. A, B, C, 4, and E
3. What happens if you import two modules that have functions with duplicate names?
   a. If you just import them and qualify the names of the functions: nothing.
   b. If you use `import *`, the second one imported overrides the first.
   c. You won't be able to use the duplicate functions in either module.
   d. You won't be able to use either module.

Answers

1. Answer c, complex numbers have imaginary and real parts.
2. Answer b, the five number systems are natural, integer, rational, real, and complex.
3. Answers a and b, the first two answers are both true; if you use import, you must qualify the names so that no possibility of conflict exists. If you use `import *`, you won't be able to use duplicate names in the first one loaded. Qualification can't be used on a module that you have already used `import *` on.

5

Exercises

For some introductory material on imaginary, complex, rational, and irrational numbers, see `http://www.math.toronto.edu/mathnet/answers/imaginary.html` and other topics on the same site.

For more advanced material on complex numbers, read Paul J. Nahin's delightful book, *An Imaginary Tale: The Story of the Square Root of -1*. A personal aside: the cover of the book features a painting by Remedios Varo, one of the greatest surrealist painters of this century. One or two Web sites are devoted to her life and work; the best is `http://csgwww.uwaterloo.ca/~dmg/remedios/`.

For a discussion of Mayan calendrical math, see `http://www.foretec.com/python/workshops/1998-11/proceedings.html`, which, among other things, discusses negative numbers and the Mayans' view of them.

For a discussion of positional number systems, such as the base 32768 system used to implement Python's long integers, take a look at Donald Knuth's *The Art of Computer Programming*, Volume 2, *Seminumerical Algorithms*. See especially Chapter 4, sections 4.1 and 4.4.

In an earlier chapter, I described a number of floating point "gotchas"; things you need to watch out for, especially when dividing floating point numbers. It would probably be useful to review those gotchas: see Chapter 3, "Basic Arithmetic with Python."

HOUR 6

Basic Data Types II: The Sequence and Dictionary Data Types

For Zen students a weed is a treasure.

—Shunryu Suzuki, Zen Mind, Beginner's Mind

Last hour, we learned about the numeric data types available in Python. In this hour, we'll continue the discussion of data types:

- Sequence data types:
    1. string
    2. tuple
    3. list
- Dictionary data type
- Arrays (a brief discussion)

Sequence Data Types

All these types are distinct from the numeric types in that they can be operated on in two general ways. The first way is similar to what you can do with numbers; that is, you can assign values of these types to variables, and you can perform operations on the variable as a unit. The second way is to view them as sequences—portions of computer memory of varying length that you can take apart, access individual items within, modify the individual components, and put together again. Although it is possible to construct sequences of the numeric types (these are called arrays; a standard module is available that contains support for them, but they aren't used much), there is little built-in support for numeric sequences in Python. In contrast, a great deal of support is available for the sequence types. At the end of this hour, I will spend a short time discussing the array module and how using an array type differs from the basic data types.

Strings

Strings are basic data types in Python, and you have seen them in use to some degree in earlier chapters. Python defines strings as "anything between quotes," which is a fairly lax definition. Most computer languages make distinctions among the different kinds of quotation marks, but Python does not. Single and double quotes are treated identically; it's simply a matter of convenience which one you choose to use.

What kind of characters can go between quotes? It depends. If you are using single quotes, anything goes except single quotes. If you are using double quotes, you can't use double quotes. Of course, there is a way to tell Python to use a quote inside a string. The backslash is called the 'escape' character and tells the interpreter that the next character is to be treated differently. In the case of a quote character, the difference is that it gets treated 'normally'—as a real character—instead of the end of the string. You'll learn about some other escape sequences later in this chapter. For example, in Figure 6.1, you can see what happens when you try to put a single quote inside a single-quoted string—and two ways to fix it.

Note also the difference when you say **`print s, s2`** and when you simply type **`s2`** and press Return; using `print` doesn't put quotes around the string it displays. That's because when you type in the name of a variable and press the Return key, Python in the interactive mode assumes that you want to see what the value of the variable is, and it puts double quotes around string values to remind you of the type. If you use `print`, Python assumes that if you want quotes, you will ask for them.

FIGURE 6.1
Mistakes were made.

```
*Python Shell*
File Edit Debug Windows Help
Python 1.5.2 (#0, Apr 13 1999, 10:51:12) [MSC 32 bit (Intel)] on win32
Copyright 1991-1995 Stichting Mathematisch Centrum, Amsterdam
>>> s = 'I'm a single-quoted string.'
SyntaxError: invalid syntax
>>> s = 'I\'m a single-quoted string.'
>>> s
"I'm a single-quoted string."
>>> s2 = "I'm a double-quoted string."
>>> print s, s2
I'm a single-quoted string. I'm a double-quoted string.
>>> s2
"I'm a double-quoted string."
>>>
```

In addition to single and double quotation marks, there is a third way to delimit a string, and that is through the use of triplets of double, or single, quotation marks. Generally referred to as "triple-quoted strings," or just "triple quotes," these are used to place large chunks of text into a string. The most frequent use is in the documentation string of a function, or docstrings, which you will learn more about in the next hour. Figure 6.2 shows a triple-quoted string in use, and you can see a couple of advantages with this style of quoting:

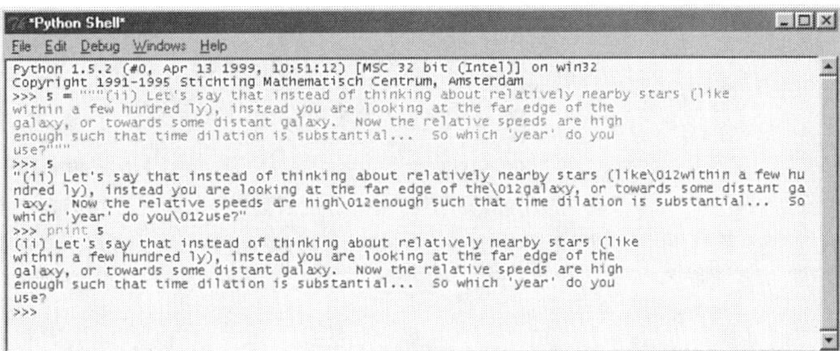

FIGURE 6.2
Triple quotes.

As before, you can see the difference when you ask Python to show you the value of the variable, by typing **s**, and using the `print` variable. Triple-quoting a string enables you to store almost anything into a string without having to escape the more troublesome parts, including the carriage returns (those are stored as the `"\012"` characters in the previous string). You can store anything you want in a triple-quoted string, except for three double quotation marks in a row—and you can easily store those by escaping each quote the same as we did in Figure 6.1. Because the backslash character inside a string always means something special to Python, Table 6.1 lists all these special meanings.

Table 6.1 Escape Codes

Backslash Code	*Meaning*
`\`	Line continuation when it appears at the end of a line; it must be the last character in the line, because putting a space after a backslash at the end of a line is a syntax error
`\\`	Converts to a single backslash
`\'`	Converts to a single quote
`\"`	Converts to a double quote
`\a`	Converts to the bell (it makes your computer beep)
`\b`	Converts to a backspace
`\e`	Converts to the escape key (`\033` or `\x1B`, not the backslash character)
`\0`	Converts to a NULL (see text)
`\n`	Converts to a linefeed
`\v`	Converts to a vertical tab (which almost no one uses)
`\t`	Converts to a horizontal tab
`\r`	Converts to a carriage return
`\f`	Converts to a form feed
`\0nn`	Converts to an octal character (see text)
`\xnn`	Converts to a hex character (see text)
`\any`	Converts to `\any`; that is, if `any` is not one of the characters listed previously, Python replaces the `\any` combination with `\any`. This is equivalent to the identity operation in mathematics

You don't have to be concerned about most of the preceding special meanings. Little use exists for a vertical tab, for instance, because the machine for which it was invented (the teletype) is obsolete. You will usually not have to care about the differences between linefeeds, carriage returns, and form feeds either, unless you happen to regularly move text files between UNIX, DOS, or Windows, and the Macintosh. In that case, I'm sure you have already heard more than enough about the differences! Listing 6.1 gives a small program that demonstrates some of the more common escape codes you will encounter.

Listing 6.1 Escape Codes (*xtst.py*)

```
s = "e:\\Beginner"
s1 = "e:" "\\" "Beginner"
s2 = s1 + \
"\\tst.py"

```

```
print "This is a DOS path:", s
print "This is a DOS path:", s1
print "This is a DOS path:", s2

s3 = "I contain 'single' quotes"
s4 = 'I contain "double" quotes'
s5 = """I am a triple-quoted string that contains \"\"\" quotes"""

print s3
print s4
print s5

s6 = "I contain\t\t\tthree\t\t\ttabs"
s7 = "I contain a\t\v\tvertical tab"
s8 = "I contain a\t\a\tBELL, which you can hear"

print s6
print s7
print s8

s9 = "I contain a BACK\bSPACE"
s10 = "I contain a BACKK\bSPACE AND a \nNEWLINE and a \rLINEFEED"
s11 = "I've got a FORM\fFEED!"

print s9
print s10
print
print s11

s12 = "If Python doesn't know what the escape code\n" \
"means, it performs the identity operation!  \identity!"
s13 = "But if you don't know what a code means, don't use it!"

print s12
print s13
```

Figure 6.3 shows what happens when you run `xtst.py` in a DOS box.

Figure 6.4 shows the results of running `xtst.py` in an IDLE window; you can see that some of the escape codes are represented differently from the DOS box.

ASCII stands for American Standard Code for Information Interchange. Originally a 7-bit code, it has been extended to 8 bits. The 7-bit ASCII table contains 128 characters from 0000000 to 1111111, but the 8-bit table extends to 11111111. In hex, this is 00 to FF.

FIGURE 6.3

`xtst.py` in a DOS box.

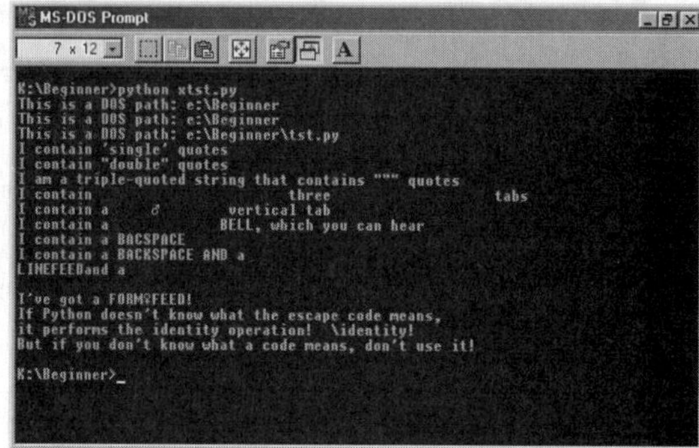

FIGURE 6.4

`xtst.py` in an IDLE Window.

```
*Output*
File Edit Windows Help
This is a DOS path: e:\Beginner
This is a DOS path: e:\Beginner
This is a DOS path: e:\Beginner\tst.py
I contain 'single' quotes
I contain "double" quotes
I am a triple-quoted string that contains """ quotes
I contain                    three                    tabs
I contain a     □       vertical tab
I contain a     □       BELL, which you can hear
I contain a BACK□SPACE
I contain a BACKK□SPACE AND a
NEWLINE and a □LINEFEED

I've got a FORM□FEED!
If Python doesn't know what the escape code means,
it performs the identity operation!  \identity!
But if you don't know what a code means, don't use it!
```

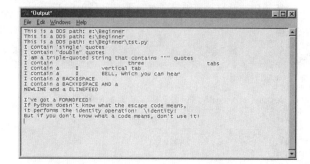

The reason for the character differences is that DOS has extended the ASCII character set. Listing 6.2, `ascii.py`, is a small Python program that you can use to find out how characters are displayed; you can run it on any platform that uses ASCII.

LISTING 6.2 Printing ASCII with *`ascii.py`*

```
#!/usr/local/bin/python

i = 0
while i < 256:
    print chr(i),
    if i != 0 and i % 8 == 0 :
        print
    i = i + 1
```

chr() is a special Python function that takes a number as input and returns the (usually) ASCII character associated with that number. The reverse function, *ord()*, takes a character as input and returns the number.

Figure 6.5 shows `ascii.py` run from a DOS box.

FIGURE 6.5
ASCII codes displayed by DOS.

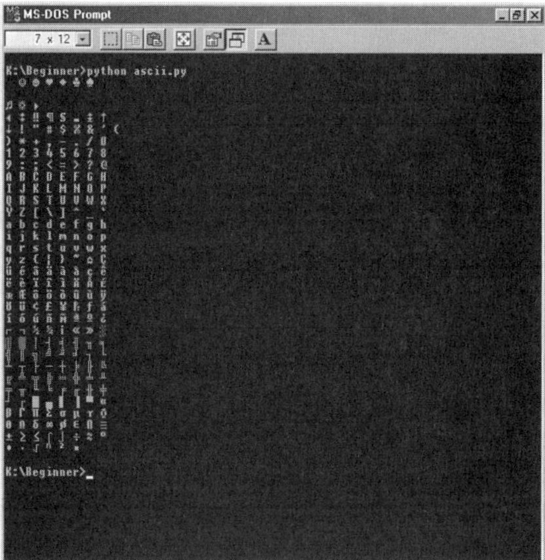

Sometimes you do not want values stored in a string variable to obey the normal character escape rules. On Windows, for example, there are occasions when you might want a variable to contain a path to a file. Paths on Windows contain backslash characters because the backslash is the normal directory separator for DOS and Windows. Backslashes in these paths might easily produce results you don't expect if, for example, you forget to double the backslashes when you enter them. Guido has used his time machine to add a new kind of string just for this purpose. They are called raw strings, and you can tell Python that a string is raw by putting an "r" before it, like this:

```
s = r"k:\Beginner"
```

Naturally, raw strings have many other uses; the real reason Guido put them into Python is because it makes writing regular expressions much easier than if raw strings weren't available. Regular expressions are not covered in this book, but you can find out about them by searching `http://www.python.org/`.

6

Guido is purported to have a time machine that he uses to add features to Python—features that people complain about not having before they have finished complaining. Attributions of temporal intervention are usually provoked by people who haven't read either the Python documentation or the Python source code (both free) and who then ask for a feature that already exists. Of course, there are many often-overlooked features in Python, so even gurus sometimes ask for things that already exist. Because Python has been so well thought out, Guido rarely has to violate the Temporal Prime Directive.

Strings are useful when you are writing a program to collect some input from a user, when you want to provide documentation to a programmer, when you want to interface with your operating system, or when you want to examine the output of some other program. You may have noticed that some of the operators, such as +, that we used with the numerical types can also be used with strings, but they do different things. This is by design. Python keeps track of the nature of all variables for you, so that at any given time, it knows exactly what you are asking it to do. `1 + 1`, for example, is obviously a mathematical statement, but what does `"string1" + "string2"` do? The + obviously means something different here; in the context of strings, + means to concatenate the two strings. The result of `"string1" + "string2"` is thus `"string1string2"`. This capability to use the same operator to mean different things in different contexts is called *operator overloading*, and when used appropriately can be one of the most valuable features of Python. Later in this book, you learn how to do your own operator overloading.

Table 6.2 shows the various operators that you can use with strings, and following the table, I discuss how to use the operators.

TABLE 6.2 Sequence Operators Used with Strings

Operator	*Meaning*	*Example*
`s1 + s2`	Concatenate `s1` and `s2`	`s3 = s1 + s2`
`s * n` or `n * s`	Repetition; repeat sequence `s` `n` times	`t = s * 5`
`u in s` `u not in s`	Is `u` a member, or not a member, of sequence `s`?	`if u in s:` *`do something`* `for u in s:` *`do something`*
`s[n]`	Index sequence `s` by `n`	`z = s[0]`
`s[i:j]`	Slice sequence `s` from `i` to `j`	`z = s[0:2]`

Operator	*Meaning*	*Example*
`len(s)`	Return length of sequence s	`l = len(s)`
`min(s)`	Return smallest item of sequence s	`m = min(s)`
`max(s)`	Return largest item of sequence s	`m = max(s)`

The first operator, +, we've already seen in use. The second, the repetition operator *, should also be obvious. Figure 6.6 shows how to use it.

FIGURE 6.6
The repetition operator.

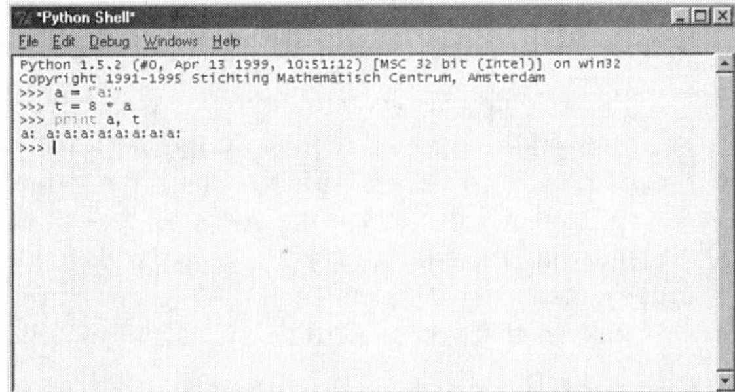

Indexing and slicing both allow you to retrieve only selected parts of a sequence. In Figure 6.7, I've used a string made up of numbers so that you can see how these two operators work.

FIGURE 6.7
Indexing and slicing.

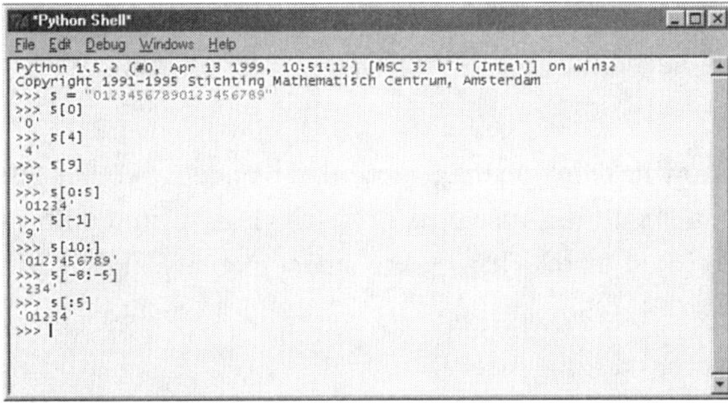

6

Unlike many other computer languages, Python allows you to use negative indexing; some languages allow negative indexing but give nonsense (or destructive) answers when you use it (C is a prime example). For Python, negative indexing means only to start counting from the end of the sequence toward the front. You can produce the same effect with more code by first finding the length of the sequence and building positive numbers from that. For example, if you wanted to find the last member of any string, you could do the following:

```
e = s[len(s) - 1]
```

If you forget the `- 1` part, Python tells you that your index is out of range; because it tracks how big sequences are, it knows when you try to go outside the boundaries of the sequence. Other languages don't know and don't care if you try to use parts of a sequence that aren't defined, but because asking to see part of a sequence that lies outside the sequence only rarely makes sense, Python lets you know that you're not making sense. Guido felt that someone ought to do it.

You will find that when you use slicing to view or copy parts of strings and other sequences you don't have to be very particular about beginnings and ends. That is, if you have a string 10 characters in length, then s[:], s[:2000], s[-2000:2000] and s[-2000:] all mean exactly the same thing, copy the whole sequence. In fact, s[:] in the Python source code is implemented using very large numbers for limits. It's only when you want a particular element from the sequence that you need to be a little more specific (and accurate).

Other languages may have functions that allow you to retrieve substrings (parts of strings), but none that I know of are as convenient as Python's slicing notation (Perl does something similar, but I don't find Perl's syntax convenient). Note that just because I used actual numbers inside those brackets, that doesn't mean you must. Any integer or integer variable may be used for indexing and slicing, which means that based on current information, you can retrieve different substrings depending on immediately calculated values.

After seeing how to index a string, you may wonder if you can use this operator in an assignment statement; the answer is no. Strings are immutable; you can't change them after you've created them. That means that something like the following is expressly forbidden:

```
s = "This string has a misteke in it."
s[ -10 ] = 'a'
```

Python will complain if you try it.

The way to change a string is not to change it (there's a little Zen for you), but to make a new one. Using the preceding artificial example, we could fix the "misteke" this way:

```
s = "This string has a misteke in it."
s1 = s[:-10]
s2 = s[-9:]
s = s1 + 'a' + s2
```

If you type the preceding code into the interpreter, you should see what is shown in Figure 6.8.

FIGURE 6.8
Mistekes were made.

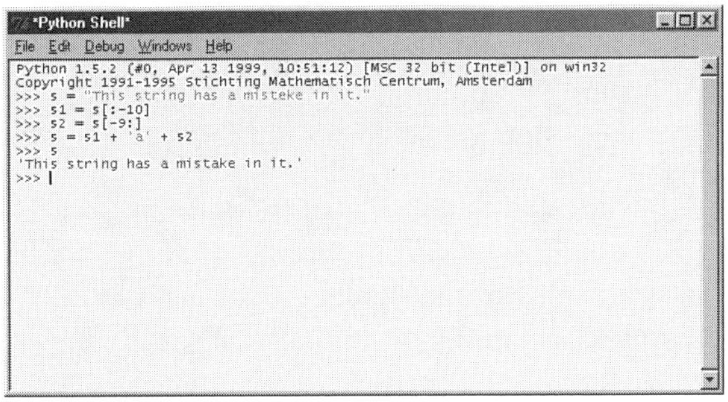

Of the remaining sequence operators, `min()`and `max()` should be pretty obvious; given any sequence, they will return either the largest or the smallest item. If we are working with strings, the minimum and maximum values for items are defined exactly by the alphabetic ordering of those characters. That is, the character A is "smaller" than the character B. Other comparison operators, which we saw previously, work the same way. Full strings may also be compared directly, unlike other languages, so that it is quite valid to say something like this:

```
if "smith" > "jones" :
    do something
```

Comparing variables containing strings is just as valid as comparing variables containing numbers. You should be aware that uppercase letters are always (in ASCII) "smaller" than lowercase ones, so you can be surprised. One way around such surprises is to always compare in lowercase, using `string.lower()`.

Finally, the `in` operator deserves some discussion. As we discussed in Chapter 4, "Variables and Control Flow," the `for` loop in Python doesn't follow the same rules as other programming languages. The syntax is

```
for <target> in <list> :
    do something
else:
    do something if no break statement was encountered.
```

<list>, however, can be any sequence. Because strings are sequences, we can legally use strings in `for` statements. Suppose we have a string that a user of one of our programs has typed into an edit box, and we want to make sure that it is a legal DOS path to an executable file. Figure 6.9 shows some quick checks we can perform on this string.

FIGURE 6.9
Membership tests.

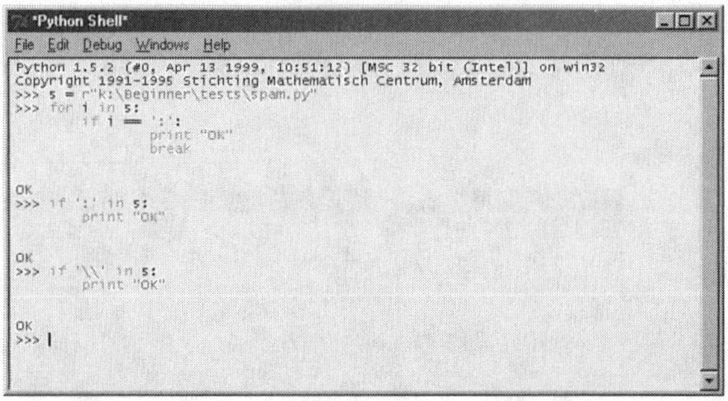

```
*Python Shell*
File Edit Debug Windows Help
Python 1.5.2 (#0, Apr 13 1999, 10:51:12) [MSC 32 bit (Intel)] on win32
Copyright 1991-1995 Stichting Mathematisch Centrum, Amsterdam
>>> s = r"k:\Beginner\tests\spam.py"
>>> for i in s:
        if i == ':':
                print "OK"
                break


OK
>>> if ':' in s:
        print "OK"


OK
>>> if '\\' in s:
        print "OK"


OK
>>> |
```

As you can see, the `for` loop is not really needed in this particular application; a simple test for membership or nonmembership is all that's really required. You will often need the `for` loop, however.

You will need to perform other string operations as well, such as converting a string into a number, but these extra operations are not operators. Instead, they are functions located in the string module. To use it, place the line import string at or near the top of your programs, and you will be able to call the functions using qualification. Table 6.3 shows the most important, and most used, functions in `string`.

TABLE 6.3 Important *string* Functions

Function	*Description*
`atoi(s[, base])`	Convert `s` to an integer using the optional *base* as the radix; return the integer.
`atol(s[, base])`	Convert `s` to a long integer using the optional *base* as the radix; return the long integer.
`atof(s)`	Convert `s` to a floating-point number (`s` may contain exponents); return the float.
`split (s[, sep[, maxsplit]])`	Look through `s` for the characters in *sep*, and split `s` into words. Returns a list of words. If `sep` is not supplied, it defaults to whitespace. If *maxsplit* is supplied, then limit to that number of words; the last word in list returned will contain the unsplit remainder of `s`.

Function	*Description*
`join (words[, sep])`	Take all the *words* (a list) and put them together, separated by *sep*, in one string, which is returned. If *sep* is not supplied, it defaults to a single space.
`find (s, sub[, start[,end]])`	Look through *s* for *sub*. If found, return the index of the first character of *sub* in *s*. *start* and *end* are optional, but if supplied, *start* is the index (location) in *s* to start the search, and *end* is where to stop looking.

Listing 6.3 shows some of these functions in use in a small program I wrote to help me manage my video collection. I number my tapes in hex, starting with tape `0000` (my brother-in-law tells me that this is the ultimate computer nerd thing to do; I don't understand why he says this), and I have a little label printer so that I can print out self-stick labels for the boxes. I can print a whole bunch at once, providing the numbers are in a particular format in a text file. The program shown, *lbm.py*, prints numbers in the right format, either one at a time or starting with the number given as an argument on the command line. Look the program over, and then I'll discuss it.

LISTING 6.3 *lbm.py*

```
#!/usr/local/bin/python
import sys
import string
def printlabel ( n ) :
    s = "%04X" % ( n )
    sys.stdout.write ( "%s\r\n" % ( s ) )
    for i in s :
        sys.stdout.write ( "%s\r\n" % ( i ) )
    sys.stdout.write ( "\r\n" )
    sys.stdout.flush ( )

if __name__ == "__main__" :
    if len ( sys.argv ) > 1 :
        if sys.argv[ 1 ] == "-h" :
            print """Usage: lbm start_number quantity
    Example:
lbm b30 100
    Start_number is hex, quantity is decimal
    if no arguments are given, lbm reads from stdin."""
            sys.exit ( 0 )
        elif len ( sys.argv ) > 2 :
            n = string.atoi ( sys.argv[ 1 ], 0x10 )
            e = string.atoi ( sys.argv[ 2 ] )
```

continues

LISTING 6.3 continued

```
            for n in range ( n, n + e ) :
                printlabel ( n )
    else :
        while 1 :
            p = sys.stdin.readline ( )
            if not p :
                break
            n = string.atoi ( p, 0x10 )
            printlabel ( n )
```

The function `printlabel()` takes an integer argument, n, which it converts into a hex string (the `%04X` part; you'll learn more about this in Hour 8) and then prints the result (the `sys.stdout.write()`) in a special way. It then uses `for i in s` (s is a sequence) to write each hex digit on a line of its own, and at the end writes a blank line. The main part of the program (all the stuff after that funny-looking `if __name…`" line) checks to see whether the user supplied arguments; if so, `lbm.py` reads one argument as hex (`the n = string.atoi(sys.argv[1],0x10)` line). (0x10 is hex; 16 is decimal), and the other argument as decimal (the "`e=string.atoi(sys.argv[2])`" line), and then just calls `printlabel()` for every number in the range the user has given it; that's the `for n in range(n, n + e):` line.

If there aren't any arguments, `lbm.py` lets the user type numbers, in hex, to the program; every number it gets that way is printed by `printlabel()`. The best way to see how this works is to try it (as with all the code for this book, you can download it from the Web site). Type

```
python lbm.py > out.txt
```

in the directory where you've saved the code (as `lbm.py`, of course). Then type hex numbers at it; when you're done, type the **`^Z`** that ends the program (**`^D`** on UNIX), and examine the output file, `out.txt`.

For further information about the string module and its functions, you will need to look at the documentation, which you can either read at `http://www.python.org` or download from there.

Tuples

Now that we've covered strings, the next type will seem easy. Tuples (rhymes with "couples") are another kind of immutable sequence, but at a larger scale than strings. In strings, the sequence is made up of individual characters, whereas in tuples the individual elements can be strings, numbers of any sort, other tuples, and any other legal kind of data type. This includes the user-defined type that will be covered in the middle part of this book. You've actually seen a few tuples here and there earlier in the book, but this section should clarify and organize your knowledge.

Tuples are enclosed in parentheses; like strings, they are immutable. The following example shows how to tell Python that a variable is a tuple:

```
t = ("this", "is", "a", 6, "element", "tuple")
e = () # This is an empty tuple
```

Like other sequences, you can index a tuple:

```
u = t[-1]
```

However, unlike strings, there are no special functions for working with tuples. That is, there is no tuple module to import. Many functions, however, return tuples. The time and date functions are good examples. Figure 6.10 demonstrates a few time functions and how to work with tuples.

```
C:\>python
Python 1.5.2 (#0, Apr 13 1999, 10:51:12) [MSC 32 bit (Intel)] on win32
Copyright 1991-1995 Stichting Mathematisch Centrum, Amsterdam
>>> import time
>>> time.localtime(time.time())
(1999, 7, 19, 9, 2, 48, 0, 200, 1)
>>> t = time.localtime(time.time())
>>> t
(1999, 7, 19, 9, 3, 6, 0, 200, 1)
>>> t[0]
1999
>>> t[1]
7
>>> type(t)
<type 'tuple'>
>>> t[0] = 1888
Traceback (innermost last):
  File "<stdin>", line 1, in ?
TypeError: object doesn't support item assignment
>>> _
```

FIGURE 6.10
Time and tuples.

One nice thing you can do in Python that few other languages support is "unpacking" a tuple. Previously, in Figure 6.10, we assigned the result of a time function to a variable and then checked the type of the variable; as you can see, that type was tuple. However, Figure 6.11 shows what we could have easily done.

The only requirement here is that the number of variables separated by commas on the left side of the assignment statement must match the number that the function returns. If, for example, you wished to retrieve only the year, you might want to do what is shown in Figure 6.12.

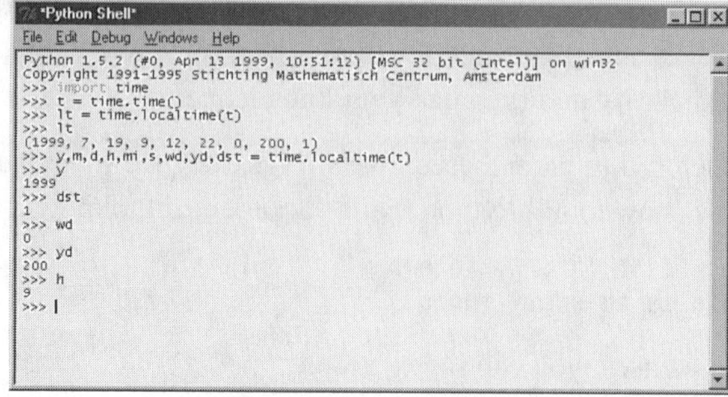

FIGURE 6.11
Unpacking the time tuple.

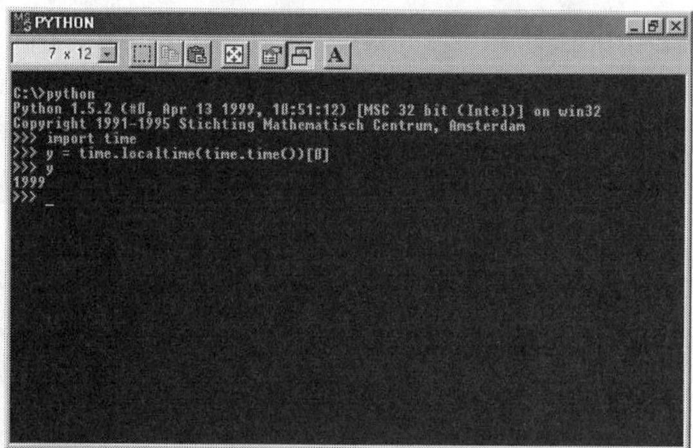

FIGURE 6.12
Just the year, Ma'am.

You're not unpacking a tuple here, but indexing; `time.time()` returns the time expressed as a floating-point number of seconds since January 1, 1970. The `time.localtime()` function takes that floating-point number as input and returns the 9-element tuple (or 9-tuple for short) that we saw in Figure 6.11. Finally, we index that 9-element tuple ([0]) and assign the value retrieved by the index operation to the variable *y*, which is the year. This demonstrates that any tuple (or any sequence) can be indexed, and any function that returns a sequence can also be indexed.

Like strings, the only way that you can change a tuple is to create a new one. If you wish to change the year in a time tuple, for instance, you need to do something like this (see Figure 6.13).

But a simpler way than you saw in Figure 6.13 is to use string concatenation in combination with slicing:

```
yt = (1888,) + u[1:8]
```

Since it is easy for Python to confuse the parenthesized number (1888) with a tuple containing only one element, (1888,) is the only way to tell Python to use a tuple. The odd trailing comma is the key here. The slicing indicated by u[1:8] tells Python that we want all members of the 9-tuple except the first, and then we use the concatenation operator to combine the two sets of tuples (the 1-tuple and the 8-tuple) into a single 9-tuple.

FIGURE 6.13
Changing a tuple.

```
*Python Shell*
File Edit Debug Windows Help
Python 1.5.2 (#0, Apr 13 1999, 10:51:12) [MSC 32 bit (Intel)] on win32
Copyright 1991-1995 Stichting Mathematisch Centrum, Amsterdam
>>> import time
>>> t = time.time()
>>> u = time.localtime(t)
>>> u
(1999, 7, 19, 9, 20, 45, 0, 200, 1)
>>> yt = (1888,u[1],u[2],u[3],u[4],u[5],u[6],u[7],u[8])
>>> yt
(1888, 7, 19, 9, 20, 45, 0, 200, 1)
>>> u = yt
>>> u
(1888, 7, 19, 9, 20, 45, 0, 200, 1)
>>> 
```

There is, however, yet an easier way that gives you the power to modify, and that is to use lists, the topic of the next section.

Lists

Lists are very much like tuples, except that they are mutable sequences; additionally, lists have methods. Methods are just like functions, except that they always belong to some data type. Remember that earlier we learned about qualification and the proper way to call a function within a module? When we call `time.time()`, we are using qualification to tell Python, "Here's the exact way I want you to get to the function `time()`." To call methods, you must also tell Python the same sort of thing: "Here's the way to get to the function I want you to call." The only difference is that one kind of qualification works on modules, and the other kind works on specific data types.

You can tell Python that a variable is a list by using square brackets instead of parentheses:

```
t = ["this", "is", "a", 6, "element", "list"]
e = [] # This is an empty list
```

6

However, notice the difference between tuples and lists in Figure 6.14.

You can see that it's much easier to change a list than a tuple, and you can also see that it is easy to convert a tuple to a list simply by using the `list()` function. Lists are, by virtue of being mutable and having methods, very often the data type of choice. Tuples are still preferred, however, whenever you have data that you're not going to want to change, because tuples take up less memory in the Python interpreter. For small programs, of course, memory is really not an issue, but it is usually wise to make variables that should not be changed into tuples instead of lists.

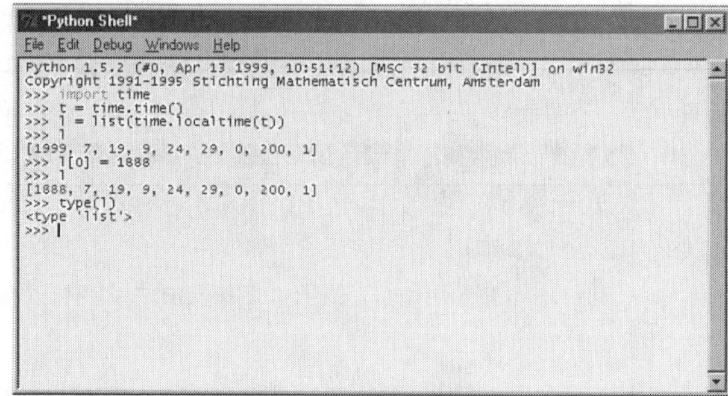

FIGURE 6.14
Lists.

Lists, as I said, have methods, and these are what make lists so attractive to use. The following table describes all the methods available for use in lists.

TABLE 6.4 List Methods

Method	*Description*	*Example*
`append(s)`	Append *s* to the end of the list.	`l.append ("item")`
`count(s)`	Count the number of times *s* appears in the list.	`l.count ("item")`
`index(s)`	Find the index of *s* in the list.	`l.index ("item")`
`insert(i,s)`	Insert *s* into the list at index *i*.	`l.insert (2,"item")`
`remove(s)`	Delete first instance of *s* from the list.	`l.remove ("item")`
`reverse()`	Reverse the order of the entire list.	`l.reverse()`
`sort([funcname])`	Sort the list in ascending order; optional *`funcname`* is the name of a `sort` function. See text for explanation.	`l.sort()`

Although you ordinarily won't need to use the optional *`funcname`* argument for the `sort()` method, sometimes the ability to control the order in which a list is sorted is very important. The *`funcname`* argument to the `sort()` method lets you do exactly this; simply pass in the name of a two-argument function to `sort()`, and *`funcname`* will be called every time that `sort()` needs to know in what order to put elements in the list. The two arguments to the function are simply elements of the list; you tell Python what order to put things in by returning 0, 1, or -1. Sorting in ascending order is the default; sorting in descending order is as simple as

```
l = ["d", "e", "f", "c", "b", "a" ]
l.sort()
l.reverse()
```

so no need exists to provide your own function for either ascending or descending order. The `srt()` function in Listing 6.4, however, places all numbers after any string, which can sometimes be useful.

LISTING 6.4 *sort.py*

```
#!/usr/local/bin/python
l = ["a", 2, "f", "b", "e", "d", "c", 0, 5]
def srt(a, b):
    if type(a) == type(0) and type(b) == type(0):
        if a < b:
            return -1
        elif a > b:
            return 1
        return 0
    if type(a) == type("") and type(b) == type(""):
        if a < b:
            return -1
        elif a > b:
            return 1
        return 0
    if type(a) == type(0) and type(b) == type(""):
        return 1
    if type(a) == type("") and type(b) == type(0):
        return -1
    return 0

print l
l.sort()
print l
l.reverse()
print l
l.sort(srt)
print l
```

Figure 6.15 demonstrates a few of the other methods that you can use when working with lists.

FIGURE 6.15
Methods and lists.

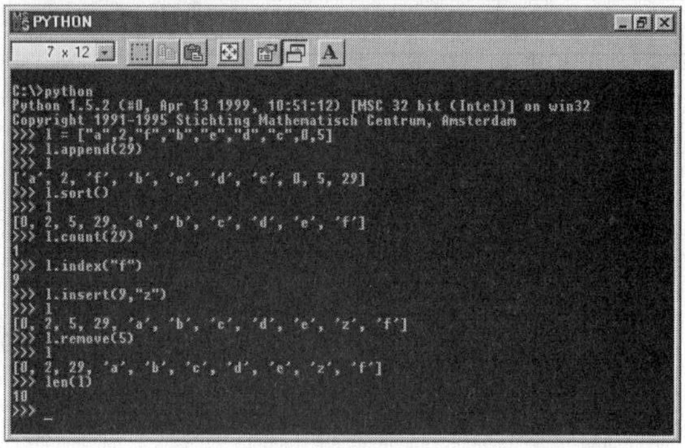

Lists are the final topic in our discussion of sequence data types. The next section features dictionaries, which are quite different but extremely useful.

Dictionaries

Dictionaries are like sequences in some respects, but the elements are not stored in any specified order. They are collections of key-value pairs: you put information into a dictionary by giving Python a key, which can be almost any valid Python type, with which to associate a value, which can be any kind of information. Strings are the most common type of key, but you can use integers, long integers, tuples. You cannot use lists or dictionaries because the key is required to be of an immutable type. That is, you can use variables as keys in dictionaries only if they end up, when evaluated, as immutable things. Numbers are considered to be immutable; "1 = 2", for example, is illegal Python syntax. The way to create an empty dictionary is this:

```
dict = {}
```

The curly brackets or braces (these are usually called "squiggles" by experienced C programmers) indicate dictionary to Python. To create a key in the dictionary with an associated value, you need to assign to a key:

```
dict["mypi"] = 3.14159
```

And to retrieve the value, simply index with the same key that you used for assignment:

```
mypi = dict["mypi"]
```

If the key does not already exist when you try to retrieve it, Python will give you an error. To create a dictionary with keys and values already in place, use this syntax:

```
dict = {"first":1, "second":2, "third":3, "eleventh":11}
```

Although you can specify the dictionary in order, Python will store the keys and values in whatever order it likes. When I entered the preceding line and then printed the variable `dict`, this is what I got:

```
{'first': 1, 'third': 3, 'eleventh': 11, 'second': 2}
```

There is neither point nor need in trying to get Python to store dictionaries in any kind of order. If you need to go through a dictionary in order, you can use the `keys()` method dictionaries have and sort the result. For the preceding dictionary, Figure 6.16 shows this process.

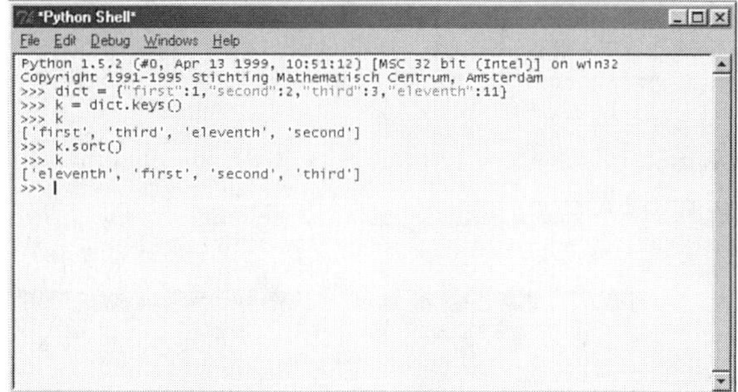

FIGURE 6.16
Sorting dictionary keys.

Most sequence operators apply to dictionaries, with the exception of the slicing operators. Other operations on dictionaries are performed with methods; Table 6.5 lists all the methods available for the dictionary data type.

TABLE 6.5 Dictionary Methods

Method	*Description*	*Example*
`clear()`	Remove all elements from the dictionary.	`dict.clear()`
`copy()`	Return a copy of all elements in the dictionary.	`newcopy=dict .copy()`
`get(`*`key`*` [,`*`default`*`])`	Just like indexing (`dict ["key"]`) but return either *`default`* or None if *`key`* doesn't already exist.	`x=dict.get ("Invalid Key")`
`has_key(`*`k`*`)`	Returns 0 if the key doesn't exist, otherwise 1.	`t=dict.has_ key("Spam")`

continues

6

TABLE 6.5 continued

Method	*Description*	*Example*
`items()`	Returns a list of tuple pairs of the form (*`key`*,*`value`*) of all elements (*`key-value`* pairs) in the dictionary.	`t=dict.items()`
`keys()`	Returns a list of all the keys in the dictionary.	`l=dict.keys()`
`update(`*`dict2`*`)`	Update the dictionary from *`dict2`*; see text for explanation.	`dict.update (dict2)`
`values()`	Returns a list of all the values in the dictionary.	`v=dict.values()`

Most of these methods are self-explanatory, with the exception of *`update()`*, which is shown in Figure 6.17.

FIGURE 6.17
Updating a dictionary.

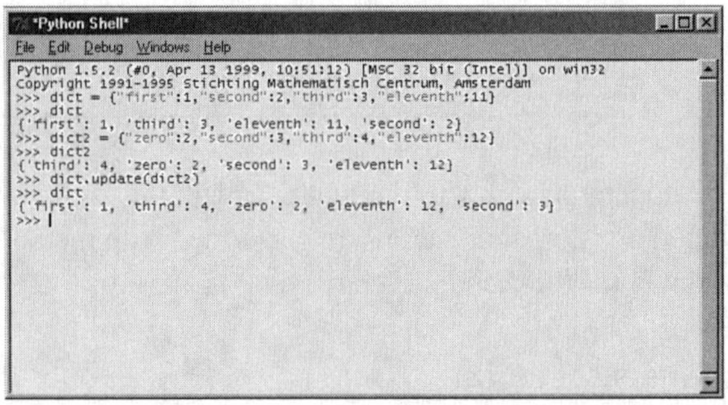

```
*Python Shell*
File Edit Debug Windows Help
Python 1.5.2 (#0, Apr 13 1999, 10:51:12) [MSC 32 bit (Intel)] on win32
Copyright 1991-1995 Stichting Mathematisch Centrum, Amsterdam
>>> dict = {"first":1,"second":2,"third":3,"eleventh":11}
>>> dict
{'first': 1, 'third': 3, 'eleventh': 11, 'second': 2}
>>> dict2 = {"zero":2,"second":3,"third":4,"eleventh":12}
>>> dict2
{'third': 4, 'zero': 2, 'second': 3, 'eleventh': 12}
>>> dict.update(dict2)
>>> dict
{'first': 1, 'third': 4, 'zero': 2, 'eleventh': 12, 'second': 3}
>>>
```

You can use dictionaries to hold any kind of information, even other dictionaries (this is something that the tuple and list data types have in common with dictionaries; all can hold elements of any other type, including their own types). Dictionaries are especially useful if you don't care how the information is stored and want users to be able to retrieve arbitrary information from them by typing in strings. For example, month names in the Mayan calendar have been spelled in many ways over the last four centuries, and most of them have now been standardized into relatively few spellings. To make sure that users of one of my programs can be certain that they are getting the right month name, I used a dictionary that contained many keys and few values. The keys listed all the variant spellings (which also included several languages) that I could find in the literature, and the values mapped these spellings to a number indicating the standard month index. This simplified the user interface dramatically over a similar version I wrote in C years ago, and the simplification gave the interface much more power and flexibility.

This month-name dictionary, for those who are interested, is found in Listing 6.5 (the new standardized names are listed first in each spelling list).

LISTING 6.5 Mayan Month-Name Dictionary

```
monthnames = {
    "pohp":0, "pop":0, "kanhalaw":0, "k'anhalaw":0,

    "wo":1, "uo":1, "ik'k'at":1, "ikk'at":1,
    "ik'kat":1, "ikkat":1,

    "sip":2, "zip":2, "chakk'at":2, "chakkat":2,

    "sots":3, "zots":3, "zotz":3, "tsots":3,
     "tzots":3, "suts":3, "suts'":3, "sutz":3, "sutz'":3,

     "sek":4, "sec":4, "zec":4, "zek":4, "tzek":4,
     "tsek":4, "kasew":4,

     "xul":5, "chichin":5,

     "yaxk'in":6, "yaxkin":6,

     "mol":7,

     "ch'en":8, "chen":8, "ik'":8, "ik":8,

     "yax":9,

     "sak":10, "zak":10, "tsak":10, "tzak":10,

     "keh":11, "ceh":11, "chak":11,

     "mak":12, "mac":12,

     "k'ank'in":13, "kank'in":13, "kankin":13, "uniw":13,

     "muwan":14, "muan":14, "moan":14,

     "pax":15, "ah k'ik'u":15, "ahk'ik'u":15, "ahkik'u":15,
     "ah kik'u":15, "ahk'iku":15, "ah k'iku":15, "ahkiku":15,
     "ah kiku":15,

     "k'ayab":16, "kayab":16, "cayab":16, "kanasi":16,
     "k'anasi":16,

     "kumk'u":17, "kumku":17, "cumku":17, "cumhu":17,
     "cum'hu":17, "ol":17,

     "wayeb":18, "uayeb":18
 }
```

Dictionaries are also very useful in building what's called a *dispatch table*, a place where you can use a key to find a function that you then call. In the preceding dictionary, you could easily change the numeric month index values into functions so that any time a user typed in a string to attempt to match a month name, a function would be called. The function could, for example, do nothing if the string that a user typed matched the standard name, but it would remap the nonstandard names to the standard one.

Another good use for dictionaries is in menu processing. Many times you may want to offer the user of one of your programs a selection of choices; using normal techniques, you might use lots of `if` statements:

```
if user_choice == 1:
    function1()
elif user_choice == 2:
    function2()
...
```

But with dictionaries, the procedure is much simpler:

```
dict = {"1":function1, "2":function2, ...}
... obtain the user's choice somehow...
dict[user_choice]()
```

Arrays

Python comes with lots of extension modules. Documentation for all the distributed modules, standard and extension, can be found at the usual place, `http://www.python.org/`. When you download Python and install it, I strongly recommend obtaining and installing the standard HTML documentation along with Python. Having it easily available on your hard drive is much more convenient than having to go out on the Internet (especially if you're limited to modem speeds), and it protects you against times when your net connection is down. An extension module of more than passing interest for those who are coming to Python from other computer languages is the array module, which provides array facilities comparable to C's. Arrays, as implemented by the array module, behave very similarly to lists and tuples, but they are mutable and constrained to contain only homogeneous data. Figure 6.18 demonstrates a few important points regarding arrays.

As you can see, arrays are easily modifiable. You can easily convert arrays of characters into strings (there's a *`fromstring()`* method, too). Any time you need to read or write binary information from or to a file, excellent array methods are available; sooner or later every programmer has to do such unpleasant tasks. For further information, refer to the array documentation; it's very helpful, and when you need arrays hardly anything else will do. Do note, however, that arrays hold only character or numeric items. This is because all elements of an array must be the same size. When you need to interface with a program written in another language, or when you need to pass information across a network connection, this restriction should not be a problem. You may have to fill a numeric array with hex numbers to make sure that the bits are exactly right when sending information over a network connection, for example, and using the array module would make this easier.

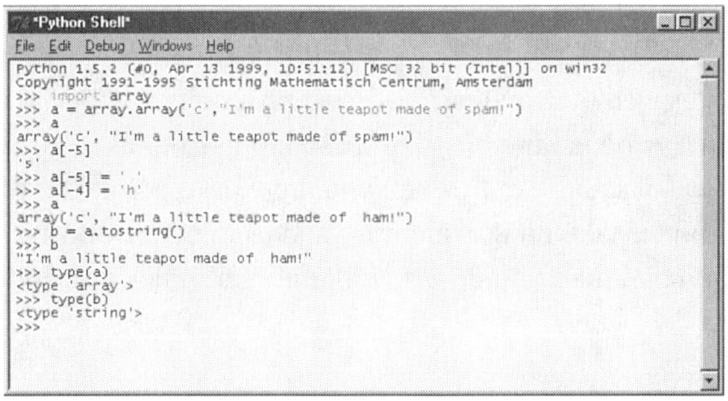

FIGURE 6.18
Arrays are mutable.

```
*Python Shell*
File Edit Debug Windows Help
Python 1.5.2 (#0, Apr 13 1999, 10:51:12) [MSC 32 bit (Intel)] on win32
Copyright 1991-1995 Stichting Mathematisch Centrum, Amsterdam
>>> import array
>>> a = array.array('c',"I'm a little teapot made of spam!")
>>> a
array('c', "I'm a little teapot made of spam!")
>>> a[-5]
's'
>>> a[-5] = ' '
>>> a[-4] = 'h'
>>> a
array('c', "I'm a little teapot made of  ham!")
>>> b = a.tostring()
>>> b
"I'm a little teapot made of  ham!"
>>> type(a)
<type 'array'>
>>> type(b)
<type 'string'>
>>>
```

Summary

In this hour, we've covered a lot of ground—far more than in other hours. You've seen how to work with strings, including many functions in the string module; we've talked about tuples and how they differ from lists. We've talked about the methods you can use with lists, and you've seen dictionaries and their methods (you will see more of them later in this book); finally, we discussed arrays. In the next hour, we will be using and defining functions, and the background you now have in Python's data types will be very helpful.

Workshop

Q&A

Q Why are Python's strings an immutable data type?

A It comes down to efficiency; Guido could have made strings modifiable, but the penalties involved would have slowed Python down too much, primarily because keeping track of the storage for changeable strings would have added prohibitive bookkeeping overhead.

Q Do other languages use dictionaries?

A Yes. SNOBOL, which is a string processing language, uses them. Two UNIX command-line shells, bash and ksh, use them, although they are called "associative arrays" in those programming languages, and AWK, another UNIX-developed small programming language, uses them extensively. Perl uses them, having AWK as one of its ancestors. There are undoubtedly many others because there are literally hundreds of programming languages with more on the way every day.

Q Is there any reason to ever use tuples?

A Yes, but given the small size of most programs that you will be working with, at least in this book, any possible reason to use tuples instead of lists is moot because those reasons apply only when you are working with very large batches of tuples at once. Tuples take up less memory and use less processing power than lists. Additionally, many functions work only on tuples and not on lists.

Quiz

1. Can strings be used in `for` statements?
   a. No.
   b. Yes, but you have to run them through a function that will turn them into sequences first.
   c. Yes. Strings are sequences.
   d. All of the above.
2. What kinds of things can be used as keys in dictionaries?
   a. Integers and long integers
   b. Strings and tuples
   c. Floats and complex
   d. All of the above
3. What does + mean for strings?
   a. Concatenate the two strings to make a new one.
   b. Find the numeric value from the ASCII values of all the characters, total each string, and add the mathematical values.
   c. Whatever you define it to mean.
   d. Combine the two strings with a '+' sign in between.

4. What is qualification?
    a. Testing your programs to make sure that they meet minimum safety standards.
    b. The function you have to use to convert arrays of characters into strings.
    c. Specifying the full name of a function, which includes the module name, to make sure you get the correct one.
    d. Changing lines of code to make your programs work on all the platforms on which Python runs.

Answers

1. c, strings are sequences, so it is perfectly legal (and often desirable) to use them in `for` statements.
2. d, you can use all the given types as keys in dictionaries; only lists, dictionaries, and user-defined types can't be used as keys.
3. a, the + sign means to concatenate the two strings to make a new one.
4. c, to make sure that you call the right function, you must use its full name, which includes the module in which it lives.

Exercises

If you can find it, the best general book on data types and structures is *Data Structures and Algorithms*, by Aho, Hopcroft, and Ullman, published by Addison Wesley, ISBN: 0-201-00023-7. Although it provides pseudocode algorithms for creating and accessing various types and structures, you will find that Python already does most of these things for you. It's always good to understand more of what's going on underneath the hood, however, and a wealth of useful information remains about the data types we have covered in this hour and the material we will cover in the central third of this book.

If you want to get a head start on topics covered later in this book, then look at the code for `lbm.py` (Listing 6.3) and see if you can figure out what all the lines are doing, including the ones we haven't talked about (look at your Python HTML documentation). Can you rewrite `lbm.py` to include less code? Throwing away code is one of my favorite ways to program—not in the sense of tossing out perfectly good working code, but in the sense that usually, when a program is written, you tend to stuff in everything in case you need it. Later, the *everything* comes back to bug you (pun intended), and you have to go through the code and get rid of stuff you no longer need; why not spend time now and then eliminating these potential bugs before they grow up and become real bugs?

For a little relaxation with a time machine, consider reading Larry Niven's latest, *Rainbow Mars*. You'll appreciate Guido's Time Machine a little more, I think.

HOUR 7

Functions and Modules

Readability counts.

—Tim Peters

Last hour, we learned about the sequence and dictionary data types available in Python. You have completed most of the basic preparation for writing functions, and in this hour you will learn how to write functions. Armed with functions in addition to what you already know, you will be able to write useful programs. We will also cover modules, which you've seen references to before; modules are files in which functions live. At the end of this chapter, not only will you be able to write functions, but you will be able to put them in modules so that you can use them over and over. What we'll cover is:

- How to define your own functions
- How to build your own modules
- How to include tests in your modules
- How to use the command line

What Do Functions Do?

A function's only purpose in life is to make the programmer's life less difficult. If we were all Klingon programmers, we would just start writing, putting it all onto one big honking lump of code, with *goto*s and *longjmp*s everywhere. Software would escape, not be released. We wouldn't read code, we would do battle with it.

`longjmp()` is an infamous UNIX function that allows what are euphemistically called "nonlocal gotos." This allows programmers in C on UNIX systems to leap out of a block of code at any point for any reason into another block of code without regard to current program state. When properly controlled, this can be art; when not so controlled, the results are about as aesthetic as small children jumping into mud puddles with both feet.

But we're not Klingons. We care about our sanity, we like to make our users comfortable, and we're not defensive (or macho) about our code. That's why we write in Python, after all. We strive to understand our own code and to make it understandable to others. Making code understandable is why functions exist; with them, you can break up those long, ugly lumps of indigestible code into small, easy-to-understand components. You can reuse those components. Function reusability is important—and possible—in all computer languages, but Python makes it easy and desirable to reuse functions written by you or by someone else. There's no sense, nor honor, in rewriting the same code for every program you write.

Breaking a program into many small parts (or at least as many as necessary) does more than just make it easier to understand each small part or let you reuse those parts; it changes the way you think about your program. It changes the way you program. For example, let me tell you about one of the first programs I ever wrote, back in 1968—spaghetti code days, remember.

I worked as a computer operator on third shift. Every week we had to sit down at the keypunch (how else did you think those holes got in the punchcards?) and make "tape label" cards for the storage tapes for an inventory program. We had to punch about 50 cards, enough for the whole week, and this could take an hour or more—depending on how good we were with the keypunch. Not long after I learned some basic COBOL programming, I realized that I could have the computer punch these tape label cards for me. All I had to do was write a program to do it.

Because the cards were useful only on workdays, I had to find out about the Gregorian calendar. I had to provide enough information so that the program could write tape label cards for years to come. I figured out that years repeat their pattern over a period of 28 years, with minor exceptions every 100 years. As my contribution to the Y2K problem, I decided to ignore those minor exceptions—which, of course, meant that I was using the Julian calendar, not the Gregorian.

This was in the days before structured programming; not being a super-genius, I didn't think of functions with arguments, and so I did what everyone else at the time did. I used a bunch of gotos; I calculated which of the 28-year types the current one was, and then jumped to a big hunk of code that was hard-coded with values for that kind of year. This means that I had 28 nearly identical pieces of code in this program, and that means that if I had had any problems with any of those pieces, I would have had to fix the problem 28 times. Nowadays, of course, the same function can be written in just a few lines of Python code as a function, replacing all those thousands of lines of impossibly wordy COBOL. Of course, we use tapes only for backups nowadays, and those we do use don't have to be specially labeled by the Operating System as valid only on a particular date.

The combination of a goto, some lines of code, and another goto that jumped back to the line after the original goto was called a subroutine; when you look at the assembler code produced by modern compilers, you can see that a suspicious similarity exists between the code produced for a function and the subroutine logic we used to use in spaghetti-code days. It's true that functions are just nice clothes for a very basic construct—a goto, some code, another goto. But it's those nice clothes that let us think more logically about the structure of our programs, and you should remember from Hour 1 that the structure of language structures thinking; this is nowhere more true than in programming languages.

Let's look at a very small function, one which you have seen pieces of before. Listing 7.1 shows you how to define a function in Python; it should mostly look very familiar.

LISTING 7.1 How to Define a Function

```
def julian_leap(y):
if (y%4) == 0:
    return 1
return 0
```

The Python keyword `def` introduces a function definition; this is followed by an arbitrary name, parentheses containing arguments, and a terminating colon. The body of the function is indented from the `def` line. The names between parentheses are the function's arguments or parameters; either name is fine. If you were a Klingon programmer, however, you would call them arguments (functions have arguments, and they always win them). Whatever you call them, they're just a convenient handle used to work with information passed to the function; the argument names aren't visible from outside the function. What this means is that a temporary variable named `y` is created for our function that exists only inside the function; some other piece of code can't call the `julian_leap()` function and then assume that a new variable called `y` has been created.

Listing 7.2 shows how you would use the preceding function.

LISTING 7.2 Using (Calling) a Function

```
year = 1999
if julian_leap(year):
    print year, "is leap"
else:
    print year, "is not leap"
```

Now, you can see that if we replaced the function call with a goto (in which case this would not be Python) and also replaced the return statements with gotos, we would have what used to be called a subroutine; in fact, you can view `return` as a kind of "goback" statement. That's all `return` is, of course; the compiler or interpreter keeps track for us of the place from which a function was called, and the `return` statement just means "goto the place in the code that you started from." Underneath, all the control flow constructs we've studied so far are just tests and gotos; even `for` loops, for instance, are translated by the Python interpreter into a set of gotos combined with tests to see if the input list to the `for` has been exhausted. It's sure a lot easier, however, to think of control flow in terms that Python has defined for us: `if`, `for`, `while`, and functions.

Our `julian_leap()` function is, of course, limited to use with a Julian calendar because it assumes that every fourth year, without exception, is leap. To modify the function for the Gregorian calendar is simple. Listing 7.3 shows the code.

LISTING 7.3 Gregorian Leap-Year Function

```
def gregorian_leap(y):
    if (y%400) == 0:
        return 1
    elif (y%100) == 0:
        return 0
    elif (y%4) == 0:
        return 1
    return 0
```

You've seen all this before, but now it's packaged nicely. Listing 7.4 shows how you might call both functions.

LISTING 7.4 Using Julian and Gregorian Functions

```
years = [1999,2000,2001,1900]
for x in years:
    if julian_leap(x):
        print "Julian", x, "is leap"
    else:
        print "Julian", x, "is not leap"
    if gregorian_leap(x):
        print "Gregorian", x, "is leap"
    else:
         print "Gregorian", x, "is not leap"
```

The variable `years` contains a list (remember these from the preceding chapter?) of years as integers; the `for` loop cruises through that list and runs both `julian_leap()` and `gregorian_leap()` on each year, printing the results to your screen.

Python permits you to supply default argument values to functions very easily; other languages, in general, either don't permit this or make it hard. Essentially, default argument values are values to use if the caller of the function doesn't supply the argument. Taking the preceding `julian_leap()` function, we could modify it slightly to give it a default value as shown in Listing 7.5.

LISTING 7.5 Default Arguments

```
def julian_leap(y=2000):
    if (y%4) == 0:
        return 1
    return 0
```

Notice that all we've done is to make the single argument `y` into what looks like an assignment statement, and that is basically what we've done. If the caller fails to supply an argument, the variable `y` will have the value 2000 assigned to it; if the caller does supply an argument value, then that value will be assigned to the variable `y`. Simple, isn't it? You can try it by running the following code:

LISTING 7.6 Calling a Function that Uses Default Arguments

```
if julian_leap():
    print "Julian 2000 yes"
```

This next listing (see Listing 7.7) puts the functions that we've talked about so far—and the code to test them—into one file. Use your favorite text editor to type these lines in and save them in a file called `leap2.py`.

LISTING 7.7 *leap2.py*

```
#!/usr/local/bin/python
import sys
import string
def julian_leap(y=2000):
    if (y%4) == 0:
        return 1
    return 0
def gregorian_leap(y=2000):
    if (y%400) == 0:
        return 1
    elif (y%100) == 0:
        return 0
    elif (y%4) == 0:
        return 1
    return 0
years = [1999,2000,2001,1900]
print julian_leap()
print gregorian_leap()
if julian_leap():
    print "Julian 2000 yes"
if gregorian_leap():
    print "Gregorian 2000 yes"
for x in years:
    if julian_leap(x):
        print "Julian", x, "is leap"
    else:
        print "Julian", x, "is not leap"
    if gregorian_leap(x):
        print "Gregorian", x, "is leap"
    else:
        print "Gregorian", x, "is not leap"
```

If you put the preceding code into a file called `leap2.py` and then type **`python leap2.py`**, you should see the output, as shown in Listing 7.8.

LISTING 7.8 Output of *leap.py*

```
C:\> python leap2.py
1
1
Julian 2000 yes
```

```
Gregorian 2000 yes
Julian 1999 is not leap
Gregorian 1999 is not leap
Julian 2000 is leap
Gregorian 2000 is leap
Julian 2001 is not leap
Gregorian 2001 is not leap
Julian 1900 is leap
Gregorian 1900 is not leap
C:\>
```

You can use other fancy tricks with arguments to functions, but you really don't need these tricks most of the time. After you've had some experience and have solved some difficult problems, you'll be able to appreciate the finer points of argument passing, and you can find out more either from other books or the official documentation that you installed with Python. For now, however, you have learned enough about functions to take care of 90 percent of your programming needs. Let's move on to the next topic, modules.

Modules

Although it's not been formal, you have seen modules before; whenever you've used `import string` or `from math import *`, you've been using modules. Put simply, a module is a filename. That filename must end in the standard Python suffix (or extension, as it is known as on Windows), which is .py. Remember the rules that we described in earlier hours; if you use import `module`, you must qualify every function or variable name that lives inside the `module` file. If you use the from `module import *`, you don't have to qualify names, but you risk getting the wrong function (remember what happened with the `math` and `cmath` modules?). The import statement requires a filename but gets mad if you include the .py suffix.

Before you can build your own module for functions that you might use more than once, you should know about one Python idiom. In fact, you've seen it before, but we didn't discuss it. Every Python program that you run has a name; even when you run a program by typing it into the interpreter started from the command line, the program has the name `"__main__"`. However, a program entered into the IDLE window has the name `"__console__"`. This is somewhat of an oddity, but it will not ordinarily affect the programs you write because you just won't normally need to test the program's name during interactive mode. You can see what a program's name is by simply printing the special variable `__name__`. In most cases, this will be `__main__`; note that `__name__` is not the filename (or the module name).

7

Use your favorite editor and put the code shown in Listing 7.9 into a file called `name.py`.

LISTING 7.9 *name.py*

```
#!/usr/local/bin/python
import leap2
print __name__
```

Make sure that it's in the same directory in which you saved `leap2.py`, and then run it in the usual way—by typing **`python name.py`**. Listing 7.10 shows what you should see.

LISTING 7.10 Output of *name.py*

```
C:\>
1
1
Julian 2000 yes
Gregorian 2000 yes
Julian 1999 is not leap
Gregorian 1999 is not leap
Julian 2000 is leap
Gregorian 2000 is leap
Julian 2001 is not leap
Gregorian 2001 is not leap
Julian 1900 is leap
Gregorian 1900 is not leap
main__
C:\>
```

What has happened here is that when Python executed the import statement, it also executed the code inside the *leap2* module. If you change the `leap2.py` file to include the following test for the program's name (be sure to properly reindent the remaining lines after the `if` line), however, you can prevent the unwanted execution shown in Listing 7.11.

LISTING 7.11 Changes to leap2*.py*

```
if _name__ == "__main__":
    years = [1999,2000,2001,1900]
    ...
```

Modules that are imported do have a `__name__` variable, but it is set to the name of the file. In this case, the *leap2* module which lives in file *leap2.py* has its __name__ set to `"leap2"`. Usually, you're not that interested in a module's name because to import, you already have to know what it is. Knowing that a module's name has been set to `__main__` by the interpreter, however, is very useful. This allows us to include test code in every module we write, which can then be run by simply executing the module instead of importing it. You can verify this by running the `leap2.py` file again, now that you've added the test of the module name; you should see the same output you did when you ran it originally. In addition, you can now use the leap-year functions in any module that imports `leap2`.

To allow `__main__` modules to interact with users, you need to be able to read command-line arguments that the user supplies when your program is run. To do this, you need to add the line **`import sys`** to the main module of any program in which you want to be able to read user-supplied arguments. Whenever a program is run, the Python interpreter collects all the command-line arguments and places them into a special list in the `sys` module; that special list's name is `argv`.

> `argv` stands for argument vector, and it has that name because on UNIX, this was the name given to the default argument supplied to C programs when the operating system ran the program for you; vector is just a fancy name for an array. C programs are expected to always have a central function where everything starts, named `main()`, and this is the historical source for the `__main__` module name. In C, UNIX, and Python, the very first member of the argument vector (`argv[0]`) is always set to the name of the program.

Because it is a list, it's very easy to get to it. You can find out how many arguments the user typed with the built-in function `len()`:

```
l = len(sys.argv)
```

As pointed out in the note, `argv[0]` always contains the program's name (the filename that we typed to execute the program). This is helpful because you can make the program behave differently if it is named differently, and the help and error messages you provide can always print `sys.argv[0]` instead of hard-coding the program's name. If the length of `sys.argv` is only one, then the user supplied no arguments, and you can modify the behavior of the program based on this fact. Listing 7.12 shows a modified `name.py` to take into account the points we've just discussed.

LISTING 7.12 Modified *name.py*

```
#!/usr/local/bin/python
import sys
import string
import leap2
if __name__ == "__main__":
    if len(sys.argv) < 2:
        print "Usage:", sys.argv[0], "year year year..."
        sys.exit(1)
    else:
        for i in sys.argv[1:]:
            y = string.atoi(i)
            j = leap2.julian_leap(y)
            g = leap2.gregorian_leap(y)
            if j != 0:
                print i, "is leap in the Julian calendar."
            else:
                print i, "is not leap in the Julian calendar."
            if g != 0:
                print i, "is leap in the Gregorian calendar."
            else:
                print i, "is not leap in the Gregorian calendar."
```

Running `name.py` without giving it any information should result in the output shown in Listing 7.13 (it may differ slightly on UNIX systems).

LISTING 7.13 Output of *name.py*

```
C:\> python name.py
Usage: .\name.py year year year...
C:\>
```

Running with an argument, such as 1900, should look like Listing 7.14.

LISTING 7.14 Output of *name.py*

```
C:\> python name.py 1900
1900 is leap in the Julian calendar.
1900 is not leap in the Gregorian calendar.
C:\>
```

You now have a program that tells you whether any given year is leap in both styles of calendar, Julian and Gregorian. I suggest that you rename it `ly.py` because `name.py` is no longer very descriptive of the program's purpose. "Any given year," of course, means "subject to the limitations of integers." That is, no year you type on the command line can be larger than `sys.maxint` or "smaller" than `-(sys.maxint -1)`. I'll show you how to get around these limits when I talk later about exceptions. Notice, in the meantime, that although `ly.py` works just fine on negative years, it doesn't work on "B.C." years. Does this mean it doesn't work properly? No, because astronomers and people who study calendars long ago settled on a standard way to number years before the year 1 A.D. Although this does not reflect common usage, it makes it much easier to calculate dates prior to a time when a calendar was actually put into use. Because the Gregorian calendar was first used in the year 1582, and the Julian calendar was first used in the year 707 A.U.C. (*ab urbe condita*, "from the founding of the city"—the city, of course, being Rome), one could quite properly make a case that using either of these calendars before their respective start dates makes no sense. Astronomers, archaeologists, theologians, and calendar students, however, very often have need to place events in time that we moderns can relate to, and thus they use what are called proleptic calendars. We simply backdate the calendars; the B.C. usage, of course, makes little sense if you're attempting to date events in Joseph and Mary's life, for example (this is one reason that many people prefer the notations C.E. and B.C.E.; C.E. stands for Common Era, and B.C.E. for Before the Common Era). In the B.C. system, the year before 1 A.D. is 1 B.C., whereas in the normal proleptic system, the year before 1 C.E. is the year zero (0), and the year before that, -1. Mathematically, this makes a great deal of sense (incidentally, if a year 0 exists, the millennium does indeed start with January 1, 2000. Depends on your viewpoint, of course).

Summary

We've covered functions and modules in this chapter, including how to define your own functions, how to build your own modules, how to include tests in your modules, and how to use the command line. In the next hour, we'll cover lots of miscellany that will be needed in the next third of the book.

Workshop

Q&A

Q Why `def`? Why not `define`?

A Like every other programmer in existence, Guido doesn't like extra typing.

Q Are *`gotos`* and *`longjmps`* ever really necessary?

A Not in a well-designed language. Even in straight C, which *was* very well designed, however, the occasional *`goto`* actually clarifies code that might otherwise be unreadable; and in the same language, some applications—notably shells or command interpreters—require the use of *`longjmp`*.

Q I've heard about assembler before. What is it? Would I ever need to know it?

A One step above actual machine language, assembler doesn't use a compiler. Instead, it uses a translator. This is because the letter codes used in assembler don't cause many other functions to be called, but are simply mnemonics that stand for a particular binary pattern that happens to be meaningful to the computer directly. You would only need to know assembler if you planned to write real-time, high-speed games programs, or if you wanted to write programs that would be used in the space program. See `http://www.s-direktnet.de/homepages/neumann/sprachen.htm` for a sample "Hello, World!" program in assembler. You won't be fooled into thinking it's Python.

Quiz

1. How do you define a function in Python?
    a. `defun` *`name(arguments)`*`(body)`
    b. `def name(`*`arguments`*`): body`
    c. `name(`*`arguments`*`){body}`
    d. Any of the above

2. If Julius Caesar made everyone in the Roman Empire use his calendar starting in 46 B.C., what year corresponds to the founding of Rome?
    a. 707 B.C.
    b. 753 A.D.
    c. 753 B.C.
    d. 0

3. What is the best way to put tests into your modules?
    a. In each module, check to see whether the `__name__` matches the name you gave the module, and if it doesn't, run the test code.
    b. In each module, check to see whether the `__name__` is `__main__`, and if it is, run the test code.
    c. Check to see whether the name is `__main__`, and run tests if it isn't.
    d. Don't bother.

Answers

1. b, the Python way to define a function is the second method, `def name(arguments): body`.
2. c, the traditional year for the founding of Rome is usually considered to be 753 B.C., or -752 Gregorian proleptic.
3. b, if a module's `__name__` is `__main__`, then run tests; never is "don't bother" acceptable when speaking of test code.

Exercises

For more information on calendars, a good place to start is `http://www.calendarzone.com/`. The calendar FAQ is to be found at `http://www.pauahtun.org/CalendarFAQ/`, where it is maintained by Claus Tonderling.

You can find out more about UNIX shells—and why `longjmp()` is sometimes necessary—in Marc J. Rochkind's book from Prentice-Hall, *Advanced UNIX Programming*. Although the book does require knowledge of C, if you persevere with it you, too, can write your own shell that is incompatible with all other shells.

Hour 8

Useful Miscellany

IMPORTANT: The Equation Editor does not solve equations for you.

—Corel WordPerfect8 Manual

In the previous seven chapters, you have learned about most of the basic functions, operators, and data types in Python. In this hour, we will cover several topics that don't conveniently fit in the categories previously described. First, we will talk about three built-in functions and a statement that can be very helpful:

- `map()`
- `reduce()`
- `filter()`
- `lambda`

These four constructs are part of Python's functional programming capabilities.

Functional programming is defined in the functional programming FAQ as the following: "Functional programming is a style of programming that emphasizes the evaluation of expressions, rather than execution of commands. The expressions in these languages are formed by using functions to combine basic values. A functional language is a language that supports and encourages programming in a functional style."

In this chapter, I'll discuss

- Printing (the `print` statement)
- Formatting (the `` `%' `` operator)
- File I/O (Input/Output)
- Catching errors (the `try` and `except` statements)

Three Functions and a Statement

The three functions are built-in functions; therefore, to use them, you never have to import any other modules. I've found them useful in about the order listed here. When we are working with tkinter in the last third of the book to build GUI applications, lambda becomes very important.

GUI, or Graphical User Interface programs, are those that present the user with some sort of menu or dialog, allowing the user to interact with an application program. Traditional programs are command-line driven. DOS programs are command-line programs, and the DOS boxes you type program names into are command-line interfaces.

Map

`map()` is the easiest to use of the three functions, and it isn't hard to understand at all. It applies a function, whose name you supply as an argument, to every element of a sequence. Its syntax is:

`map(`_`function,sequence`_`)`

Suppose you have a string given to you by another program, or one that is in a format decided on by other people. For example, you might have to decode a string that contains a date. You can look at one and see that a first cut at solving the problem would be to break up the string on spaces. Given a standard date string, such as might be displayed by the UNIX *date* command, which looks like this:

```
Thu Aug 5 05:51:55 MDT 1999
```

Then the way to split it up is this:

```
s = string.split("Thu Aug 5 05:51:55 MDT 1999")
```

The `s` variable will then be a list, looking like this:

```
['Thu', 'Aug', '5', '05:51:55', 'MDT', '1999']
```

After you have the list, you need to go through it and do some sort of processing on each item in the list. Therefore, you need to write a function that examines an item and does the right thing. Listing 8.1 shows a simplistic one.

LISTING 8.1 *look()*

```
def look(s):
if s[0] in string.digits:
    return string.atoi(s)
else:
     eturn s
```

Our `look()` function performs very simple-minded processing, yet you should be able to see what it does. It examines the first character of its argument, `s`, and if that character is a digit, converts it to a Python integer. Otherwise, it returns the same argument it was given. This is not particularly useful, as you will see when you run it, which you should do as shown in Listing 8.2.

LISTING 8.2 Running *look()*

```
import string
x = "Thu Aug 5 06:06:27 MDT 1999"
t = string.split(x)
lst = map(look,t)
print lst
```

When you run the preceding program either in the interpreter window or as a program in a file, you will see a complaint:

```
ValueError: invalid literal for atoi(): 06:06:27
```

That is, Python is complaining that you told it to convert the string "`06:06:27`" into an integer, and it can't do that because of the colons. Listing 8.3 shows a slightly improved version of the `look()` function.

LISTING 8.3 A New `look()`

```
def look(s):
        if ':' in s:
                ts = string.split(s,':')
                return map(string.atoi,ts)
        if s[0] in string.digits:
                return string.atoi(s)
        else:
                return s
```

Run it the same way as you did before, and you should see this output:

```
['Thu', 'Aug', 5, [6, 6, 27], 'MDT', 1999]
```

Notice that our time string ("`06:06:27`") has been converted into a list (`[6, 6, 27]`) within the list returned by the `map()` function, which uses our `look()` function. The map() function within the `look()` function uses `string.atoi()` and applies it to each item in the list we built with `string.splitfields()`.

I find the `map()` function most useful in situations where an input string is known to be something such as the time-of-day string (with colons) shown previously. For Mayan dates, you can expect input strings of the form `"12.19.6.7.12"`, and these are perfect candidates for simple conversion into lists:

```
s="12.19.6.7.12"
ls = string.split(s,'.')
md = map(string.atoi, ls)
```

After these two lines have been executed, the variable *md* will

```
[12, 19, 6, 7, 12]
```

Later on in the book, I'll show some other useful Mayan date functions. Meanwhile, we proceed to `reduce()`.

Reduce

This function needs the name of a function that takes two arguments, and its purpose is to combine those two arguments into one in some way. Its syntax is:

`reduce``(`*`function`*`,`*`sequence`*`)`

At its simplest, `reduce()` is an effective way to turn a list of strings into a single string. A simple example is shown in Listing 8.4.

LISTING 8.4 Using *reduce()*

```
x = ['Thu', 'Aug', '5', '06:06:27', 'MDT', '1999']
def strp(x,y):
        return x + ' ' + y
r = reduce(strp,x)
print r
```

This should print a more-or-less reconstituted date string. Listing 8.5 shows a numeric example.

LISTING 8.5 Numbers and *reduce()*

```
n = range(1,11)
def mult(x,y):
        return x * y
f = reduce(mult,n)
print f
```

This will print `10` factorial (usually written `"10!"`); the input list for `reduce()` that `range()` provides is `"[1, 2, 3, 4, 5, 6, 7, 8, 9, 10]"`; the `mult()` function is simply handed the first two arguments in the list; it returns a single one and is handed its own result and the next item in the list. The reason we call `range(1,11)` is to get a list starting at 1 and ending at 10 (`range()` always stops at one less than its ending number).

We can reduce the line count considerably by using the `lambda` statement, which we'll discuss later.

Filter

This function, like the previous two, operates a function for which you supply the name to every element in a sequence. The syntax is:

`filter``(`*`function`*`,`*`sequence`*`)`

Your function should return `1` or `0` (conventionally used to represent `true` and `false` values), depending on whether you want the element included in the new sequence built by `filter()`. The following example uses the `gregorian_leap()` function we wrote in the preceding Hour, see Listing 8.6.

LISTING 8.6 Using *filter()*

```
def gregorian_leap(y):
        if (y%400) == 0:
                return 1
        elif (y%100) == 0:
                return 0
        elif (y%4) == 0:
                return 1
              return 0
n = range(1900,2001)
ly = filter(gregorian_leap, n)
print ly
```

Running the preceding program produces a list containing as elements all leap years from 1900 to 2000.

Lambda

As I mentioned before, we can reduce the line count, under some circumstances, for all three functions we've just talked about That way is to use the `lambda` statement. This statement marks the beginning of a function definition, but of a special kind, that of an anonymous function. Anonymous means just that; the function has no name. You can still call the function, surprising as that may seem, but not in the same way that normal functions are called. Previously, we defined a small function to multiply two numbers:

```
def mult(x,y):
    return x * y
```

and then passed the function's name to a *reduce()* call. Here's how we would perform the same work with less typing:

```
f = reduce(lambda x,y: x*y,n)
print f
```

We could do the same thing for the other two, *map()* and *filter()*. The syntax for `lambda` is

lambda *parameter-list* **:** *expression*

Note that no parentheses are required around the parameters, as required for normal functions. The parameter list is composed of parameters separated by commas. After the colon, the expression is required to be on the same line, and anything that is not allowed in an expression terminates it. Expressions are simply operands and operators: *x + y*, *x * y*, *s[9]*, and so on. You can also supply default arguments to `lambdas`, much the same as you can for normal functions:

```
lambda x, y=13: x * y
```

If this `lambda` doesn't receive both its parameters, it will substitute `'13'` for the second one.

However, you should be aware of a few cautions before using `lambda`s. The first is that it is not always appropriate to use one—they are hard to read. Second, it can be difficult to use in many situations, primarily because it does not have access to as much context as normal functions. In the following example (see Listing 8.7), `lambda` will not work the way you might expect:

LISTING 8.7 Bad *lambda*

```
def myfunc(x):
        increment = x + 1
        return lambda increment : increment + 1
```

Because the `lambda` doesn't know anything about the new variable increment. It knows only about variable names supplied as parameters and variable names that are not part of any function definition. You can, however, get around this problem by using default arguments, and you'll see more of this technique in the last third of this book.

Thirdly, you cannot use statements as part of a `lambda` expression. This means that you can't use the `print` statement in one, but must use other techniques instead if you want to display values. You'll learn a bit about one of these in the "Files" section later in this chapter.

Printing and Formatting

You've seen many `print` statements, but nothing formal until now. You already know that if you put a `print` into a program, it simply displays whatever comes after the print on your DOS box:

```
x = ['Thu', 'Aug', '5', '06:06:27', 'MDT', '1999']
print x
```

The preceding code shows the following output:

```
['Thu', 'Aug', '5', '06:06:27', 'MDT', '1999']
```

You got out what you put in. This is, by the way, very Zen-like: You get nothing out of Zen practice that you don't put in.

Any variable that contains a string is easy to print because strings are what `print` produces; it doesn't have to do anything except transfer the string directly to your display. Numbers are automatically converted to strings for you, as are lists, tuples, and dictionaries. Function names, however, come out a little differently. If you have a function called *myfunc* and you attempt to `print` it (not call it), you would get a display like the following:

```
<function myfunc at 7cf8b0>
```

This is probably not what you wanted. If the function returns a value, then you can `print` what it returns:

```
print myfunc()
```

This calls `myfunc()` and then prints the return value.

However, you often need to convert numbers, sequences, or dictionaries into a string. There are, of course, ways to do this. The shortest way is to surround whatever it is you want to turn into a string in `` characters (acute accents, or, informally, "backticks"):

```
x = 23
y = `x`
```

The variable *x* contains the number 23, but the variable *y* now contains the string representing 23, and string operators can be used on it (indexing, for example). The same functionality is available using the built-in function `str()`.

```
x = 23
y = str(x)
```

You can also use the built-in function `repr()`. The difference between `str()` and `repr()` is a subtle one; `str()` returns a printable string representation of whatever it is applied to, whereas `repr()` is supposed to return a string that can be converted into an exact copy of what you started with. With numbers, sequences, and dictionaries, there is no difference; when we study user-defined objects, however, we'll talk more about what `repr()` is supposed to do. Many user-defined objects, however, don't bother to make the distinction.

Sometimes, though, you want to make several variables of differing kinds into one string, perhaps with some words or punctuation between them. You can do this, of course, with the string concatenation operator, the '+' symbol, as shown in Listing 8.8.

LISTING 8.8 String Concatenation

```
x = 20
y = 13
z = "x is " + `x` + ", y is " + `y` + " and x * y is " + `x * y`
print z
```

An easier method to use is called *formatting*. It has nothing to do with the `print` statement, but it uses the `'%'`, or format, operator. Listing 8.9 is example, producing the same output string as we just saw with the string concatenation operator.

LISTING 8.9 Formatting with the % Operator

```
x = 20
y = 13
print "x is %d, y is %d and x * y is %d" % ( x, y, x * y )
```

Inside strings, the `%` sign means something special to the format operator, which expects a string on its left side and a tuple on its right. The right side has to be made into a tuple (parenthesized) only if you have more than one argument, but it's safer to get into the habit of always parenthesizing so that you don't forget. The format operator expects to find as many `%` signs inside the string on the left side as it has arguments. These are called format specifications because they are made up of at least two characters. In the previous example, for instance, you can see that there are three `'%d'` combinations; these are the format specifiers for integers, meaning that the corresponding argument, on the right side inside the tuple, must be an integer. Table 8.1 shows the most useful format specifiers.

TABLE 8.1 Format Specifiers

Character	*Argument Expected*
c	String of length 1
s	String of any length
d	Integer, prints in base 10
u	Integer, prints as unsigned base 10
o	Integer, prints in base 8
x or X	Integer, prints in base 16 (uppercase for X)
e, E, f, g, G	Floating-point number, prints in various styles
%	Prints a literal percent sign

The format specifier also accepts special instructions between the percent sign and the character code; a number, for instance, means to pad the field to the specified number of characters using spaces. The full array, including all combinations, is quite complex because you can use multiple combinations. You won't need most of them most of the time, although I will show you some tricks later in the book; therefore, they're not covered here.

The format operator can be used anywhere that you want, not just after a print statement. Anywhere you need a formatted string, it's legal to use a `%` sign. Another thing that can make it extremely convenient is that in situations where you don't know what type a variable is, you can always use `'%s'` because the string conversion works on any kind of input. If the argument it receives is not already a string, it simply runs `str()` on that argument; this works with anything that supports `str()`—and even those that don't. In cases where `str()` isn't supported, `'%s'` reports the type of data it sees. Listing 8.10 is an example.

LISTING 8.10 Printing a Function Variable

```
def myfunc():
    pass

z = "Printing myfunc yields '%s'." % (myfunc)
print z
```

Note that we didn't call `myfunc()`; we just used its name. If you run the preceding lines in the interpreter, you should get something like this:

```
Printing myfunc yields '<function myfunc at 7f74f0>'.
```

The numbers (in hex) after "at" tell you the address of `myfunc()` in your computer's memory. This is ordinarily not useful information, but it can be helpful in some debugging situations. Debugging is not covered in this book, although I provide a few tips in the last chapter; one reason is that Python is such a clear language that you can very often find and fix bugs using simple inspection of the suspect code, but for really sticky problems, it can be an invaluable technique. Some information can be found at the Python Web site, `http://www.python.org/`.

One other useful trick you can use is shown in Listing 8.11.

LISTING 8.11

```
#!/usr/local/bin/python
import math

d={"pi":math.pi,"e":math.e,"pipi":2*math.pi,"ee":2*math.e}

print "pi %(pi)s e %(e)s 2pi %(pipi)s 2e %(ee)s" % d
```

The % operator does not have to take a tuple; you can instead use a dictionary. Notice that the dictionary variable does not have to be parenthesized. The syntax for using dictionary entries in your format string is:

```
%(varname)format-specifier
```

That is, you signal the formatting function that you want it to look up *varname* in the dictionary d and use *format-specifier* to display the value it found. If you have long, complicated formatting requirements, you can often clarify them, both for you and for the reader, by using a dictionary instead of a tuple.

File Objects

A great deal of the time, you will be perfectly satisfied to use the normal `print` statement to display the results of your programs. However, when you need to collect lots of output, read a large file efficiently, or want to modify a file without destroying it, you will need to be able to use files.

Although you haven't known it, you've been using what's called a file object every time you use the `print` statement. You're using a file object called `stdout`, another name that also has a long UNIX heritage; it's part of a trio that includes `stdin` and `stderr`, providing, respectively, input facilities and someplace to write error messages to. The `print` statement only knows how to write messages on `stdout`, so any time you want to use error messages or obtain input from your users, you need to use something else. It turns out that, like lists, file objects have methods that you can use to perform these tasks. The three standard file objects, `stdin`, `stdout` and `stderr`, live in the `sys` module, so anytime you want to use them directly, you need to `import sys` before you do so.

All file objects must be opened before you use them except for the standard three, which Python always opens for you. The function that opens files is called, logically enough, `open()`. It's one of the built-in functions; you don't need to import anything before using it. The same is true of file objects.

Opening a file is very easy; the most complicated part is remembering in which order the arguments go.

```
x = open("test.txt","r")
```

That's all you need to open a file for reading. The characters allowed for the second argument are shown in Table 8.2.

TABLE 8.2 Mode Arguments for *open()*

Character	*Meaning*
`r, rb`	Open the file for reading.
`w, wb`	Open the file for writing; this destroys anything the file already had in it.
`a, ab`	Open the file for writing, but append data written to the end of the file without destroying existing data.

Adding the `b` character tells the operating system to open the file in binary mode for you. This has meaning only on operating systems that make a distinction between ordinary text files, which can contain only character information that humans can read, and files that contain binary information, normally meaningful only to computers or programs. Windows and the Mac are examples of the latter, but UNIX couldn't care less—any file can contain anything at all. Even if you always work on UNIX systems, it can be good practice to get into the habit of using binary mode because you may have to try to use your programs on other systems sometime, or you may want others to be able to use them. The primary danger of not using it is that if you read a file on Windows that was prepared on UNIX, and then try to write back to the file, the operating system will change line endings for you unless you specify binary mode. I like to know exactly what OS my files came from, and I always prefer to retain explicit control over the line endings.

Only a few methods are attached to file objects that you're going to care about right now, and I list them all in Table 8.3, with explanations and examples. In the table, *f* is a file object.

TABLE 8.3 File Object Methods

Method	*Explanation*	*Example*
`f.read()`	Reads the entire file into a returned buffer.	`buf = f.read()`
`f.readline()`	Reads one line into a returned buffer. Line is defined as up to and including whatever constitutes an end-of-line character on the current OS.	`l = f.readline()`

Method	*Explanation*	*Example*
`f.read(n)`	Read *n* characters into a returned buffer, or however many are left in the file if it's less than *n*.	`c = f.read(1024)`
`f.write(s)`	Write string `s` to the file.	`f.write("Hello, World!\n")`
`f.writelines(list)`	Write `list`, containing multiple strings, to the file in order.	`list = ["Hello, ", "World\n"]` `f.write(list)`

All the read methods return an empty string after they have exhausted the file. Note that the `write` method, unlike the `print` statement, does not append a new line or carriage return to the end of any lines written; you must do that yourself. Listing 8.12 is a complete, although very simple, program, which merely reads lines from the file and writes each line to `sys.stdout`.

LISTING 8.12 *readit.py*

```
#!/usr/local/bin/python
import sys
if __name__ == "__main__":
        if len(sys.argv) > 1:
                f = open(sys.argv[1], "rb")
                while 1:
                        t = f.readline()
                        if t == '':
                                break
                        if '\n' in t:
                                t = t[:-1]
                        if '\r' in t:
                                t = t[:-1]

                        sys.stdout.write(t + '\n')
                f.close()
```

This program serves as a simple text-file conversion utility. It reads the input file, for which you supply the name on the command line, and it copies every line to *stdout*. No matter how the input lines are terminated, each output line is terminated with the correct line ending for your operating system. Note that even if blank lines are in the file, such lines are not "empty": they still contain the normal, end-of-line terminator for your operating system. Only when the file has actually been completely read will the `readline()` method return an empty string (`''`).

Try and Except

At this point, you should run `readit.py` and supply a filename that does not exist. You should see something like the following in Listing 8.13.

LISTING 8.13 Running *readit.py*

```
C:\> readit.py doesntexist.txt
Traceback (innermost last):
  File ".\readit.py", line 7, in ?
    f = open ( sys.argv[ 1 ], "rb" )
IOError: [Errno 2] No such file or directory: 'doesntexist.txt'
C:\>
```

If you're writing a program that another user might run, you could choose either to fail silently on such errors or supply an error message that is more informative. That's what we will discuss next.

The `try` statement's syntax is simple:

```
try:
    ...stuff to try...
```

The "stuff to try" code must be indented from the `try` statement, of course. The `try` statement cannot stand alone; there must be an `except` statement too, at the same indentation level as the `try`. Listing 8.14 shows a modified `readit.py`.

LISTING 8.14 Modified *readit.py*

```
#!/usr/local/bin/python
import sys
if __name__ == "__main__":
         if len(sys.argv) > 1:
                 try:
                        f = open(sys.argv[1], "rb")
                 except:
                        print "No file named %s exists!" % (sys.argv[1],)
                 while 1:
                       t = f.readline()
                              if t == '':
                                      break
                       if '\n' in t:
                              t = t[:-1]
                       if '\r' in t:
                              t = t[:-1]
```

```
                        sys.stdout.write(t + '\n')
                f.close()
```

Unfortunately, when we run this program, we get the results shown in Listing 8.15.

LISTING 8.15 Complain, Complain

```
C:\> readit.py doesntexist.txt
No file named doesntexist.txt!
Traceback (innermost last):
  file ".\readit.py", line 13, in ?
    t = f.readline ( )
NameError: f
C:\>
```

What has happened here? We do see that our error message has been printed, but we still got an error after that.

If you inspect the code, you see that if the `try` code fails, which "raises" an exception (the technical term for errors in Python), then variable `f` is never created; this would be fine, except that we forgot to quit execution of the program after we printed the error message. Thus, the program keeps right on running. When it sees the `f.readline()` method call, it says, quite correctly, "there isn't any such variable as *f*." A simple modification resolves the issue, as shown in Listing 8.16.

LISTING 8.16 Modified *readit.py*

```
#!/usr/local/bin/python
import sys
if __name__ == "__main__":
        if len(sys.argv) > 1:
                try:
                        f = open(sys.argv[1], "rb")
                except:
                        print "No file named %s exists!" % (sys.argv[1],)
                        sys.exit(0)
               while 1:
                       t = f.readline()
                               if t == '':
                                       break
                       if '\n' in t:
                               t = t[:-1]
                       if '\r' in t:
                               t = t[:-1]
                       sys.stdout.write(t + '\n')
               f.close()
```

Calling `sys.exit(n)` is the accepted way to terminate your programs abnormally. If *n* is `0`, that indicates that the program ended normally; any other value tells your operating system that some error occurred. You won't see many cases where a programmer has chosen to call `sys.exit(0)`; if Python reads to the end of the program file and there are no more program statements, it assumes that the program has executed correctly. It therefore calls `sys.exit(0)` for you.

In this case, when the user supplies a nonexistent or bad filename, you can either treat that as just a normal typo, or you can treat it as an error. I choose to treat the condition as a typo, and call `sys.exit(0) instead of sys.exit(-1).`

Exceptions are a fact of life in Python, as errors are in any programming language, and Python, by including the `try` and `except` statements from the beginning, has made it possible for programmers not only to allow for errors, but also to simplify their programs by providing for cleaner logic using them. We've seen, for example, that if you pass a string that is not a number to `string.atoi()`, or one that doesn't contain characters that `atoi()` expects, Python raises an exception. One way around the exception is to examine the string first and check it in detail for disallowed characters; if you find any, print an error message that the user will see. Nothing is wrong with such a procedure, but because `string.atoi()` already knows what characters it will or will not accept, why bother? It's cleaner, it uses less code and it's much more Pythonic to write such a construct as shown in Listing 8.17.

LISTING 8.17 Pythonic *atoi()*

```
s = raw_input("Enter a number: ")
try:
        n = string.atoi(s)
except ValueError:
        print "I require numbers, please."
        sys.exit(1)
  ...normal processing...
```

The `raw_input()` function is useful for collecting whatever a user types. The string argument is used as a prompt to give instructions if they're needed.

The syntax for the `except` statement is more complicated than the `try` statement (which could hardly be simpler); it allows not only for specifying the type of error you want, but for any legitimate expression. Thus, you can, for example, write an exception handler (that's the code after an `except` *`expression`*`:` clause) for opening files that allows two kinds of error, but exits on others. The `try ... except` statement has an optional `else` clause that is executed if no error was raised in the `try` clause, and that can occasionally be useful. Ordinarily, though, you know what kinds of errors are going to occur, so it's often simplest, and most readable, to code for exceptions as in the previous example.

The `try` statement also has another form entirely: `try … finally`. This is similar to the other form, but the `finally` clause is executed whether or not an exception was raised. One good application for this is as a "cleanup handler" for temporary files. You can put your entire normal block after a `try` and remove the temporary file in the `finally` clause, so that even if things go wrong, you won't be littering up the user's disk with funny filenames. If an exception does occur in the `try` clause, the exception is saved in memory, the `finally` clause is executed, and the exception is then re-raised to make sure the user knows something went wrong. Listing 8.18 shows a very simple example.

LISTING 8.18 Clean Up Your Mess

```
#!/usr/local/bin/python
import os
import tempfile

tf = tempfile.mktemp()
try:
        f = open(tf, "wb")
        f.write("I'm a tempfile.\n")
        f.flush()
        f.close()
finally:
        try:
                os.remove(tf)
        except:
                pass
```

The *`mktemp()`* function, from the `tempfile` module, returns a string to be used as a filename that is guaranteed to be a name that doesn't already exist. Whatever the temporary file is named, it will always get removed, but if the program couldn't open the file, the user will be notified of the reason. The `try … except` inside the `finally` clause is to handle the cases where Python couldn't open the file and thus didn't create it. Because the `finally` clause presents an error to the user, we want no others jumping in to confuse the issue; therefore, the `except .. pass` combination throws away any other errors that happen, such as complaints that the file doesn't exist.

Summary

In the last hour, we've covered some of Python's functional programming constructs: `map()`, `reduce()`, `filter()`, and `lambda`. You've learned about printing and formatting and about file objects, which have been used all along, without naming them. Lastly, we learned about `try` …`except` …`else` and about `try` … `finally`.

This hour is the last chapter of Part 1 of this book; in the next hour, as well as in the following seven, I will discuss objects, and you will begin to apply some of what you have learned so far.

Workshop

Q&A

Q Why `lambda`? Where did the name come from?

A Guido took the `lambda` statement directly from Scheme, a dialect of Lisp that has major support for functional programming. Alonzo Church, "A Formulation of the Simple Theory of Types," appearing in *The Journal of Symbolic Logic* in 1940 where it was used to denote the abstraction of a function, was probably the first mention of the lambda notation. He originally used a caret (^) over an x to stand for function abstraction, and later moved the caret to the left of the x. For typographical reasons, an appendage was added to the caret, and it became the Greek lambda character, λ. (Thanks to Charles G. Waldman, Michael Mahoney, Rene Grognard, and Max Hailperin for this information.)

Q Are the functional programming constructs we've talked about here the only ones in Python?

A No, there are a few more, such as *`apply()`* and *`exec()`*, but you will need to refer to a more advanced text for more information. The ones described here are the most useful. Do note that Python cannot itself be described as a functional language, even though it has these few constructs.

Q Exceptions seem to be pretty useful. Do other languages support something similar?

A Indeed they do. Most modern languages support exceptions in one form or another. The first popular language I know of to use them is C++. Exceptions are relatively recent additions to computer science.

Quiz

1. What are three of the functional programming constructs available in Python?
   a. `map(), reduce(), filter()`
   b. `compile(), exec(), apply()`
   c. `map(), reduce(), lambda`
   d. `lambda, apply(), exec()`
2. If you wish to trap some errors but let others go through unobstructed, what do you think the proper syntax for `except` would be?
   a. `except Error1 + Error2 + Error3 …`
   b. `except Error1 and Error2 and Error3 …`
   c. `except Error1 or Error2 or Error3 …`
   d. `except Error1 | Error2 | Error3 …`
3. What is the best way to convert an integer into a string?
   a. `s = str(123)`
   b. ``s = `123` ``
   c. `s = "%s" % (123)`
   d. `s = string.string(123)`

Answers

1. a,b,c and d, trick question. All the listed names can be used in a functional programming style, so the answer is "any three." Ordinary functions, as long as they return a value and have no "side effects" (such as printing something the user can read) can easily be used in an FP way.
2. c, `except Error1 or Error2 or Error3 …`is the way to trap several kinds of errors but to let others go ahead and raise on their own.
3. a,b or c, the only wrong answer here is `string.string()`. No such function exists because there are several other, faster, ways to do it.

Exercises

For more information on format specifiers, an excellent reference book is *C: A Reference Manual*, by Harbison and Steele. Now in its fourth edition, this has been a standard since it first appeared. Although not about Python, it does contain important material related to Python because several ideas, such as the format specifiers, were lifted directly from C. It also contains hints on how to write a program to demonstrate all combinations of all character codes and all the flags that go with them.

Rewrite the `look()` function in the first section of this chapter to include `try … except` to make the code simpler.

A full list of all Python's built-in exceptions can be found at `http://www.python.org/doc/current/lib/module-exceptions.html`.

Part II

Objects in Mirror Are Closer Than They Appear

Hour

Hour 9

Objects at Rest

If you are uncertain as to the language being used in your class, by all means ask.

—Audrey Thompson

In this hour we begin our grand tour of objects, occupying us for the central third of the book. This time, we will only be laying the groundwork for the chapters that follow, but at the end of this hour of study, you will be able to

- Define objects
- Understand variables as references to objects
- Understand the basics of OOP, or object-oriented programming

However, you will be doing very little programming. Instead, you will be learning about objects in general; the particular comes in the next chapter.

Everything Is an Object

In Python, everything is an object, and objects are like boxes; they contain things. In the case of built-in objects, or the basic data types, the things contained are restricted. Numbers, for example, contain no methods, only a single value. Lists are objects, and contain both methods and values, but you cannot add methods to them. Tuples have no methods, but can contain all kinds of values. Dictionaries have methods and contain values, but you can't add methods to them. So even though everything is an object in Python, there is a dichotomy between the basic data type objects and user-defined objects. User-defined objects, however, can contain whatever things you like. And "things" means anything. Your objects, called classes, can contain as many of the basic data types as you want, they can contain other objects, and they can contain functions. Inside objects, functions are called methods. A module, too, is an object, although not at quite the same level as is ordinarily thought of—they're not "first-class objects." But modules do allow you to put things inside of them: basic data type variables, other objects, and methods.

When you write a Python program, you're writing a module. When you `import` a module into your program, those modules are known by the names of the files that they live in; you've seen this, for example, in the case of the string module. Everything that lives in the `string.py` file in which the string module lives must have its name qualified by the name of the module. So you've used objects and their methods plenty of times before, such as when you've used `string.atoi()`. But the name of the module your program runs in is always called "`__main__`", which is why we often put in the check to see if our program is named that, so that we can determine whether it is a module or a program:

```
if __name__ == "__main__":
    ...program processing or test code...
else:
    ...module-specific stuff...
```

Even numbers are objects in Python. All objects must carry around with them a certain amount of information so that Python can recognize them as the types that they are. Thus, numbers carry around a little tag that says, "I'm a complex number," or whatever type is necessary. Whenever you type a number into your program and then use Python to run it, Python recognizes the number and puts it into a little box combining type information ("I'm a floating-point number") and the actual value that the number has. As you know, however, numbers don't have methods. Neither do strings or tuples. Lists and dictionaries (also called a mapping type) do have methods, such as `list.append()` or `dict.keys()`. So even though everything is an object in Python, some distinctions can be drawn. Guido and several other Python internals specialists are planning to erase these distinctions in Python 2.0, thus providing strings (and numbers and tuples) with methods, so that you will be able to do a `"'23'.atoi()"`, for example. Python 2.0, however, is a long way off, so you don't need to worry about code breakage for a long time. Knowing the way Guido does things, though, I would bet that most code will still run with minimal or no changes. The methods for strings may arrive sooner, in Python 1.6 (due out in 2000), but you will still be able to use the string module.

The "objectness" of everything is a very important part of Python's ability to do dynamic typing. Without things being wrapped inside of containers, which carry tags for type info, Python wouldn't be able to tell, except very slowly, what kind of thing a thing is. Without that, Python would be just another statically typed language, of which we have plenty. We have plenty of slow languages, too.

Objects are collections of things. Any such collection that contains variables is said to contain, or have, *state*. Think of a light switch; it's either in the off state or the on state. Most variables have far more than the two states a light switch has, but this simply makes them more useful.

Any object that contains methods is said to have behavior. As with cats, any stimulus elicits a response, and that response is, obviously, behavior. With Python objects, though, you're not likely to be scratched—except metaphorically.

You can pull a cat's tail to stimulate it. Instead of pulling an object's tail, however, you can stimulate it in less irritating ways. Strict object-oriented terminology would have it that this stimulation is called "sending a message" to the object. The cat might disagree. In Python, you don't send a message; you call a method.

In Python, some objects have state but no behavior. All the numeric data types have only state. Strings and tuples have state; because they have no methods, they, too, are behaviorless objects. Lists and dictionaries have both state and behavior: `list.append(item)` and `dict.keys()` are examples of behavior. Finally, modules that have no variables at the top level are examples of objects with behavior but no state. If a cat had state but no behavior, I'm pretty sure it would be a dead cat—so I doubt if the object/cat metaphor stretches to cover these odd combinations, other than to lead to the conclusion that the most interesting and lively objects are those which have both state and behavior.

We'll return to the properties of objects later, after we talk about variables some more.

Variables Are References to Objects

In many languages, a variable is the name given to a specific place in memory that contains a specific value. In Python, things are done differently. Values live wherever Python chooses to put them, wrapped inside their "object boxes," and a variable is just a reference to that object. This is important because it means many variables can refer to the same object. If the object changes, then every variable that refers to that object will reflect the change. Remember that even integers are objects. To conserve memory and reduce the time necessary to build a new object whenever a new integer is referred to or assigned as the value of a variable, Python "pre-boxes" the first 100 integers. Any variable that refers to the value 42, for example, refers to the same integer object. Creating a new integer object only requires using the new value—for example, 1,000,000. When we speak of integers, there is ordinarily no problem, because you cannot change the integer object 1 to anything else.

Other objects, however, are mutable. Remember our discussion in earlier chapters of the differences between mutable and immutable objects? Numbers, strings, and tuples are immutable, whereas lists, dictionaries and user-defined objects are mutable. When you change an immutable variable, you're changing what it refers to, not the object itself. Complex numbers, although they have two components that you can read individually, are just as immutable as any other number. Try these lines in your interpreter:

```
i = 3+4j
i.real
i.imag
i.real = 2.0
```

You should see an error:

```
>>> i.real = 2.0
Traceback (innermost last):
  File "<stdin>", line 1, in ?
    TypeError: object has read-only attributes
>>>
```

Variables that are references to immutable objects should, in theory, present no major confusion, because the components that make up such immutable objects cannot be modified. However, this changes when we work with lists, dictionaries, and user-definable objects.

From previous chapters, you should remember that functions can have default arguments—values supplied to be used when no value is given by the caller. A function can have a list as an argument; if no list is supplied by the caller, it might require an empty list. Thus, you could be excused for beginning a function definition like this:

```
def myfunc(l=[]):
    ...
```

This would not be a good idea, as you can see from examining and then running the following short program.

LISTING 9.1 `spam.py`

```
#!/usr/local/bin/python
def spam(n, l=[]):
    l.append(n)
    return l

x = spam(42)
print x
y = spam(39)
print y
z = spam(9999, y)
print x, y, z
```

After running the program, you should see that *x*, *y*, and *z* all point to the same object—a list that started out as an empty list. The three variables have been spammed. You can ensure that a new list is created each time the function is called by changing the function definition for `spam()` to this.

LISTING 9.2 Modifying `spam()`

```
def spam(n, il=[]):
    flist = il[:]
    flist.append(n)
    return flist
```

Running the preceding program with these changes incorporated gives us the expected behavior, returning a new list every time. Our slicing operator (`[:]`) makes a copy of the empty list, if no list argument is given, and of any list that is supplied. Copies of objects, by definition, are not the same object as the original. You can check this for yourself, using Python's `is` operator, which returns 0 if two objects are not the same and non-0 if they are. Using the first version of our `spam()` function, running `x is y` should yield 1, but with the modified function `is` should return a 0. Try it using either the interpreter or IDLE, or modify the program to print the result of `x is y`.

On the other hand, if you have a program or module that creates an empty list outside of a function, and later on you create another variable that refers to an empty list, as shown in the following listing,

```
list1 = []
...
list2 = []
...
```

then the two lists are not the same object. The reason is that these assignment statements are executed when Python encounters them. Whenever a function definition is encountered, Python transforms all the instructions into a special form, called bytecodes, that is stored for later use. Default arguments that are found in parameter lists are treated the same way that any assignment statement is treated, but it is only executed the first time the function definition is encountered. Thus, any object that is created by a default argument statement is created only once, and all other executions of that function always refer to the single object.

For the most part, problems caused by Python's view of variables as objects will not arise. You're far more likely to cause your own problems by doing something like using `i` as an integer variable, assigning a string to it, and then later on attempting to use the value of `i` where only integers are allowed.

Object-Oriented Programming

Object-oriented programming, or OOP, is the art of programming with objects. We've already seen that objects can have state and behavior, but another property is a necessity to get useful work done. It's called identity; all this means is that although you may have thousands of any given type of object, you can distinguish every individual instance of an object from all the others. Think of numbers: one 1 is indistinguishable from any other 1, which is why Python shares the 1 object it builds when it starts up among all the places 1 is needed in your program. But 1 is easily distinguished from 2; 1 is not 2. "1 is 1" is the basis for the identity property.

Although you must be able to distinguish objects from other objects, many objects share common state, common behavior, or both, to some degree. Objects that share common behavior and vary only in state may be made from a single template, called a class. You can think of a class as a cookie cutter. If you have a cookie cutter that cuts a particular shape of cookie, but no dough, the cutter is equivalent to a class. When you begin cutting out cookies, however, you are creating instances of cookies; the cookies are the real objects. Classes are not objects, but potential objects. Objects created using the class template are called instances, and the process of creating the real object is called instantiation. It follows, then, that when you tell Python to assign a value to a variable, what you're really doing with a line such as `a = 42` is saying, "Instantiate the object 42 into a variable named a." You could think of a as a cookie with 42 chocolate chips in it. Or as a 42-egg omelet, for that matter.

Of course, cookies don't have much in the way of behavior. They get eaten, and that's really about all they do. Cats, on the other hand, have lots of behavior—mostly what they darn well please. Or don't please. Working with objects in computer programs is definitely easier than persuading your cat to get off the table, which is probably why computer geeks have a higher percentage of cats than the average. Cause and effect.

Now, with cookie cutters, every time you want to have a new shape, you have to start with a new piece of metal or plastic. It would be nice if you could start with an existing shape and then stretch it, push it around a little bit, and arrive at a completely new shape with less work than building it from scratch. You can't do it with cookie cutters, but you certainly can with objects. You can define a class that has behavior and state and use that class to produce instances. If you then decide you want other objects that are mostly similar, but with some differences, you can save work by starting with the original class and only adding or deleting behavior and/or state. When one class gets most of its behavior and state from another class, the new class is said to inherit from the original. Inheritance is another primary property of objects, and it provides for the opportunity to reuse already defined classes—classes that may have been written by you or by complete strangers. When you've imported modules into your programs before, you've been able to use behavior, written by someone else, stored in the imported module. Although this is a fairly limited form of software reuse, it is not technically inheritance. It does provide for similar savings of work; you're not duplicating or rewriting code that someone else has written. In later chapters, we will see better examples of reusability and inheritance. Some languages, by the way, elevate inheritance to such a level as to make it mandatory. Java is one of these. In Java, every class you define must inherit from some other class. In Python, like C++, classes are not required to inherit from something else; objects don't have to have ancestors.

Two other useful properties of lesser importance are worth covering before we finish this hour. These are encapsulation and polymorphism. They're not difficult to understand.

Encapsulation is simply the process of defining an interface to an object and then carrying through on implementation. You've used interfaces to objects before; every time you use a function, you call that function according to a defined interface. The string module `atoi()` function, for example, requires that you call it with at least one string argument, and it allows you to add an optional integer argument. If you try to reverse the two arguments, `atoi()` complains. `atoi()`'s interface, then, can be defined by the two arguments and the return value, which is always an integer. Objects have interfaces, too, although they are almost always more complex than that of a function.

The second part of encapsulation is the implementation. Implementation is easy; when you call the `string.atoi()` function correctly according to its interface, everything that happens between the call and the return value is implementation—the stuff that does the real work. As a user of the `string.atoi()` function, you don't care how it does its work.

You care only that it does work, and works correctly.

However, encapsulation is not that simple. A function normally has only one interface that's visible to the caller. Objects, or classes, are more complex; they contain state, or variables, and behaviors, or methods. Most languages that have classes provide a way to control who sees what parts of those classes. This allows programmers to completely hide some parts of a class from meddling by those they suspect of ill intent or to open up other members of a class so that other, trusted programmers can change the internal state without problems. Encapsulation, in a stricter OOP language than Python, then, is the set of choices you make in designing public and private state and data. The goal is to expose the interface and hide the implementation. It's how you package your class. The hard part is deciding what is interface and what is implementation. My personal experience is that most programmers, with the best intentions and the best research in the world, invariably turn out to have decided incorrectly when you need to get something done right now, no excuses.

In Python, all members of a class, whether variables or methods, can be accessed from outside the class by any programmer who takes the trouble to read your code. There is no way to prevent "unauthorized entry" of a class in Python, as there is in C++, where you can unilaterally prohibit anyone from even seeing what members are there, much less changing their values. Python simply has a different approach to encapsulation than other languages. The way to expose the interface in Python is to tell people what methods and variables they should call or change. The way to hide the implementation in Python is to say in your documentation, "You don't care what's in this box over here." Encapsulation is by convention, not by proscription. The really big difference between the two styles is painfully obvious when you pass your code on to someone else, and they discover that they need a class of yours to do a job you didn't think of. If they know what they need and can read Python code, they can add what you forgot. Or maybe you did put it in, and you simply forgot to put it in your documentation. All they have to do is inspect your code, and if they need it, they have access to members of your class that in other languages would be hidden.

In the next few hours, you will gain a better understanding of how to design objects properly, which really is the essential truth of encapsulation. To design objects properly requires an understanding of objects and an understanding of the context or contexts in which they will be used. Again, the next few hours will enhance the understanding of context.

The key idea behind polymorphism is also one you've seen before. In Python, any time you wish to see a string representation of a variable (that is, print it out), you can use the `str()` function, the `` ` ` `` (backtick) trick, or you can use formatting with a `%s` format specifier. All three ways send an identical message to an object or variable; the object or variable responds appropriately, and the sender of the message always gets back a string. That's the main purpose of polymorphism: to send one message to many objects and get back the appropriate response from each of them. When you build a class, you need to implement responses to generic types of messages yourself. We'll see how to do that in a later chapter as we increase our understanding of objects and the world that supports them.

It is instructive, I think, to look at the following two listings, one of a C++ program and one of a Python program, which do precisely the same thing. Each defines a simple class and prints the year. Listing 9.3 is the C++ entry.

Listing 9.3 C++ Class now *(now.cpp)*

```
#include <stdio.h>
#include <time.h>
class now
{
    public:
    time_t t;
    int year;
    int month;
    int day;

    int hour;
    int minute;
    int second;
    int dow;
    int doy;

    now()
    {
        time(&t);
        struct tm * ttime;
        ttime = localtime(&t);
        year = 1900 + ttime->tm_year;
        month = ttime->tm_mon;
        day = ttime->tm_mday;
        hour = ttime->tm_hour;
        minute = ttime->tm_min;
        second = ttime->tm_sec;
        dow = ttime->tm_wday;
        doy = ttime->tm_yday;
    }
};

main ( int argc, char ** argv )
{
    now n ;
    fprintf ( stdout, "The year is %d\n", n.year ) ;
}
```

Listing 9.4 shows the equivalent Python.

LISTING 9.4 Python Class now *(now.py)*

```
#!/usr/local/bin/python
import time
class now:
    def __init__(self):
        self.t = time.time()
        self.year, \
        self.month, \
        self.day, \
        self.hour, \
        self.minute, \
        self.second, \
        self.dow, \
        self.doy, \
        self.dst = time.localtime(self.t)

n = now()
print "The year is", n.year
```

In the next chapter, we discuss exactly what is happening in `now.py`; for the moment, we need only look at a few of the differences.

- For outside callers to gain access to the `year` variable in the C++ version, it must be marked as `public`. In Python, all members are public (or, as Evan Simpson puts it, "Python assumes trust…there's no automatic protection mechanism for determined users to have to find an obscure way around"). Other C++ access markers are `private` and `protected`.
- In C++, every line must end with a semicolon; not so in Python.
- In C++, block structure is indicated by ugly `{}` characters `;-)` ; in Python, block structure is indicated by indentation.
- In C++, the `now` class has a hidden member, called `"this"`, which any method in the class can see and optionally use. You could, to make things perfectly clear, recode the line that reads "`year = ttime->tm_year;`" as "`this->year = ttime->tm_year;`" and so on. In Python, the equivalent is "`self`", and its use is mandatory. The reasons for preferring Python's method will become clear in the next hour.
- In C++ (also in C), you must add 1900 to the year returned by the `localtime()` call; Python takes care of this for you.

- In C++, the method that gets called when you create an instance of the `now` class is called by the name of the class, `now()`. When a class is instantiated in Python, Python looks for a method named `__init__()` and calls that; we'll learn about other funny-looking `__name__` methods later in this section of the book.

The conclusion you're expected to come to after looking at both of these class implementations is, "Gee, Python is easy." Also, please take into account that after you have typed in the code for `now.py`, you can run it. In C++, you must first compile `now.cpp` before you can run it. If you don't have a C++ compiler, you have to either buy one or spend a lot of time downloading and installing a free version of one. As Frank Stajano says, "Python comes with batteries included."

Summary

In the past hour, we have learned

- What objects are
- That variables are only references to objects
- Some of the basics of OOP

In the next hour, we will build a simple class, discuss it in detail, and learn how to communicate with it.

Workshop

Q&A

Q Is there a good way to think about polymorphism?

A You could think of polymorphic objects as being like a herd of cats. All of them are different, but if you start poking them with sticks, you will soon notice that they all respond in markedly similar ways.

Q Tuples are immutable objects, which means that after they are created, you can't change them. However, tuples are allowed to contain any other kind of object you want, including mutable ones such as lists. Does Python allow you to change lists when they are inside tuples?

A Yes. Objects that are mutable always retain their original properties. A tuple can't be changed after it's built, but you can do pretty much anything you want inside a list that you've put inside a tuple. You can't delete the whole list, but you can delete individual members of the list.

Q If strings are objects, why don't they have their own methods? Why do we have to `import string`?

A Because Python still has an artificial dichotomy between basic, or built-in, data types and other kinds of objects. Letting all objects have methods means, among other things, that users could add or change methods on all objects, not only user-defined ones. This raises many issues, some of which are in the process of being resolved by Guido and the members of the types-sig (SIG stands for Special Interest Group). Some of the work they have done will appear in Python 2.0, or possibly as early as Python 1.6.

Quiz

1. Objects must have
   a. State
   b. Behavior
   c. Self
   d. Identity
2. Object-oriented programming concepts include
   a. Ancestors, siblings, descendants, ascendants, and objects
   b. Classes, objects, inheritance, encapsulation, and polymorphism
   c. Time, space, money, style, and class
   d. Class, behavior, state, identity, and cookies
3. Objects are
   a. Collections of things
   b. Instantiations of classes
   c. More like cats than cookies
   d. Expressions of the Buddha Nature of programming

Answers

1. d, objects may have state or behavior or both, but all must have identity.
2. b, classes, objects, inheritance, encapsulation, and polymorphism is the correct answer, but I'm sure that plenty of people out there don't think it's worth it if they don't get cookies, too.
3. a, b, c, and d, all the answers are correct. If you don't understand the Buddha Nature of programming, don't worry: only those who claim to understand it don't.

Exercises

Visit the Object-Oriented FAQ at

`http://www.cyberdyne-object-sys.com/oofaq2/` for more advanced information on object-oriented programming. Remember that Python's OOP facilities are not as tight or as secure as some other languages.

Take a look at the Python types-sig page, at `http://www.python.org/sigs/types-sig/`, to see what some of the major issues are regarding the removal of the dichotomy between basic data types and user-defined objects.

HOUR 10

Defining Objects

Most bands start to suck the minute they learn to play.

—Gary Burger, lead guitarist for The Monks

This hour, we'll learn how to build objects that we can use. Then we'll learn how to send messages to our simple object, how to look at what's inside it, and how to use it in practical situations. At the end of the hour, you should be able to

- Write a class
- Create an object from the class
- Write methods for the class
- Understand how to use object inheritance

We will begin by talking about the class used at the end of the last hour, `now`.

First Class

You'll see that in Listing 10.1, I've included only the code for class now.

LISTING 10.1 Class now

```
class now:
def __init__(self):
    self.t = time.time()
    self.year, \
    self.month, \
    self.day, \
    self.hour, \
    self.minute, \
    self.second, \
    self.dow, \
    self.doy, \
    self.dst = time.localtime(self.t)
```

When an instance of a class is created in Python, the special method `__init__()` is called the same as if it were a normal function, with the exception that a special first argument, `self`, is passed when any method of a class is called. This special argument is simply a reference to the object itself. To explain what `self` means and does, we need to take a short digression into variables and functions.

As you remember, a variable is created whenever you assign a value to it; that's what we're doing in the `__init__()` method in class `now` when we say

```
self.t = time.time()
```

Here we are explicitly creating the variable `t` by assigning a number that corresponds to the current time as kept by your computer. Why can't we just create `t` and let it go at that? Because if we did, we would be creating what is called a local variable, not a member of the class. That means that if we create a variable inside a function without qualifying it, only the function can see it—and that includes the class. If we said

```
t = time.time()
```

instead of using the `self` parameter, then only the function `__init__()` would be able to see `t`, and any objects we created using class `now` could not. Imagine that any function or method is inside a box; you can put things in by calling the function or method with the right arguments, and you can get things out by using returned values. The function creates things inside the box, but unless it uses those input arguments that you give it, it can't create things outside the box. Functions and methods can't think outside the box.

Although you can call a function or method and use the return value to assign to or create a variable, the function itself cannot create something outside its box—unless the function uses the `self` parameter. We see how that's done in Listing 10.1. The way to create variables (members in OOP talk) in an object is the same way Python creates all variables—by assigning a value to them. That's what is going on Listing 10.1; `self.t`, `self.year`, `self.month`, and so on are variables being created as members of class `now`. The `localtime()` function returns a 9-tuple; an assignment such as that shown in the previous listing unpacks the tuple, placing the values into the variables on the left side of the = sign, exactly the way you would expect. *Dow* stands for "day of the week," *doy* indicates "day number of the year," and *dst* is 1 if daylight savings time is being observed, 0 if not.

After you create an instance of class `now`, you can, outside the box, look inside the instance and see that the `__init__()` method has created variables. You can inspect the variables, you can modify them, you can add new methods, and you can call any methods that are inside the class; you can even modify the methods and variables after creating an instance. However, if you do that, when you create another instance, your added methods and variables won't show up in the new instance. (There is a way to do this, but it's not something you'll be wanting to do for a long time, and it won't be covered in this book.)

As you saw in the original listing for class `now`, which was presented in the preceding chapter (see Listing 9.2), creating an instance of a class is easy:

```
n = now()
print "The year is", n.year
```

You may notice that creating an instance of a class looks very much like calling a function. That's because it is; Python does a few magic tricks behind the scenes, by fabricating a generic object and then passing that as the `self` argument to a function call that effectively looks like

```
n = now.__init__(object)
```

After you've created an instance of a class, you might think that you could call the class's `__init__()` method directly, like this:

```
n = now()
o = now.__init__(n)
print "year", o.year, n is o
```

If you run the preceding code, you'll see that you get an `AttributeError` that tells you that the object `o` is not an instance of class `now`, but a `None` object. That's because the `self` argument you provided to `__init__()` was not really a reference to itself. Only Python can construct a generic object that will really work in such a call. Chalk it up to magic.

Modifying the Class

Although the class we talked about in the last section is somewhat useful, because it wraps two function calls into one easy-to-use object creation, it would be more useful if it provided more information with as little work. That's what we're going to do now (no pun intended)—build a new class that does more. We'll begin this class in this hour and add to its functionality both in the next hour and in the hour in which we discuss special class methods.

What should our new class do? Here's a small list:

- The main requirement, naturally, is to tell us the current date and time.
- However, it should handle noncurrent dates within the limits of the current machine architecture.
- It should support simple date arithmetic.
- It should be easy to extend.

More additions will occur later, but this is enough for a start.

Listing 10.2 shows our class only slightly revised.

LISTING 10.2 Class now

```
#!/usr/local/bin/python
import time
class now:
    def __init__(self):
        self.t = time.time()
        self.storetime()
    def storetime(self):
        self.year, \
        self.month, \
        self.day, \
        self.hour, \
        self.minute, \
        self.second, \
        self.dow, \
        self.doy, \
        self.dst = time.localtime(self.t)
n = now()
print "The year is", n.year
print n
```

All we've done here is to provide a simple method that we can use at any time to stuff the time values into the appropriate member variables. This means that even after we've created an instance of the `now` class, we can update it by setting the current time:

```
n = now()
n.t = time.time()
n.storetime()
```

An alternative implementation could store the current time as the tuple returned by the call to the `localtime()` function; it could then provide methods to retrieve each required time unit by name. Listing 10.3 gives a partial implementation using this method.

LISTING 10.3 Another Way to Implement Class `now`

```
class now:
    def __init__(self):
        self.t = time.time()
        self.current = time.localtime(self.t)
    def year(self):
        return self.current[0]
    def month(self):
        return self.current[1]
    ...
```


This way of defining the class, however, requires users of the class to do more typing when they access parts of dates, although it's a more traditionally OOP approach. You would access the year, for example, like this:

```
n = now()
print n.year()
```

Python isn't always as traditional as other languages, though.

When you run `now.py` (from Listing 10.2), however, you'll see that when the last line is executed (`print n`), what is printed is not very helpful:

```
<__main__.now instance at 7fa450>
```

All this tells us is that `n` is a class instance, and we already knew that. What we need is a way to tell Python what we want to have happen when we try to print an instance. Python being Python, there is a way to do this. We're going to use what's called a special class method. A whole hour will be devoted to these in Hour 13, "Special Class Methods in Python," so you can treat this as a teaser for that chapter.

You've seen a special class method already; `__init__()` is one. Whenever you instantiate a class, Python looks for this method in the class definition and runs it if it exists. If it does not exist, nothing bad happens, but there is not much point in defining a class that doesn't perform some sort of initialization when it's created. There are uses for such beasts, but they are arcane, used mostly in the metaphysical atmosphere of Python introspection (and other topics I don't understand), so I won't go into them in this book.

Whenever you type something such as `print n` and `n` is an instance of a class, Python looks at the class definition for a special class method named `__str__()`. This method needs to return a string that represents your class instance; it is perfectly acceptable, if no reasonable string representation exists, to return a simple description. In the case of our `now` class, however, a perfectly good (and expected) string representation is available. The time module (which we are using anyway) contains a function to provide this for us; `time.ctime()` returns a string that serves our needs just fine. Modify `now.py` as shown in Listing 10.4.

LISTING 10.4 Modifying Class `now`

```
#!/usr/local/bin/python
import time
class now:
   def __init__(self):
       self.t = time.time()
       self.storetime()
   def storetime(self):
       self.year, \
       self.month, \
        self.day, \
        self.hour, \
        self.minute, \
        self.second, \
        self.dow, \
        self.doy, \
        self.dst = time.localtime(self.t)
   def __str__(self):
        return time.ctime(self.t)

n = now()
print "The year is", n.year
print n
s=`n`
print s

```

Run `now.py`; you should see the output shown in Figure 10.1 (making allowances for the different time, of course).

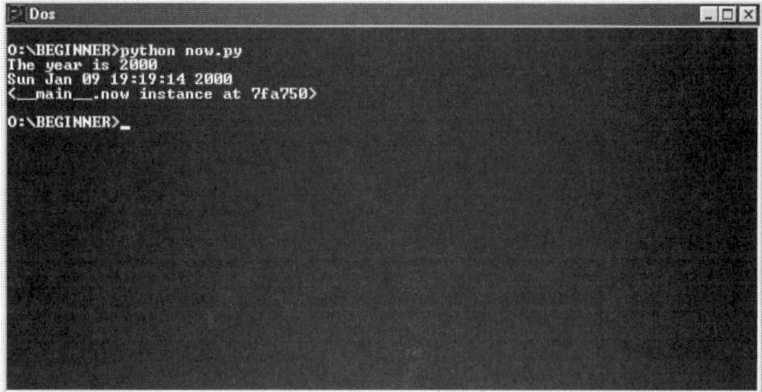

FIGURE 10.1
Output of modified `now.py`.

Besides calling `str()` implicitly when you issue a `print` statement, you can call `str()` explicitly:

```
n = now()
s = str(n)
print s
```

Another special class method dealing with string representations is `__repr__()`. This is called whenever you put a class instance in `` (backticks); it differs from the `__str__()` method in that, by convention, `__repr__()` is supposed to return a string that can be used later to re-create the instance. In other words, the output of `repr(n)`, where *n* is an instance of class `now`, should be convertible using some as-yet unwritten function or method back into an instance of class `now`. For the present, simply add the following lines to your class definition:

```
def __repr__(self):
    return time.ctime(self.t)
```

You'll notice that it is the same as the definition for the `__str__()` method; classes are often set up this way. Since Python makes a distinction between the two forms, __str__() and __repr__(), though, as you can see by examining the previously shown Figure 10.1, we need to provide both versions.

A Class Divided

Listing 10.5 shows the class as you should have it now, and newly wrapped test code.

LISTING 10.5 Now.py with `__repr__()` and `__str__()` Methods

```
#!/usr/local/bin/python
import time
class now:
```

continues

LISTING 10.5 continued

```
    def __init__(self):
        self.t = time.time()
        self.storetime()
    def storetime(self):
        self.year, \
        self.month, \
        self.day, \
        self.hour, \
        self.minute, \
        self.second, \
        self.dow, \
        self.doy, \
        self.dst = time.localtime(self.t)
    def __str__ ( self ) :
        return time.ctime ( self.t )
    def __repr__ ( self ) :
        return time.ctime ( self.t )
if __name__ == "__main__":

    n = now()
    print "The year is", n.year
    print n
    x = now()
    s = `x`
    print s
```

Because we've added the `if __name__...` test, that means that we can `import now` in other modules and in the interpreter, as shown in Figure 10.2.

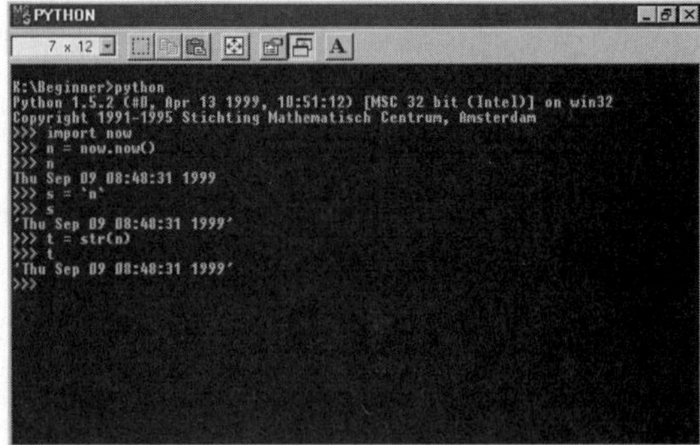

FIGURE 10.2
Using class now *in the interpreter.*

We can use class now in any module; it's not very flexible because it only builds an object containing the time and date fields for the moment we create a new object.

To build a more useful class, we're going to add one more special method to it. Add the following lines to `now.py`, after the `def __repr__` line:

```
def __call__(self,t=-1.0):
    if t < 0.0:
        self.t = time.time()
    else:
        self.t = t
    self.storetime()
```

This new method will enable us to do two things:

1. Update the class instance to the current time.
2. Set the time the instance uses to any time in the standard UNIX time range (1970 through 2038).

You can see how this works in Figure 10.3.

FIGURE 10.3
Adding a `__call__()` method to class `now`.

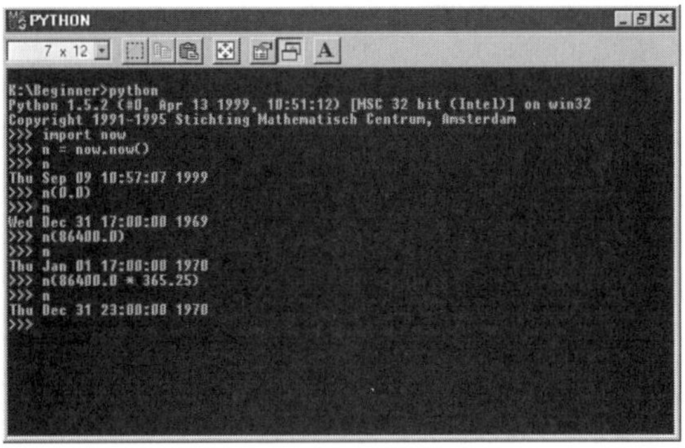

```
K:\Beginner>python
Python 1.5.2 (#0, Apr 13 1999, 10:51:12) [MSC 32 bit (Intel)] on win32
Copyright 1991-1995 Stichting Mathematisch Centrum, Amsterdam
>>> import now
>>> n = now.now()
>>> n
Thu Sep 09 10:57:07 1999
>>> n(0.0)
>>> n
Wed Dec 31 17:00:00 1969
>>> n(86400.0)
>>> n
Thu Jan 01 17:00:00 1970
>>> n(86400.0 * 365.25)
>>> n
Thu Dec 31 23:00:00 1970
>>>
```

What we've done here is to add a special method that lets us call an instance of the class as if it were a function. Creating an object from class `now` always gives us the current time, as you can see in Figure 10.3. When I call object *n* and provide a time value (parameter *t*) of 0.0, I'm setting n to the epoch, or zero point, of UNIX time. This is defined as January 1, 1970, at the very beginning of the day, or 1 January, 1970 at 00:00:00 hours. The reason 0.0 is shown as 5 p.m. on December 31, 1969 is that I'm in the Mountain Timezone, and I used the `localtime()` function from the `time` module. All United States time zones are behind UTC by some number of hours and can vary from those standards by fiddling with day light saving time.

UTC used to be called Greenwich mean time, or GMT. The prime meridian (0 degrees longitude) goes directly through the Royal Observatory at Greenwich (pronounced "grennich"), England and provides the baseline from which all times are counted. It was chosen as "The Prime Meridian of the World" by everyone but the French in 1884 at the International Meridian Conference. In 1970, a new conference was held by the International Telecommunication Union. GMT began each day at noon, but when the name was changed to UTC, the beginning of the day was also changed to 00:00:00 hours. UTC means Coordinated Universal Time, but the letters don't match the words. The UTC abbreviation was chosen precisely because it doesn't stand for anything in any language.

Changing the Name of Arkansas

Our simple class will now go on to become the basis for a new class, which will inherit from class now. As you remember from the last hour, inheritance is one of the attributes of object-oriented programming; we are now ready to see how it works. Listing 10.6 shows how to define our new class, today, that inherits from the old one.

LISTING 10.6 Class today

```
#!/usr/local/bin/python
import time
import now
class today(now.now):
    def __init__(self, y = 1970):
        self.t = time.time()
        self.storetime()
if __name__ == "__main__":
    n = today()
    print "The year is", n.year
    print n
    x = today()
    s = `x`
    print s
```

When a class inherits from another one and Python calls the `__init__()` method for the inheritor, all the methods that are already defined for the inheritee (also called the *parent* class) are immediately available in the new class, the same as if we had written them into the new class. Class variables, on the other hand, do not exist until we either create them in the child *or* call the parent's `__init__()` method. Listing 10.5 shows the first method—that of creating the variables explicitly. We can simplify the preceding code a bit by changing the code to use the second method, calling the parent's `__init__()` method in the child's `__init__()` method, as follows:

```
def __init__(self, y = 1970):
    now.now.__init__(self)
```

This calls the `now` class's `__init__()` method for us, avoiding duplication of code—always a good thing. By doing this, we can change class `now` anytime we want and be assured that the changes will automatically transfer to any module or class that imports it.

Before moving on to the next chapter, let's add one method to the new `today` class; we'll add an `update()` method, which lets us set today's date to any time from 1970 to 2038, as shown in Listing 10.7.

Listing 10.7 Adding a New Method to Class `today`

```
#!/usr/local/bin/python
import time
import now
class today(now.now):
    def __init__(self, y = 1970):
        now.now.__init__(self)
    def update(self,tt):
        if len(tt) < 9 :
            raise TypeError
        if tt[0] < 1970 or tt[0] > 2038:
            raise OverflowError
        self.t = time.mktime(tt)
        self(self.t)
if __name__ == "__main__":
    n = today()
    print "The year is", n.year
    print n
    x = today()
    s = `x`
    print s
    tt = (1999,7,16,12,59,59,0,0,-1)
    x.update(tt)
    print x
```

Our new method, `update()`, takes a tuple that represents some arbitrary time, runs some simple-minded checks, and tries to convert the tuple into a time, using the `time.mktime()` function; times in Python are represented as floating-point numbers, and the number representing the date shown here is 932151599.0. Figure 10.4 shows the results of running `today.py`.

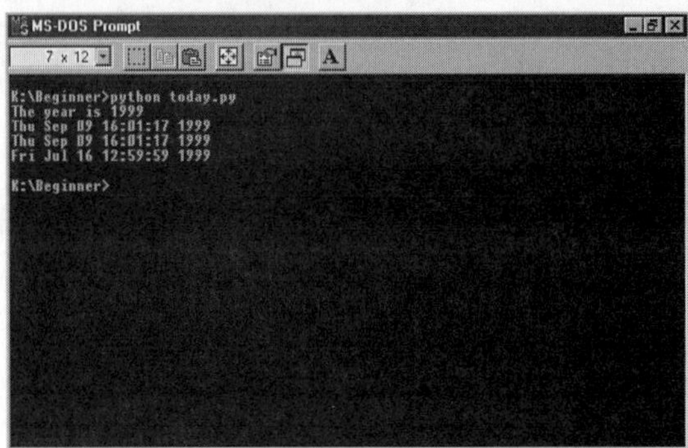

FIGURE 10.4
Running `today.py`.

In the next hour, we'll start adding more methods to the `today` class to make it more useful; we still need to be able to add and subtract changes in time from our `today` objects.

Summary

During this hour, I've shown

- How to write a class
- How to create an object from the class
- How to write methods for the class
- How to use object inheritance

Workshop

Q&A

Q Why are 1970 and 2038 special dates for UNIX?

A January 1, 1970, 00:00:00 hours is the base time for all UNIX dates. The current time is always stored in an integer on UNIX systems; in most cases, the integer is 4 bytes, or 32 bits, in size. Because the time is stored as the number of seconds since the epoch and has a sign, there is generally room for only 31 bits; this means that on many UNIX systems, the time counter will wrap around to zero on January 19, 2038. Some implementations of UNIX have dropped the sign from the time counter, adding another 68 years, and others have simply widened the time type from 4 bytes to 8 bytes, effectively removing practical limits.

Q Where do I get detailed information about the `time` module?

A You can download all the documentation for Python at `http://www.python.org/doc/current/download.html`. Select the style of documentation you prefer. If you have no preference, probably the easiest to get started with is the HTML version, which you can view in any Web browser. Follow the directions for installing, then look at the index page and follow the link to the "Global module index." Click the link for `time`. If you prefer reading online, go directly to `http://www.python.org/doc/current/modindex.html` and click `time` there.

Quiz

1. What is the difference between `t = time.time()` and `self.t = time.time()`?
   a. The first creates a variable visible throughout the containing module, and the second creates one visible only inside a class definition.
   b. The first creates a temporary variable and the second creates a permanent one.
   c. There is no difference.
   d. The first creates a variable visible only in the containing method or module, and the second creates a variable visible to any function or module that knows the definition of the class.
2. What is the difference between the `__str__()` and `__repr__()` methods?
   a. None.
   b. The `__str__()` method can return any old string at all, but the `__repr__()` method is supposed to return a string that can be used to rebuild the object.
   c. The `__str__()` method must return a string, but `__repr__()` can return binary data.
   d. The `__str__()` method writes or prints, but `__repr__()` reads.
3. When one class inherits from another, which part do you have to call the parent's `__init__()` method to create?
   a. The parent's methods
   b. The parent's member variables
   c. Both methods and variables
   d. The parent's parent

Answers

1. d, `t = time.time()` used inside a function creates a variable local to the function. Inside a module, it creates a variable local to the module. Used inside a class, `self.t = time.time()` creates a class variable that is visible anywhere that the class is visible.
2. b, the `__str__()` method can return any string you feel is appropriate, but `__repr__()` is supposed to return a string that you can use to rebuild the originating object. Often, though, there isn't any real difference between the two.
3. a, you have to either call the parent's `__init__()` method, which creates member variables, or explicitly create them in the child's `__init__()` method.

Exercises

Rewrite class `today` using the alternative implementation shown in Listing 10.3. Which style do you like better? Why?

You can find out more about the Royal Observatory at Greenwich (which no longer maintains an observatory at Greenwich, by the way) at `http://www.rog.nmm.ac.uk/index.html`, and you can read about UTC at `http://liftoff.msfc.nasa.gov/academy/rocket_sci/clocks/time-gmt.html`, NASA's Space Academy page.

You can find out about "Changing the Name of Arkansas" by tracking down Mack McCormick's recording from Raglan, *The Unexpurgated Folk Songs of Men*. It's out of print, sadly (and the record company is out of business), and it is not for the faint of heart.

You can find out who The Monks are at

`http://www.the-monks.com/`

HOUR 11

Object-Oriented Programming Concepts

Throw the big part.

—Introduction to Grenade Throwing

In this hour, we'll discuss some more object-oriented programming (OOP) concepts that you'll need to understand later, both in this book and in your programming life. These will include

- Identity
- Encapsulation, interfaces, and contracts
- Namespaces and scope

Identity

When you think about numbers, it's not hard to see that each number has its own individual character. As pointed out in Hour 9, the notion that "1 is 1" (implying that "1 is not 2") is the basis for the identity property of objects. Note that this identity property of objects is not the same as the identity operation in mathematics, which is simply an operation that leaves the operand unchanged. When you think about objects, it's a little less clear, at least until you remember that all numbers are objects in Python. Any numerical object can always be easily distinguished from any other numerical object.

Let's perform a small experiment and create a few simple objects in Python. Run the program shown in Listing 11.1.

LISTING 11.1 bunch.py

```
#!/usr/local/bin/python
class bunch:
    def __init__(self):
        pass
if __name__ == "__main__":
    b = []
    for i in range (0,25):
        b.append (bunch())
    print b
```

You can see that this makes a list containing instances of a class. When you run this program, you will be able to see two things. First, the list `b` contains 25 instances of class `bunch`. Second, you can distinguish any given instance from any other in one of two ways: by position in list `b` or by "ID." The ID is what Python prints out when it displays something like this:

```
<__main__.bunch instance at 7f7f00>
```

The "`7f7f00`" is the ID number; those of you with some C experience will recognize this as an address or a pointer, but as far as Python is concerned, it's just a unique identifier, a way to track objects so that it can throw them away at the right time.

Another thing you may have noticed is that instances of class `bunch` are worthless. Although you can tell each instance apart from its neighbors, there is not much point in doing so because the class has neither state nor behavior. Like bad managers, the list of `bunch`es sits around occupying space and waiting to expire, doing nothing at all in the meantime.

Listing 11.2 does the same thing as `bunch.py`, except that instead of instances of class `bunch`, it creates instances of class `today`, which we built in the last chapter.

LISTING 11.2 `todays.py`

```
#!/usr/local/bin/python
import today
if __name__ == "__main__":
    b = []
    for i in range (0,25):
        b.append (today.today())
    print b
```

Of course, when you run this one, you can see that these instances are of no more use than our previous bunch of `bunches`! To get something that at least looks useful, modify the `b.append()` line of the loop body to look like this:

```
x = today.today()
x(i*86400)
b.append (x)
```


(Remember to maintain indentation.) Then run the program. You'll see that each instance of class `today` represents the same time on a different day. At last, we see that all these different, distinguishable instances have at least the potential to be interesting and useful. As Gregory Bateson has pointed out, "information is any difference that makes a difference." Our modified `todays.py` program presents us with differences that make a difference. We could, for example, cruise through our list of instances and calculate tide levels at the same time each day, or eclipse possibilities, or even fish-catching probabilities. This is the essence of the identity property of objects: it's not enough to be able to tell objects apart if the differences among them don't make a difference.

Encapsulation

In Hour 9, encapsulation, one of the components of OOP, was defined as the combination of two parts: interface and implementation. By looking at our `today` class, we can examine what these ideas really mean. What is the interface for our class? Remember that an interface simply defines how to call a function or a method or how to instantiate an object. Bearing these concepts in mind, let's inspect our class, see Listing 11.3.

LISTING 11.3 Class today

```
class today(now.now):
    def __init__(self, y = 1970):
        now.now.__init__(self)
    def update(self,tt):
        if len(tt) < 9 :
            raise TypeError
        if tt[0] < 1970 or tt[0] > 2038:
            raise OverflowError
        self.t = time.mktime(tt)
         self(self.t)
```

The basic interfaces to class `today` are two:

1. `__init__(self,y=1970)`
2. `update(self,tt)`

These two interfaces represent a contract between the programmer and the user, or caller. The contract says, in effect, "if you, the user, activate the interface correctly according to the published interface, I, the program, will give you back the answer you contracted for." The contract also, notably, does not specify how the internals will be implemented, only that they will be. You could, for example, write your own version of `time.mktime()` instead of using the one that lives inside the time module. It wouldn't even have to behave the same way or return the same kind of value, provided that you documented what it actually did. Class now exposes the following five interfaces:

1. `__init__(self)`
2. `storetime(self)`
3. `__str__(self)`
4. `__repr__(self)`
5. `__call__(self,t=-1.0)`

Therefore, the total number of interfaces for class `today` is seven, because we need to count all the interfaces available. Because Python exposes not only the behaviors of a class but the state of a class, it's only fair to count the variable, `t`, that holds the time as part of the interface. By convention, however, the state of a class is usually not modified by the user/caller unless the programmer documents how to do it and what the restrictions are when doing so. Unlike other OOP languages, Python has no mechanism that prohibits absolutely the modification of a class instance from the outside. It is even possible for users of a class to add both state and behavior to any given object at any time. You as a programmer can discourage this through the means of your documentation, but you cannot prevent it.

I've mentioned documenting methods and functions, but you haven't seen one of the more valuable ways to do such documentation in Python, the `docstring` facility. Any function, method, or module can have a documentation string built into it which, when it exists, can be viewed by any interested party. Listing 11.4 shows a modified `storetime()` method for class now.

LISTING 11.4 Modified `storetime()`

```
def storetime(self):
    """storetime():
    Input: instance of class now
    Output: None
    Side effects: reads the member variable t and converts t into
    9 member variables representing the same time as t.
    """
    self.year, \
    self.month, \
    self.day, \
    self.hour, \
    self.minute, \
    self.second, \
    self.dow, \
    self.doy, \
    self.dst = time.localtime(self.t)
```


As you can see, a triple-quoted string explaining what `storetime()` does has been added to the method. Remember that even functions and methods in Python are objects. All objects, other than the primitive or basic ones, can have state and behavior. Here, when we add the triple-quoted string, we are adding the definition of a special variable to the `storetime()` method: it even has a name, `__doc__`. The way to read the docstring for our method would be something like what's shown in Figure 11.1.

Notice that the docstring doesn't say anything about how `storetime()` is implemented. That is intentional. `Storetime()`, a published interface, has contracted to provide a certain service, but the users of that service are not supposed to care how the service gets performed. You could, for example, write your own version of `mktime()`, or even do the math right inside `storetime()`. To convert the time stamp provided in `self.t` directly into a number of days, just divide `self.t` by 86400 (the number of seconds in a day). You'll have some seconds left over, of course, which you can determine by taking `self.t modulo 86400`. You can see that those leftover seconds can be converted into a time of day. Given the number of days and the time of the current day, it's entirely possible (if not exactly easy), to determine the year, the month, and the day, and in fact, everything required by our published interface. In our case, it is straightforward to use the `mktime()` function from the `time` module, but nothing prevents you from rolling your own version of `mktime()` if you wish to.

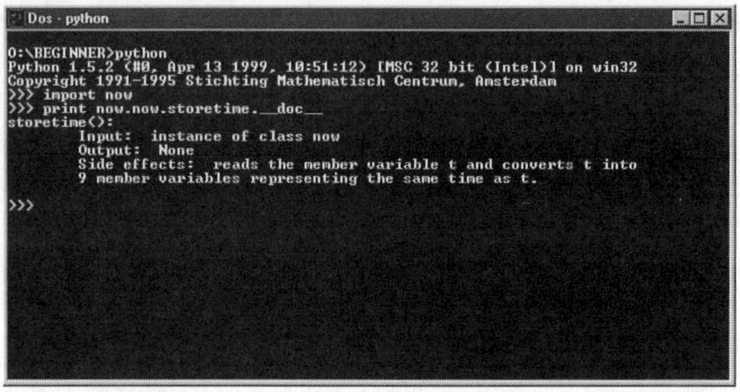

FIGURE 11.1
Printing a docstring (__doc__).

```
Dos - python
O:\BEGINNER>python
Python 1.5.2 (#0, Apr 13 1999, 10:51:12) [MSC 32 bit (Intel)] on win32
Copyright 1991-1995 Stichting Mathematisch Centrum, Amsterdam
>>> import now
>>> print now.now.storetime.__doc__
storetime():
        Input:  instance of class now
        Output:  None
        Side effects:  reads the member variable t and converts t into
        9 member variables representing the same time as t.

>>>
```

The docstring is an important feature of Python. You should attempt to provide them for most of your programs, at least if they are going to be used by even one other person. Besides the obvious benefit of helping someone else understand your programs, an added benefit is help for yourself when you find that you must revisit, rewrite, or debug an older program of your own.

To document an entire module that you've written, simply provide a docstring as the first line or lines in the file, coming immediately after any opening comments. Here's a simple one for `now.py`:

```
"""This is a test documentation string for the now module."""
```

You would print this out by typing

```
print now.__doc__
```

which is simple and obvious. Classes can have documentation too, in addition to the `__doc__` variable (or attribute) attached to every function and method. Here's how:

```
class now:
    """This line demonstrates how to add class documentation.
    """
```

You would print this out by (first importing the class file)

```
print now.now.__doc__
```

Remember that the first `now` is the module, the second `now` is the class that lives inside the `now` module, and `__doc__` is the docstring attribute for the `now` class. I trust that is all very clear. ;-)

Namespaces and Scope

Where do variables live? Functions and methods? Classes and modules? I think that we can examine these questions best by looking more closely at the docstrings, which we discussed in the previous section. Let's begin by simply starting the interpreter, either in IDLE or in your command window (DOS or shell, as appropriate). After you get your >>> prompt, type `dir()`. You should see this response:

```
['__builtins__', '__doc__', '__name__']
```

What are we looking at here? Well, it looks like a list. Is it? Let's check.

```
>>> type(dir())
<type 'list'>
>>>
```

So yes, we have a list. A list of what? For that answer, we need to turn to the Python documentation and find out what it is that `dir()` does:

> Without arguments, return the list of names in the current local symbol table. With an argument, attempts to return a list of valid attributes for that object.

Attributes is another term for names, as in function, variable, or class names. In your interactive session, create a variable and rerun `dir()`:

```
>>> dir()
['__builtins__', '__doc__', '__name__']
>>> spam = 42
>>> dir()
['__builtins__', '__doc__', '__name__', 'spam']
>>> spam
42
>>>
```

Without arguments, the built-in function `dir()` returns a list of all the names it knows about. Simple enough, but what does "current local symbol table" mean? For that, let's look at another built-in function, `locals()`, and see what the documentation says:

> Return a dictionary representing the current local symbol table.

Ah. A symbol table is a dictionary—that is, one of our basic data types that contains names (often called keys) and values. If you try the `locals()` function in your interactive session, you should see something like this:

```
>>> locals()
{'spam': 42, '__doc__': None, '__name__': '__main__', \
     '__builtins__': <module '__builtin__' (built-in)>}
>>>
```

You can see that the variable spam, which you just created, is listed and is associated with the value 42. Notice that the dictionary key __builtins__ is also listed, and it has a value of <module '__builtin__' (built-in)>. If __builtins__ is a module, it should have attributes, just like our current interactive session. Try dir(__builtins__) in your interactive session. You ought to get something like this:

```
>>> dir(__builtins__)
['ArithmeticError', 'AssertionError', 'AttributeError', 'EOFError', 'Ellipsis',
'EnvironmentError', 'Exception', 'FloatingPointError', 'IOError', 'ImportError',
'IndexError', 'KeyError', 'KeyboardInterrupt', 'LookupError', 'MemoryError',
'NameError', 'None', 'NotImplementedError', 'OSError', 'OverflowError',
'RuntimeError', 'StandardError', 'SyntaxError', 'SystemError', 'SystemExit',
'TypeError', 'ValueError', 'ZeroDivisionError', '__debug__', '__doc__',
'__import__', '__name__', 'abs', 'apply', 'buffer', 'callable', 'chr', 'cmp',
'coerce', 'compile', 'complex', 'delattr', 'dir', 'divmod', 'eval', 'execfile',
'exit', 'filter', 'float', 'getattr', 'globals', 'hasattr', 'hash', 'hex', 'id',
'input', 'int', 'intern', 'isinstance', 'issubclass', 'len', 'list', 'locals',
'long', 'map', 'max', 'min', 'oct', 'open', 'ord', 'pow', 'quit', 'range',
'raw_input', 'reduce', 'reload', 'repr', 'round', 'setattr', 'slice', 'str',
'tuple', 'type', 'vars', 'xrange']
>>>
```

Hmmm. Our dir() function tells us that __builtins__ has a docstring; try printing it out:

```
>>> print __builtins__.__doc__
Built-in functions, exceptions, and other objects.

Noteworthy: None is the `nil' object; Ellipsis represents `...' in slices.
>>>
```

What is it that we've learned here?

- __builtins__ is a module ("type(__builtins__)")
- …that has a symbol table ("dir(__builtins__)")
- …that has an entry for __doc__ and also __name__
- If we type dir(), we get the names in a symbol table
- …that has an entry for __doc__ and __name__
- Are we in a module?

As a matter of fact, we are. Still in your interactive session, type import now and rerun dir(). Now is now a name in the list, and if you type type(now), you should get <type 'module'>. What this all shows is that we're always in a module; if you're running directly in the interpreter in an interactive session or running a program from a file, Python does everything you tell it inside a special module. Modules all have the special attribute __name__; now.__name__ is, of course, *now*. If you print the name of the module that you're in when running the interpreter, it will say *`__main__`*. There's one difference between the `__main__` module and other modules, though; you can't use the name *`__main__`* as a means to qualify a name. You can use `now.__doc__`, for example, but you can't say `__main__.__doc__`. You can only use `__doc__`. Thus, the absence of a qualifying name means "the current `__main__` module."

When you type `dir()` and `dir(now)`, the second version is provided with the name of a module (one that you've imported), whereas the first version uses the current `__main__` module by default. In both cases, you will see that several names are listed in every list. For `dir()`, you'll see

```
['__builtins__', '__doc__', '__name__']
```

If you then import `now` and run `dir(now)`, you will see this:

```
['__builtins__', '__doc__', '__file__', '__name__', 'now', 'time']
```

The names common to the two modules are `__builtins__`, `__doc__` , and `__name__`. Here's what is going on.

- When Python starts, it creates a module named `__main__`, which has a dictionary attached to it (this is what you're seeing when you run `dir()`).
- Every time you run an `import` *`name`* statement, Python creates another module that has its own dictionary attached (dir(now)).
- Because some names are the same in both modules, there must be a way to distinguish which name is which.
- The way to tell Python which name you want is through qualification: `__doc__` versus `now.__doc__`.
- Names, whether variable, function, or class names, are simply keys, or attributes, in a dictionary associated with a particular module.
- The shorthand for the dictionary in which these names reside is called a *namespace* (I bet you thought we'd never get to it!)
- The built-in function `dir()` simply lists all the names in a namespace.

11

Every module has a namespace of its own; each function has its own namespace. In fact, most objects in Python have their own namespaces (the basic data types don't, of course). Very often, you'll see references to Python having only two or only three namespaces. This is not strictly accurate; Python has two or three levels of namespace.

You can actually see namespace dictionaries, although it takes a little work. It turns out that Python keeps an internal list of modules that are loaded, and you can access that list without too much difficulty. Listing 11.5 shows how to do this.

LISTING 11.5 namespace.py

```
#!/usr/local/bin/python
import sys
import now
k = sys.modules.keys()
print "Keys:", k
print "---------------"
for i in k:
    if i == "__main__":
        print ">>>", i, "__dict__", sys.modules[i].__dict__
print dir()
```

I've restricted the output to printing only what is in the `__main__` module's namespace. You can take out the `if` test here, but it'll print out a lot of stuff in which you may not be interested if you do that.

Functions have namespaces, too, but you can't get at them the same way. In Listing 11.5, we're able to see all the module namespaces, but if you try to look at a function's namespace from outside you must use the `dir()` function. That is, you can't do the following:

```
def f():
    "doc string"
    z = 42

print sys.modules["__main__"].__dict__["f"].__dict__
```

even though it seems like the logical thing to do. You'll get an `AttributeError` if you try it.

However, if you change the preceding `print sys.modules...` line to this

```
print "DIR", dir(f)
print "DIR", dir(sys.modules["__main__"].__dict__["f"])
```

you'll see that both lines print out the same thing.

Inside function `f()`, however, you can print what the function itself sees for its local namespace. Modify `f()` to read as follows:

```
def f():
    "doc string"
    z = 42
    print "f", dir()
```

If you run the modified function and compare it with `dir(f)`, you'll see that they are quite different. In fact, the only thing you'll see as the output of `f()` is a list containing the name `z`. Although `dir(f)` includes a reference to the `__doc__` attribute, `dir()` inside `f()` does not. This means that functions can't see their own docstrings.

Functions also can't see inside other functions. Add this to your file for `namespace.py`:

```
def d():
    "another doc string"
    z = 44
    x = 9.999
    print "d", dir()
```

Running these functions one after another, you can see that their perceived namespaces are different:

```
f ['z']
d ['x', 'z']
```

Although a variable named `z` is in each function, the `z` that is inside `f()` is not at all the same as the `z` inside function `d()`. Functions can, however, see and modify things that are not in their namespaces.

```
def e():
    "yet another doc string"
    z = 22
    global z
    z = 9999
    print "e", dir()
```


When you run this last function, it should be clear that there are two `z`s here: one that lives at the module level and one that lives inside function `e()`. We can make it clear to the function which `z` it should be referring to. The `global z` line tells the function to look for `z` not in the function's own namespace, but in the enclosing namespace. No `local` keyword does the reverse, so after you use `global` in a function to mark a variable as living in a nonlocal namespace, you're stuck.

There are (on my view) three levels of namespace in Python. They are

- The `__builtins__` namespace. All modules, functions and classes can see this, but it's transparent to them.
- The `global` namespace. This is the namespace that a module is created with. Although you cannot see inside some other object's local namespace, you can see, use, and modify anything in the `global` (or `module`) namespace using qualification.
- The `local` namespace. This is what classes, methods in classes, and functions see.

You'll get slightly different views from other books and other Pythonistas, but this is the view that works for me.

There are only a few more points to make, and then we'll be through with namespaces.

Listing 11.6 shows two things:

1. Functions nest. You can build functions that live only inside another function.
2. Namespaces do not nest. The inner function cannot see variables that live inside the outer function. From a namespace perspective, `inner()` and `outer()` are two unrelated functions living in the enclosing module, namespace.

LISTING 11.6 `nesting.py`

```
#!/usr/local/bin/python
import sys
global_var = 9999
def outer():
    z = 42
    def inner():
        global z
        y = 666
        z = 99
        print dir()
    inner()
    print dir(), z
print dir()
outer()
print z
```

The inner function cannot see variables created in the outer function's namespace. The `global z` line tells function `inner()` to ignore the local namespace when it sees a reference to `z`. The first reference to `z` is the `z = 99` line, which doesn't change the value of `outer()`'s `z` but instead creates a *new* variable `z` in the enclosing, global namespace.

Classes have the same rules for namespace that functions do. Classes can nest, but namespaces don't. Each class instance gets its own local namespace, and thus cannot see variables or methods in another classes' namespace, even when a class is built inside an existing class.

Finally, we should discuss scope. In many texts, you'll see scope and namespace used interchangeably, but they aren't the same. Scope properly defines both the namespace in which a variable, class, or function lives, and the lifetime of the object. A variable created inside a function has both a local namespace and a local scope; when the function ends, any variables created in the local namespace go out of scope—that is, they cease to exist. Python reclaims any memory used by out-of-scope variables. Because the namespace itself has gone out of scope, Python knows that it should go through the namespace, track down any resources used by names in the namespace, and throw them away before disposing of the namespace.

Summary

In this hour, we've learned about objects and identity, about encapsulation, and about namespaces and scope. In the section on identity, we learned that it's not enough to be able to tell objects apart; the differences have to mean something. Under encapsulation, we learned about interfaces and contracts, and in the last section, we learned that namespaces control both the visibility of an object and what is visible to an object.

Workshop

Q&A

Q I thought encapsulation had something to do with hiding information?

A It often does in other programming languages, but in Python the term primarily refers to the way objects are packaged and called, not how information is hidden. This is because Python has a fundamentally different view that, in general, programmers and users can ordinarily be trusted not to mess things up.

Q Why is there a __builtins__ namespace? Couldn't these built-in functions have been placed in every new object's namespace?

A They certainly could have, but the result would have meant lots of names in every object; this could mean a certain degree of namespace pollution. By placing only a reference in each new namespace to the built-in one, namespace slots are kept to a minimum.

Quiz

1. What does "<__main__.bunch instance at 7f7f00>" mean?
   a. Something to do with broccoli.
   b. The __main__ module has a bunch class instance with an ID of 7f7f00.
   c. It's the namespace for the __main__ module.
   d. It's the identity property for the __main__ module.
2. What is the proper syntax for a docstring?
   a. docstring = "Documentation"
   b. __doc__ = "Documentation"
   c. """Documentation"""
   d. doc = Don't quote me

3. What built-in function(s) can you use to inspect a namespace?
   a. `namespace()`
   b. `dir(`*`namespace`*`)`
   c. `locals()`, `globals()` and `dir(`*`namespace`*`)`
   d. `scope()`

Answers

1. b, "<__main__.bunch instance at 7f7f00>" means that `__main__` has an instance of class `bunch` with the id shown.

2. b, docstrings are strings, properly quoted, that occupy a specific position in a module, class, class method, or function.

3. b, the `dir()` function only gives you a list of names that exist in a namespace; `locals()` and `globals()` return a dictionary that mirrors the namespace. You can look at the `dir()` function as being similar to the dictionary method `keys()` followed by a sort.

Exercises

Write a replacement `mktime()` routine. As a hint for a direction to take, search the Web for **`Julian Day`** and **`Joseph Justus Scaliger`**. Another possible starting point is Peter Meyer's Calendar pages, which can be found at `http://www2.papeterie.ch/serendipity/hermetic/cal_stud.htm`.

Only marginally related to Python and the concepts presented in this chapter, the article found at this link, `http://www.inf-gr.htw-zittau.de/~wagenkn/Natasha_Chen.html`, "High School Computing: The Inside Story," is fascinating and telling. If you substitute "Python" for "Scheme" in the text, the article's point may strike a little closer to home.

Hour 12

More OOP Concepts

Mistakes are almost always of a sacred nature. Never try to correct them.

—*Salvador Dali*

In the previous hour, we discussed several OOP concepts: identity, encapsulation, and namespaces. In this hour, you will learn about more OOP concepts, such as

- Data hiding with "private" variables
- Polymorphism
- Multiple inheritance

Data Hiding with "Private" Variables

Python is not really built to enforce traditional ideas of data hiding (also called access control). Many other OOP languages have simple ways to explicitly hide or publicize class variables and methods. Java and C++, for example, employ special keywords that do nothing but inform their compilers that some data is to be exposed—or not. For these two languages, the keywords are

- `public`
- `private`
- `protected`
- no keyword, which gives "private" access by default in C++, and "friendly package" access in Java

A brief rundown of what these keywords stand for and why they might be useful is in order before we proceed with Python.

- Public means just what it says: any function or method that uses a class can both read and modify any variable or function that is marked public. Methods in other classes can reach right in and change things around. The danger here, according to proponents of data hiding, is that classes might be open to accidental or purposeful manipulation that may subvert or destroy the internal consistency of an object.
- Private means that the only class methods that are allowed to change or use state and behavior marked private are those in the class itself. Nothing outside the class can read or write variables. The benefit is, supposedly, that the programmer always knows exactly what is going on with the class, and it is protected from unauthorized access.
- Protected means that the class itself and any classes that inherit from the class can read and write the information. Protected methods may be called only by other methods in the class or by classes that inherit from it. A benefit here is that only "approved" classes can change state and call methods. For example, in a class that handled disk I/O it might be prudent to protect an object from receiving monitor (display screen) I/O.
- Friendly package access, in Java, means that any class that originates in a file in the same directory as the target class can change state and behavior and use methods.

Python does not have any special marker keywords to control access to members of a class. Most access control is done by convention, with a small amount being performed by taking advantage of class, variable, and method naming techniques, using one or more leading underscores to signal Python that it's not supposed to just blindly expose all classes, variables, and methods. In Python, there are some special reserved groups of names, which we will discuss, all beginning with an underscore. Only one underscore limits data exposure in Python, but it doesn't actually prevent access; anyone knowledgeable can get to and modify any variable anywhere if they want.

The first special name is the _; it exists only when you're running the interpreter interactively. Whenever you evaluate a statement, such as "1 + 1", interactive Python stores the result in the _ variable, which does not exist until some evaluation takes place. You can use the `'_'` as a name that you create only in a noninteractive session, but it's smarter not to do so.

The second special name, or actually group of names, is any name beginning with a single underscore. This is the only special name you actually need to care about. Any name beginning with a single underscore is not imported into the importing module's namespace when you use `from <module> import *`. To see how this works, take a look at Listing 12.1.

LISTING 12.1 `imptest1.py`

```
#!/usr/local/bin/python
_CHANGEOVER="Sep 3 1752"
from today import *
```

This is a very simple program; all it does is create a variable that is visible only in the file `imptest1.py`. Listing 12.2 shows attempts to use the variable.

LISTING 12.2 `imptest2.py`

```
#!/usr/local/bin/python
from imptest1 import *
x = today()
print x
print dir()
try:
    print _CHANGEOVER
except:
    try:
        print imptest1._CHANGEOVER
    except:
        print "Can't find _CHANGEOVER"
```


If you need to, refer to Hour 8 where we discussed `try` and `except` to see how this works. Figure 12.1 shows the output of running `imptest2.py`.

As you can see from the output of `dir()`,no variable is named `_CHANGEOVER` in `imptest2.py`'s namespace. The `imptest1` module can see and use this variable, but no one else can.

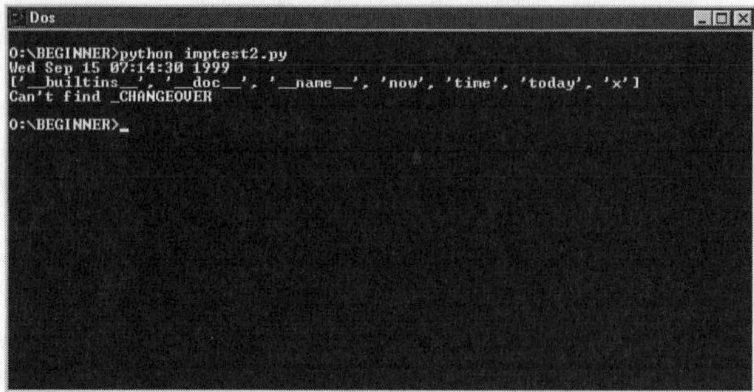

Dos
O:\BEGINNER>python imptest2.py
Wed Sep 15 07:14:30 1999
['__builtins__', '__doc__', '__name__', 'now', 'time', 'today', 'x']
Can't find _CHANGEOVER
O:\BEGINNER>_

FIGURE 12.1
Running `imptest.py`.

However, it is possible to modify the variable, although we have to modify `imptest2.py` as shown in Listing 12.3.

LISTING 12.3 Modified `imptest2.py`

```
#!/usr/local/bin/python
import imptest1
x = imptest1.today()
print x
print dir()
print dir(imptest1)
try:
    print _CHANGEOVER
except:
    try:
        print imptest1._CHANGEOVER
    except:
        print "Can't find _CHANGEOVER"
```

Figure 12.2 shows what happens now:

```
O:\BEGINNER>python imptest2.py
Wed Sep 15 07:30:50 1999
['__builtins__', '__doc__', '__name__', 'imptest1', 'x']
['_CHANGEOVER', '__builtins__', '__doc__', '__file__', '__name__', 'now', 'time'
, 'today']
Sep 3 1752
O:\BEGINNER>_
```

FIGURE 12.2
Running the modified `imptest.py`.

As you can see, if `from <module> import *` is avoided, it is perfectly simple to see (and therefore change) the `_CHANGEOVER` variable.

The next group of special names is that comprising names that begin and end with two underscores. These are called special class method names, and you will learn all about them in the next hour. You have, of course, seen a few of these already: `__call__`, `__init__`, and so on. All these special class method names are defined by Python, but you need to implement the actual methods if you wish to take advantage of the functionality they allow.

The final group is a set that you really won't need to worry about at all because it is a fairly advanced concept. In the interests of completeness, however, here is a quick overview. Names that are members (either variables or methods) of a class and which begin, but do not end, with two underscores are subject to something called class-private name mangling by Python. Mangling, a term taken from C++, simply means changing. The idea is that if you don't want users of the class to see some variables or methods in a class you create, you put two underscores in front of their names. Programmers who use your class can see and modify members with ordinary names, but they can only see double-underscore names by using Python's name mangling rules themselves. You can find out more at the usual place, `http://www.python.org/`, but I won't go into any more detail in this book.

In the next section, we talk about Python and polymorphism.

Polymorphism

In Hour 9, we defined polymorphism as the capability to send one kind of message to many objects and get back the appropriate response from each object. You've seen examples already, such as the `__init__()` method that the classes `now` and `today` have used. Python sends each class a message when it creates an instance; programmers who write classes in Python must build the `__init__()` method into them so that they can control exactly what happens when the class is created. You should realize, however, that it is not always necessary to have an `__init__()` method; sometimes you want only objects that have certain kinds of behavior, and you couldn't care less what state the object has. Polymorphism, then, is not automatic; programmers have to do something so that their objects will respond appropriately.

In the case of the `__init__()` method, every class is free to do whatever it wants in order to create, or not create, itself properly. You can change the number of arguments that `__init__()` takes, except for the first. All class methods require the first argument to be an instance of the class. This first argument is, by convention, always called `self`. No law or restriction in Python says it has to be called `self`, but nearly everyone calls it that. To make your programs as readable as possible, it is highly recommended that you go with tradition in this matter.

The `__init__()` method does not return a value. If for some reason your initialization routine fails to do what it is supposed to do, you should throw an exception. (I suspect the reason that it's called "throw an exception" is because it's a bit like sticking a log into moving bicycle spokes.) Probably the best one in such a case is `AttributeError`, although you may want to look into defining your own. Exceptions are classes, too, so inheriting from them to build your own is not too difficult. Other polymorphic methods require adhering to an interface (remember encapsulation?). For instance, the `__add__()` method, which is used when two objects are added using the + operator, requires two arguments—`self` and `other`—and must return a new instance of the class being added. We will cover these specified interfaces in detail in the next hour.

Although Python provides many kinds of polymorphic messages, as we will see in the next hour, they don't cover all possible responses you might wish to obtain from your own objects. Most objects that you build, in fact, will have methods that you define that provide different kinds of behavior than the built-in special methods do. With inheritance, it's easy to build an entire class hierarchy of objects that respond to a single message that you've specified. For example, dates and numbers in Mayan mathematics have many characteristics in common, but at the same time, they have some important differences. Numbers are a uniform base 20, but dates are mixed-radix: they're base 20 except in the second place, which is base 18. Dates, therefore, could inherit from numbers and still share a great deal of behavior and almost all the state. Sometimes you would need to convert between the types. The easiest way to do this is to have the `number` class have a method called (surprise) `convert()`, which automatically returns a date. The `date` class, inheriting from the `number` class, would have an identically named method, but it automatically returns a number. You send an instance the same message in either case (`<instance>.convert()`), but you would get back the appropriate object in return.

In the next section, we're going to talk about inheritance and we will see how to inherit from multiple classes.

Multiple Inheritance

In Hour 10, we saw how normal inheritance worked. Listing 10.5, to which you should refer, showed class `today`, which inherited from class `now`. In this section, we're going to learn how to do multiple inheritance; that is, how to build a class that inherits state and behavior from more than one class.

By far the most common usage for multiple inheritance is what are called *mixin* classes; that is, classes that are so generic that they can be mixed into almost any sort of class. For instance, you could define a class with a method that goes through an object's namespace, finds all the attributes, and returns a list of printable strings representing each attribute. You could mix this class into virtually all classes you build, and by naming the method `__repr__`, you could avoid having to write a new `__repr__()` method for every new class you define. Depending on the size of your classes or project, this could be a serious timesaver.

In computer science, the term *token* is used to describe very small bits of input to a *parsing engine*, which is a program, or part of one, that reads structured input and decides what that input means based on what the tokens stand for and the order of the tokens. In your DOS command prompt, for example, the \ token has a special meaning, and so does the | token. Like subway or bus tokens, the more you put in, the longer the ride you get in exchange. Sometimes, you get where you weren't going.

Because class `today` already has a `__repr__()` method, however, we'll add a different mixin class. You've seen old movies where the copyright date is in Roman numerals, right? Let's build a class that does nothing except convert the year into a Roman numeral (converting into Roman numerals is a lot easier than converting Roman numerals into ordinary base 10 numbers). Table 12.1 shows the components (also called elements, or in the language of computer science, tokens) of the Roman numerals that we're going to use.

12

TABLE 12.1 Elements, or Tokens, of Roman Numerals

Token	*Value*
I	1
V	5
X	10
L	50
C	100
D	500
M	1000

This is an incomplete list of all the possible tokens, by the way. Monks during the Middle Ages elaborated on the system substantially, adding not only new tokens but modifiers that acted as multipliers to an existing meaning. For example, X with a bar over it stood for 10,000, so the bar was a 1000× multiplier. We're only trying to provide movie dates here, so we won't go into anything more complicated in this book. Listing 12.4 shows a simple mixin class that converts a year into a Roman numeral.

LISTING 12.4 roman.py

```
#!/usr/local/bin/python
import string
import sys
class roman:
    def __init__(self,y):
        if y < 1:
            raise ValueError
        self.rlist = []
        ms = y / 1000
        tmp = y % 1000
        if ms > 0:
            self.rlist.append("M" * ms)
        ds = tmp / 500
        tmp = tmp % 500
        if ds > 0:
            self.rlist.append("D" * ds)
        cs = tmp / 100
        tmp = tmp % 100
        if cs > 0:
            self.rlist.append("C" * cs)
        ls = tmp / 50
        tmp = tmp % 50
        if ls > 0:
            self.rlist.append("L" * ls)
        xs = tmp / 10
        tmp = tmp % 10
        if xs > 0:
            self.rlist.append("X" * xs)
        vs = tmp / 5
        tmp = tmp % 5
        if vs > 0:
            self.rlist.append("V" * vs)
        js = tmp
        if js > 0:
            self.rlist.append("I" * js)
    def ryear(self):
        s = ""
        for i in self.rlist:
            s = s + i
        return s
if __name__ == "__main__":
    if len(sys.argv) > 1:
```

```
        yr = string.atoi(sys.argv[1])
    else:
        yr = 1999
    x = roman(yr)
    print x.ryear()
```

The preceding `append()` lines offer a simple solution to selecting the proper number of characters; we take advantage of the * operator's knowledge of strings by just multiplying the correct letter times the number of thousands, five hundreds, hundreds, and so on. `"C" * 4` yields a string that reads "CCCC," which is just what we want here.

Running this program without an argument will translate 1999 into a Roman numeral. Providing an argument shows you the Roman numeral for whatever year you want. Figure 12.3 shows what happens when you run it with 2000 as the year.

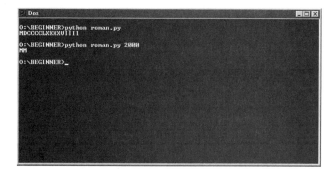

FIGURE 12.3
Running `roman.py`.

Note that although the Roman year equivalents produced by `roman.py` are technically correct, they are only so in the most literal sense. Although you do occasionally see the nineteenth century written as "MDCCCC," you more often see it written as "MCM," and you never see nine decades written as "LXXXX," but always as "XC." And of course, it's not "VIIII" but "IX." Taking advantage of these shortcuts, then, 1999 would more properly be written as "MCMXCIX." Our `roman` class, then, is kind of dumb. It does work, though, at least enough for purposes of demonstration. Class `roman` could be built in another way, too—one without any state variables, having only behavior. All the code that converts base 10 into a Roman numeral string could be moved into a method other than `__init__()`, and classes that inherited from `roman` would get that method without having to call the `__init__()` method.

OK, let's mix in class `roman`. Listing 12.5 shows class `today`, modified for multiple inheritance.

LISTING 12.5 Modifying `today`: `today-roman.py`

```
#!/usr/local/bin/python
import time
import now
import roman
class today(now.now,roman.roman):
    def __init__(self, y = 1970):
        now.now.__init__(self)
        roman.roman.__init__(self,y)
    def update(self,tt):
        if len(tt) < 9 :
            raise TypeError
        if tt[0] < 1970 or tt[0] > 2038:
            raise OverflowError
        self.t = time.mktime(tt)
        self(self.t)
        roman.roman.__init__(self,self.year)
if __name__ == "__main__":
    n = today()
    print "The year is", n.year
    print n
    x = today()
    s = `x`
    print s
    tt = (1999,7,16,12,59,59,0,0,-1)
    x.update(tt)
    print x, x.t
print "Roman", x.ryear()
    st=`x`
    print st
```

Figure 12.4 demonstrates what you get when you run it.

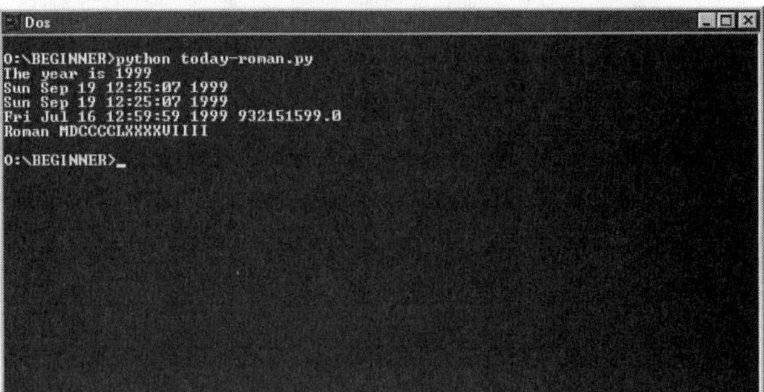

FIGURE 12.4
Running *`today-roman.py`*.

Let's add a __repr__ method to class roman. Add the following lines to roman.py, right after the ryear() method:

```
def __repr__(self):
    return(self.ryear())
```

Then run today-roman.py. You shouldn't see any difference in the output at all. However, if you now change the order of inheritance in the class line from this:

```
class today(now.now,roman.roman):
```

to this:

```
class today(roman.roman,now.now):
```

you ought to see a difference when you run it. Figure 12.5 shows what you should see.

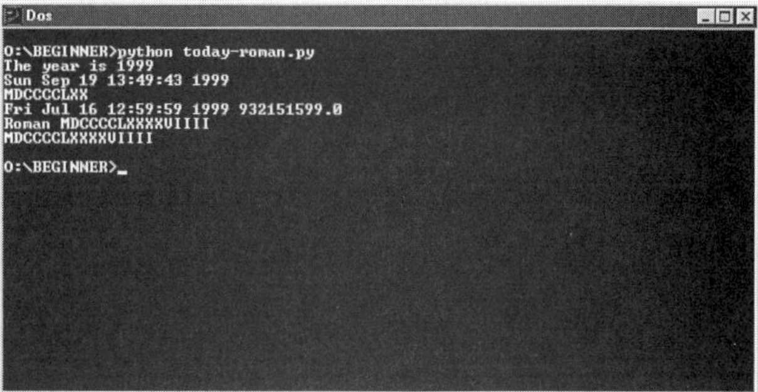

FIGURE 12.5
today-roman.py, showing changed inheritance order.

The first time, the __repr__() method called was the one that lives in class now, but the second time, after we changed the order of inheritance, the method called was the one we just added to class roman. This demonstrates that the order of classes inherited from is important, and that you can have classes that inherit from each other with methods named the same in all of them (otherwise, polymorphism wouldn't work). Whenever you create an object that uses multiple inheritance, Python searches through the various classes in a left-to-right order. Whenever a name is encountered that duplicates one already found, the second one is ignored. You need to be careful when using multiple inheritance, because otherwise you might very well call a method that you shouldn't have—and obtain peculiar results.

Summary

In this hour, we've learned that even though you can't prevent anyone who is really determined, you can take some steps to hide classes and variables from the view of another program. We learned a bit more about polymorphism and learned how to use multiple inheritance to build mixin classes. In the next hour, we talk in more detail about special class methods, which you've seen only in passing.

Workshop

Q&A

Q Isn't life complicated enough without multiple inheritance?

A Why, sure. But multiple inheritance can sometimes pay off in big ways, especially if you're writing a large number of classes that are related. It can be a good way to save yourself lots of code duplication.

Q Roman numerals? What happened to the Mayan numbers?

A They shall return. You can work on Roman ones for homework.

Q How different from Python is multiple inheritance in other languages?

A It's mostly very similar, but the syntax is usually more complicated; in languages such as C++, it can turn an object into just as much of a spaghetti-code nightmare as `goto`s can. Properly used and vigorously documented, however, it can simplify programmers' lives immensely.

Quiz

1. What is signified by a variable name that begins with a single underscore?
    a. Not even Python can see such a variable.
    b. When it's inside a class, no other classes can see it.
    c. It's not imported with `from <module> import *`.
    d. Such names are "mangled" by Python.
2. What is `self`?
    a. An illusion made up of the five aggregates.
    b. The same as C++'s `this` pointer with a new name.
    c. A way that an object can modify itself.
    d. An example of polymorphism at work.

3. When using multiple inheritance, what should you be most careful of?
    a. Don't have any names the same in any of the classes you're mixing in, either of variables or methods.
    b. Never build a class that calculates Easter.
    c. Don't have any recursive classes.
    d. The order in which classes are specified determines which duplicately named methods or variables end up in the resulting object.

Answers

1. a, variables that begin with a single underscore are not visible when the module they live in is imported with `from <module> import *`.
2. b, in Python, `self` is the same as the C++ `this`, and it allows objects to modify themselves. Buddha says it's also an illusion, but he may be wrong when the `self` is an object.
3. d, the order in which classes are specified determines which duplicately named methods or variables end up in the resulting object; without allowing duplicate names, polymorphism wouldn't exist. The remaining two choices probably represent good advice, too.

Exercises

Write the mixin class described at the beginning of the "Multiple Inheritance" section that provides a `__repr__()` method to any class that inherits from it. Modify the `today` class to take advantage of your mixin class. Hint: Mark Lutz and David Ascher cover this topic in their book from O'Reilly, *Learning Python*. You may need to change the name of the method from `__repr__` to something else if you want `today` to continue to display the date it represents.

Track down all the symbols or tokens that have been used over the last 2,000 years to build Roman numerals. Decide on easy ways to represent these tokens when your program is limited to the command-line interface. See if you can figure out a way to read in a Roman numeral, decode it, and print out the equivalent base 10 number.

Rewrite class `roman` to use the shortcuts described. While you're at it, work on coming up with a less wordy way of converting from a base 10 number into a Roman one. Hint: use lists or arrays.

For more on the Buddhist conception of no-self, see Buddhadasa Bhikkhu's *Heartwood of the Bodhi Tree: The Buddha's Teaching on Voidness*, which you can find at Wisdom Publications (`http://www.channel1.com/users/wisdom/index.html`).

HOUR 13

Special Class Methods in Python

Heh, asking a bunch of Buddhists to judge "good" and "bad", good luck!

—Brian Dowcet

In this hour, we will start putting things together. We'll talk about special class methods—those funny-looking functions inside classes that have underscores in front and after their names. At the end of this hour, you should be able to add your own special class methods to classes you write or modify.

Operators and Operator Overloading

Back in Hour 3, you learned about operators and operands. You also learned about operators, such as the + operator, that behaved differently depending on what their operands were. For example, `1 + 1` and `"Hello, " + "World!"` behave differently; when given numbers, + adds them, and when given strings, + concatenates them. This is a clear example of polymorphism; you're sending an "add" message to different kinds of objects. In the first case, it goes to two numbers, and in the second case, it goes to two strings. What's going on here is something called *operator overloading*, which means that you can define what an operator does in many contexts. Now, you can't redefine what operators do when given two operands of the basic data types (strings, lists, numbers, and so on), but anytime you define a class, you can specify exactly what will happen for any operator you want. And not only can you specify what happens when both operands are of your own class, but you can do the same for any context in which either one of the operands is an instance of your class. Operator overloading, through the use of special class methods, is one of the most powerful features of Python. Other languages also allow operator overloading, but in my opinion, none are as simple to understand and use as Python's method.

Being able to define what an object of your own design does in response to different kinds of messages is extremely useful. With the C language, you can't overload operators; you can define functions that do the same job, but there's no way to tell C what function to call when the operands are of a certain type. You can just call the functions, of course, but that's not all that convenient. So you can think about the abstract view, but that's as close as you can get. You can't write down what you think. For instance, in my first research into the Mayan calendar, I had to track down a special library that allowed the creation and use of arbitrary-length integers (I was tired of calculations pooping out after reaching only a billion or two years). These fulfilled the same function that long integers do in Python; you can work with gigantic numbers. Because the library—and my code—was in C, I had to call the functions directly because I couldn't use operator overloading. I could think, "I want to multiply `mm` and `tt`, and then divide the result modulo 13," but I had to write stuff like this:

```
Mint * tmpn = mpIntToMint ( 0 ) ;
Mint * q = mpIntToMint ( 0 ) ;
Mint * r = mpIntToMint ( 0 ) ;
Mint * tx = mpIntToMint ( 13 ) ;
Mint * mm = mpIntToMint ( 20 ) ;
Mint * tt = mpIntToMint ( 819 ) ;
mpMultiply ( mm, tt, tmpn ) ; /* Put output in tmpn */
mpDivide ( tmpn, tx, q, r ) ; /* mod answer 13, output in r */
mpPtrFree ( mm, modname ) ; /* free tmp variables */
mpPtrFree ( tt, modname ) ;
mpPtrFree ( q, modname ) ;
mpPtrFree ( tmpn, modname ) ;
mpPtrFree ( tx, modname ) ;

return ( r ) ;
```

Later on, after I began using C++, I thought about converting the library to use C++-style operator overloading. Luckily, before I could act on this self-damaging impulse, I discovered Python, where I could do the same job this way:

```
r = ( 20L * 819L ) % 13
return r
```

or even:

```
return ( 20L * 819L ) % 13L
```

But better yet, when I figured out how to define my own classes and special methods within them, I found that it was easy to do things like this:

```
from mayalib import *

x = mayanum()
x()
x = x + "13.0.0.0.0"
x()
print x.gregorian()
```

That would have taken many more lines of code in C, it would have taken far, far longer to write and debug, and it would not have been nearly so clear. (The code, by the way, prints the famous "end date" of the Mayan calendar in our own Gregorian calendar; download the code from the book's Web site at `http://www.pauahtun.org/TYPython/` and run it.)

Sometimes, what a class should do in response to any particular message or operator is obvious; in the case of Mayan dates, for example, the + operator's function is clear. It should add a Mayan date and either another Mayan date or something that can be converted to a Mayan date. But sometimes it's not so clear. In Hour 15, for instance, we will be constructing a class to help track TV programs that have been taped on video cassettes, and it's not so clear what the + operator should do. Spending a little time on the design up front, however, can pay off later by drastically reducing the amount of cut-and-try time. If you think about what's on VHS cassettes and what they do in real life, a solution offers itself.

Tapes are containers. They can be empty, they can contain one or more programs, and sometimes you tape over all or part of one. Sometimes your VCR eats them (if your VCR eats a *Star Trek* tape, it's time for capital punishment!). Therefore, we need a `cassette` class, which can be empty or can contain instances of `program` classes. Think about what you do with the real cassettes; you add programs to them, and sometimes you delete programs. See? You can define classes that know what to do with other classes and can operate on those contained classes in all kinds of useful ways. Now, it's always good to spend time on design issues up front, but Python gives you such extraordinarily powerful tools that you can often spend time trying—and discarding—many implementations of an idea, and in doing so, you can see exactly how a class behaves when you really use it. You can work out what a class should do by trying it and by modifying behavior until you and Python find out what that class is really supposed to do. Sometimes this can be a real surprise, such as when you find out that a class does best something you had no idea of at all when you started building it. This sort of person-machine dialectic can be extremely rewarding—but sometimes it can bite you, too. You just have to be willing to take risks and to throw away code that doesn't work. Usually, with Python, development time that you invest in an implementation is so short that you are helped into the attitude that you can afford to take these kinds of risks. By the way, the kind of analysis we just did—looking at an object, determining what it is and what it contains—is an important tool in OOP design. Constructing an object that is a thing of some sort and that contains other things (which are subject to analysis in the same way) is the ground zero from which you start building classes and their implementation. For all its simplicity, the *is a/contains* method of analysis can take you a very long way in OOP design.

We'll revisit the cassette and program classes later on in Hour 15, but in the meantime, let's move on to learning more about special class methods.

Using Special Methods

In Appendix D, you will find an alphabetic list of all possible special class methods, current as of Python 1.5.2; any user-defined classes (that is, any classes that you as a programmer want to build) can implement, or not implement, them in any way that you want. It does help if the "way you want" makes sense, though. Many times, it's perfectly clear that implementing a specific class method for an object would be a waste of time. For instance, in the cassette class, what would the * operator do? Nothing prevents you from defining it to be the way in which a cassette and all its programs are destroyed, but no user of your class objects would ever dream that that's what it meant. It's much better to stick to methods, such as + and -, that offer at least the possibility that people will think, "Oh, that makes sense," rather than make them look up the meaning of every single operator and have them think, "Why in the world did she do it that way?"

Many of the special class methods require arguments of a particular kind, in a specific order, and are required to return certain kinds of values. Other methods are much more flexible, with the only requirement being that they accept the standard `self` argument. `Self`, you remember, is just a simple, explicit way that a method can tell what kind of object it is and that gives it a way to change its own state and/or behavior. You've already seen one example of the latter case; the `__init__()` method is only required to accept `self` and return nothing. Any other arguments that you want to add are optional—not required; you're the one designing the class, so you can require any other arguments you want. Python will enforce your requirements for you after you tell it what they are, but Python itself has no additional requirements for the `__init__()` method.

What this means is that you can define the `__init__()` method for your class to do nothing at all, and you can define other methods that will add state and/or behavior later on-the-fly. The way to define a do-nothing method is easy; just use `pass`:

```
class egg:
    def __init__(self):
        pass
```

The `pass` keyword does the same thing in a class definition that it does in `if` statements and `try/except` statements; it simply tells Python explicitly, "I really want you to do nothing here."

Class methods, especially ones meant for the numeric-style operators, often have more stringent requirements. For a simple example, look at the `__add__()` method, which must take exactly two arguments (`self` and `other`) and return a new object that is the result of adding or concatenating `self` and `other`. Of course, you could define it to do something else entirely and still meet the requirements, but that "something else entirely" really ought to make some sort of sense. Don't define an `__add__()` method that multiplies, for instance! It can make sense to sometimes bend the rules a little bit, though. Set theory, for example, defines joins, unions, and intersections of sets, and has specific operators to represent them, but these specialized operators don't exist in Python's character set. In cases like this, then, you are justified in defining the + operator to mean a join of two sets, the | operator to mean the union and the & operator to mean the intersection. Anyone who understands even a little set theory will rapidly grasp what these operators do and will make the mental adaptations necessary to work with your implementation of sets.

Working in conjunction with `__add__()` and other methods, the `__coerce__()` method is a very powerful way to let your class turn objects of other types, basic types, or other kinds of classes entirely, into instances of your class. It too has stringent requirements; it takes `self` and `other` as arguments and must return `self` and `other` as a tuple (`self,other`). `Other` can be an instance of a basic data type, an instance of the same class `self` is, or some other user-defined class. You must check for all the different types that you support, do the appropriate thing in your `__coerce__()` method, and finally return the required tuple. In that returned tuple, the `other` member should be a new instance of the same type as `self`. (Although it is permissible to convert `self` into the same type as `other`, it's kind of weird, so you ought to have a really good reason to do so. I can't think of any good reasons offhand.)

Before moving on to a detailed discussion of the most useful methods, it's worthwhile to discuss a method that has some built in gotchas, `__del__()`. Many other OOP languages have something called *garbage collection*, which simply means that from time to time the interpreter will look over all the objects that have been created, find all the ones that you aren't using anymore, and then get rid of them. Python has a mechanism to get rid of junk you don't need anymore, but it's not garbage collection at all. It's called *reference counting*, and all that means is that every time an object is *created*, Python keeps track of it in a hidden way, adding a special counter to the object so that it knows how many functions, classes, or methods are using it. When no one is using an object, Python throws it away, freeing up memory space that it can use for other objects. In the following code, you see a function definition that contains a local variable, `i`:

```
def spam(y):
    i = y * 400
    ...do whatever is needed...
```

When `i` is created, the little object box that `i` is inside has a hidden counter that is set to 1, representing the number of users of the variable. At the end of the function, when `i` goes out of scope and it's obvious that you're not going to be using it anymore, Python subtracts one from the hidden counter. When it does that, it sees that the reference counter for `i` is 0, so it deletes the object completely. Although many very sophisticated garbage collectors are around, the reference counter mechanism is stable, robust, and very easy to understand. From Guido's viewpoint, its major advantage is that it is extremely portable, whereas the sophisticated garbage collectors are almost all very machine or OS specific, which require more time to get running on new or even slightly different OSes. Additionally, most garbage collectors have to pause the operation of the interpreter at periodic intervals to sweep through memory, looking for objects to delete, which doesn't happen with reference counting. Such pauses can lead to unacceptable delays in the response of the program to the user's commands. The major disadvantage of reference counting, in such a dynamic language as Python, is that, for reasons I won't go into here, it's not always possible to determine whether the counter is completely accurate. In such cases, Python errs on the conservative side and does not delete the suspect memory. All of this means that you could end up with objects in Python's memory that no one is using and can't be referenced by anyone. Such objects will take up memory space but are otherwise harmless. With most computers nowadays, memory is not nearly the expensive, precious commodity it once was, so a little wasted memory here and there is not a major problem.

The `__del__()` method is called whenever an object is about to be deleted by Python. There is a built-in function called `del()`, but all that does is decrement the reference counter on the object. If it still hasn't gone to zero, the `__del__()` method won't be called. Listing 13.1 shows an example to try.

LISTING 13.1 Deleting Objects, `del.py`.

```
#!c:\python\python.exe

class spam:
    def __init__(self,s):
      self.s=s
    def __del__(self):
      print self.s,"is about to be deleted!"

a = spam("one")

def eggspam():
    z = spam("two")

if __name__ == "__main__":
    print "Calling eggspam()"
    b = eggspam()
    t = []
    for i in range(10):
      t.append(a)

    for i in range(9,-1,-1):
      print "Calling del() on number", i
      del(t[i])

    x = spam("three")
```

Figure 13.1 shows the result of running `del.py`.

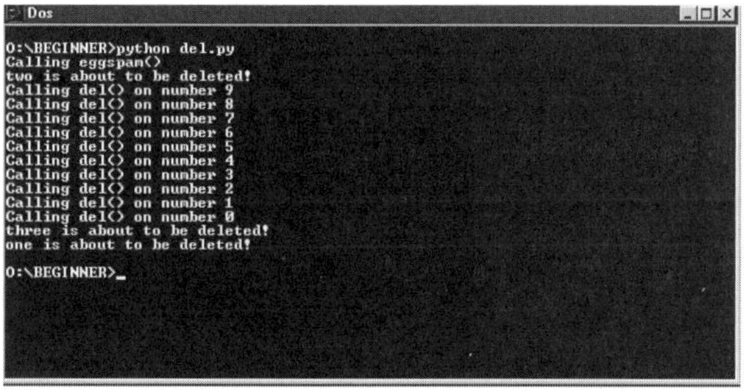

FIGURE 13.1
Running `del.py`.

```
Dos
O:\BEGINNER>python del.py
Calling eggspam()
two is about to be deleted!
Calling del() on number 9
Calling del() on number 8
Calling del() on number 7
Calling del() on number 6
Calling del() on number 5
Calling del() on number 4
Calling del() on number 3
Calling del() on number 2
Calling del() on number 1
Calling del() on number 0
three is about to be deleted!
one is about to be deleted!

O:\BEGINNER>_
```


As you can see from examining the code, the function `eggspam()` creates a `spam` object, but immediately throws it away. The list `t`, on the other hand, has 10 references to the `spam` object `a`. When the items in the list are deleted in reverse order, all that happens is that a's reference count is decremented. Only when the counter reaches zero is a really thrown away. And finally, we create one last `spam` object, which we don't explicitly delete; Python, when it exits, tosses away all remaining objects, as we can see because `spam` tells us so.

Whenever you need to go through a list and delete items in it, you should always do so in reverse order, as the second `for` loop does in Listing 13.1. This is good because every time an item is deleted from the list, it changes the length of the list, which means that if we went through from 0 to 9, by the time we got to 5, no items would be left after index 5. You can see how this works by simply changing the second `for` loop to this:

```
for i in range(10):
    delete(t[i])
```

and running `del.py` again.

The Special Methods

Numeric Special Class Methods

In this section, we will expand on our trivial `spam` class to demonstrate the most important numeric special class methods. Similar methods are grouped together for similar types, such as numeric methods for numeric types, class methods for class types, and sequence and mapping methods for other types. Of the numeric methods covered in this section, the first is `__add__()`.

As you remember, `__add__()` requires `self` and `other` arguments and must return a new `spam` object (well, must is perhaps too strong a word; it is permissible to modify `self` in place and then return it instead of a new object, but this is not considered good practice). To see the effects, let's add some state to our class. The next listing, 13.2, shows the needed changes.

LISTING 13.2 Implementing add () in spam.py

```
#!/usr/local/bin/python
class spam:
    def __init__(self):
        self.eggs = 1
    def __del__(self):
        pass
    def __add__(self,other):
        rt = spam()
        rt.eggs = self.eggs + other.eggs
        return rt
```

```
if __name__ == "__main__":
    a = spam()
    b = spam()
    a = a + b
    print "a now has", a.eggs, "eggs"
```

When you run `spam.py`, it should tell you that a now has two eggs. You can see pretty easily that a `__sub__()` method would be just like the `__add__()` method except for subtracting instead of adding. Multiplication and division of `spam` objects, using the `__mul__()` and `__div__()` should also be clear. Most of the numeric methods are pretty obvious. The complete list of all methods is in Appendix D.

However, what do you do when you want to add a `spam` object and a string?

```
a = spam()
a = a + "24"
a = "24" + a
print a.eggs
```

To implement this behavior, you will need to add two additional methods to class `spam`: the `__coerce__()` method and the `__radd__()` method. To keep it simple, we will add types to `__coerce__()` only as we need them, so for this first exercise, we will add only a string type. Listing 13.3 shows you how.

LISTING 13.3 Spam with More Eggs

```
#!/usr/local/bin/python
import string

class spam:
    def __init__(self):
        self.eggs = 1
    def __del__(self):
        pass
    def __add__(self,other):
        rt = spam()
        rt.eggs = self.eggs + other.eggs
        return rt
    def __coerce__(self,other):
        rt = spam()
        if type(other) == type(rt):
            return (self,other)
        elif type(other) == type(""):
            e = string.atoi(other)
            rt.eggs = e
```


continues

LISTING 13.3 continued

```
            return(self,rt)
        else:
            return None
    def __radd__(self,other):
         return self + other

if __name__ == "__main__":
    a = spam()
    b = spam()
    a = a + b
    print "a now has", a.eggs, "eggs"
    a = a + "24"
    print "a now has", a.eggs, "eggs"
    a = "24" + a
    print "a now has", a.eggs, "eggs"
```

Figure 13.2 shows the output you get by running the modified `spam.py`.

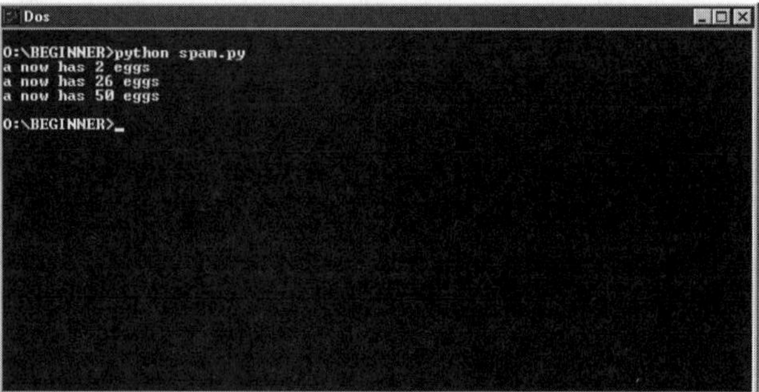

FIGURE 13.2
Eggs and spam.

Notice that in the `__radd__()` method, we didn't need to do anything special or weird; Python ensures that the order of arguments remains the same as in the `__add__()` method. Because we've already implemented that `__add__()` method, we can leverage that method by simply making sure that it's called inside the `__radd__()` method. You can treat this as a general rule. If you implement the normal methods and the `__coerce__()` method, the `__r*__()` methods can be implemented by calling the normal methods and taking advantage of the work you've already done. This is a prime example of Python's ability to do the right thing under most circumstances.

Because our `spam` class has numeric characteristics, we can build more numeric methods into it; `__abs__()` is a good example. Listing 13.4 shows this and some other numeric special class methods.

LISTING 13.4 Numeric Special Class Methods

```
#!c:\python\python.exe
import string

class spam:
    def __init__(self):
      self.eggs = 1
    def __del__(self):
      pass
    def __add__(self,other):
      rt = spam()
      rt.eggs = self.eggs + other.eggs
      return rt
    def __coerce__(self,other):
      rt = spam()
      if type(other) == type(rt):
          return (self,other)
      elif type(other) == type(""):
          e = string.atoi(other)
          rt.eggs = e
          return(self,rt)
      elif type(other) == type(0):
          rt.eggs = other
          return(self,rt)
      else:
          return None
    def __radd__(self,other):
      return self + other
    def __abs__(self):
      return abs(self.eggs)
    def __long__(self):
      return long(self.eggs)
    def __float__(self):
      return float(self.eggs)
    def __int__(self):
      return int(self.eggs)
    def __complex__(self):
      return complex(self.eggs)
    def __divmod__(self,other):
      return divmod(self.eggs,other.eggs)
    def __and__(self,other):
      return self.eggs & other.eggs

if __name__ == "__main__":
    a = spam()
    b = spam()
    a = a + b
    print "a now has", a.eggs, "eggs"
```

continues

LISTING 13.4 continued

```
    a = a + "24"
    print "a now has", a.eggs, "eggs"
    a = "24" + a
    print "a now has", a.eggs, "eggs"
    b = b + "13"
    print divmod(a,b)
    print a & b
```

Implementation of the remainder of the numeric special class methods is left as an exercise, but doing so should not be too hard.

Sequence and Mapping Special Class Methods

For this section, we will build a class of modifiable, or mutable; these can be quite useful sometimes. Listing 13.5 shows our first cut at class `parrots`.

LISTING 13.5 Parrots

```
#!c:\python\python.exe

import string
import sys

class parrot:
    def __init__(self,s=""):
      self.s = list(s)
    def __repr__(self):
      t = ""
         t=string.join(self.s,'')
      return t
    def __str__(self):
      return parrot.__repr__(self)
    def __add__(self,other):
      rt = parrot(`self`)
         rt.s = rt.s + other.s
      return rt
    def __radd__(self,other):
      return self + other
    def __coerce__(self,other):
      if type(other) == type(self):
           return (self, other)
      elif type(other) == type(""):
           rt = parrot(other)
           return (self, rt)
      elif type(other) == type([]):
```

```
          print "type list"
          rt = parrot()
          for i in other:
              if len(i) > 1:
                  for j in i:
                      rt.s.append(j)
              else:
                  rt.s.append(i)
          return (self, rt)
      elif type(other) == type({}):
          return None
      else:
          rt = parrot(str(other))
          return (self, rt)
    def __getitem__(self, key):
      if type(key) == type(0):
          return self.s[key]
      else:
         raise TypeError
    def __getslice__(self,i,j):
      s = self.s[i:j]
      t = ""
      for k in s:
          t = t + k
      return t
    def __setitem__(self, key, value):
      if type(key) == type(0):
          self.s[key] = value
      else:
         raise TypeError
    def __setslice__(self,i,j,value):
      self.s[i:j] = list(value)
    def __len__(self):
      return len(self.s)

if __name__ == "__main__":
    if len(sys.argv) > 1:
      s = sys.argv[1]
    else :
      s = "I'm a little teapot!"
    p = parrot(s)
    print p
    q = parrot (" I'm not schizophrenic!")
    print "Add:", p + q
    x = ['N', 'o', ", that bird's not dead", "!"]
    print "Add:", p + ' ' + x
    print "Index[9]: ", p[9]
    print "Index[-9]: ", p[-9]
```

13

continues

LISTING 13.5 continued

```
76      p[11], p[13] = p[13], p[11]
77      p[14], p[16] = p[16], p[14]
78      print p
79      pa = p[11:17]
80      print pa
81      print "Add:", p + ' ' + q
82      p[11:17] = "parrot"
83      print p, len(p)
84
```

Quite a few special methods are used in the `parrot` class, but many other useful ones are also available. For instance, we haven't implemented `__cmp__()`, and that can be helpful when sorting an assorted bunch of parrots. Or raptors…

You should take special note of the technique used in line 74, reading `p[11], p[13] = p[13], p[11]`, and in the next one, 75. You can use this any time you need to exchange the values of any two variables. Other languages make you create a temporary variable in which to store a value to be saved, like this:

```
tmp = a;
a = b;
b = tmp;
```

But Python allows you to do the same thing this way:

```
a, b = b, a
```

Which is a good deal less verbose.

If you implement more special methods, you will have a class of mutable strings that you can use anywhere you want. In the next hour, you'll learn more about reusing components, such as the `parrot` class, in other programs you write.

Access and Special Class Methods

The two final varieties of special class methods to look at are access and class methods. Access methods are those that are called when users of a class try to get or set members of the class, and class methods are those such as `__call__()`, `__del__()`, and so on, which define behavior for an object when it is operated on as a whole unit. The `__cmp__()` method is a class method because it is called whenever a comparison is made between two objects, such as

```
if a < b:
    ...
```

The class methods are self-evident, except possibly for `__init__()`, which you have already seen, and `__hash__()`, which should only be used if you know that you really want your object to be used as a dictionary key, and your objects are not mutable. Most user-defined objects are mutable, so usually this won't apply. If it does, however, you can find out more at the Python Web site (`http://www.python.org/`), as usual.

The access methods, though, are more interesting. You can use them to intercept requests to add members to a class you've built and thereby limit the amount of damage users of your class can do (if you suspect them of wishing to do damage). The access methods are `__delattr_()`, `__getattr__()`, and `__setattr__()`.

The first is called when some attribute of a class is deleted, with `del()`. To prevent this, you can raise an exception of some sort after printing a message. If deleting the attribute is permitted, you need to operate directly on the object's dictionary. In other words, you can't define your `__delattr__()` method like this:

```
def __delattr__(self,name):
    ...decide if operation is permitted...
    del(self.name)
```

Doing so will give Python heartburn because the `__delattr__()` method is called every time the `del()` method is called for attributes. Instead, implement it like this:

```
def __delattr__(self,name):
    ...decide if operation is permitted...
    del(self.__dict__[name])
```

Both Python and you will be much happier. A word that we haven't used yet in this book is recursive. Put simply, recursion occurs when a function calls itself. Infinite recursion happens when a function keeps calling itself over and over and has no way to stop. Recursive functions can be very useful, but they must include a way to stop when they're finished. That's what's wrong with calling `del()` in your `__delattr__()` method; it's infinitely recursive.

13

The second, `__getattr__()`, is called any time someone tries to access an attribute that doesn't already exist. For example, in the `parrot` class shown previously, which has only one state attribute (the list `s`), you could add a `__gettattr__()` method that would return the string value corresponding to the list `s` whenever someone tried to get at an attribute other than `s`. Like this:

```
def __getattr__(self,name):
    return str(self.__dict__["s"])
```

Finally, the third, `__setattr__()`, is called whenever someone tries to add a new attribute (that is, create a new variable) to a class. Here again, as in the previous two methods, you must be careful to use the class's dictionary to get to the real attribute. This method, however, could be a little more complicated in use than you might expect; don't forget that it will be called every time an attribute is created, even the ones you want to create. Listing 13.6 shows examples of all three access special class methods; examine the `__setattr__()` method closely.

LISTING 13.6 Eggs Without Spam

```
#!/usr/local/bin/python
import string
import sys
class egg:
    def __init__(self):
        self.yolks = 1
        self.white = 1
        self.brains = 0
        self.spam = 0
    def __delattr__(self, name):
        if name == "spam":
            print "All eggs must have spam!"
            raise AttributeError
        print "deleting", name
        del(self.__dict__[name])

    def __setattr__(self, name, value):
        try:
            s = self.__dict__[name]
        except KeyError:
            if name not in [ "yolks", "white", "brains",
                "spam", "salt", "pepper" ] :
                print "you're not allowed to add", name, "to eggs"
            else :
                s = self.__dict__[name] = value
        else :
            s = self.__dict__[name] = value
    def __getattr__(self,name):
        if name != "yolks":
            return self.__dict__["spam"]
        else:
            raise AttributeError

x = egg()
print x.yolks
x.spam = 1
x.snot = 1
try:
    del x.spam
```

```
40  except AttributeError:
41      print "I couldn't get rid of the spam!"
42  print x.spam
43  x.spam = 1000
44  print x.spam
45  del x.yolks
46  try:
47      print x.yolks
48  except AttributeError:
49      print "No Yolks!"
50  x.white = 29
51  print "Snot is", x.snot, "white is", x.white
```

Notice that to keep the code as simple as possible, we're using `try - except - else` in the `__setattr__()` (starting at line 17) method.

Summary

In this hour, we've learned about special class methods. You should be able to

- Use special class methods to implement operator overloading.
- Implement special class methods to handle class initialization and other housekeeping tasks in classes.
- Recognize the different categories of special class methods and how and when to use them.
- Prevent anyone but you from adding, deleting, or reading attributes of one of your classes.

In the next hour, we'll learn about reusable components—when to use them, when to build them, and where to get some that you don't want to build if you don't want to.

Workshop

Q&A

Q Why do we have to have `pass`?

A It would have been just as easy for Guido to leave it out and allow programmers to define classes and methods without any body at all, and the same for other control flow statements, too. Making `pass` required, however, means that you must take an explicit step that indicates to Python that you really do mean to do nothing and that you didn't just forget.

Q Can I have classes that refer to each other? That is, can `spam` contain `eggs` and `eggs` contain `spam`?

A Absolutely. However, you should be aware that this practice creates circular references, which is impossible for Python's reference counting mechanism to keep track of correctly. This is one of the ways that applications can waste memory. Nonetheless, there are situations in which creating circular references is nearly unavoidable.

Quiz

1. What are the four categories of special class methods?
   a. Numeric, string, class, and access
   b. Numeric, sequence/mapping, class, and access
   c. Homeric, ionic, doric, and corinthian
   d. Being, nonbeing, not nonbeing, and not not nonbeing
2. What are the three access special class methods?
   a. `__del__()`, `__init__()`, and `__cmp__()`
   b. `__add__()`, `__radd__()`, and `__mul__()`
   c. `__delattr__()`, `__getattr__()`, and `__setattr__()`
   d. `__and__()`, `__or__()`, and `__xor__()`
3. What's the most efficient way to swap the values of two variables?
   a. `tmp = a, a = b, b = tmp`
   b. `a ^ b`
   c. `a, b = b, a`
   d. `swap(a, b)`

Answers

1. b, we covered numeric, sequence/mapping, class, and access special class methods. Python 1.6 or 2.0 may add to or change some of these categories.
2. c, the three access methods are `__delattr__()`, `__getattr__()` and `__setattr__()`.
3. c, the best way in Python is the third one, `a, b = b, a`, because it allows you to avoid the use of temporary variables entirely.

Exercises

Implement the rest of the numeric special class methods for class `spam`, working from Listing 13.4 as a base.

Implement more special class methods for class `parrot`, working from Listing 13.5. Although the code shown does include all but two of the sequence and mapping types, you might wish to build a `__sub__()` method, for example, which looks through the `self` string and subtracts the `other` string from `self` if it matches. At the least, you should implement the `__cmp__()` method.

See if you can come up with a simpler way than `try - except - else` to build the `__setattr__()` method in the `egg` class in Listing 13.6.

You can download the code for `mayalib`, which contains classes and functions for manipulating dates and numbers in the Mayan calendar at the Web site for this book, `http://www.pauahtun.org/TYPython/`. You'll also find information about the Mayan calendar itself at the default page for the same Web site, `http://www.pauahtun.org/`.

HOUR 14

The Laboratory of Dr. Frankenstein

Never turn something on that you don't know how to turn off.

—Advice given to farm children

(Courtesy of Darryl Nelson)

Last hour, we talked about special class methods, one of the ideas that makes Python especially OOP friendly. This time, we're going to apply another OOP concept, software reusability, and learn some of the ways in which Python makes it easy to reuse software. Although we won't use classes for this project, you will be exposed to a process for developing software. Not everything's going to fit, so our "Frankenstein" will spill over to the next hour. At the end of these two hours, you should be able to

- Build a module specifically designed for reusability
- Document that module
- Add built-in tests to the module
- Track down parts built by others that you can use

Making Reusable Components

Anytime that you find yourself writing a function or method to do something you need more than once, consider building a module. Anytime you consider building a module that you can reuse, consider making it public; other people might very well find it as useful as you do.

Just a couple of days ago, I discovered that a few of the Python programs on my Web server weren't working. I tracked down the problem to an incorrect first line in the files; I'm running the Apache Web server on Windows NT. One of the benefits of doing this is supposed to be that configuration and management of your Web site is similar, if not identical, to the UNIX/Linux version. I like this, and although the server that the world sees runs on NT, I mirror it on two different Linux systems—one at work and one at home. There are just enough dissimilarities in the Apache versions to be irritating, and the necessity to update the first lines of each CGI program every time I copy from one system to another is something I often forget—resulting in users being unable to use my Mayan calendar tools (`www.pauahtun.org/tools.html`) and sending me hate mail, which I dislike as much as anyone. This time when it happened, I used Python to write a short program to update these files for me.

NEW TERM *Common Gateway Interface*, or *CGI*, is a way for Web server applications to collect information from users, usually by putting forms on a Web page and using a CGI script to process the information so collected. Also known as cgi-bin programs, these scripts are commonly written in Perl, sometimes in C, and increasingly, in Python. Later in the book, you will see some examples of Python CGI programs.

Because others may find themselves in the same fix, I decided to clean it up and provide it to the public. This began as a fairly simple program with pretty much one purpose in mind. We'll add a little functionality, but it's not really meant to be the ultimate in versatility—it's very close to a one-trick pony. The steps I went through in designing and building it may be helpful. Following is the list of questions I asked myself before I even started work:

- What is the problem I'm trying to solve?
- Has anyone else written a program to do what I need?
- What is the absolute minimum necessary to effect the changes?
- How do I avoid changing files that don't require modification?
- Has anyone written modules that will make it easier to write what I need?

The details of the problem are that Apache, on Windows or on UNIX, requires that any CGI program that isn't an actual executable (that is, it's not machine language) must begin with two special characters, `#!`, followed by the absolute path to the program. For my Red Hat Linux system, that means that the first line of any Python program has to be `#!/usr/bin/python` and on my NT system, the same line has to be `#!c:\python\python.exe`. Other UNIX systems and Linux distributions often put Python in `/usr/local/bin`, so on those systems, the first line would have to read `#!/usr/local/bin/python`. Running a quick search on the Python Web site told me that no one else had written anything specifically for this problem, but in the process, I turned up a reference to the `sys` module, which contained a variable that was just what I needed: `sys.executable` contains the full path to the Python interpreter. So I had the first few lines of my program, as follows:

```
import sys

pbang = "#!" + sys.executable
if sys.platform == "win32" :
    sys.stderr.write ( "Python Version " + sys.version + " Running on Windows\n" )
elif sys.platform == "linux2" :
    sys.stderr.write ( "Python Version " + sys.version + " Running on Linux\n" )
else :
    sys.stderr.write ( "Python Version " + sys.version + " Running on " + \
sys.platform + "\n" )

print pbang
```

The `#!` character combination is generally referred to as *hash-bang* or *pound-bang* (other entertaining programmer names for non-alphanumeric characters include shplat for "*", suck for <, spit for >, and squiggles for { and }). We want to know what the `pbang` variable should contain, but we assume that we don't know it when we run it, so the proper way to run the preceding script would be as shown in Figure 14.1.

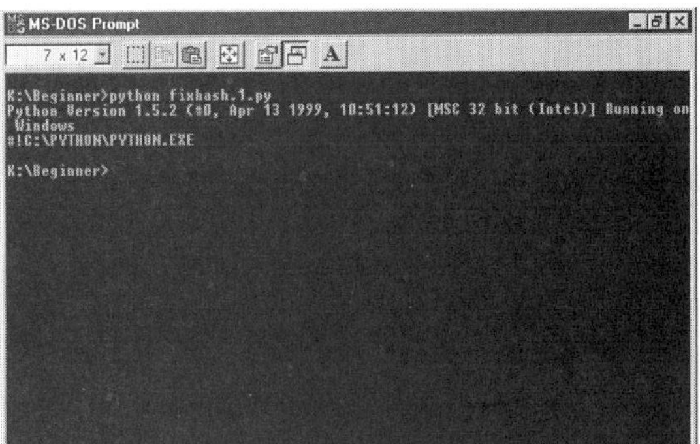

FIGURE 14.1
Where does Python live?

14

I also printed out the version, just for informational purposes. I used `sys.stderr.write()` instead of the usual `print` statement because I want to be sure that users can always read certain messages; `print`, which uses `sys.stdout`, can easily be redirected someplace else. If a user ran `python fixhash.py > tempfile`, I didn't want her to end up with no messages coming to the screen and a file telling her where she went wrong. That's not good user-interface practice.

`stdin`, `stdout`, and `stderr` are three special names inherited from UNIX for pre-opened objects that are treated like files. The names mean standard input, standard output, and standard error; in UNIX, all programs have these objects available at all times, but this is not the case with applications running on Windows. Programs with a UNIX heritage, such as Python, will make special efforts to provide these streams even on Windows.

Because I wanted to modify a potentially large number of files, I knew that the basic structure of the program would be like this:

```
for i in list_of_files :
    if i is not this_program :
        check first line of file
        if line is not equal to pbang
            modify the file
```

Note that the preceding listing is not real Python, but what's called pseudo code. *Pseudo code* is a shorthand way of describing the broad structure of a program. When you're outlining the structure of a program, you don't want to spend any time at all worrying about syntax; because it will never actually be run, you don't have to worry about errors and program failures. First, outline using pseudo code, and then implement the real code, usually from the outside in, getting ever more specific as you go through however many code-and-test iterations as you need to get it working.

The first step is how to obtain the list of files. This was easy since I remembered that the `os` module contained a function specifically for this: `os.listdir()`. Therefore, I knew that the first lines of the main part of the program were going to be the following:

```
dlist = os.listdir (".")
nfiles = 0
for i in dlist:
    if i != program name
        ...
```

How to get the program name? I definitely did not want to modify the program's file while it was running—this smacks a little too much of do-it-yourself brain surgery to make me comfortable. Again, I knew that the `sys` module provides access to the `argv` list—that is, all the arguments with which the program had been called—and that, by convention, the first element of the `argv` list is always the name of the program. Because this official name of the program always includes the full path to the file, I knew I'd have to throw away all but the last part of the name, keeping only the name and not the path. This can be done easily, as shown here:

```
nm = os.path.split (sys.argv[0])[1]
```

Because `os.path.split()` returns a list containing the path and the program name, in that order, applying the index operators (`[1]`) to the list returned by the function is easy and straightforward. By ignoring index 0, the *nm* variable ends up with only the program name in it. At this point, our code looks like this:

```
nm = os.path.split (sys.argv[0])[1]
dlist = os.listdir (".")
nfiles = 0
for i in dlist:
    if i == nm:
        continue
    ...check first line of file...
```

One way to check the first line of the file is to `open()` the file and read in one line, then compare that line with what we stored in the `pbang` variable. But thinking ahead a little, what we want is not just a path checker, but a path modifier, too. With other languages, such as C, we would have to check that line, and if we needed to modify it, write out not only the new line, but the whole rest of the file, too. Additionally, we don't want to copy a whole file if we don't have to, and this is where software reuse comes in. I ran a search on `www.python.org` in the documentation and ran across the `fileinput` module. This module contains methods that allow you to read a file a line at a time and includes a way to allow you to rewrite a file in place (that is, without creating a temporary file before renaming the temp file to your old file). That was exactly what was required in this situation. I decided to write a function that would rewrite the file when it was determined to be necessary; the main part of the code was changed to this:

```
dlist = os.listdir ( "." )
nfiles = 0
for i in dlist :
    if i == nm :
        continue
    if len ( i ) > 4 :
        if i[ -3 : ] == ".py" :
            sys.stderr.write ( "Checking " + i + "...\n" )
            for line in fileinput.input ( i ) :
                if fileinput.isfirstline ( ) :
                    if line[ : -1 ] != pbang :
```

14

```
                    fileinput.close ( )
                    t = os.access ( i, os.W_OK )
                    if t == 0 :
                        sys.stderr.write ( i + " is not writable;
                        skipping.\n" )
                    else :
                        sys.stderr.write ( "Modifying " + i + "...\n" )
                        rewritefile ( i )
                        nfiles = nfiles + 1
                    break
                else :
                    fileinput.close ( )
                    break
sys.stderr.write ( "Files modified: " + `nfiles` + "\n" )
```

Comments: The os module contains a method, `access()`, which allows us to check to see if the file is writable. If it's not writable, we just skip the file but tell the user we're doing so. The `os.W_OK` is a special flag, or symbol, that tells the `access()` method that we want to determine if the file is writable. The `isfirstline()` method just tells us if we're working on the very first line, and the line after that compares that first line with `pbang`. If the first line and `pbang` are equal, close the file and go on to the next file (that's why the `break`, which bails out of the `for` loop); otherwise, we close the file and call the `rewritefile()` function with the name of the file as an argument. I did consider making a case-insensitive comparison between the first line and `pbang`, but because case is important on UNIX systems, I decided to leave it; I'd rather modify a few extra files on Windows systems than miss even one on UNIX systems. The last line tells the user how many files were modified.

To test such code, you could easily write what's called a `stub` function to stand in for the `rewritefile()` function. *Stubs* are functions or methods that have the same signature that they will eventually have in the completed program, but that either do nothing or else simply print debugging information. You should write a stub function that at least prints the name of the file, insert that function into your `fixhash.py` file, and run the program to test your logic (actually, you're testing my logic and your typing, but you get the idea).

Here is the real `rewritefile()` function:

```
def rewritefile ( fip ) :
    mode = os.stat ( fip )[ ST_MODE ]
    for line in fileinput.input ( fip, inplace = 1 ) :
        if fileinput.isfirstline ( ) :
            if line [ : 2 ] == "#!" :
                sys.stdout.write ( pbang + "\n" )
            else :
```

```
                sys.stdout.write ( pbang + "\n" )
                sys.stdout.write ( line )
        else :
            sys.stdout.write ( line )
    fileinput.close ( )
    os.chmod ( fip, mode )
```

Comments: Because this is a function, variables in the module can be referenced inside the function, but you can't assign to them, which is why we can get away with using `pbang` without having a `global pbang` statement in the function—we only assign a value to it in the module context and don't have to change it after that. The `os` module includes a `stat()` function, which allows us to retrieve lots of information about files and directories; all we're interested in is the mode of the file. To obtain the definition for `ST_MODE`, though, we have to import it from the stat module: `from stat import *` is appropriate in this case; we don't actually care what the modes are, we just want to save them and restore them later. The modes, in this case, tell us if files are executable, writable, and/or readable. We obtain the mode before we modify the file and restore it after we do so, because the process of modification will often change these modes; this is usually the case on UNIX-style systems, not Windows, but in the interests of portability, you should always save and restore them.

The `for line in fileinput.input(fip, inplace=1):` statement takes advantage of a particularly nice feature of the `fileinput` module. The `inplace=1` is a keyword argument that tells the module we want to rewrite the file in place; after we call `fileinput.input()` with this special argument, the module makes a copy of the file and reopens the original for writing. From then on, any `write()` calls or `print` statements that go to `stdout` are sent to the new file. After that's done, we check the first line of the file, and if it contains the "hash-bang" syntax, we replace the line. If it doesn't start that way, we prepend the hash-bang line to the file. From then on, for all the rest of the lines in the file, we just write each line to `stdout`, and they automatically go to the new file. When `fileinput.close()` is called, the new file is closed and the internal copy of the original file is deleted.

Listing 14.1 shows the program so far.

LISTING 14.1 A Complete `fixhash.py`

```
import os
import sys
import fileinput
from stat import *
pbang = "#!" + sys.executable
```

continues

LISTING 14.1 contined

```
if sys.platform == "win32" :
    sys.stderr.write ( "Python Version " + sys.version + \
    " Running on Windows\n" )
elif sys.platform == "linux2" :
    sys.stderr.write ( "Python Version " + sys.version + \
    " Running on Linux\n" )
else :
    sys.stderr.write ( "Python Version " + sys.version + \
    " Running on " + sys.platform + "\n" )
nm = os.path.split ( sys.argv[ 0 ] )[ 1 ]
def rewritefile ( fip ) :
    mode = os.stat ( fip )[ ST_MODE ]
    for line in fileinput.input ( fip, inplace = 1 ) :
        if fileinput.isfirstline ( ) :
            if line [ : 2 ] == "#!" :
                sys.stdout.write ( pbang + "\n" )
            else :
                sys.stdout.write ( pbang + "\n" )
                sys.stdout.write ( line )
        else :
            sys.stdout.write ( line )
    fileinput.close ( )
    os.chmod ( fip, mode )
dlist = os.listdir ( "." )
nfiles = 0
for i in dlist :
    if i == nm :
        continue
    if len ( i ) > 4 :
        if i[ -3 : ] == ".py" :
            sys.stderr.write ( "Checking " + i + "...\n" )
            for line in fileinput.input ( i ) :
                if fileinput.isfirstline ( ) :
                    if line[ : -1 ] != pbang :
                        fileinput.close ( )
                        t = os.access ( i, os.W_OK )
                        if t == 0 :
                            sys.stderr.write ( i + \
                        " is not writable; skipping.\n" )
                        else :
                            sys.stderr.write ( "Modifying " \
                            + i + "...\n" )
                            rewritefile ( i )
                            nfiles = nfiles + 1
                        break
                    else :
                        fileinput.close ( )
                        break
sys.stderr.write ( "Files modified: " + `nfiles` + "\n" )
```

As the preceding code shows, `fixhash.py` is a complete, working application that performs its job admirably; no other changes are really necessary, as long as it's meant to be used by only one or two people. It will be instructive to go through the steps for making it into a module for public consumption, however, because others might very well find it useful. Even if they don't, it could come in handy for other maintenance tasks of your own in the future, especially if we add some more functionality to expand its usefulness.

The very first additional thing we can do is to add a command-line argument for the directory to operate upon. Doing so will allow us to store `fixhash.py` in a directory that is always searched for executable programs and scripts and not have to copy it to the directory every time we need it. On UNIX, this means putting the program in either your personal `bin` directory or in some central, well-known location such as `/usr/local/bin`. On Windows, however, no comparable standard locations exist; my solution, because I use the MKS toolkit on Windows to give me UNIX-like tools, is to always place such common tools into my `mksnt` directory (this is ordinarily `c:/mksnt` for any Windows platform). Your solution, however, should be a response to your needs, not mine.

If we examine the main part of the program, it should be fairly easy to determine what the needed changes are to support a command-line argument. Listing 14.2 shows the few changes necessary.

LISTING 14.2 Adding Command-Line Arguments to `fixhash.py`

```
def fixdirectory ( d ) :
    dlist = os.listdir ( d )
    nfiles = 0
    for i in dlist :
        if i == nm :
            continue
        if len ( i ) > 4 :
            if i[ -3 : ] == ".py" :
                sys.stderr.write ( "Checking " + i + "...\n" )
                for line in fileinput.input ( i ) :
                    if fileinput.isfirstline ( ) :
                        if line[ : -1 ] != pbang :
                            fileinput.close ( )
                            t = os.access ( i, os.W_OK )
                            if t == 0 :
                                sys.stderr.write ( i + \
                            " is not writable; skipping.\n" )
                            else :
                                sys.stderr.write ( \
                             "Modifying " + i + "...\n" )
```

continues

LISTING 14.2 continued

```
                                rewritefile ( i )
                                nfiles = nfiles + 1
                            break
                        else :
                            fileinput.close ( )
                            break
    return nfiles
if __name__ == "__main__" :
    nmod = 0
    if len ( sys.argv ) > 1 :
        dirnames = sys.argv[ 1 : ]
    else :
        dirnames = [ "." ]
    for s in dirnames :
        nmod = nmod + fixdirectory ( s )
    sys.stderr.write ( "Files modified: " + `nmod` + "\n" )
```

After applying the preceding changes, I ran `fixhash.py` first on the current directory, which worked fine, and then on a directory someplace else. Figure 14.2 shows what happened in the second case.

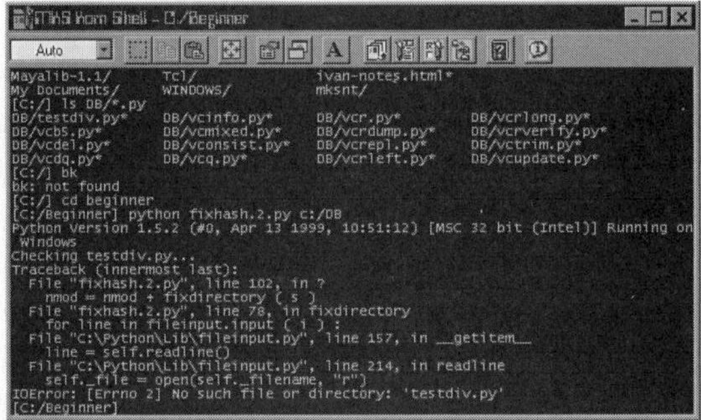

FIGURE 14.2
Oops!

As you can see, I forgot something (this is nowhere near as uncommon as I would like to think), so we have to revise a few more assumptions. Obviously, the command-line arguments are working, but even though it finds the directory (otherwise, how could it know which file it was supposed to open?) it can't open the file. This is because we only passed the filename without the directory name to the `fileinput` module. This is easy to fix, as you can see in Listing 14.3.

LISTING 14.3 Fixing *fixhash.py*

```
def fixdirectory ( d ) :
    dlist = os.listdir ( d )
    nfiles = 0
    for i in dlist :
        if i == nm :
            continue
        if len ( i ) > 4 :
            fname = d + "/" + i
            if fname[ -3 : ] == ".py" :
                sys.stderr.write ( "Checking " + fname + "...\n" )
                for line in fileinput.input ( fname ) :
                    if fileinput.isfirstline ( ) :
                        if line[ : -1 ] != pbang :
                            fileinput.close ( )
                            t = os.access ( fname, os.W_OK )
                            if t == 0 :
sys.stderr.write ( fname + \
" is not writable; skipping.\n" )
else :
sys.stderr.write ( "Modifying " \
 + fname + "...\n" )
                                rewritefile ( fname )
                                nfiles = nfiles + 1
                            break
                        else :
                            fileinput.close ( )
                            break
    return nfiles
```

If we apply these changes and run it again, Figure 14.3 shows what we get.

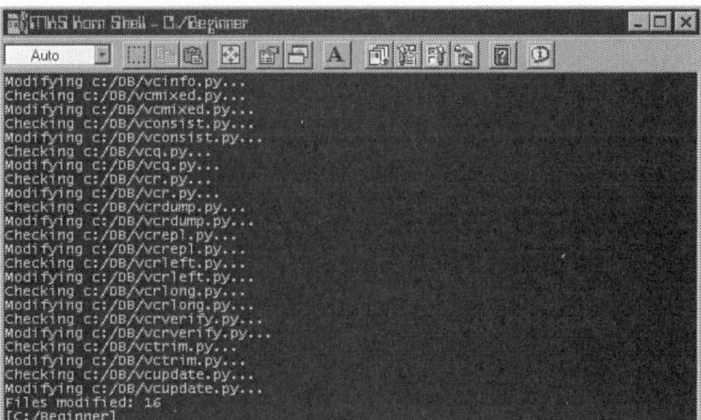

FIGURE 14.3
A corrected *fixhash.py.*

14

Notice that even on Windows, it's not required to use those awful backslashes; Python turns the much more aesthetic forward, UNIX-style slashes into backslashes if the underlying operating system requires them.

Well, now what? We've added command-line arguments (the `for s in dirnames:` line, by the way, ensures that multiple directory names on the command line get processed correctly), but have we really done all we can to widen the appeal of `fixhash.py`? What about recursive fixes? That is, suppose we want the `fixdirectory()` function to start at a particular directory and then not only fix all the Python files in the directory, but fix all the Python files in all the subdirectories below, as well?

Well, it's not that hard to provide this capability. I did a search through the available modules in the Python documentation and came up with the `path.walk()` function in the `os` module, which is exactly what we want. Because we're already using the `path.split()` function from the `os` module, we don't even have to import any new modules. At the same time, we can also substitute the `path.join()` function for our simple string concatenation operations in Listing 14.3; `path.join()` is smart enough that it will put in slashes where necessary:

```
fname = d + "/" + i
```

becomes

```
fname = os.path.join(d, i)
```

That way, if the directory name, `d`, happens to have a trailing slash on it, `join()` doesn't add an extra one like our original string concatenation would.

Our `fixdirectory()` function accepts only a single argument right now, but to use it with the `os.path.walk()` function, we need to modify it; here's the syntax and description for the function from the Python documentation:

> `walk` (path, visit, arg)
>
> Calls the function `visit` with arguments (arg, dirname, names) for each directory in the directory tree rooted at `path` (including path itself, if it is a directory). The argument `dirname` specifies the visited directory; the argument `names` lists the files in the directory (gotten from `os.listdir(dirname)`).

To use the `walk()` function, then, all we have to do is to call it in the main part of our program, passing it the directory to start at (`path`), our modified `fixdirectory()` function (`visit`), and something else (`arg`). That last argument is just a way for you to pass something to the `visit` function—normally, you won't need it, but under some circumstances, it could be helpful to have a way to pass in information that might change on a per-tree basis. Listing 14.4 shows the modified `fixdirectory()` function.

LISTING 14.4 Modifying *fixhash.py*

```
def fixdirectory ( arg, d, dlist ) :
    global nfiles
    nfiles = 0
    for i in dlist :
        if i == nm :
            continue
        if len ( i ) > 4 :
            fname = os.path.join (d, i)
            if fname[ -3 : ] == ".py" :
                sys.stderr.write ( "Checking " + fname + "...\n" )
                for line in fileinput.input ( fname ) :
                    if fileinput.isfirstline ( ) :
                        if line[ : -1 ] != pbang :
                            fileinput.close ( )
                            t = os.access ( fname, os.W_OK )
                            if t == 0 :
sys.stderr.write ( fname + \
" is not writable; skipping.\n" )
else :
sys.stderr.write ( \
"Modifying " + fname + "...\n" )
                                rewritefile ( fname )
                                nfiles = nfiles + 1
                            break
                        else :
                            fileinput.close ( )
                            break
```

Notice how few things we had to change; simply add the extra arguments, eliminate the call to `os.listdir()`, and add a `global nfiles` line. This last is required to track the number of files modified, and this necessitates adding an extra function to our module to retrieve that number. Here it is:

```
def getnfiles():
    return nfiles
```

We could, of course, tell users to get the number of files by accessing `fixhash.nfiles`, but it's a cleaner interface if we provide a simple function. Changing the main part of the program is almost as simple, see Listing 14.5.

LISTING 14.5 Modifying `fixhash.py` to Use `os.path.walk()`

```
if __name__ == "__main__" :
    nmod = 0
    if len ( sys.argv ) > 1 :
        dirnames = sys.argv[ 1 : ]
    else :
        dirnames = [ "." ]
    for s in dirnames :
        os.path.walk ( s, fixdirectory, 0 )
        nmod = nmod + getnfiles ( )

sys.stderr.write ( "Files modified: " + `nmod` + "\n" )
```

Figure 14.4 shows the result of running our modified program on a directory containing another directory, both containing Python files.

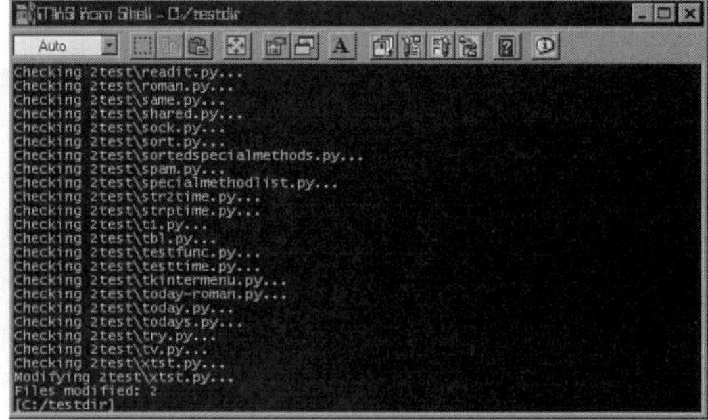

FIGURE 14.4
Running `fixhash.py` on a tree.

Summary

In this hour, we've covered the process of developing modules for reusability. We built a module, `fixhash`, and refined it. In the next hour, we'll finish up the module and document it.

Workshop

Q&A

Q Why does Python live in different places on different unices?

A Most of the different locations stem from differences in the two main branches of UNIX-like systems, BSD and System V. System V didn't really have a place to put locally developed tools, of which there were a lot, so Berkeley (BSD) developed the /usr/local location. System V later came up with both /var and /opt (with elaborate rules governing program placement within these directories), and the different distributions of Linux freely adopted some or all of these locations from both BSD and System V.

Quiz

1. What's the best way to obtain a list of files in a directory?
    a. os.path.list()
    b. os.listdir()
    c. sys.listdir()
    d. sys.dir()
2. What is sys.platform used for?
    a. It tells you what operating system you're running on.
    b. It tells you the hardware you're running on.
    c. It tells you whether you're using the Active Desktop.
    d. No one uses it.

Answers

1. b, the best (and really the only choice, unless you want to write your own) is to use os.listdir(). The dir() function does something entirely different.
2. a, the sys.platform variable tells you what operating system your program is running on. This can help you avoid functions that aren't available on all operating systems.

Exercises

You can see a nice example of a form in use at http://www.ithaca.edu/library/Training/wwwquiz.html. A decent Internet term glossary is also available at the same Web site.

After examining the rewritefile() function, you should have better ideas regarding the usefulness of stub functions. What expanded information could you put into a rewritefile() function that would make it easier to develop or to debug?

14

In line 35 of Listing 14.1, you can see that we obtain a listing of all files in a directory ending with the standard Python file suffix, .py. You should also be able to imagine what happens if someone names a directory something like spam.py. Search the Python documentation for a way to find out if a file is really a file and not a directory; add the proper lines of code to the listing. Add the new code to the final version of `fixhash.py`. Hint: Check the documentation for `os.stat()`.

Add a case-insensitive comparison to the `fixdirectory()` function, but activate it only on Windows systems. Hint: Check the documentation for the `string` module.

Hour 15

The Laboratory, Part II

Blank lines are no good.

—Natalie Goldberg

Last hour, we started building a reusable module, which we're going to finish in this hour. At the end, you'll learn more about the process of developing software, and you'll learn how to

- Build a module specifically designed for reusability
- Document that module
- Add built-in tests to the module
- Track down parts built by others that you can use

Making Reusable Components, Continued

Last hour, we finished up with a working `fixhash.py`, which would start at any of the directories given on the command line and work its way down through the directory structure, fixing all Python files it encountered.

Of course, users of this module might not always want to do a recursive fix (in this case, *recursive* means to start at the given directory and visit every directory and subdirectory in the tree; there are other meanings of recursive, but not ones we'll use in this book), so let's add a command-line argument that will turn this feature on or off. Listing 15.1 contains the new code for the main part of the program.

LISTING 15.1 Adding a Command-Line Flag to `fixhash.py`

```
if __name__ == "__main__" :
    nmod = 0
    recurse = 0
    if len ( sys.argv ) > 1 :

        if sys.argv[1] == '-r' :
            recurse = 1
        if recurse and len ( sys.argv ) > 2 :
            dirnames = sys.argv[ 2 : ]
        elif recurse and len ( sys.argv ) <= 2 :
            dirnames = [ "." ]
        else :
            dirnames = sys.argv[ 1 : ]
    else :
        dirnames = [ "." ]
    for s in dirnames :
        if not recurse :
            dlist = os.listdir ( s )
            fixdirectory ( 0, s, dlist )
        else :
            os.path.walk ( s, fixdirectory, 0 )
        nmod = nmod + getnfiles ( )

sys.stderr.write ( "Files modified: " + `nmod` + "\n" )
```

Figure 15.1 shows the result of running `python fixhash.py -r`.

And the next one, Figure 15.2, shows the result of running `python fixhash.py`.

One more thing still must be done. The main part of the program should be placed in a wrapper so that users of the module don't have to write their own. Here, in Listing 15.2, is the final modification to `fixhash.py`.

FIGURE 15.1
Running `fixhash.py -r`.

```
Checking .\nesting.py...
Checking .\ork.py...
Checking .\classes.py...
Checking .\imptest2.py...
Checking .\roman.py...
Checking .\shared.py...
Checking .\today-roman.py...
Checking .\del.py...
Checking .\parrots.py...
Checking .\access.py...
Checking .\spam.py...
Checking .\tkintermenu.py...
Checking .\dict.py...
Checking .\pvp.py...
Checking .\str2time.py...
Checking .\fixhash.1.py...
Checking .\tv.py...
Checking .\newnow.py...
Checking .\testtime.py...
Checking .\strptime.py...
Checking .\newtree.py...
Checking .\today.py...
Files modified: 0

E:\Beginner>
```

FIGURE 15.2
Running `fixhash.py`.

LISTING 15.2 The Final `fixhash.py`

```
#!/usr/local/bin/python

import os
import sys
import fileinput
from stat import *


pbang = "#!" + sys.executable
nfiles = 0
nm = ""

def initial ( v = 0 ) :
    global nm
    if v != 0 :
        if sys.platform == "win32" :
```

continues

LISTING 15.2 continued

```
            sys.stderr.write ( "Python Version " + sys.version + \
            " Running on Windows\n" )
        elif sys.platform == "linux2" :
            sys.stderr.write ( "Python Version " + sys.version + \
            " Running on Linux\n" )
        else :
            sys.stderr.write ( "Python Version " + sys.version + \
            " Running on " + sys.platform + "\n" )

    nm = os.path.split ( sys.argv[ 0 ] )[ 1 ]

def getnfiles ( ) :
    return nfiles

def rewritefile ( fip ) :
    global pbang
    mode = os.stat ( fip )[ ST_MODE ]
    for line in fileinput.input ( fip, inplace = 1 ) :
        if fileinput.isfirstline ( ) :
            if line [ : 2 ] == "#!" :
                sys.stdout.write ( pbang + "\n" )
            else :
                sys.stdout.write ( pbang + "\n" )
                sys.stdout.write ( line )
        else :
            sys.stdout.write ( line )
    fileinput.close ( )
    os.chmod ( fip, mode )

def fixdirectory ( arg, d, dlist ) :
    global nfiles
    nfiles = 0
    for i in dlist :
        if i == nm :
            continue
        if len ( i ) > 4 :
            fname = os.path.join ( d, i )
            if fname[ -3 : ] == ".py" :
                if arg != 0 :
                    sys.stderr.write ( "Checking " + fname + "...\n" )
                for line in fileinput.input ( fname ) :
                    if fileinput.isfirstline ( ) :
                        if line[ : -1 ] != pbang :
                            fileinput.close ( )
                            t = os.access ( fname, os.W_OK )
                            if t == 0 :
                                if arg != 0 :
                                    sys.stderr.write \
                ( fname + " is not writable; skipping.\n" )
```

```
                            else :
                                if arg != 0 :
                                    sys.stderr.write \
                ( "Modifying " + fname + "...\n" )
                                rewritefile ( fname )
                                nfiles = nfiles + 1
                            break
                        else :
                            fileinput.close ( )
                            break
    return nfiles

def fixhash ( d, r, v ) :
    nmod = 0
    if type ( d ) != type ( [] ) :
        dl = list ( d )
    else :
        dl = d
    initial ( v )
    for i in dl :
        if not r :
            dlist = os.listdir ( i )
            fixdirectory ( v, i, dlist )
        else :
            os.path.walk ( i, fixdirectory, v )
        nmod = nmod + getnfiles ( )
    return nmod

if __name__ == "__main__" :
    nmod = 0
    recurse = 0
    if len ( sys.argv ) > 1 :

        if sys.argv[1] == '-r' :
            recurse = recurse + 1
        if recurse and len ( sys.argv ) > 2 :
            dirnames = sys.argv[ 2 : ]
        elif recurse and len ( sys.argv ) <= 2 :
            dirnames = [ "." ]
        else :
            dirnames = sys.argv[ 1 : ]
    else :
        dirnames = [ "." ]
    nmod = fixhash ( dirnames, recurse, 1 )

    sys.stderr.write ( "Files modified: " + `nmod` + "\n" )
```

This last modification makes it possible to import the module. Listing 15.3 shows how.

LISTING 15.3 testhash.py

```
#!/usr/local/bin/python

import sys
import fixhash4

if __name__ == "__main__" :
    nmod = 0
    recurse = 0
    verbose = 0
    if len ( sys.argv ) > 1 :

        if sys.argv[1] == '-r' :
            recurse = recurse + 1
        if recurse and len ( sys.argv ) > 2 :
            dirnames = sys.argv[ 2 : ]
        elif recurse and len ( sys.argv ) <= 2 :
            dirnames = [ "." ]
        else :
            dirnames = sys.argv[ 1 : ]
    else :
        dirnames = [ "." ]
    nmod = fixhash4.fixhash ( dirnames, recurse, verbose )

    if verbose :
        sys.stderr.write ( "Files modified: " + `nmod` + "\n" )
    else :
        sys.exit ( nmod )
```

Documenting Your Components

One of the major tasks you can do to improve your modules and enhance the possibility that others will use them is to document what they do. This means that you'll have to add the docstrings to your functions, classes, and methods. This is the least that you should do. I prefer to add the docstrings and also provide HTML documentation. Often, you can copy your docstrings directly into whatever HTML editor you use, do some minimum formatting, and distribute both the Python code and the HTML file in one archive file.

You'll find that documentation can make all the difference between someone using your code and not using it. Not too long ago, I put together some quick shell scripts that I thought were very useful, but didn't bother documenting much of it. I announced it on a mailing list I belonged to at the time, and the next day I received three letters saying that it looked interesting, but because there was no documentation, they weren't going to use it. Three was enough to push me over the edge. I finished the documentation and reposted the code. I never did hear from the three complainers, though.

Rather than reproduce all the code with the new docstrings, I'll simply provide one example of a function with its docstring; Listing 15.4 shows the documented `fixhash()` function.

LISTING 15.4 Documenting `fixhash()`

```
def fixhash ( d, r, v ) :
    """This function runs fixdirectory() on each directory
    in d (a list).  If r is non-zero, os.path.walk() is
    used to recursively fix the entire tree rooted at each
    directory in the list.  If v is non-zero, messages
    are printed to stderr.  Returns # of files modified.
    """
    nmod = 0
    if type ( d ) != type ( [] ) :
    dl = list ( d )
    else :
    dl = d
    initial ( v )
    for i in dl :
    if not r :
        dlist = os.listdir ( i )
        fixdirectory ( v, i, dlist )
    else :
        sys.stderr.write ( "here fixdirectory " + i + "\n" )
        os.path.walk ( i, fixdirectory, v )
        nmod = nmod + getnfiles ( )
    return nmod
```

Figure 15.3 shows a sample page of the HTML documentation. The rest of the HTML documentation is available at this book's Web site, along with the full code for everything in this and the previous chapter, at `http://www.pauahtun.org/TYPython/`.

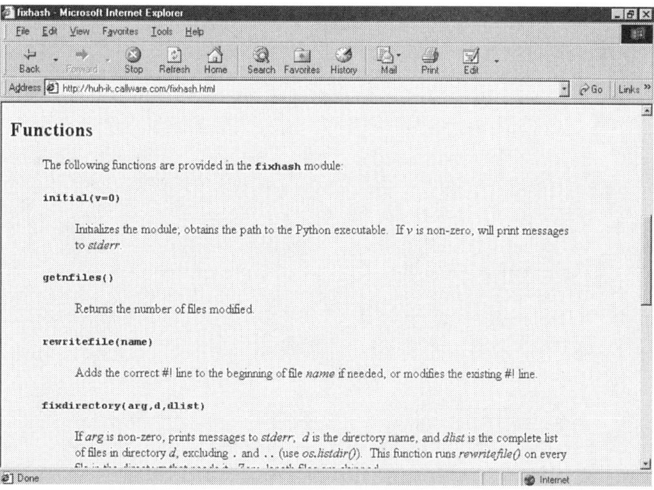

FIGURE 15.3
Sample documentation for the `fixhash` module.

Although I firmly believe in documentation, there's a difference between documentation and comments in code. Years ago, when I was first learning how to program, I often asked a senior engineer where I worked for help. At first, I would comment the code heavily; the engineer would look at the code, run his fingers through his beard, and say, "I have a hard time reading this stuff; you've got so many comments that don't match what the code does that they get in the way." I guess it just didn't take, because I kept on commenting like mad. One day, I went to him with some more chatty code, and he looked at it with disgust. "OK, that's it," he said. I thought he was going to refuse to help me anymore. Instead, he started writing a program of his own. In a few minutes, while I grew increasingly anxious, his new program was ready. He ran my code through his program and put the output into a new file. "That's better," he said. "Now I can read it." He had written a program to remove the comments from my code. He scowled at me. "The code is supposed to speak for itself," he said. "If you can't look at it and figure out what it does, no amount of commenting is going to help."

So now, when I speak of documentation, what I mean is that the interface must be documented. Don't explain what code in functions is doing; limit yourself to describing how to use the function and what it returns. For example, this is a worthless comment:

```
i = i + 1 # Add one to i
```

See? Too many of those and you start screaming. Use the docstring attribute for functions to remind yourself and any one else who reads the code of what the function is supposed to do, how it is supposed to be called, and what it returns (if anything). So in the code for the next chapter, you're going to see docstrings, but almost no comments; comments should be limited to a minimum and used only to explain particularly complex code or to put in markers to remind yourself to do some more work at a specific location. Listing 15.4 shows an explanatory docstring and a single useful comment.

LISTING 15.4 A Useful Comment

```
def FindYear ( s ) :
    """Search string s for year of the form "(1999)",
    with leading whitespace.  Returns the string without
    the year part, followed by the numeric year.  If there's
    no year, returns None.
    """
    global _yearre
    global _yearrec
    if _yearrec == 0 :
        _yearrec = re.compile ( _yearre )
    so = _yearrec.search ( s )
    if so == None :
        return None
```

```
    st, ep = so.span ( )
    st = st + 1 # skip whitespace
    y = string.atoi ( s[ st + 1 : ep - 1 ] )
    rt = s[ : st - 1 ] + s[ ep : ]
    return rt, y
```

All the comment does is call your attention to the reason for a line of code that might not be completely evident—we're skipping over unwanted whitespace.

One other function that comments in code may serve is to provide hints or documentation for functions, modules or classes that may be very poorly documented (written by other programmers, naturally, never by you). Sometimes, this need can be served by the docstrings, but other times you will want to provide a comment near a particularly opaque function call, for example.

Testing Your Components

I think that you've seen, over the course of this chapter, how important testing is. The `fixhash` module has its own test built in, as the `if __name__ == "__main__":` code in Listing 14.7 shows. But during each step of the development process for this module, you saw that we ran test after test, gradually refining the code to come closer and closer not only to what works properly, but to what others might consider useful.

The following list describes several ways to improve your testing as you develop modules:

- Test boundary conditions. For example, if you have a function that accepts a certain range of numbers, test the function with numbers inside the range, outside the range, and exactly on the boundaries.
- Test with unplanned `for` input. For example, if you have a function that expects a numeric string, feed it an alphabetic one.
- If you're developing a module, build in a test.
- If you're importing a module, try setting variables from the calling program that you aren't expecting users to set. For example, you might try setting the *`nm`* variable in the `fixhash` module to `""` or to a number.
- Run your test programs from a different directory than the one in which you developed it. If it expects directories, hand it both absolute and relative paths.
- Always be on the lookout for suspect code that could break your program. Someone will find the bugs if you don't.

- The very best advice you can follow is this: When someone has a problem with your software, assume that it is your fault. There is simply no room in software engineering for people who think they're always right and that problems are someone else's fault.

Finding Components Built by Others

As we developed the `fixhash` module, I tried to expose as much of the process of development as possible. A great part of that was trying to find out two main things. One, had anyone else built the tool already? Two, had anyone else developed modules that could be used in the development of the tool we wanted? As usual, the best place to find this information is at `http://www.python.org/`, which has a search facility built right into the front page. You can limit your search to the Python Web site, to Usenet postings, or you can search the whole Net. Usenet postings contain a wealth of announcements for new software, tricks, idioms, and help. The hardest part is knowing what to search for; refining searches is not in the scope of this book, but the Python search page (`http://www.python.org/search/`) has a lot of help available, which, if you have some idea of what you're looking for, can help you narrow the field quite a bit.

If you join the Python mailing list or the Python-tutor mailing list, you can post queries asking if anyone has built or is working on something that you can use. See `http://www.python.org/psa/MailingLists.html`.

Summary

In the last two hours, we've covered the process of developing modules for reusability. We built a module—`fixhash`—refined it, tested it, and documented it. You should be able, after you have an idea of what you're trying to do, to find out if other people have developed either what you want or tools that you can use to build what you want. Posting queries on mailing lists (or Usenet news groups) is also a good way to find out if others are interested in something you would like to build.

In the next hour, the last chapter in this third of the book, we're going to build a complete class and try out our OOP concepts more fully. I won't be talking very much; most of what you will see will be code.

Workshop

Q&A

Q Is reusable software really such a great thing?

A If you like reinventing the wheel all the time, no. However, if you'd rather write code only once and then be able to use it time and time again without worrying about it, it starts to look a lot better.

Quiz

1. How often should you test your programs?
   a. 25 times
   b. 50 times
   c. Until it works
   d. Until it works, you make it break, and then you make it work again
2. Given two software packages that purport to do the same job but only one is documented, which one should you use?
   a. The one by the better programmer
   b. The one that's fastest
   c. The one that's documented
   d. The one that everyone else says you should use

Answers

1. d, you need to test your programs to try to make them break. Every time something breaks, you get to fix it; eventually, you will develop a great deal of confidence in your code (or else you give up and throw it away).
2. c, this should be a no-brainer. Use the one that's documented. No matter how good the programmer is who wrote it or how many gurus swear by it, if it's not documented, it is not worth the risk until you are so good at reading code you can understand the Linux kernel in a day.

Exercises

Add another command-line option to `testhash.py` to enable users to turn on or off the `verbose` variable. You might want to take a look at the `getargs` module, which can be found at `http://www.pauahtun.org/ftp.html`, near the bottom of the page. It's fully documented, of course; see `http://www.pauahtun.org/getargs.html`.

Find yourself a good archiving program and stick with it. I prefer WinZip, available at `http://www.winzip.com/`. I use it instead of tar and gzip, even for distributing applications that are UNIX only, because gzip can unpack WinZip archives and the files are smaller than gzip's.

If you're interested in testing software, perhaps the best book I know of is Brian Marick's *The Craft of Software Testing*, Prentice-Hall, 1999. Brian has an unusual viewpoint and a lively writing style. At the very least, read Brian's revealing paper, "Classic Testing Mistakes," which can be found at `http://www.rstcorp.com/marick/classic/mistakes.html`. Check out Brian's Web site for more testing references: `http://www.rstcorp.com/marick`.

HOUR 16

Objects in Motion

This may sound complicated, but if you're using VIM to begin with you obviously have a pathological lack of any fear of complexity to begin with.

—Alan Daniels

In the previous two hours, we concentrated on building reusable components. This time, we're going to examine a complete application composed of two classes and lots of "glue" functions. The main purpose of this hour is not necessarily for you to actually accomplish something, but for you to gain more exposure to working code that solves real problems. Despite the aphorism that says one should learn by doing, it is often true that one learns just as much by reading. This is especially true for code; the ability to read and understand code is perhaps the most useful skill you can acquire in the programming field. Reading Python code, unless the author has deliberately made the code obscure, is easy. At the end of this hour, you should have acquired more experience in reading code and in visualizing how a larger program than those you have seen before fits together.

A Complete Application

You may remember from Hour 6 that I tape lots of shows from TV. In fact, I have more than 5,000 videotapes, and therefore I really need something to keep track of the programs on these tapes. All the tapes are numbered, as you may also remember, in hex. In Hour 13, when we discussed special class methods, we also talked about a concept of OOP design, the `is a/contains` relationship, and we discussed it using cassettes and programs. A videocassette is a container, which can be empty, holds programs, and can be reused. Cassettes and programs are the two classes used in our complete application.

I've been taping programs for years, and I haven't always had Python to help out; but I did need some sort of computer assistance. The "database" was simply a text file, in a particular format, which was read by a C program that could perform a number of tasks. It wouldn't update the text file, however, so all additions to the text file were carried out in a text editor. The C program would sort the records, duly place the programs inside their proper cassettes, and then print out listings alphabetically or numerically, as desired. I added sophisticated searching capabilities but soon realized that had been a waste of time; all the searching I needed could be done faster and more efficiently with grep (a UNIX program that looks for patterns of text inside a text file). After I started using Windows machines, however, I wanted to make something more portable than the C program; Python was the natural choice.

Despite the use of classes in the program shown in this chapter, many of the supporting functions were translated in a fairly straightforward way from their corresponding C versions. Some of the functions are new to the Python version, but overall, the program is more an example of something that "just grew" to solve practical problems than an example of good design. If I were to start from scratch today, the program would be a good deal more object-based. Given my deeper understanding of Python, I am sure that it would also be a good deal shorter.

`shelve`

The overall architecture of the program is relatively simple. Videocassettes are contained inside a dictionary, with the hex number being the key for each tape, and each cassette maintains a dictionary of the programs on the tape, with the sequence number being the key. From a text-based input file, we will build a database in memory; after the memory database is created, we will use the `shelve` module to store the database on disk. Storing a database this way is called *persisting*.

What the `shelve` module does for us is to allow us to store arbitrary Python objects in binary format and to treat the resulting store as a dictionary. Ordinary, in-memory dictionaries can use any read-only Python type as a key, but the on-disk dictionary, or *shelf*, is able to use only strings—no numbers and no tuples; only strings. To find out more about the details, you can visit `http://www.python.org/doc/current/lib/module-shelve.html` and begin reading there. I won't describe the interface, but you'll be able to see how it's used in code later on in this chapter.

16

Input Record Format

To make entry of programs as simple as possible, the file format for input records was originally designed to be easy for C programs to parse. Here's an example:

```
0001;0;sp,T120;89,89: Masterpiece Theatre: Last Place on Earth, The: 1: Poles Apart
```

Everything from position 0 to the first colon is the header, giving information on cassette number, program position on tape, speed, size of tape, minutes used, and minutes actually used for the program. Everything after the first colon gives specific program information: series (*Masterpiece Theatre*), program title ("The Last Place on Earth"), episode number (1), and episode title ("Poles Apart"). These are fields and are separated by the character combination `:\t`, or colon-tab. Any valid program contains at least one field, but it can have any number of additional fields after that. For movies, we need to track the date (1999). Comments are enclosed in {} characters and search keywords in [] characters. Finally, there must be a way to indicate that a program has been superseded with a better copy. The entry shown next describes a program exercising all these optional characteristics:

```
0045;2;ep,T120;139,139: Hidden Fortress, The [Japanese] {Xd} (1958): ->119
```

Sequence number 2 on tape 45, *The Hidden Fortress* is a Japanese movie (directed by Akira Kurosawa) from 1958. Unfortunately, the end of the movie is missing (`Xd`), so when the opportunity arrived to obtain a better copy, I did so, and that better copy is on tape 119.

Naturally, parts of this format were added later; the `ep,T120` was originally just `ep`, for example. The minutes field was originally only minutes used on tape, not an indicator of minutes used followed by the commercial-free length (`59,46` would be a minutes entry for a Star Trek program; 59 minutes long, but without commercials it's really only 46 minutes). And all the add-ons had to be compatible with earlier records. The "glue" part of our vcr program reads the input file and parses each record, creating new cassette classes as needed; the cassette classes know how to create the appropriate programs. The glue is described later; first let's talk about the two classes we need.

Classes

We need two classes for the vcr application. These classes are `cassette` and `program`, as outlined previously. Listing 16.1 shows class `program` (the line numbers indicate where the class definition goes into the `vcr.py` file).

LISTING 16.1 Class *program*

```
284 class program :
285     def __init__ ( self, s = "", n = 0 ) :
286         if s == "" and n == 0 :
287             self.seq = -1
288             self.year = None
289             self.comments = None
290             self.keywords = None
291             self.rplcd = None
292             self.tape = n
293         else :
294             self.year = None
295             self.comments = None
296             self.keywords = None
297             self.rplcd = None
298             self.tape = n
299             i = string.index ( s, ":" )
300             h = header ( s[ 0 : i ] )
301             self.seq = string.atoi ( h[ 0 ] )
302             sp, tlen = parts ( h[ 1 ], n )
303             self.sp = tspeed ( sp )
304             if self.sp == -1 :
305                 print "UNDEFINED Tape speed:", n, sp
306                 self.sp = 1 # Default speed
307             self.tlen = tsize ( tlen )
308             if self.tlen == -1 :
309                 print "UNDEFINED Tape size:", n, tlen
310                 self.tlen = _tsizes[ "T120" ]
311             self.ttime, self.ctime = tuple ( map ( string.atoi, \
312                 list ( parts ( h[ 2 ], n ) ) ) )
313             stuff = s[ i + 2 : ]
314             self.fields = [ ]
315             q = string.splitfields ( stuff, ":\t" )
316             # loop through list of fields, alpha and numeric
317             for k in q :
318                 if alldigits ( k ) :
319                     if k == "" :
320                         print h, "empty string", n
321                         k = 0
322                     self.fields.append ( string.atoi ( k ) )
323                 else :
324                     r = FindReplaced ( k ) # Returns [ list, ]
```

```
                    if r != None :
                        self.rplcd = r
                    else :
                        e = Extract ( k )
                        if e == None :
                            print "TAPE %04X Hosed." % ( n )
                            raise ValueError
                        if e[ 1 ] != None :
                            self.year = e[ 1 ]
                        if e[ 2 ] != None :
                            self.comments = e[ 2 ]
                        if e[ 3 ] != None :
                            self.keywords = e[ 3 ]
                        self.fields.append ( e[ 0 ] )

    def __len__ ( self ) :
        return self.ttime

    def speed ( self ) :
        return speedname ( self.sp )

    def size ( self ) :
        return sizename ( self.tlen )

    def __repr__ ( self ) :
        s = "%02d: " % ( self.seq )
        n = 0
        for i in self.fields :
            if type ( i ) == type ( 0 ) :
                s = s + `i`
            else :
                s = s + SwapThe ( i )
                if n == 0 :
                    if self.year != None :
                        s = s + " (%4d)" % ( self.year )
                    if self.comments != None :
                        s = s + " {%s}" % ( self.comments )
                    if self.keywords != None :
                        s = s + " [%s]" % ( self.keywords )
            s = s + ','
            n = n + 1
        return s
```

The `__init__()` method, by far the largest, is broken into two sections. The first is chosen when `program()` is called with no arguments, and the second when it's called with an input string and a cassette number. With no arguments, a dummy record is created, which can later be filled in with the exact information; when an input string and tape number are provided, the input string is parsed to fill in all the members of the class, including however many fields there are. The actual data members are the following:

- `seq`—The program sequence number on the tape.
- `year`—If this is a movie, the year of publication.
- `comments`—If comments are found, they are placed here.
- `keywords`—If keywords are found, they are placed here.
- `rplcd`—If the program has been superseded, the new tape number is here.
- `tape`—Each program knows what cassette number it's attached to.
- `sp`—The speed at which this program was taped.
- `tlen`—The size of the tape (T120, T30, and so on).
- `ttime`—The actual time occupied on tape by the program.
- `ctime`—The running time of the program, exclusive of commercials.
- `fields`—From 1 to *n* descriptive program information fields; these are subdivided into titles of some sort and numeric fields.

Comments: most of the functions that are called inside this class's `__init__()` method are self-explanatory—or will be when you see the code for them later on, but note the `string.splitfields()` call on line 315. This is the part where Python really shines; it takes the input string ("stuff") and breaks it up into a list on `:\t` boundaries. Because the resulting list now contains all the fields for this particular program, and because the separators are so clearly marked, you can see that each field can have any characters at all in it. The field is examined later (`if alldigits(k)`) to see whether it's a numeric field for episode numbers and the like. Movie titles such as *2001* are indicated simply by placing a backslash in front of the title: `\2001`.

The next class, `cassette`, is shown in Listing 16.2 (again, the line numbers indicate where the class definition is to be inserted into `vcr.py`).

LISTING 16.2 Class *cassette*

```
431  class cassette :
432      def __init__ ( self, n = 0, s = None ) :
433          self.num = n
434          self.l = { }
435          if s == None :
436              pass
437          else :
438              t = program ( s[ 5 : ], self.num )
439              self.set ( t )
440
441      def key ( self ) :
442          return "%04X" % ( self.num )
443
```

```
    def keys ( self ) :
        if len ( self.l ) == 0 :
            return None
        k = self.l.keys ( )
        k.sort ( )
        return k

    def cat ( self, s ) :
        if s != None :
            t = program ( s[ 5 : ], self.num )
            self.set ( t )

    def __len__ ( self ) :
        t = 0
        k = self.l.keys ( )
        k.sort ( )
        for l in k :
            i = self.l[ l ]
            if i != None :
                t = t + i.ttime
        return t

    def speed ( self ) :
        s = tapespeed ( self )
        return speedname ( s[ 0 ] )

    def size ( self ) :
        return tapesize ( self )

    def programs ( self ) :
        return len ( self.l )

    def programlist ( self ) :
        if isdummy ( self ) :
            return None
        rslt = [ ]
        for i in self.l.keys ( ) :
            rslt.append ( self.l[ i ] )
        return rslt

    def sequence ( self, n ) :
        if type ( n ) == type ( 0 ) :
            k = "%02d" % ( n )
        elif type ( n ) == type ( "" ) :
            k = n
        else :
            k = "%s" % ( n )
        if self.l.has_key ( k ) :
```

16

continues

Listing 16.2 continued

```
            return self.l[ k ]
        return None

    def set ( self, p ) :
        try :
            n = p.seq
        except AttributeError :
            return
        k = self.sequence ( n )
        if k == None :
            self.l[ "%02d" % ( n ) ] = p
        else :
            self.l[ "%02d" % ( n ) ] = p

    def __repr__ ( self ) :
        s = "%04X\n" % ( self.num )
        if len ( self.l ) == 0 :
            s = s + "*No Tape*"
        else :
            j = self.l.keys ( )
            j.sort ( )
            for k in j :
                i = self.l[ k ]
                s = s + `i` + "\n"
        return s

    def nreplaced ( self ) :
        if len ( self.l ) == 0 :
            return 0
        n = 0
        k = self.keys ( )
        for i in k :
            p = self.l[ i ]
            if p.rplcd != None :
                n = n + 1
        return n

    def getreplaced ( self ) :
        if len ( self.l ) == 0 :
            return None
        d = { }
        k = self.keys ( )
        for i in k :
            p = self.l[ i ]
            if p.rplcd != None :
                d[ i ] = p.rplcd
        if len ( d ) == 0 :
            return None
        return d
```

```
    def numeric ( self, fld = 0 ) :
        x = self.programlist ( )
        return x

    def alphabetic ( self, fld = 0 ) :
        x = self.programlist ( )
        return x
```


The data members in class `cassette` are

- `num`—The number of the cassette
- `l`—The dictionary in which programs are stored

And that's it. The real information is stored in the program dictionary, l. The `cassette` class really is only a container, as it should be. It has methods, but nothing really complex; the most important method is the `set()` method, which inserts a program into l at the right place, determined by the sequence number. That sequence number is the key into the dictionary—remember, the key must be a string because we're going to store all this information in a file database. Storage in a file database, by the way, is referred to in Python as *pickling*. In fact, the `pickle` module handles the details of actually storing Python objects for us; the `shelve` module insulates us from having to learn any of these details. This is a good thing.

Glue

You can define *glue* as all the stuff that makes everything else work. We can have these two nice classes, but without the code that reads the input file, builds the databases, and parses the strings, we really don't have anything except some abstract objects that do nothing. Listing 16.3 shows the rest of the code in the `vcr.py` module (note the holes in the line numbering where the class definitions are to be inserted).

LISTING 16.3 Glue for *vcr.py*

```
#!/usr/local/bin/python

import os
import sys
import math
import string
import re

_defaultdbfilename = ""

```

LISTING 16.3 continued

```
if sys.platform == 'win32' :
    _defaultdbfilename = "/DB/vcrdb"
else :
    _defaultdbfilename = "/bigtmp/DB/vcrdb"

_tsizes = { "T10" : 10,
    "T15" : 15,
    "T20" : 20,
    "T30" : 30,
    "T60" : 60,
    "T90" : 90,
    "T120" : 120,
    "T130" : 130,
    "T160" : 160,
    "T180" : 180,
    "T200" : 200,
  }

_tspeeds = { "sp" : 1, "lp" : 2, "ep" : 3, "slp" : 3, "mx" : 4 }

```

> The next 10 lines are regular expressions. You're not expected to understand them, but they do work.

```
_yearre = r"[ \t]\([0-9][0-9][0-9][0-9]\)"
_yearrec = 0
_commentre = r" {.*}"
_commentrec = 0
_keywordre = r" \[.*\]"
_keywordrec = 0
_there = r", The$|, A$|, An$|, The\s\(|, The\s\[|, The\s{|, A\s\(|,"
    "A\s\[|, A\s{|, An\s\(|, An\s\[|, An\s{"
_therec = 0

def FindYear ( s ) :
    """Search string s for year of the form "(1999)",
    with leading whitespace.  Returns the string without
    the year part, followed by the numeric year.  If there's
    no year, returns None.
    """
    global _yearre
    global _yearrec
    if _yearrec == 0 :
        _yearrec = re.compile ( _yearre )
```

```
    so = _yearrec.search ( s )
    if so == None :
        return None
    st, ep = so.span ( )
    st = st + 1 # skip whitespace
    y = string.atoi ( s[ st + 1 : ep - 1 ] )
    rt = s[ : st - 1 ] + s[ ep : ]
    return rt, y

def FindComment ( s ) :
    """Search string s for a comment of the form
    " {comment}"; if not found, return None.  Otherwise,
    return tuple of string with comment removed and
    the comment string.
    """
    global _commentre
    global _commentrec
    if _commentrec == 0 :
        _commentrec = re.compile ( _commentre )
    so = _commentrec.search ( s )
    if so == None :
        return None
    st, ep = so.span ( )
    st = st + 1
    comment = s[ st + 1 : ep - 1 ]
    rt = s[ : st - 1 ] + s[ ep : ]
    return rt, comment

def FindKeyword ( s ) :
    """Search string s for keywords of the form
    " [keywords]".  If not found return None,
    else return tuple of string with keywords
    removed and the string of keywords.
    """
    global _keywordre
    global _keywordrec
    if _keywordrec == 0 :
        _keywordrec = re.compile ( _keywordre )
    so = _keywordrec.search ( s )
    if so == None :
        return None
    st, ep = so.span ( )
    st = st + 1
    keyword = s[ st + 1 : ep - 1 ]
    rt = s[ : st - 1 ] + s[ ep : ]
    return rt, keyword

def SwapThe ( s ) :
    """If string s ends in ", A" or ", An" or ", The", then
```

continues

LISTING 16.3 continued

```
    eliminate the comma and prepend A, An or The to the string,
    which is returned.  Otherwise, return the original string.
    """
    if s :
        global _there
        global _therec
        if _therec == 0 :
            _therec = re.compile ( _there )
        so = _therec.search ( s )
        if so == None :
            return s
        st, ep = so.span ( )
        rb = s[ : st ]
        ws = string.strip ( s[ st + 1 : ] )
        if ws[ 0 ] == 'T' :
            rb = "The " + rb
        elif len ( ws ) == 1 :
            rb = "A " + rb
        elif ws[ 0 ] == 'A' and ws[ 1 ] == 'n' :
            rb = "An " + rb
        else :
            rb = "A " + rb
        return rb
    return s

def Extract ( s ) :
    """Searches string s for year, comments and keywords.
    Returns tuple of (string, year, comments, keywords);
    string will have all the others removed, and any item
    not found will be None.
    """
    if s :
        if s[ 0 ] == "\\" :
            ss = s[ 1 : ]
        else :
            ss = s[ : ]
        year = None
        comments = None
        keywords = None

        tm = FindYear ( ss )
        if tm != None :
            year = tm[ 1 ]
            ss = tm[ 0 ]
        cm = FindComment ( ss )
        if cm != None :
            comments = cm[ 1 ]
            ss = cm[ 0 ]
```

```
        km = FindKeyword ( ss )
        if km != None :
            keywords = km[ 1 ]
            ss = km[ 0 ]
        return ss, year, comments, keywords
    return s

def FindReplaced ( s ) :
    """Searches string s for replacement markers, of the
    form "->1200" and "->1200,1355".  Returns list of the
    cassettes pointed to or None, if there are no replacements.
    """
    i = string.find ( s, "->" )
    n = 0
    if i == 0 :
        i = i + 2
        c = string.find ( s[ i : ], "," )
        if c < 0 :
            try :
                n = string.atoi ( s[ i : ], 0x10 )
            except ValueError :
                return None
            return [ "%04X" % ( n ) ] # make into dict key
        else :
            t = string.splitfields ( s[ i : ], "," )
            tl = [ ]
            for u in t :
                try :
                    n = string.atoi ( u, 0x10 )
                except ValueError :
                    pass
                us = "%04X" % ( n )
                tl.append ( us )
            return tl
    else :
        return None

def speedname ( v ) :
    """Returns the string representing the speed of
    the tape.  200 returns "T200" and so on.  Returns
    None if the speed is bogus.
    """
    for i in _tspeeds.keys ( ) :
        if v == _tspeeds[ i ] :
            return i
    return None

def sizename ( v ) :
```

continues

LISTING 16.3 continued

```
    """Returns the string representing the size of
    the tape.  1 returns "sp" and so on.  Returns
    None if the speed is bogus.
    """
    if type ( v ) == type ( "" ) :
        return v
    for i in _tsizes.keys ( ) :
        if v == _tsizes[ i ] :
            return i
    return None

def minutize ( m ) :
    """Converts used tape minutes into string
    representing used minutes or used hours
    and minutes.
    """
    t = int ( m )
    h = t / 60
    hm = t % 60
    if h != 0 :
        if h == 1 :
            ss = ""
        else :
            ss = "s"
        if hm == 1 :
            mm = ""
        else :
            mm = "s"
        s = "%2d hour%s %02d minute%s" % ( h, ss, hm, mm )
    else :
        if t == 1 :
            ss = ""
        else :
            ss = "s"
        s = "%02d minute%s" % ( t, ss )
    return s

def tupleize ( m ) :
    """Converts used tape minutes into tuple
    of hours and minutes.
    """
    t = int ( m )
    h = t / 60
    hm = t % 60
    return ( h, hm )

def tsize ( s ) :
    """Converts name of a tape size (T120, T160, etc.) into a
```

```
    number, indicating minutes at sp.  Returns -1 for bogus
    strings.
    """
    if _tsizes.has_key ( s ) :
        return _tsizes[ s ]
    return -1

def tspeed ( s ) :
    """Converts name of a speed (sp, ep, etc.) into
    number--1, 2, etc.  Returns -1 for bogus strings.
    """
    if _tspeeds.has_key ( s ) :
        return _tspeeds[ s ]
    return -1

def header ( s ) :
    """Converts string s into list by splitting on semicolons.
    """
    x = string.splitfields ( s, ";" )
    return x

def parts ( s, n ) :
    """Splits s on "," characters; if there's not two,
    representing used time/time less commercials, raise
    an error.
    """
    x = string.splitfields ( s, "," )
    if len ( x ) != 2 :
        print "Panic: %d 0x%04x:  %s %s %d" % ( n, n, s, x, len ( x ) )
        raise ValueError
    return tuple ( x )

def alldigits ( s ) :
    """Checks s; return a 0 on the first non-digit character found.
    """
    for i in s :
        if i not in string.digits :
            return 0
    return 1

```

Class program goes here.

```

def fieldcmp ( l1, l2 ) :
    """Used in sorting.  The usual thing.  -1, 0, 1
```

continues

LISTING 16.3 continued

```
    for field comparison.
    """
    ll1 = len ( l1 )
    ll2 = len ( l2 )
    n = max ( ll1, ll2 )
    for pl in range ( 1, n ) : # The field[0]s are always
                               # equal when we get here
        try :
            f1 = l1[ pl ]
        except :
            f1 = None
        try :
            f2 = l2[ pl ]
        except :
            f2 = None
        if f1 != None and f2 == None :
            return -1
        if f1 == None and f2 != None :
            return 1
        if type ( f1 ) == type ( 0 ) and type ( f2 ) == type ( 0 ) :
            if f1 < f2 :
                return -1
            if f1 > f2 :
                return 1
            return fieldcmp ( l1[ pl : ], l2[ pl : ] )
        if type ( f1 ) == type ( "" ) and type ( f2 ) == type ( "" ) :
            if f1 < f2 :
                return -1
            if f1 > f2 :
                return 1
            return fieldcmp ( l1[ pl : ], l2[ pl : ] )
        if type ( f1 ) == type ( 0 ) :
            return 1
        return -1
    return 0

def alphasort ( p1, p2 ) :
    """Compare programs p1 and p2
    """
    if p1.fields[ 0 ] < p2.fields[ 0 ] :
        return -1
    if p1.fields[ 0 ] > p2.fields[ 0 ] :
        return 1
    return fieldcmp ( p1.fields, p2.fields )

def numsort ( p1, p2 ) :
    """#
    numsort ( p1, p2 ) :
```

```
    class program p1, p2
    returns -1, 0 or 1 depending on numeric sequence in tape.
    """
    if p1.tape < p2.tape :
        return -1
    if p2.tape < p1.tape :
        return 1
    if p1.seq < p2.seq :
        return -1
    if p2.seq < p1.seq :
        return 1
    return 0

```

Class cassette goes here.

```

def isdummy ( t ) :
    """Returns 1 if the cassette t is a dummy record
    0 otherwise.
    """
    if len ( t.l ) == 0 :
        return 1
    return 0

def ismixed ( t ) :
    """class cassette t
    Returns a list containing speeds used in the cassette,
    or None if only one speed is used.
    """
    k = t.keys ( )
    sp = 0
    n = 0
    rt = [ ]
    if isdummy ( t ) :
        return None
    for j in k :
        p = t.sequence ( j )
        if n == 0 :
            sp = p.sp
        else :
            if p.sp != sp :
                if sp not in rt :
                    rt.append ( sp )
                if p.sp not in rt :
                    rt.append ( p.sp )
```

continues

LISTING 16.3 continued

```
        n = n + 1
    if len ( rt ) > 0 :
        rt.sort ( )
        return rt
    else :
        return None

def makekey ( n ) :
    """Returns valid shelve dictionary key of 4 hex digits
    from number n.
    """
    if type ( n ) == type ( 0 ) :
        k = "%04X" % ( n )
        return k
    elif type ( n ) == type ( "" ) :
        k = string.upper ( n )
        while len ( k ) < 4 :
            k = "0" + i
        return k
    else :
        raise KeyError

def dummyrecord ( n ) :
    """Creates a dummy cassette--placeholder.
    """
    if type ( n ) == type ( 0 ) :
        x = cassette ( n, None )
    else :
        i = string.atoi ( n, 0x10 )
        x = cassette ( i, None )
    return x

def tapenumber ( s ) :
    """Returns number from string s, where s
    has the form "12D3;......"
    """
    n = string.splitfields ( s, ";" )
    return string.atoi ( n[ 0 ], 0x10 )

def percentoftape ( tp ) :  # A cassette record
    """Returns percent of cassette used.
    """
    n = len ( tp )
    pt = 0.0
    if len ( tp.l ) == 0 :
        return pt
    j = tp.l.keys ( )
    j.sort ( )
```

```
    for k in j :  # Program records
        i = tp.l[ k ]
        m = i.sp * i.tlen # total length of tape in speed minutes
        if m == 0 :
            print "Divide by Zero: Tape %s sequence %s" % \
                ( tp.num, i.seq )
            raise ZeroDivisionError
        p = float ( i.ttime ) / float ( m )
        pt = pt + p
    return pt

def percentleft ( tp ) : # Cassette record
    """Returns percent of cassette unused.
    """
    pt = percentoftape ( tp )
    return 1.0 - pt

def tapesize ( tp ) :
    """Returns string representing size of tape;
    T90, T120, etc.
    """
    if isdummy ( tp ) :
        return "T0"
    b = tp.l[ "00" ].tlen
    return sizename ( b )

def tapespeed ( tp ) : # Cassette record
    """Returns tuple of tape speed index
    and length of tape at that speed.
    """
    sp = 0
    tlen = 0
    if isdummy ( tp ) :
        return sp, tlen
    j = tp.l.keys ( )
    j.sort ( )
    for k in j :  # Program records
        i = tp.l[ k ]
        sp = i.sp
        tlen = i.tlen
    return sp, tlen

def minutesleft ( tp ) : # Cassette record
    """Returns minutes left at the ruling tape speed.
    """
    if isdummy ( tp ) :
        return 0.0
    if len ( tp.l ) == 0 :
```

continues

16

LISTING 16.3 continued

```
        return 0.0
    sp, tlen = tapespeed ( tp )
    l = percentleft ( tp )
    mins = sp * tlen # Total number of minutes at final tape speed

    m = mins * l
    return m

try :
    _vcrfile = os.environ[ "VCRLIST" ]
except :
    print "$VCRLIST not set in environment!"
    sys.exit ( 0 )

_thedict = { }
global _total_t
_total_t = 0

def creatememdb ( fname = None ) :
    """Creates an in-memory database from the file.
    """
    global _total_t
    global _thedict
    lineno = 0
    commentdict = { }
    nodisc = 0
    if fname == None :
        ff = open ( _vcrfile, "r" )
    else :
        ff = open ( fname, "r" )
        nodisc = 1
    swt = -1
    current_t = -1

    ct = cassette ( -1, None )

    while 1 :
        b = ff.readline ( )
        lineno = lineno + 1
        if not b :
            _thedict[ "%04X" % ( ct.num ) ] = ct
            if swt != current_t :
                _total_t = _total_t + 1
            break
        b = b[ : len ( b ) - 1 ]  # Remove newline
        if len ( b ) < 1 :          # Skip blank lines
            continue

        if b[ 0 ] == '#' :
```

```
            ck = "%08d" % ( lineno )
            commentdict[ ck ] = b
            continue
        swt = tapenumber ( b )
        if swt != current_t :
            if ct.num != -1 :
                _thedict[ "%04X" % ( ct.num ) ] = ct
            if nodisc == 0 :
                while swt != current_t + 1 :
                    print "Discontinuity: got 0x%x expected 0x%x" % \
                        ( swt, current_t + 1 )
                    current_t = current_t + 1
                    ct = dummyrecord ( current_t )
                    _thedict[ "%04X" % ( ct.num ) ] = ct
                    _total_t = _total_t - 1
            current_t = swt
            ct = cassette ( current_t, b )
            _total_t = _total_t + 1
        else :
            ct.cat ( b )
    if len ( commentdict ) > 0 :
        _thedict[ "COMMENTS" ] = commentdict

    ff.close ( )
    return _thedict, _total_t

import shelve

def createfiledb ( fname = None ) :
    """Create the file database from
    the memory database.
    """
    global _thedict
    global _defaultdbfilename
    if len ( _thedict ) == 0 :
        creatememdb ( fname )
    if fname == None :
        db = shelve.open ( _defaultdbfilename )
    else :
        db = shelve.open ( fname )
    print "Number keys:", len ( _thedict.keys ( ) )
    for i in _thedict.keys ( ) :
        try :
            db[ i ] = _thedict[ i ]
        except :
            print "ERROR.  ERROR"
            print _thedict[ i ]
    db.close ( )
    return db
```

continues

LISTING 16.3 continued

```

def openfiledb ( fname = None ) :
    global _defaultdbfilename
    if fname == None :
        db = shelve.open ( _defaultdbfilename )
    else :
        db = shelve.open ( fname )
    return db

def closedb ( db ) :
    if type ( db ) == type ( { } ) :
        pass
    else :
        db.close ( )

def getkeys ( vdb ) :
    """Returns the keys for the database.
    """
    if vdb == None :
        return None
    k = vdb.keys ( )
    for i in range ( len ( k ) - 1 ) :
        if k[ i ] == "COMMENTS" :
            k = k[ : i ] + k[ i + 1 : ]
            break
    if "COMMENTS" in k :
        print "COMMENTS NOT REMOVED in", len ( k ), "KEYS", k
        raise IndexError
    return k



def findtape ( s, db = None ) :
    """Look for tape s, assumed to be a hex number as a string.
    """
    global _thedict
    i = string.upper ( s )
    while len ( i ) < 4 :
        i = "0" + i
    if db == None :
        try :
            return _thedict[ i ]
        except :
            return None
    else :
        try :
            return db[ i ]
        except :
```

```
            return None

def dumptape ( j, vdb ) :
    """Dump the database in the input file format.
    """
    i = findtape ( j, vdb )
    n = i.key ( ) # Already formatted
    ks = i.keys ( ) # List of sequences, in order
    if ks == None :
        sys.stdout.write ( "# %s:\t*NO TAPE*\n" % ( n ) )
        return
    for r in ks :
        p = i.sequence ( r )
        # Use write to prevent trailing space.
        sys.stdout.write ( "%s;%d;%s,%s;%d,%d" % ( n, p.seq, speedname \
            ( p.sp ), sizename ( p.tlen ), p.ttime, p.ctime ), )
        u = 0
        for f in p.fields :
            if type ( f ) == type ( "" ) :
                if alldigits ( f ) :
                    sys.stdout.write ( ":\t\\%s" % ( f ), )
                else :
                    sys.stdout.write ( ":\t%s" % ( f ), )
            else :
                sys.stdout.write ( ":\t%s" % ( f ), )
            if u == 0 and ( p.year or p.comments or p.keywords ) :
                if p.keywords :
                    sys.stdout.write ( " [%s]" % ( p.keywords ), )
                if p.comments :
                    sys.stdout.write ( " {%s}" % ( p.comments ), )
                if p.year :
                    sys.stdout.write ( " (%04d)" % ( p.year ), )
            u = u + 1
        if p.rplcd :
            sys.stdout.write ( ":\t->" )
            nn = len ( p.rplcd )
            nr = 0
            for q in p.rplcd :
                sys.stdout.write ( "%s" % ( q ) )
                if nr != nn - 1 :
                    sys.stdout.write ( "," )
                nr = nr + 1
        sys.stdout.write ( "\n" )

def reprprog ( p ) :
    """Printable string representation of a program object.
    """
    rs = ""
```

continues

LISTING 16.3 continued

```
    if p != None :
        rs = rs + "%04X;%d;%s,%s;%d,%d" % ( p.tape, p.seq, speedname \
            ( p.sp ), sizename ( p.tlen ), p.ttime, p.ctime )
        u = 0
        for f in p.fields :
            if type ( f ) == type ( "" ) :
                if alldigits ( f ) :
                    rs = rs + ":\t\\%s" % ( f )
                else :
                    rs = rs + ":\t%s" % ( f )
            else :
                rs = rs + ":\t%s" % ( f )
            if u == 0 and ( p.year or p.comments or p.keywords ) :
                if p.keywords :
                    rs = rs + " [%s]" % ( p.keywords )
                if p.comments :
                    rs = rs + " {%s}" % ( p.comments )
                if p.year :
                    rs = rs + " (%04d)" % ( p.year )
            u = u + 1
        if p.rplcd :
            rs = rs + ":\t->"
            nn = len ( p.rplcd )
            nr = 0
            for q in p.rplcd :
                rs = rs + "%s" % ( q )
                if nr != nn - 1 :
                    rs = rs + ","
                nr = nr + 1
    return rs

def reprtape ( j, vdb ) :
    """Printable string representation of a cassette object.
    """
    rs = ""
    ns = 0
    i = findtape ( j, vdb )
    if i == None :
        rs = "Couldn't find %s in the database." % ( j )
        return rs
    n = i.key ( ) # Already formatted
    ks = i.keys ( ) # List of sequences, in order
    if ks == None :
        rs = "# %s:\t*NO TAPE*" % ( n )
        return rs
    ls = len ( ks ) - 1
    for r in ks :
        p = i.sequence ( r )
```

```
            rs = rs + reprprog ( p )
            if ns != ls :
                rs = rs + "\n"
            ns = ns + 1
        return rs

    def onlyspeed ( t, ssp ) :
        """Check to see if cassette t is ssp only.
        """
        xl = ismixed ( t )
        if xl == None :
            sp, tlen = tapespeed ( t )
            if ssp == sp :
                return ssp
        return 0

    def isspeed ( t, ssp ) :
        """See if cassette t has some or all programs recorded
        at ssp speed.
        """
        xl = ismixed ( t )
        if xl == None :
            sp, tlen = tapespeed ( t )
            if ssp == sp :
                return ssp
        elif ssp in xl :
            return ssp
        return 0

    if __name__ == "__main__" :
        if len ( _thedict ) == 0 :
            creatememdb ( )
        print "Total tapes:  %d 0x%x" % ( _total_t, _total_t )
        print "----------------------------------------"

        createfiledb ( )
        print "----------------------------------------"
```

Most of these glue functions are self-explanatory; read the docstrings. The other functions are

- `creatememdb()`—Create an in-memory database from the input file, the location of which is expected to be found in the environment variable `VCRLIST`.
- `createfiledb()`—Create the shelved disk database from the in-memory database.
- `openfiledb()`—Open a created file database for both reading and writing.
- `closedb()`—Closes the file database.

After the file database has been created, other programs can use it by importing `vcr.py` and opening and closing it with the preceding functions. I'll show how to do that in the next section.

Command-Line Interface

Because the original C program is more or less the model for `vcr.py`, Listing 16.4 shows the help output from the C program.

LISTING 16.4 Help Output from the C Version of vcr

```
vcr options [-h?vioarS+KkEFHdcNTIPefRpnlLVO] are:
        -h)              Help, stderr.
        -?)              Help, stdout.
        -v)              Print version & die.
        -i<file>)        Input file if not '~/VcrList'.
        -o<file>)        Output file (default stdout).
        -a)              Sort by program title.
        -r)              Reverse sense of sort.
        -S<string>)      Select by matching <regular expression>.
        -+)              Extend search/select to include fields.
        -K)              Confine search/select to keywords only.
        -k)              Print keywords.
        -E)              Don't print description.
        -F<string>)      Print output using %Format <string>.
        -H)              Help, %Format.
        -d<string>)      Debug function:level.
        -c)              Case-insensitivity off in RE searches.
        -N<string>)      Range [x, x-x, -x, x-] (hex) of tape #s to
                         select.
        -T<string>)      Produce HTML files for entries selected.
        -I<string>)      Produce HTML index files for entries selected.
        -P)              Produce PostScript labels for entries selected.
        -e)              PostScript:  edge labels only.
        -f)              PostScript:  face labels only.
        -R)              Report total running time of tapes.
        -p<string>)      .pro file to use instead of default.
        -n##)            Number of character columns wide.
        -l)              Report and show longest single field.
        -L)              Report and show only the longest single field.
        -V)              Don't put a, an and the first at print time.
        -O)              Write output file in input format.
```

We're going to implement only a couple of these facilities for the vcr database. I don't ever intend to implement all of these because some of them don't make a lot of sense and some are no longer useful. Other useful things turn up because of using a database instead of a sorted list, as was used in the C program. The ones that we do build won't actually reside in the `vcr.py` module, but will instead import that module. The first one is a very simple one: query the database for the contents of a particular tape. Listing 16.5 shows the code.

LISTING 16.5 *vcq.py*

```
#!/usr/local/bin/python

import os
import sys
import shelve
import string
import time
from vcr import cassette
from vcr import program
import vcr

try :
    _vcrfile = os.environ[ "VCRLIST" ]
except :
    print "$VCRLIST not set in environment!"
    sys.exit ( 0 )

if len ( sys.argv ) > 1 :
    vdb = vcr.openfiledb ( )
    for i in range ( 1, len ( sys.argv ) ) :
    t = vcr.findtape ( sys.argv[ i ], vdb )
    if t != None :
        print t, "Length:", len ( t ), "speed", t.speed ( ), "size", \
           t.size ( ), \
        "minutesleft", vcr.minutesleft ( t )
        print "~~~~~~~"
        k = t.keys ( ) # Auto sort
        for j in k :
        y = t.sequence ( j ) # sequence will take either ints or strings.
...
        if y.fields[ 0 ] != None :
            for z in y.fields :
            if type ( z ) != type ( 0 ) :
                print vcr.SwapThe ( z )
            else :
                print z
            if y.year != None :
            print "(%04d)" % ( y.year ),
            if y.comments != None :
            print "{%s}" % ( y.comments ),
```

continues

Listing 16.5 continued

```
            if y.keywords != None :
            print "[%s]" % ( y.keywords ),
            print "%s~~~~~~~" % ( j )

    vcr.closedb ( vdb )

```

In the preceding program, notice that we both `import vcr` and `from vcr import cassette` (and program); we do this because the `shelve` module needs to know the classnames of the Python objects we are putting into and reading from the file database. The program simply assumes that any command-line arguments it encounters are tape numbers to search for, and this is done by using the `findtape()` function. The original C program allowed for ranges; for example, 1000-1FFF or -1FFF. Eventually, I plan to add ranges to `vcq.py` (unless you want to, of course).

This next command-line program goes through the database and finds all the tapes with more than a certain amount of time left on them. This can be quite useful when you're looking for a one-hour space, for example, on which to tape Star Trek. Listing 16.6 shows this.

Listing 16.6 *vcrleft.py*

```
#!/usr/local/bin/python

import os
import sys
import shelve
import string
from vcr import cassette
from vcr import program
import vcr

try :
    _vcrfile = os.environ[ "VCRLIST" ]
except :
    print "$VCRLIST not set in environment!"
    sys.exit ( 0 )

spd = 0

howmuch = 28.0
lessthan = 9999.0
tlist = [ ]
mlist = [ ]
```

```

def prlist ( list ) :
    tpr = 0
    n = len ( list )
    z = 0
    i = 0
    for z in range ( n ) :
    print list[ z ],
    tpr = tpr + 1
    i = z % 3
    if i == 2 :
        print ""
    else :
        print "\t",
    if i != 2 :
    print ""
    print "-----------------------------------------------------------"
        "-------------------"

if len ( sys.argv ) > 1 :
    howmuch = float ( string.atoi ( sys.argv[ 1 ] ) )
    if len ( sys.argv ) > 2 :
    try :
        lessthan = float ( string.atoi ( sys.argv[ 2 ] ) )
    except :
        if sys.argv[ 2 ] == "sp" :
        spd = 1
        elif sys.argv[ 2 ] == "lp" :
        spd = 2
        elif sys.argv[ 2 ] == "ep" or sys.argv[ 2 ] == "slp" :
        spd = 3
        else :
        print "I don't understand", sys.argv[ 2 ]
        raise ValueError
    if len ( sys.argv ) > 3 :
    if sys.argv[ 3 ] == "sp" :
        spd = 1
    elif sys.argv[ 3 ] == "lp" :
        spd = 2
    elif sys.argv[ 3 ] == "ep" or sys.argv[ 3 ] == "slp" :
        spd = 3
    else :
        print "I don't understand", sys.argv[ 3 ]
        raise ValueError
vdb = vcr.openfiledb ( )
lst = vcr.getkeys ( vdb )
lst.sort ( )
print "Looking for", howmuch, "<", lessthan, "minutes, in", \
    len ( lst ), "Keys"
```

continues

LISTING 16.3 continued

```
print "----------------------------------------------------------------"
    "----------------"
for j in lst :
    i = vcr.findtape ( j, vdb )
    t = vcr.minutesleft ( i )
    if spd != 0 :
    if not vcr.onlyspeed ( i, spd ) :
        continue
    if howmuch < t < lessthan :
    x, y = vcr.tapespeed ( i )
    hl, ml = vcr.tupleize ( t )
    st = "T%04X %s -- %03dm %02d:%02d" % ( i.num, vcr.speedname ( x ), t, \
       hl, ml )
    mlist.append ( st )
    st = "%03dm %02d:%02d -- T%04X %s" % ( t, hl, ml, i.num, \
       vcr.speedname ( x ) )
    tlist.append ( st )

tlist.sort ( )
mlist.sort ( )


prlist ( mlist )
prlist ( tlist )

vcr.closedb ( vdb )

```

Most of this code should be self-evident. The command-line arguments are expected to be the amount of time you're looking for in minutes, followed by the speed; if the amount of time is left out, then the program assumes you just provided the speed. The default amount of time to search for i, by default, 28 minutes.

Summary

In this hour, the last one in this third of the book, I've shown you a great deal of code. Some of this code, such as the regular expressions, doesn't really have to be understood; if it piques your interest, by all means figure out what those regular expressions do. See the exercises for a hint. What I expect you to gain from reading all this code is exposure and experience in visualizing how the parts go together. All the code is downloadable from the book's Web site; I've provided a small sample as an input file, along with a readme that explains what you need to do to get it running on your own system. Naturally, I'm not providing my entire video database. And no, none of my tapes are available for loan.

Workshop

Q&A

Q All we've done this hour is read code. Do we really have to have a quiz?

A No. You deserve a break.

Exercises

The definitive book on regular expressions is *Mastering Regular Expressions,* by Jeffrey E.F. Friedl, from O'Reilly & Associates. David Ascher said of this book, "Jeffrey Friedl's book is IMO one of the few that I own that I think are worth the price, even though its Python knowledge is obsolete and I use regexps as sparingly as I possibly can. If nothing else, it is proof that the human mind will delve obsessively into arcane knowledge for no other reason than because it can." High praise, indeed.

Add ranges to `vcq.py`. Hint: look at my `getargs` module, which can be found at `http://www.pauahtun.org/ftp.html`, near the bottom of the page. It's fully documented, of course: see `http://www.pauahtun.org/getargs.html`. When you add the ranges, send the changes to me, and I'll give you a credit on the Web page for this book. This is your chance for fame and fortune.

PART III

Introducing the Python GUI

Hour

Hour 17

Introducing the Python GUI

I reshot some head [pictures] today. I have to tell you, pythons do not like to behave for closeups of their heads. It was a battle all the way, but no serious lacerations to either them or me.

—John Hollister

This is the first chapter in the last third of the book, the third in which you learn about Python's official GUI, Tkinter. I'm sure you remember that GUI stands for Graphical User Interface. You will find that for several reasons, GUI programming is somewhat different from command-line interface programming, so we'll talk about the programming model and a bit of underlying theory (trust me, this theory won't be hard) before we move on to actual programming. At the end of this hour, you should be able to

- Describe the differences between command-line and GUI programming
- Explain what an `event queue` is
- Explain what events are
- Explain what callbacks are

This is another one of those boring chapters where you don't get to write any code; the next few chapters will more than make up for the lack.

The GUI Programming Model

I remember when Apple brought out the Lisa computer. One of the vice-presidents of the company I worked for at the time bought one and brought it in to work. He put it in the common computer lab, and everyone was allowed to try it out. This was a company where even the secretaries were computer geeks, so you can imagine how much of a workout this machine got. Naturally, I tried it out and had a great time. Some months later, the Macintosh debuted; based on their experiences with the Lisa, several engineers went out and bought Macintoshes. I couldn't afford one, however, so my initial experiences with the Mac GUI were limited to working with the PostScript printer attached to the single unit the company bought. I stayed late most evenings that summer, learning PostScript.

Much later, after X Windows came out, I transferred to the graphics project and received a Sun workstation—which I promptly named "Phssthpok" after the Pak character in Larry Niven's novel *Protector*. This turned out to be a good choice, even though most of the other engineers insisted on referring to it as "fishhook," because not too long after I got the machine, the timeserver software on several of our machines turned out to have a really terrible bug in it.

Timeserver software is supposed to keep time on a network in sync; our code would work fine for several hours and suddenly jump back in time by well over an hour, or sometimes more. The bug in the software was eventually tracked down; it turned out to be a sign where no sign should have been. That is, one branch of an `if` that was supposed to add a correction subtracted it. At least four people had looked at the offending code, not just once but several times, before someone took the time to actually step through it and was able to see when the time correction fell back when it should have gone forward. Although Python is far easier to debug than many other languages, and even though debugging is a topic not covered in this book, you should remember this story. Step through your code line by line and make certain that it is doing what you think it is doing. Four people (including me) failed to do this for critical code, and for several months the company's network was working less than optimally because of it.

My first GUI program would go out on the Net and query one of the U.S. Naval Observatory's sites for the current time; it set the time on my Sun, which I made the master timeserver on our local net, and my Sun would set the time for all of our other machines. Thus, Phssthpok was acting as the protector for our network, overriding our own buggy software.

Working with X on that Sun was my first real exposure to GUI programming (I think this was X11 Release 2, but it might have been the final release of X10), and it was very educational. The graphics part wasn't too difficult, but I had a hard time getting used to an event-driven paradigm, which is the way that all GUIs operate. In the programs we've been writing up until now, the program actually drives the logic flow. A user runs the program, and the program, in effect, tells the user what to do, based on the initial set of conditions provided by the user; when the program is finished, it exits.

GUI programs, on the other hand, run when the user tells them to. They display graphical objects, such as a dialog or an edit window, or something like that. They do nothing at all after the display is shown, and they wait until the user tells them what to do. When the user is finished, she tells the program to exit.

Logic in command-line programs is usually relatively straightforward. When such a program is run, it starts at point A, steps to point B, and so on to point Z, and then it exits. This main part of such programs is probably the most important part: start here, go there, end here. GUI programs typically have a start-here section, but the main part is ordinarily extremely simple and often looks like this (this is pseudocode, not real Python):

```
while there are events:
    do something with those events
```

The emphasis here is on the events, not on the logic flow. This may seem like a small distinction, but it is essential to grasp just how fundamental it is. Command-line programs go through a strict sequence: A, B, C,...Z, and then exit. GUI programs perform an initial setup and then wait for events; because the user governs how the program behaves in practice, there is no predicting which events will arrive when. Finally, a GUI program exits only when the user tells it to. I think the basic distinction is predictability: command-line programs are (theoretically) perfectly predictable, given a set of initial conditions. GUI programs aren't, because every run of such a program may have identical initial conditions, but users can do entirely different things in every run.

How are events delivered? This role is somewhat different in the various windowing systems that exist; under X Windows events are received by a server program and delivered to a separate client program. Both programs here are what are termed "user-level" programs; that is, they are not part of the actual operating system, but are instead ordinary programs started by the user. On Windows (all varieties), the windowing system is integrated into the operating system; X Windows is layered as just another application program on (or under) the UNIX operating system. The Macintosh operating system, or at least the earlier versions that I've used, also has the windowing system integrated into it.

Earlier versions also had no command-line interface, although I understand that the situation is changing now; in fact, the newest version (MacOS X) separates the OS and GUI layers. As you may have guessed, I haven't used a Macintosh for years.

But in all cases, events are generated by the user in various ways: by moving the mouse, by pressing keys, or by clicking mouse buttons. The generated events are placed into a queue, pulled off by the server (which may or may not be part of the OS), and placed into another queue where the user application program pulls them out of that queue. It seems important, therefore, to understand what a queue is in programming terms.

You can think of event queues as straws into which dried peas (or spitballs, if you prefer) are inserted. After a pea is inserted, the only way to get it out is to take it out of the other end of the straw; you can't fiddle with it inside the straw. After you've taken the pea out, you can make soup with it or do whatever else you want, including inserting it into another straw, or queue, without otherwise doing anything to it. A program or a server can insert events into a queue, but once in, they don't come out until a program or server comes along and takes the event out at the other end; this is done by polling. Our pseudocode `while` loop shown previously demonstrates this; it's just an endless loop that pulls an event out of the queue, works on it, and goes right back to wait for more events.

This brings us to another topic. There are two kinds of "working on an event": *synchronous* and *asynchronous*. In the `while` loop shown previously, the `do` portion of the loop can call functions synchronously or asynchronously. In a synchronous model, the `do` would call a function to do some work and then wait for the return value. Nothing else would happen while it was waiting for the function to end, except for processing in the function. In an asynchronous model, the `do` would call the function and then immediately go on to check to see whether another event had arrived. If so, that `do` could go right on and call another function. This means, then, that two functions could be running at the same time—a completely different situation from that of a synchronous model. Command-line interface programs are mostly synchronous.

On UNIX, a class of command-line programs called daemons (using the old-fashioned spelling on purpose) runs asynchronously. Similar programs are called services on Windows. The timeserver software I described earlier is such a daemon on UNIX. Timeserver services are also available for NT. When the program structure of daemons or services is analyzed, it becomes clear that they are nearly identical with windowing systems because they, too, go into `while` loops (or something very similar) and wait for events.

Event-driven windowing systems, however, are inevitably of the asynchronous variety. To maintain a reasonable degree of responsiveness to user actions, windowing systems cannot afford to sit around and wait for functions to finish (if they ever do) before turning their attention back to such details as making the mouse move when the user moves her hand. Additionally, things happen in the background that users don't ordinarily know or care about; some process has to draw such things as the window borders and keep them up-to-date. Files sometimes need updating—Windows `.ini` files are a good example—and some events that occur mean that other events (called *messages* on Windows) must also be delivered.

The terms *background* and *foreground*, when applied to tasks that a computer is performing, are terms that go back to the very earliest multiprocessing computers. IBM 360 computers split memory into two parts, foreground and background, and the parts were referred to as memory *partitions*. Programs had to be specially recompiled to run in the background partition. Background programs ran much more slowly than foreground ones, and the foreground ones were slowed down substantially. As a first step, it was acceptable, but by today's standards, such an approach is not feasible. It's worth remembering, however, that the largest IBM 360 I ever worked on had 256KB of memory. That's kilobytes, not megabytes. The machine I'm writing this book on has 320 megabytes of RAM.

Windows 95/98 and NT spend lots of time behind your back updating the system registry, which is what has largely replaced .ini files now. The principle is the same, however; settings change and programs need to track information, so such items and settings are stuffed into the registry whenever you're not looking (which is most of the time). Unlike X Windows, which does only so much of this because the UNIX OS takes care of most of it, Windows also has to do things such as run your keyboard, run the video display, operate your hard disks, and so on. None of these things can afford to wait until your solitaire game is completely drawn.

Events

Now that you've learned how events are generated and delivered and have incidentally learned about another of the traditional data structures—queues—it's time to find out what events are good for. You need to know the sorts of things that produce events. In the next section, we'll also look at the information that can accompany different kinds of events on UNIX, running both X Windows and Python/Tkinter.

All windowing systems run your display, which consists of one or more monitors, the keyboard, and the mouse. The monitor is (normally) a passive device—an output-only device—that needs to have windows and dialogues drawn upon it; wallpaper, clocks, and taskbars are examples of other items to be drawn. Keyboards and mice, however, are active devices (as are the "touch" part of touch-screen monitors). You can press keys on the keyboard, you can move the mouse pointer, and you can click mouse buttons. Each one of these actions generates an event, and most possible actions have events associated with them. That is, a keypress has a press action and a release action, and some way is always available to determine whether other keys, such as Shift or Ctrl, are held down at the same time. Mouse pointer movements always have X and Y coordinates associated with them, where X is the location in the width of your monitor and Y is the location in the height of the monitor's display. Mouse button clicks have X and Y coordinates, the number of the button, whether it's a press or a release action, and some indication of keyboard keys that are held down at the same time. The latter are usually limited to what are called modifier keys—Shift, Ctrl, Alt, and so on.

Because we are interested in the kinds of events available when running Python/Tkinter, I won't describe the (hundreds) of extra events defined under Windows; most of these aren't available in Python unless you use Mark Hammond's Win32 extensions. The best place to read about and download these is `http://starship.python.net/crew/mhammond/`.

Table 17.1 lists events as used in Tkinter.

TABLE 17.1 Tkinter Events

Event	*Action*
`Activate`	This window/widget is now the active window.
`ButtonPress, Button`	Mouse button pressed; `Button1` = mouse button 1, and so on.
	`Double-Button-1` = double-click mouse button 1.
	You can even use `Triple-Button-1`.
`ButtonRelease`	Mouse button released.
`Circulate`	The window/widget's Z-order position has changed.
`Colormap`	Colormap changed; I don't think this one happens on Windows.
`Configure`	Size, shape, or location changed.
`Deactivate`	This window/widget is no longer the active window.
`Destroy`	This widget is about to be destroyed.
`Enter`	The mouse pointer has entered the boundaries of this window/widget.

Event	*Action*
`Expose`	Some or all of this window/widget has changed exposure.
`FocusIn`	This widget has keyboard focus.
`FocusOut`	This widget lost keyboard focus.
`Gravity`	You don't care about this one.
`KeyPress, Key`	Key pressed; `Key`*a* = keyboard key *a* and so on.
`KeyRelease`	Keyboard key released.
`Motion`	Mouse pointer moved.
`Leave`	The mouse pointer was moved out of this window/widget ("Elvis has left the building").
`Map`	This window/widget was displayed.
`Property`	Some property of the window/widget changed, such as color.
`Reparent`	Parent window/widget changed to another window/widget.
`Unmap`	This window/widget was undisplayed.
`Visibility`	Visibility changed; iconified, maximized, and so on.

17

As you can see, there are lots of events. Not all of them are useful, and it is unlikely that you will use all of them in any single program. As we progress, the meanings of the useful ones will become clear. To respond to these events, however, you need to register and provide handlers, or callbacks, for the events you're interested in. If your program doesn't register for an event, it won't be notified when the event occurs; callbacks and registering for events are the topics for the next section.

Callbacks

To register for an event, you need to create a *widget* of some sort. Widgets are windows that have special properties; any time you run a GUI program, you can see widgets, or the equivalent, that do different things. Buttons are widgets, and so are edit fields, menus, scrolled windows, and icons. Windows that have smaller windows inside them are parent widgets; the parent of all the windows and widgets on your display screen is the root window, and all widgets must have parents. Whenever you run IDLE, you can see lots of widgets—most of them menus and menu selections. IDLE is written entirely in Python/Tkinter. Before you can create widgets, however, you need to do some minimal initialization, like this:

```
from Tkinter import *
root = Tk()
```

These lines initialize Tkinter and stuff the root variable with everything you need to know about the root window; it's an object. After you initialize and get back the root object, you're ready to create a widget:

```
button = Button(root)
```

That's certainly simple enough, isn't it? Of course, `button` won't do anything (and in fact won't be visible until later), so we have a bit more work to do. For one thing, if we showed the button right away, it wouldn't have any text on it. Here's how to add that:

```
button["text"] = "Ave atque vale!"
```

What this line does is treat `button` like a dictionary (it may not actually be one, but we can pretend it is, because the button object has the `__getattr__()` method; see Chapter 13, "Special Class Methods"), find the "text" attribute, and set its value to **`Ave atque vale`** ("Hail and farewell" in Latin). At this point, we could show the button, but it still wouldn't do anything. To enable it to do something, we have to register for an event and supply a callback. Here's how:

```
def die(event):
    sys.exit(0)
...
button.bind("<Button1>", die)
```

That's all there is to it. We define a function, `die()`, which we provide as the callback function name for the `button.bind()` method. The `bind()` method requires two parameters, the first of which is the event, as a string that you want to register your callback for. The < and > parts of the string are required, but otherwise match the names given in Table 17.1. The second parameter is the name of your callback function, which takes one parameter, `event`. This `event` parameter isn't used in `die()`, but we will be using it later in many other callback functions.

There is another way to specify callbacks. Many of the widgets have special attributes to which you can directly assign a callback. In the case of buttons, the alternate method would be like this:

```
def die():
    sys.exit(0)
...
button["command"] = die
```

When we do it like this, we don't have to use the `event` parameter for `die()`.

Using either method to assign a callback, we need to do only two things before we have an actual working program that does something. The following are the two lines to add:

```
button.pack()
root.mainloop()
```

That's it. The `pack()` method is what's called a geometry manager method; it sends a message to the button telling it to figure out how big it should be and to adjust the button to be an appropriate size to hold the text we gave it, plus a little padding for aesthetic purposes. The `mainloop()` method for the `root` widget sends a message that says, "OK, I'm done with setup and initialization; now start receiving and processing events." This is our event loop—the one that says "`while` *`there are events`*, `do` *`something with the events`*." (Remember our previously shown pseudocode `while` loop?)

You could type the few previous lines into Python by hand, if you want, or put them into a file. Listing 17.1 shows the entire file.

LISTING 17.1 `ave.py`

```
#!/usr/local/bin/python

import sys
from Tkinter import *

def die(event):
    sys.exit(0)

root = Tk()
button = Button(root)
button["text"] = "Ave atque vale!"
button.bind("<Button-1>", die)
button.pack()
root.mainloop()
```

Figure 17.1 shows how it all looks when you run it.

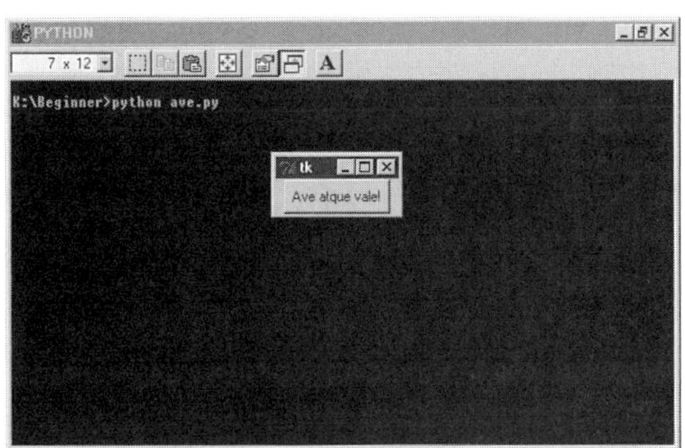

FIGURE 17.1
Running `ave.py`.

So far, you've seen that callbacks are simply functions in Python. In C and C++, callbacks are also functions, but a good deal more complicated, both to register and in the function itself. A sample C callback function is shown next:

```
static void
ButtonCallback(Widget w, XtPointer cd, XtPointer dd)
{
    /* Exit processing. ... */
    exit(0);
}
```

And the way you would register the callback is

```
XtAddCallback(w, XmNactivateCallback, ButtonCallback, (XtPointer)cd);
```

The C callback function is drastically simplified; a real one could run to many lines of code. Of course, you would also have to have much more support code for startup and initialization, to build widgets, and to configure the widgets properly; after all that was done, however, the main event loop would be only minimally more complex than a `while ... do` loop. Finally, you would have to compile a C program, a step that would add yet more delays into the process. By contrast, Python/Tkinter lets you create a fully functional program in just a few minutes. An X Windows program written in C that would be equivalent to `ave.py` would take a minimum of 100 lines of code and would be much more prone to bug infestation.

Summary

We've covered a little history of GUI programming, the differences between command-line programming and GUI programming, what events are, what callbacks are, and what an event queue is. In the next hour, we will be writing some introductory GUI programs using Tkinter.

Workshop

Q&A

Q Hey, I thought you said we wouldn't be doing any programming?

A So I did. I guess I lied, didn't I?

Q What's the largest IBM 360 that you ever heard of?

A The IBM 360/90 Model I had a megabyte of memory. As far as I know, there was only one—in Washington DC; it was so large and ran so hot that it had to be water cooled. From the pictures I remember, it filled a large room. Like a basketball court, maybe.

Quiz

1. What is a good metaphor for how an event queue operates?
   a. It's like a stack of plates at a cafeteria; you push a pile of plates down and take them off the top.
   b. It's like a rope; you pull on one end and something gets yanked at the other.
   c. It's like a straw full of spitwads; push one in and it comes out the other end.
   d. It's like a flat tire; all tread and no go.
2. Who decides when a GUI program is finished?
   a. The programmer. When the job is finished, the program exits.
   b. The computer. When memory is exhausted, the computer crashes.
   c. The OS. When the OS gets bored, it jumps to the Blue Screen of Death.
   d. The user. When the user is finished processing, she tells the program to exit.
3. What are callbacks?
   a. Someone with an answering machine who really does answer messages.
   b. A method or a function that is registered to be called whenever an event arrives.
   c. A method or a function that calls a method or a function that you supply when you call it.
   d. A part of the Windows OS that dials your telephone.

Answers

1. c, a straw full of spitwads. The plates are a metaphor for a FIFO (First In, First Out) stack, yet another of the classic data structures. Queues maintain the same order throughout; that is, if event A precedes event B, then that will be true at the other end of the queue when events are removed.
2. d, the user. Command-line programs are those in which the programmer usually decides when the job is finished.
3. b, when an event arrives from the event queue that your program has registered for, it activates a callback function or method.

Exercises

You can get a taste of what it was like in the '60s working on IBM mainframes by visiting Dave Nichols's Place at `http://www.geocities.com/SiliconValley/Lakes/5705/360.html`. I'm thinking about getting one of his T-shirts—the one that says "I helped create the Y2K bug." Too bad the Y2K bug turned out to be nearly invisible.

Hour 18

Tk Widgets I

Life is much too short to spend time programming in lousy languages.

—Robert Meegan

In this hour, we start learning about windows and widgets in Tkinter. At the end of the hour, you will be able to

- Discriminate between windows and widgets
- Identify different several kinds of widgets
- Use callbacks in Tkinter applications

Windows and Widgets

The distinction between windows and widgets is clear: a window is simply an area of your screen that is marked off in some way, usually by visible borders added by either your window manager (in X Windows) or by the Windows OS. A widget is the same as a window, but it has added behavior—sound familiar? It should. A widget is usually a smaller part of a window. Figure 18.1 should make the distinction visible:

FIGURE 18.1
Windows and widgets.

The object on the left is a simple window; it does nothing but occupy screen real estate because there aren't any buttons or menus. The code—what there is of it—is

```
from Tkinter import *
root = Tk()
root.mainloop()
```

The only way to exit this program is to push the X button at the upper right-hand corner. On the other hand, the object on the right is a window that contains a widget—a button that says "I am a widget." It actually does something; if you push the button, it exits the program (you should remember this from the last chapter). Listing 18.1 shows the code.

LISTING 18.1 `tkt3.py`

```
#!/usr/local/bin/python

from Tkinter import *
import sys

root = Tk()
button = Button(root)
button["text"] = "I am a widget"
button.pack()
root.mainloop()

```

Again, this listing should look familiar because it's very close to `ave.py` from Chapter 17, "Introducing the Python GUI."

As I pointed out before, widgets have behavior and state; they have methods that you can call and properties that you can set. The root window that appears on the left in Figure 18.1 is not really a true window; it is instead a Tkinter encapsulation of a window; because all widgets in Tkinter are children of this root, or top level, window, it has some properties and some behavior, which all children inherit. Remember our earlier discussion of Python's object inheritance? All widgets in Tkinter are objects, and thus, all have state (properties) and behavior (methods); you can subclass them and modify the behavior to suit your needs.

Reference pages for the Tkinter widgets can be found at `http://www.pythonware.com/library/tkinter/tkclass/index.htm`. These pages list the various kinds of widgets, their properties, and their methods. All the different widgets are described and pictured next, alphabetically. Simple test scripts are given, along with some comments; in the section on scrollbars and text widgets, in Chapter 19, Tk Widgets II, I'll present a complete application that actually does something useful. The Button widget, shown in Figure 18.2, is fairly simple to use. Listing 18.2 shows how:

The Button Widget

FIGURE 18.2
A Button widget.

LISTING 18.2 tkbutton.py

```
1  #!/usr/local/bin/python
2
3  from Tkinter import *
4  import sys
5
6  def die(event):
7      sys.exit(0)
8
9  root = Tk()
10 button = Button(root)
11 button["text"] = "Button"
12 button.bind("<Button>",die)
13 button.pack()
14
15 root.mainloop()
```

As you can see, it's essentially the same as `tkt3.py`, shown in Listing 18.1. However, we could create the button another way: We could use Tkinter's `option` syntax, which works like this:

```
button = Button(root,text="Button",command=die)
```

This single line would replace lines 10 through 12 in Listing 18.2. When any widget is created, you can set as many options as you want by using the "`keyword=value`" syntax shown previously. The only glitch for `tkbutton.py` is that the `command` option expects to be given a callback function that takes no arguments, so `die()` must be modified to eliminate the `event` parameter. For creating this Button widget, then, this alternate method doesn't really get us much, but it doesn't cost much either. The `option` method can, however, be both easier and more readable in many situations; some widgets have a great many options. You should get into the habit of using actual event bindings instead of the `command=callback` style; callbacks that can be installed as options this way are limited to just one event and one specific argument list. Using event bindings lets you have callbacks for exactly what you need. The Canvas widget, shown in Figure 18.3, is simple (and boring) to look at in its natural state. Drawing things in it, which is what it's good for, is a subject for in-depth treatment in a later chapter.

The Canvas Widget

FIGURE 18.3
A Canvas widget.

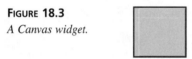

The simplest possible program showing how to display one is shown in Listing 18.3.

LISTING 18.3 tkcanvas.py

```
#!/usr/local/bin/python

from Tkinter import *
import sys

def die(event):
    sys.exit(0)

root = Tk()
button = Button(root)
button["text"] = "Button"
button.bind("<Button>",die)
button.pack()
canvas = Canvas(root)
canvas["height"]=64
canvas["width"]=64
canvas["borderwidth"]=2
canvas["relief"]=RAISED
canvas.pack()

root.mainloop()
```

The height, width, and so on could be set using the option method we used in the alternate method for Button widgets, but again, it doesn't make much difference in such a small demo program anyway. Many of the options are covered in a later chapter.

The Checkbutton Widget

The Checkbutton widget, as shown in Figure 18.4, is used for yes-no conditions, or *toggle* variables (from toggle switches) that have only two states: on and off.

FIGURE 18.4
A Checkbutton widget.

Listing 18.4 shows how to use it.

LISTING 18.4 `tkcheckbutton.py`

```
#!/usr/local/bin/python

from Tkinter import *
import sys

def die(event):
    sys.exit(0)

root = Tk()
button = Button(root)
button["text"] = "Button"
button.bind("<Button>",die)
button.pack()
checkbutton = Checkbutton(root)
checkbutton["text"] = "Checkbutton"
checkbutton.pack()

root.mainloop()
```


Many, if not most, of the widgets I'm showing you will look different on different platforms. For example, Figure 18.5 shows how the Checkbutton would look on UNIX, and it would appear differently on a Mac, too.

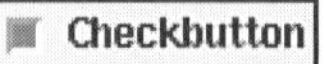

FIGURE 18.5
A Checkbutton widget on UNIX.

The Entry Widget

The Entry widget shown in Figure 18.6 obtains text input from a user. It's limited to a single line, whereas the Text widget that you will see later can have multiple lines. Listing 18.5 shows a simple way to use it.

FIGURE 18.6
An Entry widget.

LISTING 18.5 `tkentry.py`

```
 1  #!/usr/local/bin/python
 2
 3  from Tkinter import *
 4  import sys
 5
 6  def die(event):
 7      print entry.get()
 8      sys.exit(0)
 9
10  root = Tk()
11  button = Button(root)
12  button["text"] = "Button"
13  button.bind("<Button>",die)
14  button.pack()
15
16  entry = Entry(root)
17  entry.insert(0,"Entry")
18  entry.pack()
19
20  root.mainloop()
21
```

When you exit the program by pressing the button, the program prints the text that you typed into the Entry widget; line 7 shows how to read the value—with the `get()` method. The `get()` method is common to many widgets, as is the `set()` method.

The Frame Widget

The Frame widget, shown in Figure 18.7, holds things. It is also used to occupy space; that is, it can be used either as a placeholder or as a separator for aesthetic reasons.

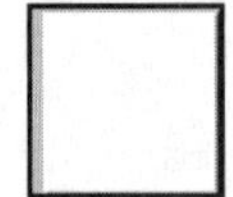

FIGURE 18.7
A Frame widget.

Listing 18.6 shows a simple program that displays a Frame widget; notice that height and width must be set.

Listing 18.6 `tkframe.py`

```
#!/usr/local/bin/python

from Tkinter import *
import sys

def die(event):
    sys.exit(0)

root = Tk()
button = Button(root)
button["text"] = "Button"
button.bind("<Button>",die)
button.pack()
frame = Frame(root)
frame["height"]=64
frame["width"]=64
frame["background"] = "white"
frame["borderwidth"]=2
frame["relief"]=RAISED
frame.pack()

root.mainloop()
```


The Label Widget

The Label widget, shown in Figure 18.8, is one of the most useful widgets.

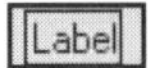

Figure 18.8
A Label widget.

It holds noneditable text and is extremely easy to use, as Listing 18.7 shows.

Listing 18.7 `tklabel.py`

```
#!/usr/local/bin/python

from Tkinter import *
import sys

def die(event):
    sys.exit(0)
```

continues

LISTING 18.7 continued

```
root = Tk()
button = Button(root)
button["text"] = "Button"
button.bind("<Button>",die)
button.pack()
labelx = Label(root)
labelx["height"] = 1
labelx.pack()
label = Label(root)
label["text"] = "Label"
label["borderwidth"] = 1
label["relief"] = SOLID
label.pack()
root.mainloop()
```

This program uses an extra label (`labelx`), with no text, as a separator; the Frame widget could have been used just as easily.

The Listbox Widget

A listbox widget, shown in Figure 18.9, is used to provide users with multiple choices. When building the widget, it's easier to use the regular method of construction instead of the option way.

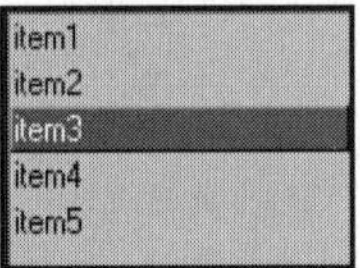

FIGURE 18.9
A Listbox widget.

Listing 18.8 shows how.

LISTING 18.8 `tklistbox.py`

```
#!/usr/local/bin/python
from Tkinter import *
import sys
elements = [ "item5", "item4", "item3", "item2", "item1" ]
```

```
8  def die(event):
9      sys.exit(0)
10
11 root = Tk()
12 button = Button(root)
13 button["text"] = "Button"
14 button.bind("<Button>",die)
15 button.pack()
16 labelx = Label(root)
17 labelx["height"] = 1
18 labelx.pack()
19
20 listbox = Listbox(root)
21 for i in elements :
22     listbox.insert(0, i)
23 listbox.pack()
24
25 root.mainloop()
```

The `for` loop in line 21 inserts the text for each item into the list. You could add elements or items to the listbox in many ways; this is just one way.

Tkinter Variables

To use variables with the Tkinter widgets, you must first understand that all Tk/TCL variables are strings. Therefore, any time a widget requires a variable that it can modify (we'll see a use for this in the description of menu widgets, next), you have to use a set of special variables designed especially for interfacing between Python and Tkinter. What you need to know about them is that they are objects, not simple strings; all of them inherit from a class called `Variable`, which has certain basic methods and states that are common to all the different kinds. Each particular kind knows how to get and set its own value, taking into account its own special needs. Table 18.1 lists the Tkinter variables, along with a description and a short example of how to create one.

TABLE 18.1 Tkinter Variables

Name	*Description*	*Example*
`StringVar()`	Holds string values	`x = StringVar("Text")`
`IntVar()`	Holds integer values	`x = IntVar(42)`
`DoubleVar()`	Holds floating-point values	`x = DoubleVar(3.14159)`
`BooleanVar()`	Holds `true` and `false` values	`x = BooleanVar("true")`

To retrieve the value of any of these variables, you would simply use the *get()* method: `print x.get()`, for example. To set the value, use the `set()` method: `x.set(2*pi)`. Any time you need to send a variable value into or get a value out of a widget, you will need to use a Tk variable, as we'll see next.

The Menu and Menubutton Widgets

The Menu widget is not displayable on its own; it must contain Menubutton widgets. You can think of the Menu widget as something like a Frame widget that holds things. There are two major kinds of menus: menu bars and option menus. A menu bar looks like the one shown in Figure 18.10.

FIGURE 18.10
A menu bar.

You've seen these in all kinds of Windows applications. Listing 18.9 shows the code for a standard menu bar.

LISTING 18.9 tkmenu.py

```
#!/usr/local/bin/python

from Tkinter import *
import tkMessageBox
import sys

def die():
    sys.exit(0)

def callee():
    print "I was called; few are chosen"

def about():
    tkMessageBox.showinfo("tkmenu","This is tkmenu.py Version 0")

root = Tk()
bar = Menu(root)

filem = Menu(bar)
filem.add_command(label="Open...", command=callee)
filem.add_command(label="New...", command=callee)
filem.add_command(label="Save", command=callee)
filem.add_command(label="Save as...", command=callee)
filem.add_separator()
```

```
25 filem.add_command(label="Exit", command=die)
26
27 helpm = Menu(bar)
28 helpm.add_command(label="Index...", command=callee)
29 helpm.add_separator()
30 helpm.add_command(label="About", command=about)
31
32 bar.add_cascade(label="File", menu=filem)
33 bar.add_cascade(label="Help", menu=helpm)
34
35 root.config(menu=bar)
36 root.mainloop()
37
```

Lines 13 and 14 show a special callback for the `About` menu entry; the MessageBox widget is discussed later in this chapter. Line 19 creates a Menu widget, which is the container for several Menubutton widgets, which are added to it in lines 20 through 25. In line 24, we add a separator—which is just a line, giving some kind of visual separation between the other menu entries and the Exit selection. As you can see, we don't ever call `Menubutton()` directly, but instead, use methods built into the Menu widget; `add_command()` has easier-to-use syntax than `Menubutton()`.

Lines 27 through 30 create and fill another Menu, and in lines 32 and 33, we add the two created menus to the menu bar, which we created in line 17 as a child of the root window. The `add_cascade()` method puts a label into the menu bar and then attaches the specified menu to that label; clicking the label pops up the appropriate "cascade" menu. Figure 18.11 shows what the cascade looks like popped up.

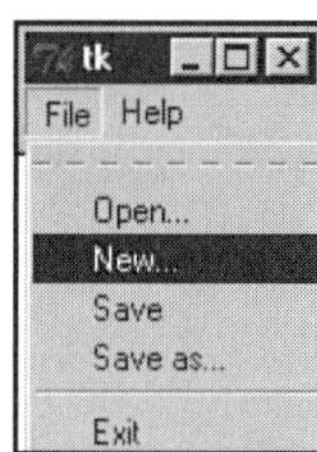

FIGURE 18.11
A cascade menu.

It's also possible for such a cascade menu to have other cascading menus hanging off individual Menubuttons, but I'm not particularly fond of designs like that. Menus are usually touchy things, so the more dependent menus you have, the more opportunity the user has to get annoyed because the menu decides to evaporate underneath the pointer. By the way, the ellipses in the menus (the "..." in "`New...`") means, by convention, that if you choose such an item, a dialog will pop up. An arrow, or some similar indicator, means that another menu will appear if you choose that selection. Menus can include submenus, check boxes, regular selections, and separators.

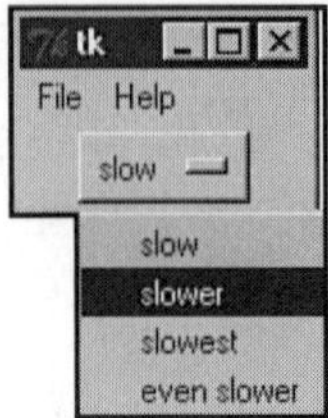

FIGURE 18.12
An option menu.

An option menu, however, is a little more complicated (see Figure 18.12). Although it's not mandatory, it is generally necessary to provide a Tkinter variable to set the label of the option menu. Option menus can appear anywhere within a Tk container widget, not just within a menu bar at the top of the application's main (or a dialog) window. Listing 18.10 shows the code for the option menu shown in Figure 18.12.

LISTING 18.10 `tkoptionmenu.py`

```
#!/usr/local/bin/python

from Tkinter import *
import tkMessageBox
import sys

def die():
    global xx
    print xx.get()
    sys.exit(0)

def callee():
    print "I was called; few are chosen"

def about():
    tkMessageBox.showinfo("tkmenu","This is tkmenu.py Version 0")

root = Tk()
bar = Menu(root)

filem = Menu(bar)
filem.add_command(label="Open...", command=callee)
filem.add_command(label="New...", command=callee)
filem.add_command(label="Save", command=callee)
filem.add_command(label="Save as...", command=callee)
filem.add_separator()
filem.add_command(label="Exit", command=die)

helpm = Menu(bar)
helpm.add_command(label="Index...", command=callee)
helpm.add_separator()
helpm.add_command(label="About", command=about)

```

```
34 bar.add_cascade(label="File", menu=filem)
35 bar.add_cascade(label="Help", menu=helpm)
36
37 root.config(menu=bar)
38 frame = Frame(root)
39 frame.pack()
40 xx = StringVar(frame)
41 xx.set("slow")
42
43 fm = OptionMenu(frame,xx,"slow","slower","slowest","even slower")
44 fm.pack()
45 root.mainloop()
46
```

As you can see, it contains the same menu bar code as Listing 18.9 does, in addition to new code for the option menu. Line 40 sets up a Tkinter string variable, and in line 43 it is used; the second argument to `OptionMenu()` must be a Tkinter variable, and here it is set to `slow`. This provides the default setting for the menu, and thus, the initial label for the option menu. When another choice is selected from the menu, the value of the *xx* variable is also changed. Lines 8 and 9 show how to retrieve that value and print it out.

The MessageBox Widgets

MessageBox widgets are known as "dialogs" because they are windows that pop up from your main application and stay in front of them until the user pushes a default button. This default button, for most dialogs and message boxes, is usually labeled "OK," but it does not have to be. For instance, the "yesno" message box has buttons labeled only "Yes" and "No," but of course, that's logical. The easiest way to use most message boxes, as you can see in Listing 18.10 in line 16, is to use convenience functions. We will see how to use the actual `Messagebox()` call later, so that question boxes can be customized. Note that all the pictures here are of Windows message boxes; the UNIX versions differ quite a bit, notably in using monochrome icons instead of color ones, but their function and usage remains the same.

The Info MessageBox

LISTING 18.11 `tkmessage.info.py`

```
#!/usr/local/bin/python

from Tkinter import *
```

continues

LISTING 18.11 continued

```
 4  import tkMessageBox
 5  import sys
 6
 7  def die(event):
 8      tkMessageBox.showinfo("tkMessageBox","tkMessageBox.showinfo")
 9      sys.exit(0)
10
11  root = Tk()
12  button = Button(root)
13  button["text"] = "Button"
14  button.bind("<Button>",die)
15  button.pack()
16
17  root.mainloop()
```

The first parameter in the convenience function `showinfo()` (line 8) is the title of the box, and the second parameter is the text to be displayed in the box itself. Figure 18.13 shows what it looks like in action.

FIGURE 18.13
An Info MessageBox widget.

Most of the remaining message boxes are just as simple to use.

The Warning MessageBox

The warning box shown in Figure 18.14, for example, is used almost identically.

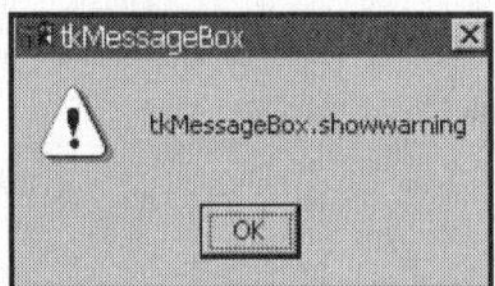

FIGURE 18.14
A Warning MessageBox widget.

Listing 18.12 shows the code.

LISTING 18.12 `tkmessage.warning.py`

```
#!/usr/local/bin/python

from Tkinter import *
import tkMessageBox
```

```
5  import sys
6
7  def die(event):
8      tkMessageBox.showwarning("tkMessageBox","tkMessageBox.showwarning")
9      sys.exit(0)
10
11 root = Tk()
12 button = Button(root)
13 button["text"] = "Button"
14 button.bind("<Button>",die)
15 button.pack()
16
17 root.mainloop()
```

Only line 8 differs at all.

The Error MessageBox

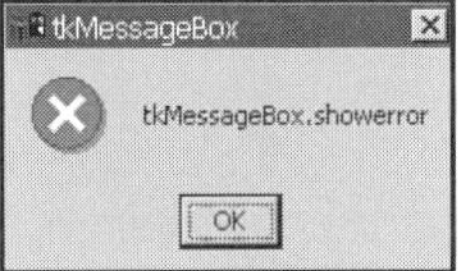

FIGURE 18.15
An Error MessageBox widget.

The same situation holds in the case of the error box (see Figure 18.15), which again has a single button. Listing 18.13 shows how simple it is to use.

LISTING 18.13 tkmessage.error.py

```
#!/usr/local/bin/python

from Tkinter import *
import tkMessageBox
import sys

def die(event):
    tkMessageBox.showerror("tkMessageBox","tkMessageBox.showerror")
    sys.exit(0)

root = Tk()
button = Button(root)
button["text"] = "Button"
button.bind("<Button>",die)
button.pack()

root.mainloop()
```

Again, only line 8 differs. The three boxes we've been talking about have much in common because they have only one button; the user isn't really expected to do anything except acknowledge that they've seen the box. In the case of an error box, it's usually a good idea to exit the application unless you are certain (you the programmer) that there will be no ill effects; that is, the user will not lose any data. In most cases, it's better to exit and annoy the user a little bit than to keep running and run the risk of either destroying or distorting data. The next set of message boxes, however, uses more than one button because the user is expected to make a decision, and the program is expected to respond properly to the user's decision.

The Yesno MessageBox

The message box shown in Figure 18.16, naturally enough, asks a yes–or-no question.

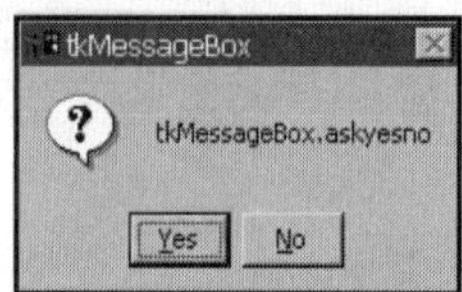

FIGURE 18.16
A Yesno MessageBox widget.

The code is shown below in Listing 18.14.

LISTING 18.14 `tkmessage.askyesno.py`

```
#!/usr/local/bin/python

from Tkinter import *
import tkMessageBox
import sys

def die(event):
    response = tkMessageBox.askyesno("tkMessageBox",
        "tkMessageBox.askyesno")

    print response
    sys.exit(0)

root = Tk()
button = Button(root)
button["text"] = "Button"
button.bind("<Button>",die)
button.pack()

root.mainloop()
```

If you run this code, you will see that pushing the Yes button results in a 1 being printed out; when the No button is pushed, the result is a 0. The `askyesno()` function returns a value indicating which button the user pushed, and that value is collected in line 8. By adding an `if` statement to check the response, you could decide whether to exit the program, based on the user's choice.

The Okcancel MessageBox

In this message box, shown in Figure 18.17, you can see that we also have only two buttons, although they're labeled differently.

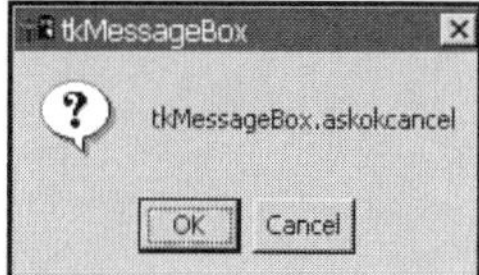

FIGURE 18.17
An Okcancel MessageBox widget.

Listing 18.15 shows the code (and its similarity to the other two-button message box).

LISTING 18.15 `tkmessage.askokcancel.py`

```
#!/usr/local/bin/python

from Tkinter import *
import tkMessageBox
import sys

def die(event):
    r = tkMessageBox.askokcancel("tkMessageBox", \
        "tkMessageBox.askokcancel")
    print r
    sys.exit(0)

root = Tk()
button = Button(root)
button["text"] = "Button"
button.bind("<Button>",die)
button.pack()

root.mainloop()
```

When you run this code, you'll see that the response is the same as the previous box: either 1 or 0.

The Retrycancel MessageBox

This box, shown in Figure 18.18, is another two-button message box and also behaves the same way.

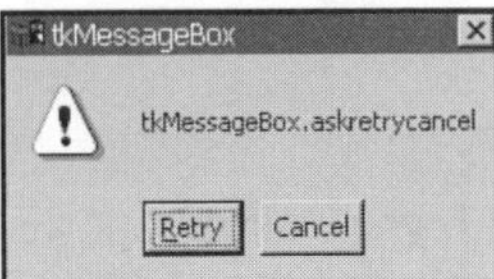

FIGURE 18.18
A Retrycancel MessageBox widget.

Listing 18.16 shows the code.

LISTING 18.16 `tkmessage.askretrycancel.py`

```
#!/usr/local/bin/python

from Tkinter import *
import tkMessageBox
import sys

def die(event):
    r = tkMessageBox.askretrycancel("tkMessageBox", \
        "tkMessageBox.askretrycancel")
    print r
    sys.exit(0)

root = Tk()
button = Button(root)
button["text"] = "Button"
button.bind("<Button>",die)
button.pack()

root.mainloop()
```

The usage for all three two-button convenience functions is the same: Put up a standard question dialog so that the user can answer a simple question one of two (limited) ways. These dialogs all return 0 or 1, which means that you should remember which button returns which value: 0 means no, cancel, or ignore, and 1 indicates yes, OK, or retry.

The Question MessageBox

For a three-button message box, as shown in Figure 18.19, we must resort to calling the `Message()` method directly; there are no convenience functions for message boxes with more than two buttons. Notice that here we use the keyword style of setting options.

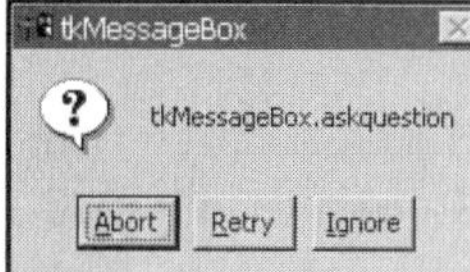

FIGURE 18.19
A Question MessageBox widget.

Listing 18.17 shows the code.

LISTING 18.17 `tkmessage.askquestion.py`

```
 1 #!/usr/local/bin/python
 2
 3 from Tkinter import *
 4 import tkMessageBox
 5 import sys
 6
 7 def die(event):
 8     x = tkMessageBox.Message(root,type=tkMessageBox.ABORTRETRYIGNORE,
 9         icon=tkMessageBox.QUESTION,
10         title="tkMessageBox",
11         message="tkMessageBox.askquestion")
12     r = x.show()
13     tkMessageBox.showinfo("Reply", r )
14     sys.exit(0)
15
16 root = Tk()
17 button = Button(root)
18 button["text"] = "Button"
19 button.bind("<Button>",die)
20 button.pack()
21
22 root.mainloop()
```

Lines 8 through 11 show the keyword arguments; we specify the type (three buttons) and the icon (the `QUESTION` icon) using special constants defined in the `tkMessageBox` module. The title and the message, although passed as keyword options, are ordinary strings, the same as we would have used if there were a convenience function. Because no convenience function is available, what we have to do is create the message box (`x = tkMessageBox.Message()`) and then call the `x.show()` method. We retrieve the value returned by `show()` in line 12 and then use the `showinfo()` convenience function to display the button pressed by the user. When you run this program, notice that `r` is a string; this is a consequence of not using a convenience function.

You can use this same style for all the message boxes; convenience functions are just that—merely convenient, not necessary.

Summary

We've talked about various kinds of basic `Tkinter` widgets, from the Button widget to the different kinds of message boxes. In the next hour, we'll discuss more Tkinter widgets (from Radiobuttons to Text), put together a complete application, and demonstrate Toplevel widgets.

Workshop

Q&A

Q Why do Windows, X Windows, and Mac widgets all look so different?

A Originally, Windows and X Windows widgets looked fairly similar because they evolved from a common ancestor developed by HP. On X Windows, the HP widgets transformed in a relatively straightforward way into Motif widgets. Windows widgets, influenced by Mac widgets (which grew out of similar objects developed at Xerox's Palo Alto Research labs), mutated into Windows classes, which changed appearance yet again in the transition from Windows 3.1 to Windows 95. The developers of Tk/TCL originally used widgets that looked the same on all three platforms, but recently they have changed to using the native widget sets for the three differing platforms. The reason for the change, I suspect, is that the portable widgets looked so clunky.

Q One kind of widget I see a lot of on Windows is a list combined with a scrollbar. What are these, and are they available in Tkinter?

A These are usually called combo boxes, and they are not available in Tkinter itself. However, Greg McFarlane, in Australia, has put together an extremely nice package called "Python Megawidgets," which does include combo boxes; it can be found at `http://www.dscpl.com.au/pmw/`. Greg says, "It consists of a set of base classes and a library of flexible and extensible megawidgets built on this foundation. These megawidgets include notebooks, comboboxes, selection widgets, paned widgets, scrolled widgets, dialog windows, etc." They're also written in pure Python, with no C extensions needed (this is important if you don't have a C compiler on your machine).

Quiz

1. What kind of widget operates like a toggle switch?
    a. Button
    b. List

c. Check box

d. Entry

2. What's the difference between menu bars and option menus?

   a. Menu bars run across the whole top of the application's main window; option menus are in a bar at the bottom of the window.

   b. Menu bar menus pull down; option menus pull sideways.

   c. Option menus can appear anywhere in a window, whereas menu bars have to be at the top.

   d. Only the names are different; they are otherwise the same.

Answers

1. c, check box widgets operate like toggle switches; they only have two states: checked and unchecked.
2. c, option menus can be used anywhere in a window; menu bars run across the top.

Exercises

Take out Alien Abduction Life Insurance, in case you get kidnapped by the Heechee. Make Scott Meyers the beneficiary. Get abducted. Try to file a claim.

Research the history of GUI programming; an excellent starting point is Michael S. Hoffman's interesting Web page, "The Unix GUI Manifesto," to be found at `http://www.cybtrans.com/infostrc/unixgui.htm`.

HOUR 19

Tk Widgets II

The Trans Am was ten, with the dents and glitches to prove it,
but it still hugged corners like a python.

—Sara Paretsky, in Hard Time

In the last hour, we started learning about many kinds of basic Tkinter widgets. This hour, we continue the discussion. At the end of the hour, you will be able to

- Identify more basic widgets
- Combine more than one widget into small applications
- Write a complete application, tkeditor

The Radio Button Widget

I doubt if many of you are old enough to remember old-style pushbuttons on car radios, but they are the direct ancestor of radio button widgets. Car radio buttons were entirely mechanical in nature (as anyone who has disassembled one can tell you); push one in, and another one that had been pushed in popped out—with a distinctive "thock" sound. Widget radio buttons (see Figure 19.1) are "wired" the same way, which is why you never have a single radio button—"a lone baboon is a dead baboon," as they say in primatology. UNIX radio buttons are set up the same way, but they have diamond-shaped buttons (see Figure 19.2).

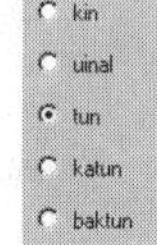

FIGURE 19.1
Radio buttons.

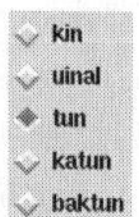

FIGURE 19.2
UNIX radio buttons.

Even on Windows, however, you can specify that the radio buttons should take on a normal button-like appearance (see Figure 19.3).

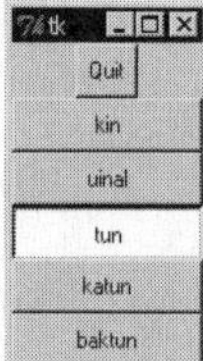

FIGURE 19.3
Un-radio button radio buttons.

In the code shown in Listing 19.1, you can see that running it without an argument gives you the default, round (or diamond) radio buttons, whereas giving the program any command-line argument at all produces expanded regular buttons.

LISTING 19.1 `tkradiobutton.py`

```
#!/usr/local/bin/python

from Tkinter import *
import sys

def die(event):
    global v, periods
    print periods[v.get()][0]
    sys.exit(0)
```

```
10
11  root = Tk()
12  button = Button(root)
13  button["text"] = "Quit"
14  button.bind("<Button>",die)
15  button.pack()
16
17  v = IntVar()
18  v.set(2)
19
20  periods = [
21      ("kin", 0),
22      ("uinal", 1),
23      ("tun", 2),
24      ("katun", 3),
25      ("baktun", 4),
26  ]
27
28  if len(sys.argv) > 1:
29      indicator = 0
30      filler=X
31      expander=1
32  else:
33      indicator = 1
34      filler=None
35      expander=0
36  for t, m in periods :
37    b = Radiobutton(root, text=t, variable=v, value=m, \
38          indicatoron=indicator)
39      if indicator == 1 :
40          b.pack(anchor=W)
41      else :
42          b.pack(expand=expander,fill=filler)
43
44  root.mainloop()
```


In lines 17 and 18, we're using a Tk variable; this time, it's an integer. There is no reason at all, however, that we could not have used a `StringVar()` call and specified our list of period tuples like this: `("kin", "kin"), ("uinal", "uinal")`. We could then have printed the value as a string, using `v.get()`, or used the `showinfo()` convenience function to display the chosen value in a message box.

The Scale Widget

Scale widgets can be displayed in either horizontal style (see Figure 19.4 or vertical style (see Figure 19.5).

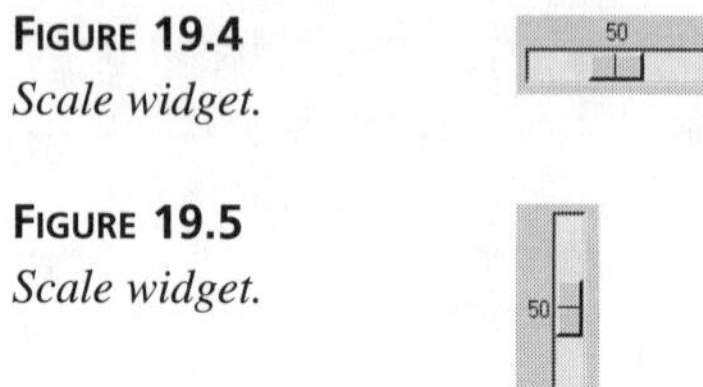

FIGURE 19.4
Scale widget.

FIGURE 19.5
Scale widget.

They are used whenever you want users to be able to select a value from a continuous range in specific boundaries. The ones shown here use the default range, 0 through 100 (giving 101 discrete values). Listing 19.2 shows how to code both styles, with the vertical version using a different range:

LISTING 19.2 `tkscale.py`

```
#!/usr/local/bin/python

from Tkinter import *
import sys
import string

def die(event):
    sys.exit(0)

def reader(s):
    f = string.atoi(s)
    f = f - 32
    c = f/9.
    c = c * 5.
    print "%s degrees F = %f degrees C" % (s, c)

root = Tk()
button = Button(root)
button["text"] = "Quit"
button.bind("<Button>",die)
button.pack()

scale1 = Scale(root, orient=HORIZONTAL)
scale1.pack()
scale2 = Scale(root, orient=VERTICAL,from_=-40,to=212,command=reader)
scale2.pack()

root.mainloop()
```

If you run this program, you'll see that the vertical scale widget has been set up to convert from degrees Fahrenheit to degrees Celsius (I always *think* Centigrade, myself, because that's what it was called when I learned it, but names have changed). You'll also notice that -40 is the same temperature in both scales; this is called a *gosh* number, because when you learn about it, you say, "gosh." There doesn't seem to be a lot else to say, does there?

Printing information to `stdout` the way we do in Listing 19.2 isn't the most elegant way to provide answers to users' questions in a GUI, however, so let's modify `tkscale.py` to update a couple of labels in the callback; this will keep the user interface located all in one window. While we're at it, let's get rid of the extra scale widget and title the window appropriately. Listing 19.3 shows our modified code.

LISTING 19.3 `tkscale2.py`

```
#!/usr/local/bin/python

from Tkinter import *
import sys
import string

def die(event):
    sys.exit(0)

def reader(s):
    global label
    f = string.atoi(s)
    f = f - 32
    c = f/9.
    c = c * 5.
    flabel["text"] = "Degrees Fahrenheit:  %s" % (s)
    label["text"] = "Degrees Celsius:  %d" % (int(c))

root = Tk()
button = Button(root,width=25)
button["text"] = "Quit"
button.bind("<Button>",die)
button.pack()

flabel = Label(root,text="Degrees Fahrenheit:")
flabel.pack(anchor=W)
scale2 = Scale(root, orient=VERTICAL,from_=-40,to=212,command=reader)
scale2.pack()
label = Label(root,text="Degrees Celsius:")
label.pack(anchor=W)

root.title("Fahrenheit to Celsius")

root.mainloop()

```

Figure 19.6 shows how the whole application looks when running.

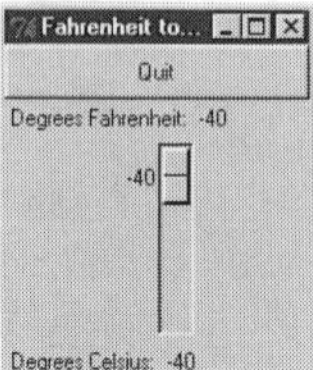

FIGURE 19.6
tkscale2.py.

The Text, Scrollbar, and ScrolledText Widgets

Text widgets (see Figure 19.7) are like multiline entry widgets. They also come with a full complement of *bindings*—that is, actions bound to mouse clicks and keypresses. Copying a block of highlighted text is bound to the appropriate keystroke on the current platform (Ctrl+C on Windows), as is cutting and pasting, and so on. Listing 19.4 shows minimal code to get a text widget running.

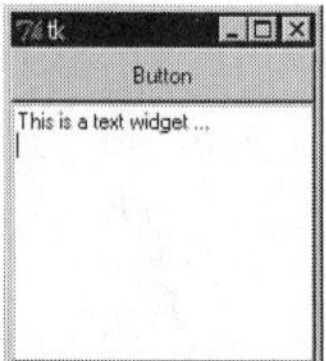

FIGURE 19.7
Text widget.

LISTING 19.4 `tktext.py`

```
#!/usr/local/bin/python

from Tkinter import *
import sys

def die(event):
    sys.exit(0)

root = Tk()
f = Frame(root)
f.pack(expand=1, fill=BOTH)
button = Button(f,width=25)
button["text"] = "Button"
button.bind("<Button>",die)
button.pack()
t = Text(f,width=25,height=10,relief=RAISED,bd=2)
t.pack(side=LEFT, fill=BOTH, expand=1)
```

```
18
19  root.mainloop()
20
```

In line 16, the option keyword `bd` is shorthand for borderwidth. A few (not many) option keywords do have shorthand forms.

Scrollbars

Scrollbars are used to move things such as text widgets up and down (see Figure 19.8). You can orient them horizontally, but very little support is built into Tkinter for them. Most scrollbars are used in conjunction with the text widget to give a ScrolledText widget, with the Canvas widget to provide scrolling of drawings, and with the FileDialog widget, which enables users to scroll sideways in the native Windows version and up and down in the pure Tkinter version.

FIGURE 19.8
Scrollbar.

Rather than provide code to display a scrollbar all by itself, which is not useful, Listing 19.5 shows you how to use the ScrolledText widget (a *composite* widget—that is, made up of two or more basic widgets) in a simple way.

LISTING 19.5 `tkscrollbar.py`

```
#!/usr/local/bin/python

from Tkinter import *
from ScrolledText import *
import sys

def die(event):
    sys.exit(0)
```

continues

LISTING 19.5 continued

```

root = Tk()
f = Frame(root)
f.pack(expand=1, fill=BOTH)
button = Button(f,width=25)
button["text"] = "Quit"
button.bind("<Button>",die)
button.pack()

st = ScrolledText(f,background="white")
st.pack()

root.mainloop()

```

These few lines of code, although not providing a way to save the text that you enter into the widget, accomplish in very little space what it used to take hundreds of lines of C code to do (and really, it still does; each line of Python/Tkinter code here calls into a full-scale widget written in C). Widgets are pretty smart objects, and you can take advantage of that while freeing yourself from having to worry about low-level details (such as where to position the cursor, how and where to draw the letter Q, and so on); this is called *abstraction*, and it is one of the best reasons to use a high-level language such as Python. Running `tkscrollbar.py` gives us the ScrolledText widget shown in Figure 19.9.

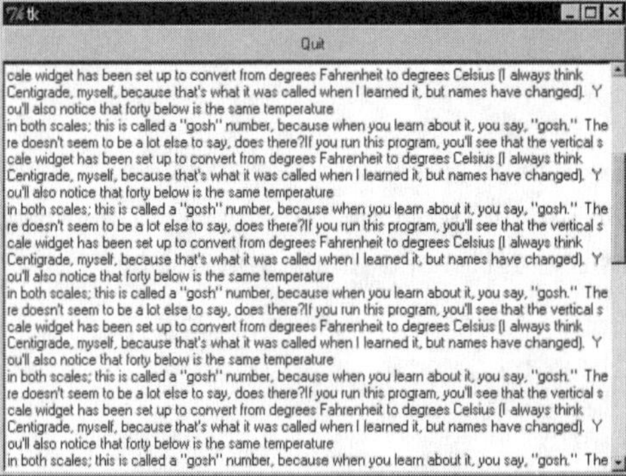

FIGURE 19.9
A ScrolledText widget.

In the interests of completeness, let's add a way to save the file that we create in our ScrolledText widget. This means that we'll have to add a menu bar, and while we're at it, we can go ahead and add an About box, too. Only one part is new here, and that is the way to save and open files. Listing 19.6 shows the complete code for our tkeditor application.

LISTING 19.6 `tkeditor.py`

```
#!/usr/local/bin/python

from Tkinter import *
from ScrolledText import *
import tkMessageBox
from tkFileDialog import *
import fileinput

st = None

def die():
    sys.exit(0)

def openfile():
    global st
    pl = END
    oname = askopenfilename(filetypes=[("Python files", "*.py")])
    if oname:
        for line in fileinput.input(oname):
            st.insert(pl,line)

def savefile():
    sname = asksaveasfilename()
    if sname:
        ofp = open(sname,"w")
        ofp.write(st.get(1.0,END))
        ofp.flush()
        ofp.close()

def about():
    tkMessageBox.showinfo("Tkeditor", "Simple tkeditor Version 0\n"
        "Written 1999\n"
        "For Teach Yourself Python in 24 Hours")


if __name__ == "__main__":
    global st
    root = Tk()
    bar = Menu(root)

    filem = Menu(bar)
    filem.add_command(label="Open...", command=openfile)
    filem.add_command(label="Save as...", command=savefile)
    filem.add_separator()
    filem.add_command(label="Exit", command=die)

    helpm = Menu(bar)
    helpm.add_command(label="About", command=about)
```

continues

LISTING 19.6 continued

```
    bar.add_cascade(label="File", menu=filem)
    bar.add_cascade(label="Help", menu=helpm)
    root.config(menu=bar)

    f = Frame(root,width=512)
    f.pack(expand=1, fill=BOTH)

    st = ScrolledText(f,background="white")
    st.pack(side=LEFT, fill=BOTH, expand=1)
    root.mainloop()
```

Figure 19.10 shows `tkeditor.py` running (and containing its own code) and its associated file dialog as displayed by the `openfile()` callback.

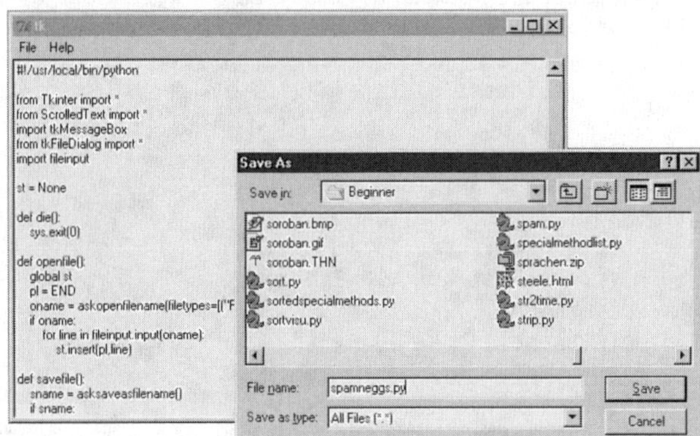

FIGURE 19.10
Running `tkeditor.py`.

Listing 19.5 has 59 lines of code, some of them blank. Just a few years ago, obtaining the same level of functionality in a program would have required hundreds of lines of code, and a few years before that, thousands.

There are many features left to implement, but none of them are hard to do. For instance, it's entirely possible to embed pictures into your documents; you would have to modify the way in which files are saved, but even that wouldn't be difficult (think `pickle`). A list of possible features you might want to implement can be found in the exercises at the end of this chapter.

The Toplevel Widget

Toplevel widgets are widgets that act just like main windows of an application; you could, for example, add a `New ...` menu entry to `tkeditor.py` that would open up a completely new editor window, which would look exactly like the original window (later, we'll add this feature). `IDLE` does this; selecting `New` … from the menu opens a new window with a new Python interpreter already running inside it. Listing 19.7 shows one simple way to have multiple Toplevel widgets.

LISTING 19.7 `tktoplevel.py`

```
#!/usr/local/bin/python

from Tkinter import *
import sys

wl = []

def die():
    print "You created %d new toplevel widgets" % (len(wl))
    sys.exit(0)

def newwin():
    global root
    wl.append (Toplevel(root))

root = Tk()
bar = Menu(root)
filem = Menu(bar)
filem.add_command(label="New...", command=newwin)
filem.add_separator()
filem.add_command(label="Exit", command=die)

bar.add_cascade(label="File", menu=filem)
root.config(menu=bar)
root.mainloop()

```


In Figure 19.11, you can see how this works in practice; I selected `New` … four times.

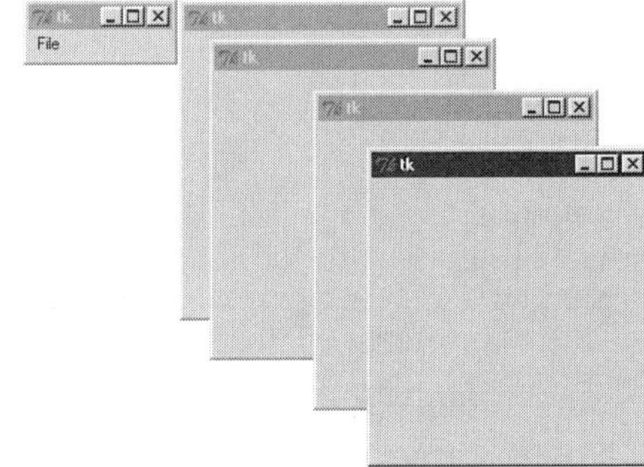

FIGURE 19.11
Multiple Toplevel widgets from `tktoplevel.py`.

Naturally, it doesn't do us much good to have multiple toplevel windows doing nothing but occupying space; it would be much more valuable to have the extra windows do something. If we combine our tkeditor with Toplevel widgets, we can edit one file and select `New...` from the menu to create more edit windows. There are several ways to do this, but the most elegant is to create a class that instantiates an editor window for us. If we do that, not only do we reduce the size of the main part of our program to just a few lines, but we can import the module and instantiate an editor any time we need one in any kind of Tkinter program at all. Listing 19.8 shows the code, which includes an editor class (beginning in line 20) with its associated methods and three functions, which don't need to be part of the class (`die()`, line 12; `about()`, line 15; and `neweditor()`, line 71).

LISTING 19.8 `multi-editor.py`

```
1  #!/usr/local/bin/python
2
3  from Tkinter import *
4  from ScrolledText import *
5  import tkMessageBox
6  from tkFileDialog import *
7  import fileinput
8
9  tl = []
10 root = None
11
12 def die():
13     sys.exit(0)
14
15 def about():
16     tkMessageBox.showinfo("Tkeditor", "Simple tkeditor Version 1\n"
17         "Written 1999\n"
18         "For Teach Yourself Python in 24 Hours")
19
20 class editor:
21     def __init__(self, rt):
22         if rt == None:
23             self.t = Tk()
24         else:
25             self.t = Toplevel(rt)
26         self.t.title("Tkeditor %d" % len(tl))
27         self.bar = Menu(rt)
28
29         self.filem = Menu(self.bar)
30         self.filem.add_command(label="Open...", command=self.openfile)
31         self.filem.add_command(label="New...", command=neweditor)
32         self.filem.add_command(label="Save as...", \
33             command=self.savefile)
34         self.filem.add_command(label="Close", command=self.close)
35         self.filem.add_separator()
```

```
36          self.filem.add_command(label="Exit", command=die)
37
38          self.helpm = Menu(self.bar)
39          self.helpm.add_command(label="About", command=about)
40
41          self.bar.add_cascade(label="File", menu=self.filem)
42          self.bar.add_cascade(label="Help", menu=self.helpm)
43          self.t.config(menu=self.bar)
44
45          self.f = Frame(self.t,width=512)
46          self.f.pack(expand=1, fill=BOTH)
47
48          self.st = ScrolledText(self.f,background="white")
49          self.st.pack(side=LEFT, fill=BOTH, expand=1)
50
51      def close(self):
52          self.t.destroy()
53
54      def openfile(self):
55          pl = END
56          oname = askopenfilename(filetypes=[("Python files", "*.py")])
57          if oname:
58              for line in fileinput.input(oname):
59                  self.st.insert(pl,line)
60              self.t.title(oname)
61
62      def savefile(self):
63          sname = asksaveasfilename()
64          if sname:
65              ofp = open(sname,"w")
66              ofp.write(self.st.get(1.0,END))
67              ofp.flush()
68              ofp.close()
69              self.t.title(sname)
70
71  def neweditor():
72      global root
73      tl.append(editor(root))
74
75  if __name__ == "__main__":
76      root = None
77      tl.append(editor(root))
78      root = tl[0].t
79      root.mainloop()
```


You can also see that whenever we're editing a file or have saved a file, we retitle the current editor window; this is done in lines 60 and 69, using the Toplevel widget's `title()` method. Toplevel widgets have many more useful functions; the Tkinter documentation lists them all.

Again, notice that our multiple-window editor has only 79 lines. Sometime around 1984, I spent a few weeks trying to write an editor. I quit at around 10,000 lines or so because I couldn't keep track of the entire project in my head; there was no abstraction going on, so it's no wonder I got lost. This little editor application, put together in less than a day, is far more powerful than what I had written. (To be fair, the 1984 editor was a special-purpose editor, intended for editing nodes and connections in a directed graph system; but I did get lost in the actual editing part, which could be replaced almost entirely by these 79 lines of Python.) Figure 19.12 shows our multi-editor application running.

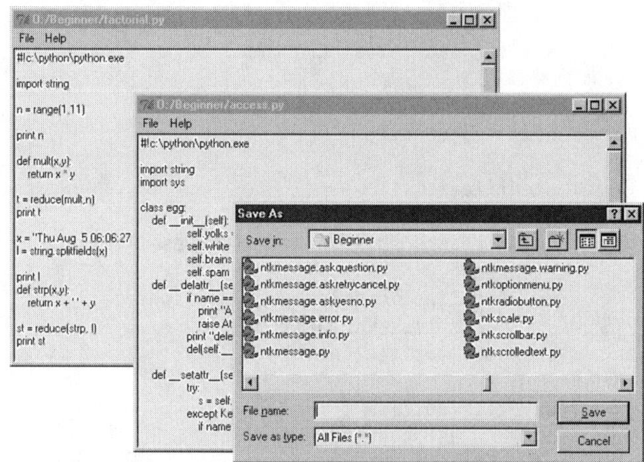

FIGURE 19.12
The multiple-window editor running.

This concludes our discussion of the many kinds of basic Tkinter widgets.

Summary

We've covered the remaining basic Tkinter widgets and have written two programs (`tkscale2.py` and `multi-editor.py`), one of which (`multi-editor.py`) is remarkably useful for so few lines of code. In the next chapter, we cover Tk graphics, using the Canvas widget. Later, we will write a program to calculate Mandelbrot sets and display them in a Canvas widget.

Q&A

Q On Windows machines, I notice that a common look for larger applications is that of a single large window that contains many smaller windows, such as editors. Is there any support for this in Tkinter?

A You mean MDI, or Multiple Document Interface, by Microsoft. There really isn't anything like that available in Tkinter. Perhaps you should write some support classes? If I were doing this, I would start with Greg McFarlane's excellent PMW library, described in the previous hour.

Q I ran `multi-editor.py` on my Linux box, and the file open/save dialogs are as ugly as a 1972 Thunderbird. Why do I have to put up with this?

A You don't; you could write your own. You could wait until Tk/TCL starts using the KDE or GNOME toolkits for their implementation of the basic widgets. If you know some C or C++ programming, you could contribute to the effort to make Tk/TCL widgets bearable to look at. A good place to start for this is at the K Desktop Environment's home page, at `http://kde.fnet.pl/` or at the GNOME Developer's site, at `http://developer.gnome.org/`.

Workshop

Quiz

1. What's the difference between the root window and Toplevel widgets?
    a. The root window can't contain any other widgets.
    b. The Toplevel widget can contain only a limited set of child widgets.
    c. Nothing.
    d. The root window doesn't have a parent, but Toplevel widgets use the root window as their parent.
2. Why are some of the callbacks in `multi-editor.py` class methods instead of functions?
    a. Functions can't be used as callbacks, only methods.
    b. If functions were used, we'd never know which window called us.
    c. It seemed like a good idea at the time.
    d. Methods are faster.

Answers

1. d. There's always only one root window in a Tkinter application; it has no parent (`Tk()`) and the Toplevel widgets use the created root window as their parent.
2. b. Methods belong to classes. Therefore, we can store the proper Text widget in the class, and the called method always knows the Text widget it's supposed to update.

Exercises

A pleasant way to learn a little about gosh numbers is to read Fred Pohl's *Heechee* books, beginning with *Gateway*. There are five books altogether:

1. *Gateway*
2. *Beyond the Blue Event Horizon*
3. *Heechee Rendezvous*
4. *Annals of the Heechee*
5. *The Gateway Trip*

I won't tell you in which book gosh numbers first appear. If you want to start in strict chronological order, the first story is "The Merchants of Venus," in *The Gateway Trip* (a collection of stories).

There is a small bug in our implementation of `tkeditor.py` and `multi-editor.py`: When a file is saved, an additional blank line may appear at the end of the saved version. Find the bug and fix it.

Add more features to `tkeditor.py`. Here is the beginning of a list; you can add to it as you see fit:

- Add command-line parsing so that users can specify filenames at startup.
- Add the capability to embed pictures into the text widget.
- Fix the `Save as...` command to save pictures, too.
- Add a `Save` command.
- Add a way to choose fonts.
- Add a way to color different areas of text.
- Figure out what it would take to turn `tkeditor.py` or `multi-editor.py` into a full-featured editor for HTML documents.
- Document the finished editor.
- Give your code away.
- Sit back and bask in the benefits of fame and fortune.

HOUR 20

Tk Graphics I

Beware of programmers who carry screwdrivers.

—Constantinos A. Kotsokalis

In the previous two hours, we learned about many kinds of basic Tkinter widgets. In this hour, we continue the discussion for one section and then move into graphics. At the end of the hour, you will be able to

- Use new kinds of menus (pop-up and built-to-order)
- Combine a list box and scrollbar into one useful unit
- Use prebuilt graphical images in Tk widgets
- Understand the different kinds of objects in Canvas widgets

New Menus

In Hour 18, we learned about Menu widgets, which are containers for Menubutton widgets. However, we learned only about two very standard types: the menu bar (at the top of most applications) and the option menu (which can appear anywhere within an application's window). Before we move on to graphics, we need to cover the following:

- Pop-up menus, which pop up from a specific mouse click—usually the right button
- Built-to-order menus, or menus built "on-the-fly"

Plenty of applications use such pop-up menus. The code in Listing 20.1 shows how to build one.

LISTING 20.1 tkpopup.py

```
#!/usr/local/bin/python

from Tkinter import *
import string
import sys

def die(event=None):
    sys.exit(0)

def getxy(something):
    s = something.geometry()
    return map(int, string.splitfields(s[1+string.find(s,"+"):],'+'))

def new_file(event=None):
    print "Opening new file"

def open_file(event=None):
    print "Opening existing file"

def activate_menu(event=None):
    x, y = getxy(root)
    menu.tk_popup(x+event.x, y+event.y)

root = Tk()
root.canvas = Canvas(root, height=100, width=100)
root.canvas.pack()
menu = Menu(root)
menu.add_command(label="New...", underline=0, command=new_file)
menu.add_command(label="Open...", underline=0, command=open_file)
menu.add_separator()
menu.add_command(label="Exit...", underline=0, command=die)
menu['tearoff'] = 0

root.canvas.bind("<Button-3>", activate_menu)

root.mainloop()
```

Only one line here really needs explanation because you've seen nearly everything else before. In line 12, you see about the nearest thing to obfuscated code that I normally write. We need in this callback to obtain the geometry of the main window (root), and that is returned by the call to `s = something.geometry()` in line 11; this method returns a string in the format "`100x100+64+64`", the standard geometry string used under X Windows. The `100x100` represents the width and height of the window—in this case, 100 by 100 pixels. The `+64+64` represents the x location and y location, again in pixels, from the left and top edges of the screen. Because we have a string, we need to decode parts of it into numbers. When we actually pop up the menu, in line 22, all we need from the geometry string is the *x* and *y* locations, so it's more efficient to perform as much processing as possible on one line. The `string.find()` call searches our returned string for the first occurrence of a + sign; we add 1 to that (because the return value is the position of the found +) and use the result to slice the string from the digit after the + to the end. That would give us "64+64", for example, and we then split that into a list of strings, again using the +, so our return value from the `string.splitfields()` call is going to be "['64','64']". We then pass our list of strings to the `map()` call, which converts each string to an int using the `int()` call. Finally, the `return` takes the list of integers and returns them to the caller, which is looking for the *x* and *y* locations; these are added with the appropriate `event.x` and `event.y` values to obtain the screen coordinates of the mouse click (not the root window coordinates). The call to `menu.tk_popup()` requires screen coordinates.

Normally, pop-up menus are not equipped with `Exit…` functions; that is more properly supplied by the standard menu bar. For such a small program as this demonstration, however, it's OK; just remember that it's easy to slip and select the wrong function on pop-up menus. Figure 20.1 shows the program running.

FIGURE 20.1
A pop-up menu from `tkpopup.py`.

A useful technique is to be able to build menus on-the-fly; that is, instead of hard-coding what goes into a menu, you peer around and see what should go into the menu based on prior actions by the user. The hardest part of this is setting up your callbacks, and this provides the context for the return of `lambda` (anonymous functions). The use of the `lambda` statement strikes me as peculiarly appropriate when used to build callbacks for anonymous menus. Listing 20.2 shows how to build menus on-the-fly, how to build cascading menus, and—as a bonus—how to use prebuilt graphics in your program.

LISTING 20.2 tkcascadingmenu.py

```
#!/usr/local/bin/python

from Tkinter import *
import os
import string

img = None

def die():
    sys.exit(0)

def listgifs(d="."):
    l = os.listdir(d)
    rl = []
    for i in l:
        t = string.lower(i)
        g = string.rfind(t,".gif")
        if g >= 0:
            rl.append(i)
    if len(rl)<1:
        rl = None
    else:
        rl.sort()
    return rl

def setimage(s):
    global elements
    global lb
    global img
    if s in elements:
        img = PhotoImage(file=s)
        lb["image"] = img

def main():
    global elements
    global lb
    elements = listgifs()
    if not elements:
        print "No gifs"
    n = len(elements)
    nm = n / 10
    no = n % 10
    if no:
        nm = nm + 1
    print "For %d files, I'll make %d menus" % ( n, nm )
    root = Tk()
    mb = Menu(root)
    cb = Menu(mb)
    cb.add_command(label="Exit",command=die)

```

```
51      gm = Menu(mb)
52      for i in range(nm):
53          tm = Menu(gm)
54          if i == nm - 1 and no != 0:
55              lim = no
56          else:
57              lim = 10
58          for j in range(lim):
59              ne = (10 * i) + j
60              tm.add_command(label=elements≠,
61                  command=lambda m=elements≠:setimage(m))
62          gm.add_cascade(label="List gifs %d" % (i),menu=tm)
63
64      mb.add_cascade(label="File", menu=cb)
65      mb.add_cascade(label="Gifs", menu=gm)
66
67      lb = Label(root,text="No gif")
68      lb.pack()
69      root.config(menu=mb)
70      root.mainloop()
71
72  if __name__ == "__main__":
73      main()
```

The `listgifs()` function in lines 12–25 returns a sorted list of all the GIF files in the current directory by making use of the `os.listdir()` method. Because Python lacks a non-case-sensitive string-compare function, we roll our own by using `string.lower()` on every item in the list we get back from `listdir()` and comparing the lowercase result with the suffix we're looking for. Alternatively, you could use the `fnmatch` module, which provides facilities for locating files in a platform-dependent way. For example, you could code the `listgifs()` function as shown in Listing 20.3.

LISTING 20.3 `listgifs()` Using the `fnmatch` Module

```

def listgifs(d="."):
    l = os.listdir(d)
    rl = []
    for i in l:
        if fnmatch.fnmatch(i,"*.gif"):
            rl.append(i)
    if len(rl)<1:
        rl = None
    else:
        rl.sort()
    return rl

```

The second parameter to `fnmatch()` is a "shell wildcard" or "shell expression," common on UNIX systems. DOS provides limited ("challenged" might be a better word) for wildcards, but it's not the same. Table 20.1 explains the special characters usable in an `fnmatch()` pattern.

TABLE 20.1 UNIX-Style Shell Wildcards

Pattern	*Matches*
*	0 or more occurrences of any character.
?	Any single character.
`[abc]`	Any one of the characters listed inside the [].
`[a-z]` or `[0-9]`	The - is shorthand so you don't have to list every single character between the start and stop characters.
`[!`*`seq`*`]`	Any character that does not occur in `seq`.

GIF files, or Graphic Interchange Format pictures, were originally intended only as a picture format for CompuServe; it is now the most common graphics format on the Internet. Much controversy has arisen regarding its use, mainly because of the rather inexplicable behavior of Unisys, owners of the patent on the Lempel-Ziv-Welch (LZW) compression method used to keep the size of the files to a minimum. See the exercises to find out more about GIF and the controversy; the bottom line is that programs that read and render the format have no strings attached, but those that write it using compression have complicated conditions (and royalty fees) imposed upon the authors. Tkinter does not provide a `write()` method for GIF files.

The `setimage()` function in lines 26–32 is the function that actually lets us use GIF files; we're using the `PhotoImage()` function that's built in to Tkinter to read the file and produce an image that's understood by all Tkinter widgets. The `elements` variable is simply a list of all the GIF files found in the current directory, which is made using `listgifs()`. The `lb` variable holds a Label widget. There's a gotcha here; the `img` variable that holds the image must be a global; if it's not, when the `setimage()` function ends, the variable evaporates, and the widget that uses the image throws it away.

This program also demonstrates an alternative coding style; C programs always have a `main()` function, which is where the program starts when it is executed. The technique shown here imitates that C style, even though Python doesn't follow that convention. The `if __name__ == "__main__":` line is Python's convention, and here it merely calls the `main()` function. I don't ordinarily use this style (believing that Python is not C, or PINC for short), but it's a technique you will encounter and should know the history of.

In lines 37–50, we build our GIF list, assign it to a global variable, decide how many cascaded menus to build, and construct the File menu. Lines 51–63 show the basic method of constructing cascading menus: Create a Menu widget, add 10 GIF filenames as commands, and then call `add_cascade()` to add a submenu to the containing Menu widget. After completion of the loop, we add our menus to the menu bar in lines 64 and 65. The tricky part appears in lines 60 and 61, where we build a command Menubutton widget and use `lambda` to make our callback.

What we want to have happen in the callback is for the name the user selected on the menu to be passed in so that it can be looked up in the list of GIF files. It would be nice if the Menubutton widgets were smart enough to keep track of the text when they were selected, but they're not; therefore, we must. We cannot use `setimage()` directly, then, because there is no way to pass in the name; the command callback cannot have any parameters. The trouble with `lambda`, however, is that it cannot use assignments. We must use the default argument trick, which we can see if we examine only the `lambda` statement itself.

```
lambda m=elements≠:setimage(m)
```

When we build the submenus, we know what the name of the image is; that's `elements-`. To tell `lambda` what that name is, we must pass it in when we know it (at the time of construction) by using `m=elements≠—`; `m` is replaced by the actual name of the file. Later, when the callback is activated, `setimage()` is called with the `m` variable, which, because of the default argument, is the appropriate filename as determined when we built the menu. From here on out, it's simple. Figure 20.2 shows `tkcascadingmenu.py` running.

FIGURE 20.2
Running `tkcascadingmenu.py`.

The `PhotoImage()` function, by the way, understands only two formats: GIF and PPM. Few people on Windows would have PPM files lying around, but those on Linux/UNIX might very well have; an enhancement here would be to add support in the `listgifs()` function to list PPM files in addition to GIF (or it would be an enhancement if you had any PPM files).

Portable Pixmap (PPM) format was developed a few years ago by Jeff Poskanzer. It was intended to be the absolute lowest common denominator for color graphics files and to be the natural successor to his PBM format (Portable Bitmap) for single-color images. It's not really supposed to be used as a format for storing files (although it sometimes is) because it's very fat, using no compression at all. See the exercises for more information.

Any menu can have submenus, and submenus can have submenus, too. Ordinarily, it's not a good idea to depend on this style of menu for your user interfaces, but in some circumstances it can serve a useful purpose, primarily to reduce the size of menus. People get irritated when there's too much stuff on a menu, especially if they can't see the top and/or bottom entries, which can happen if you plan and implement your menus on a 1280×1024 display (or 1600×1280 like a friend of mine does; he claims no one else ever looks at his screen long enough to figure out he's not working. If there's a larger resolution, you can bet he'll use that one, too) and they're running them on 640×480.

Scrolling a Listbox Widget

Scrolled Listbox widgets are not the same as combo boxes that you see on many Windows applications; those are editable and usually are only one line in height. Scrolled Listboxes, on the other hand, are list boxes of a specified size that have a scrollbar attached so that you can use the scrollbar to move the list in the list box up and down. Both Listbox and Scrollbar widgets have special functions built in to them to support such behavior, so it's not difficult to connect the two. Listing 20.4 shows how to do it.

LISTING 20.4 `tkscrolledlistbox.py`

```
#!/usr/local/bin/python

from Tkinter import *
import sys
import os
import string

def setn(event):
    global elements
    global listbox
```

```
    global lb
    global img
    x = listbox.curselection()
    n = string.atoi(x[0])
    img = PhotoImage(file=elements[n])
    lb["image"] = img

def listgifs(d="."):
    l = os.listdir(d)
    rl = []
    for i in l:
        t = string.lower(i)
        g = string.rfind(t,".gif")
        if g >= 0:
            rl.append(i)
    if len(rl)<1:
        rl = None
    else:
        rl.sort()
    return rl

def die(event):
    sys.exit(0)

root = Tk()
button = Button(root)
button["text"] = "Quit"
button.bind("<Button>",die)
button.pack()
labelx = Label(root)
labelx["height"] = 1
labelx.pack()

elements = listgifs()

frame = Frame(root,bd=2,relief=SUNKEN)
frame.pack(expand=1,fill=BOTH)
scrollbar = Scrollbar(frame, orient=VERTICAL)
listbox = Listbox(frame,exportselection=0,height=10,
    yscrollcommand=scrollbar.set)
listbox.bind("<Double-Button-1>",setn)
for i in elements :
    listbox.insert(END, i)
scrollbar.config(command=listbox.yview)
listbox.pack(side=LEFT)
scrollbar.pack(side=LEFT, fill=Y)
listbox.select_set(0)
listbox.see(0)
lb = Label(root,text="No gif")
lb.pack()

root.mainloop()
```

We build on the generic framework of `tkcascadingmenu.py` by reusing some of the code; `listgifs()` is the same, and `setn()` is similar to `setimage()`. Because we're not using `lambda` and don't need to, we can use `setn()` as a callback directly. We bind it to a double-click event in line 51 so that it takes a double-click to load a new picture. The new stuff is between lines 49 and 59. When we create our Listbox widget in lines 49–50, we assign the `scrollbar.set()` method to the built-in `yscrollcommand` for the Listbox. When we configure the scrollbar (configure takes options and applies them after the widget has already been created) in line 54, we assign the built-in `yview()` method to the scrollbar's command variable. Those two conditions are all that is required to take care of the scrolling capabilities. In line 57, we make sure the very first item is selected in the Listbox widget, and in line 58 we tell the box to make sure that the selected item is shown. To load in a new image, all that is required is to double-click an image name in the scroll box. Figure 20.3 shows how it appears when running.

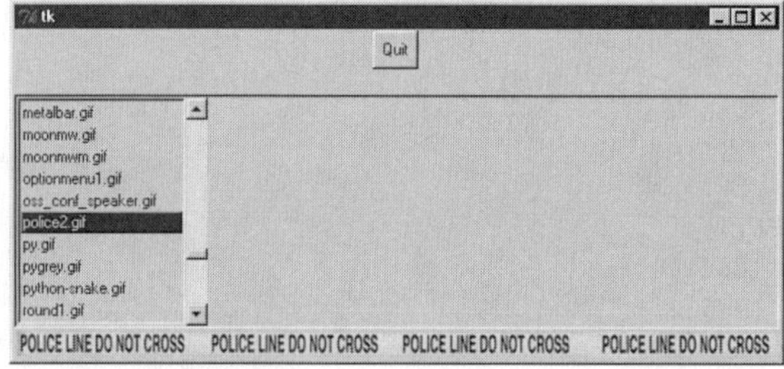

FIGURE 20.3
Running `tkscrolled listbox.py`.

If you added the PPM enhancement for `tkcascadingmenu.py`, you could transfer your modified `listgifs()` function directly to `tkscrolledlistbox.py`.

The Python Imaging Library

If you want to use more than two graphics formats, however, you should download and install the Python Imaging Library, which can be found at `http://www.pythonware.com`. Installation instructions for Windows are nonexistent, so, in brief, here they are:

1. Download the package from `http://www.pythonware.com/downloads.htm#pil`.
2. Unzip the package into a temporary directory; you'll find a new directory in the temp directory, which contains PIL, Scripts, and `tkinter.dll`.
3. Copy all the files in the PIL directory into your Python/Lib directory (such as `C:\Python\Lib`).
4. Copy all the files in the Scripts directory into your `Python/Tools/Scripts` directory.
5. Copy `tkinter.dll` into your Python directory.

After you've done this, you have access to many more graphical image formats. On Linux or other UNIX platforms, you'll have to compile it yourself; full build instructions are included with the source package (available at the same download page). To use it after you've installed it is extremely easy, especially for our limited use of it. Simply continue to import Tkinter, but add an additional line: `import Image, ImageTk`. After that, the only real change (other than how you find your files) is to change the line that used to read `img = PhotoImage(…)` to be `img = ImageTk.PhotoImage()`. That's it. You now have access to several more image formats. Listing 20.5 shows a complete application.

LISTING 20.5 `tkpil.py`

```
#!/usr/local/bin/python

from Tkinter import *
import sys
from tkFileDialog import *
import os
import string
import Image, ImageTk

def buildmenu(xx=0):
    global pwd
    global root
    global lg
    global bar
    if pwd != None:
        lg = listgifs()
        if lg != None:
            n = len(lg)
            gifm = Menu(bar)
            if n < 20:
                n = 0
                for i in lg:
                    gifm.add_command(label=i,
                      command = lambda m=i: setimage(m))
                    n = n + 1
            else:
                nm = n / 20
                no = n % 20
                if no:
                    nm = nm + 1
                for i in range(nm):
                    tm = Menu(gifm)
                    if i == nm - 1 and no != 0:
                        lim = no
```


continues

LISTING 20.5 continued

```
                    else:
                        lim = 20
                    for j in range(lim):
                        ne = (20 * i) + j
                        tm.add_command(label=lg≠,
                          command=lambda m=lg≠:setimage(m))
                    gifm.add_cascade(label="List gifs %d"%(i),menu=tm)

            if xx == 0:
                bar.delete(2)
            bar.add_cascade(label="Gifs",menu=gifm)

class MyDialog:
    def __init__(self, parent,txt):
        top = self.top = Toplevel(parent)
        Label(top, text="Enter new directory").pack()
        self.e = Entry(top)
        self.e.insert(0,txt)
        self.e.pack(padx=5)
        b = Button(top, text="OK", command=self.ok)
        b.pack(pady=5)

    def ok(self):
        global pwd
        global root
        global lg
        npwd = self.e.get()
        if npwd and npwd != "":
            pwd = npwd
            os.chdir(pwd)
            root.title(pwd)
            buildmenu()
        self.top.destroy()

def cd():
    global pwd
    global root
    d = MyDialog(root,pwd)
    root.wait_window(d.top)

def listgifs(d="."):
    l = os.listdir(d)
    rl = []
    for i in l:
        t = string.lower(i)
        g = string.rfind(t,".gif")
        if g >= 0:
            rl.append(i)
    if len(rl)<1:
```

```
            rl = None
        else:
            rl.sort()
        return rl

    def setimage(s):
        global lg
        global img
        global pwd
        if s in lg:
            _label["image"] = img = ImageTk.PhotoImage(file=s)
            pwd = os.getcwd()
            root.title(pwd+'/'+s)

    def die():
        sys.exit(0)

    def sv():
        global _label
        global img
        pl = END
        oname = asksaveasfilename(initialfile="untitled.ppm",filetypes=[
            ("PPM files", "*.ppm"),
        ])
        if oname:
            img.save(oname)

    def ls():
        global _label
        global img
        pl = END
        oname = askopenfilename(filetypes=[("Gif files", "*.gif"),
            ("Jpeg files", "*.jpg"),
            ("PNG files", "*.png"),
            ("PPM files", "*.ppm"),
            ("XBM files", "*.xbm"),
            ("All files", "*.*")
        ])
        if oname:
            _label["image"] = img = ImageTk.PhotoImage(file=oname)
            root.title(oname)

    def main():
        global _label,img,root
        global lg
        global pwd
        global gifm
        global bar
        global img
```

20

continues

Listing 20.5 continued

```
133     img = None
134     lg = listgifs()
135     root = Tk()
136     if len(sys.argv)>1:
137         fn = sys.argv[1]
138         img = ImageTk.PhotoImage(file=fn)
139     else:
140         try:
141             fn = "X_oc.gif"
142             img = ImageTk.PhotoImage(file=fn)
143         except:
144             if lg and lg[0]:
145                 fn = lg[0]
146                 img = ImageTk.PhotoImage(file=fn)
147     pwd = os.getcwd()
148     root.title(pwd+'/'+fn)
149     bar = Menu(root)
150     filem = Menu(bar)
151     filem.add_command(label="Open...",command=ls)
152     filem.add_command(label="Save as...",command=sv)
153     filem.add_command(label="Change directory...",command=cd)
154     filem.add_separator()
155     filem.add_command(label="Exit",command=die)
156 
157     bar.add_cascade(label="File", menu=filem)
158     if lg != None:
159         buildmenu(1)
160     else:
161         bar.add_cascade(label="None")
162     root.config(menu=bar)
163     if img:
164         _label = Label(root,image=img)
165     else:
166         _label = Label(root,text="No gif files found")
167     _label.pack()
168 
169     root.mainloop()
170 
171 if __name__ == "__main__":
172     main()
173 
```

You've seen almost all of this before: I've moved the menu creation code to the `buildmenu()` function, added a file dialog (in `function ls()`, line 111), and added a small dialog (lines 47–67) to allow users to change the current working directory. The little dialog is called in the `cd()` function, line 69, but all the work is done in the dialog code itself, in the `ok()` function. Lines 62–67 do the real work, calling `os.chdir()` to go to the new directory, then building a new list of files, and so on. Figure 20.4 shows the Enter New Directory dialog.

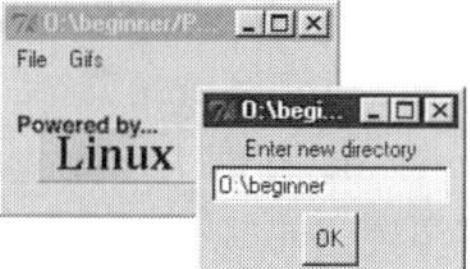

FIGURE 20.4
`tkpil.py` *and the Enter New Directory dialog.*

I also added a Save As… menu entry, which allows you to save any image in PPM format (the ImageTk class only offers that format for writing; other formats are available for writing in the PIL, but they require different ways of loading files, which are covered in the PIL documentation). Figure 20.5 shows the `askopenfilename()` dialog, which is very similar to the `asksaveasfilename()` dialog.

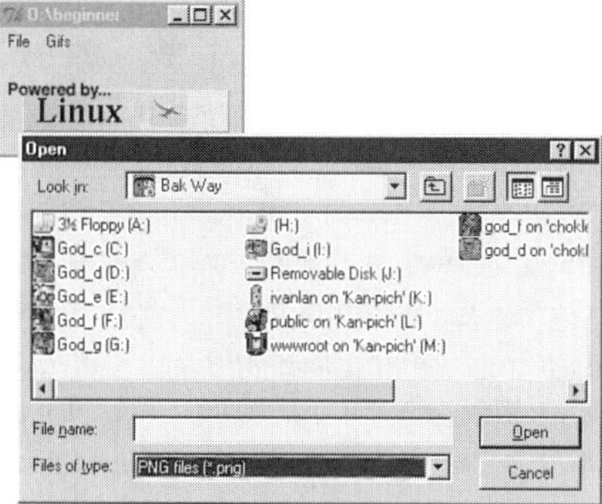

FIGURE 20.5
`tkpil.py` *and the Open File dialog.*

(That's the flying penguin in the Linux button, by the way.) Downloading and installing the Python Imaging Library is a worthwhile endeavor; the biggest advantage is that you can create your own drawings or images, use them, and distribute them without having to resort to GIF files, which is problematic at best. Note that some problems exist with it, particularly in the UNIX-specific graphic formats such as XBM and XPM. If you don't use files of those two formats, you probably won't notice any peculiarities. In the next section, you begin learning how to create your own drawings and images using the Canvas widget.

The Canvas Widget

The Canvas widget, designed expressly for drawing, has a great many methods available. Some documentation exists at `http://www.pythonware.com`, but it's not complete and can be fairly sparse. Before you can use it, however, you must first understand the drawing paradigm. As with most graphics toolkits, you ordinarily don't draw things pixel by pixel; instead, you make up a data structure of some sort, pass it to a window or a widget with the appropriate command, and then the drawable (the window or widget) does the work for you. If you've had experience with other toolkits, the Tkinter Canvas widget may seem to offer fewer methods of drawing than others, but anything you want can be drawn by combining the right basic instructions. For example, there's no command to draw a single pixel; what you must use instead is either a `Rectangle()` or a `Line()` method. This should encourage you to find ways to combine several requests into one (an approach I did not take for the `Mandelbrot.set` displayer that you'll see later).

The basic paradigm that the Canvas widget uses for drawing objects is slightly different from other GUI systems. In most other systems, you can draw to an onscreen drawing area or an offscreen one using points and lines or other drawing primitives, and such drawing happens right away. With the Canvas widget, you describe an object, such as a rectangle, and place that description into the widget's list of objects to be drawn. The drawn object does not appear until the widget is updated, and it is drawn on top of any objects that already exist. You can delete drawn objects, which disappear on the next update. Drawn objects can also be extremely complex but, once drawn, can be moved anywhere on the Canvas with very little work. This makes it simple, for example, to add crosshairs on top of another drawing, which can be moved or withdrawn trivially. Later, in the Mandelbrot drawing application, we'll see exactly this. The disadvantage of this style of drawing is that any given Canvas widget can potentially contain thousands of objects; drawings that contain individual pixels attain this level of complexity easily. Memory usage is high, and updates can be painfully slow. Nonetheless, the flexibility attained is normally enough to offset the memory and speed issues.

The following sections describe the graphical objects that are contained within the Canvas widget; in every case, although there is a method of the Canvas widget to create the object, it is easier to use the convenience functions provided. The underlying Canvas methods take the form `create_rectangle()` or `create_line()`.

The `Rectangle` Object

Rectangles are specified by four coordinates; x and y for the upper-left corner and x1 and y1 for the lower-right corner. An x,y of 0,0 refers to the upper-left corner of the Canvas; to see the pixels drawn at 0,0, however, you must set the `borderwidth` and `highlight-thickness` options to 0. If you don't, the focus highlight will be drawn on top of the Canvas widget (taking away from the viewable area). If you want a border of some sort, the best practice is to enclose the Canvas widget in a Frame widget and apply your border options to that.

The syntax for a `Rectangle()` call is

```
Rectangle(cv,x,y,x1,y1,options...)
```

A typical call might be something like this:

```
Rectangle(cv,100,100,200,200,fill="red")
```

This would draw a red rectangle on the Canvas `cv` that was 100 pixels square, with the upper-left corner (or NW for northwest, in Tk parlance) set at coordinates 100 and 100. For reference, the corresponding `create_rectangle()` call would be

```
cv.create_rectangle(x,y,x1,y1,options...)
```

Several useful options are available, but rather than cover them in this book, I've built a demonstration program that can be downloaded at this book's Web site: `http://www.pauahtun.org/TYPython/CanvasDemo.html`. Instructions and screen shots show you how to use all available options for Canvas drawing objects in detail.

The `Line` Object

Lines are also specified with four coordinates, the same as Rectangles; x and y are the starting point for the line, and x1 and y1 are the ending point. The syntax is

```
Line(cv,x,y,x1,y1,options...)
```

A typical call might be

```
Line(cv,100,100,200,100,fill="blue")
```

The `Arc` Object

Arcs are not circles; you can draw them so that they take up 360 degrees, but the correct object for drawing circles is the `Oval` (covered later). Figure 20.6 shows a screen shot of `CanvasDemo.py` (the downloadable demonstration program) and explains why.

The arcs at the top of the picture are `"pie slice"` style; the other two styles are `"arc"` and `"chord"`. The calls to draw all three of the right arcs are

```
Arc(cv,x,y,x1,y1,extent=90,fill="#808080",style="pieslice")
Arc(cv,x,y,x1,y1,extent=90,fill="#808080",style="arc")
Arc(cv,x,y,x1,y1,extent=90,fill="#808080",style="chord")
```

Options make all the difference. Note that you can draw arcs that go from 0–359 degrees, but you have to use more parameters than you would if you used the `Oval` object.

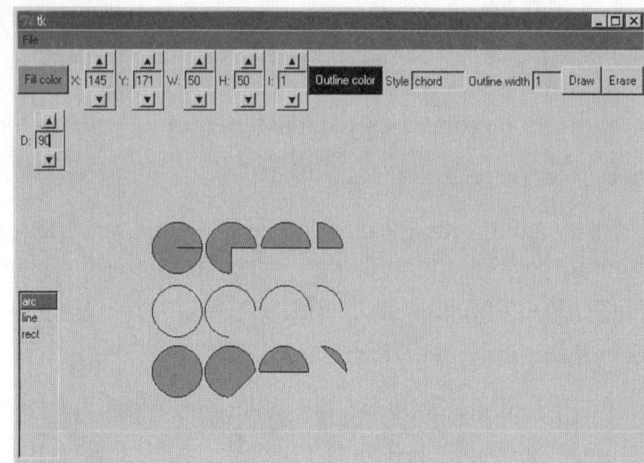

FIGURE 20.6
Drawing circles with `Arc` *objects.*

The `Oval` Object

To draw the same circle as in the preceding example, you could use this code:

```
Oval(cv,x,y,x1,y1,fill="#808080")
```

You need to remember that neither circles, arcs, nor ovals are drawn with respect to their centers (ellipses have two foci instead of a meaningful "center"); instead, their bounding boxes determine where they are drawn, and the centers are thus available only through calculation (if you care). It is therefore easy to transform a perfect circle into a perfect ellipse, merely by changing the dimensions of the bounding box. Figure 20.7 shows the result of changing only the bounding box.

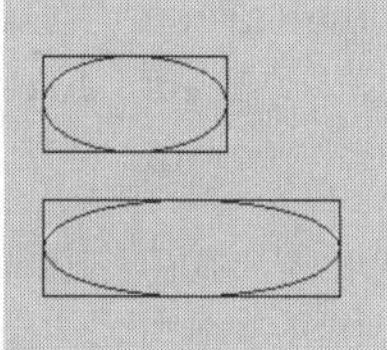

FIGURE 20.7
Stretch the box, stretch the `Oval` *object.*

The `Polygon` Object

Polygons are closed figures made up of line segments. You can have as many segments as you want, but a diagram composed of only two lines cannot be a polygon; to close the figure, it must have at least three line segments. Polygons that have lines and angles all the same are known as "regular" polygons; hexagons and pentagons are good examples. Of course, polygons with enough sides and shallow enough angles are indistinguishable from circles, but you wouldn't want to specify a circle by making a list of several thousand points (it could be done, however). Triangles are the simplest polygons and, like most polygons useful in drawing, are more often irregular than not. The `Polygon` object can be used to draw both regular and irregular polygons, but if you want to draw regular ones, you'll need a program to help you calculate where the vertices go; several such programs are available for free on the Internet, but of course they're not written in Python (see the exercises for more information).

A *vertex* is the point where two lines meet. If the two lines meet at a 180 degree angle, there is no vertex, just a line. The plural of vertex is *vertices*.

That's because Tkinter doesn't do the calculation for you, as it does in the case of circles, arcs, or ellipses; you hand Tkinter a list of points (x,y) and it draws lines between them. If you have a polygon composed of nine sides, you need to tell Tkinter about all nine of the vertices; you do not, as with some graphics systems, need to include the starting vertex as the tenth vertex in the list. Tkinter will assume that you want to close the polygon, so it will connect the last and first vertices. The following code draws a simple three-sided polygon:

```
Polygon(cv,130,130,130,258,258,258,130,30,fill="#FFFFFF")
```

This code assumes you're drawing on a 400x×400 Canvas widget and that the background color of the widget is something other than white (some shade of gray is typical). We'll talk more about polygons later.

The `Bitmap` Object

Bitmaps are what are termed "single-plane" images. That is, no colors are built in to the picture; instead, the image is composed of bits that are either on or off. The most common storage format for these pictures is one popularized by X Windows, the X Bitmap format, or XBM. Tkinter provides support for these kinds of images, as you've seen before, using the `ImageTk` object. With the `Bitmap` object, however, you don't have to build the image first; you can merely specify the name of the file from which to get the bitmap. You can also specify the foreground and background colors when you create the object. The following code does just that:

```
bmpn = "@GVI.xbm"
item = Bitmap(cv,368,368,bitmap=bmpn,foreground="#808080")
```

The @ sign tells the `Bitmap()` call to search for a file rather than use one of its built-in bitmap images—again, assuming that you are drawing on a 400×400 Canvas widget. The result of this call is shown in Figure 20.8.

FIGURE 20.8
A `Bitmap` object.

The `Image` Object

Like `Bitmap` objects, `Images` are pictures, but with color values embedded in them; the standard Tk `PhotoImage` method supports them, but only in GIF and PPM formats. For other formats, you need the PIL, as mentioned earlier in this chapter (and in the exercises). The following code shows a color image placed at the same location on the same Canvas as the preceding bitmap:

```
img = PhotoImage("GVI.ppm")
item = ImageItem(cv,368,368,image=img)
```

Because the name `Image` is already used by Tkinter, the convenience function has been named `ImageItem`. Figure 20.9 shows the resulting `Image` object.

FIGURE 20.9
An `Image` object.

The `CanvasText` Object

Text objects are simple—give a set of coordinates, the text, the color, and your text is displayed. The following code does simply that:

```
item = CanvasText(cv,368,368+48,fill="#007090",text="The image is of god GVI of
Palenque")
```

Figure 20.10 shows the result.

FIGURE 20.10
`Image` and `Text` objects.

Note that the default placement for the `Text` object is centered about the coordinates you supply. To use a more usual placement, you would supply the `anchor=NW` option when creating your `Text` object.

The `Window` Object

`Window` objects are used to place any Tkinter widgets you want inside a `Canvas` object, including another `Canvas` object. The following code shows how to include a simple button:

```
btn = Button(cv,text="Image",command=drawImage)
item = Window(cv,368,368,anchor=SW,window=btn)
```

Figure 20.11 shows the `Canvas` containing the Button widget.

FIGURE 20.11
A `Window` object. (Remember that a Button widget is a window object too.)

Summary

We've covered several kinds of menus, built a scrolled Listbox, touched on some of Tkinter's image capabilities (including a little on the Python Imaging Library), reviewed the Canvas widget's drawing paradigm, and discussed the various kinds of objects available for drawing in the Canvas widget.

In the next chapter, we cover simple graphics and animation.

Workshop

Q&A

Q One of those pie slices looks a lot like Pacman. Can you do games in Python?

A Sure. They won't be very fast if you write them entirely in Python, so you would want to do at least parts of it in C. The 7th International Python Conference, in 1998 in Houston, featured an article on Virtual World simulation with Python. For more information, see `http://www.foretec.com/python/workshops/1998-11/proceedings/papers/asbahr/asbahr.html`.

Q Figure 20.6 shows some pretty fancy widgets; why didn't you cover those?

A Those are examples of the Python MegaWidgets, which are beyond the scope of this book. See the PMW Web site at `http://www.dscpl.com.au/pmw/`.

Quiz

1. How do you scroll a Listbox widget?

   a. You have to implement three different callbacks, one for the Scrollbar widget and one for the Listbox widget.

   b. You have to build only one callback for the scrollbar.

   c. You have to draw the scrollbar yourself, otherwise it won't work.

   d. All you have to do is take advantage of prebuilt callbacks that come with the Scrollbar and Listbox widgets.

2. What is the difference between `Bitmaps` and `Images`?

   a. Nothing—they're all the same underneath.

   b. `Images` are `Bitmaps` with color.

   c. It depends on how you use them.

   d. `Bitmaps` are faster.

Answers

1. d. The correct callbacks are already built in; all you have to do is to assign them to the right options.
2. b. `Images` are, indeed, `Bitmaps` with color; each pixel in a `Bitmap` takes up one bit, whereas `Images` require at least 8 bits to store the color of the pixel.

Exercises

You can learn more about obfuscated code at `http://www.ioccc.org/`, the home page for the International Obfuscated C Code Contest. Although the emphasis is on C, it is possible to write obfuscated code in any language. It is more difficult to do in Python, but with the determined application of only average mediocrity, anyone can do it.

For information on the GIF format and the controversy, see the Burn All Gifs Web site: `http://burnallgifs.org/`. Eric S. Raymond has a number of interesting articles at his Web site, `http://www.tuxedo.org/~esr/`, some of them having to do with the GIF problem.

For some information on netpbm and other graphics formats, visit the Graphics Muse at `http://www.graphics-muse.org/`.

A new site that just opened up is the Vaults of Parnassus, `http://www.vex.net/parnassus/` by Tim Middleton. It promises to be the best place to locate Python modules. It's very well done, and some of the most arcane stuff around is easily tracked down here. It also promises to be the Python equivalent of the CPAN archives, a standardized site for locating Perl modules—a heck of a lot cooler, though. (Parnassus, by the way, is the mountain where Python, of Greek mythology, lived in caves.)

For information on regular polygons and tilings, visit `http://www.scienceu.com/geometry/articles/tiling/`. The definitive book on the subject is *Tilings and Patterns*, by Branko Grungbaum and G.C. Shephard. Published by W.H. Freeman, it is now, unfortunately, out of print, but any decent library will have (or be able to get) a copy.

HOUR 21

Tk Graphics II

I wish we all communicated with one another with India ink and watercolor brushes; takes a while to get the knack, but from then on everything's simple. It also encourages people to stuff more meaning into fewer words!

—Don Arnstine

Last hour, we started learning about Tk graphics. This hour, we continue with a discussion of color and some simple animations. At the end of the hour, you will be able to

- Understand a little bit about color
- Use the Canvas widget for simple animations

Color

Color is a vast subject; hundreds, if not thousands, of books are out there on many topics in color. Charles Poynton's *Digital Video* is probably the place to start if you want to get a basic understanding of computers and color.

The point of this is that I will be able to touch only lightly on a very few ideas because most everything else in color is outside the scope of this book. For real understanding, you should be prepared to invest years in the study of color (instead of half an hour).

Here's a blitzkrieg introduction to color (hold on to your hat). In 1931, the *Commission Internationale de L'Éclairage (CIE)* described mathematical models for the description of colors, and these models provide the standards against which all other colorspaces are measured. Because the human eye contains three color photoreceptors (known as cones, for those of you who remember a bit of high school biology), any color in the CIE system can be pinpointed with only three dimensions; these three dimensions are sufficient to describe any colorspace. I'll confine the discussion to RGB (red-green-blue) colorspace, because that's the one almost exclusively used by computers. RGB colorspace is linear; that is, each dimension can be divided into equal-sized portions, and the length of each axis is the same. Be aware that not every visible color can be pinpointed in RGB colorspace; in fact, only CIE has models sufficiently complex to specify every visible color. All other colorspaces make compromises for practical or economic reasons; for example, one colorspace that is particularly useful for television broadcasting is called YIE. However, these other colorspaces are not useful to you right now and are beyond the scope of this book. Figure 21.1 shows the RGB colorspace; here on the printed page it appears in shades of gray, so to see it in color, run the accompanying program.

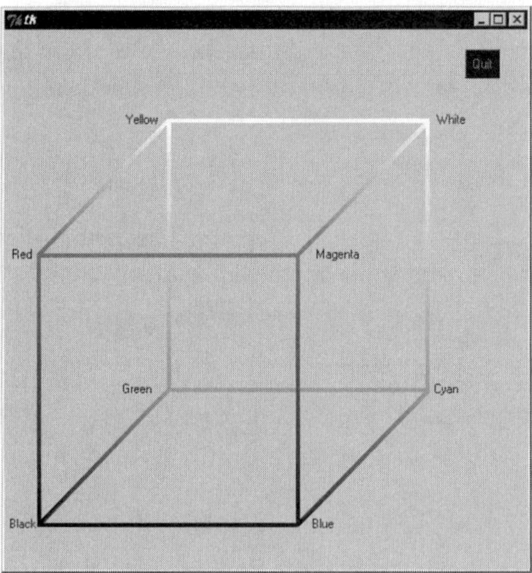

FIGURE 21.1
The RGB color cube.

In color, of course, you'll see black shading into red on the left-front vertical edge, green shading into yellow on the back vertical edge, and so on. Listing 21.1 shows the code for ccube.py, which draws the two-dimensional representation of the three-dimensional color cube shown in Figure 21.1.

LISTING 21.1 ccube.py

```
#!/usr/local/bin/python
import sys
from Tkinter import *
from Canvas import Rectangle,Polygon,Window,CanvasText

def GreenCyan():
    global bll,cv
    brl = [0,0xFF,0]
    tmp = bll[:]
    for i in range(ncolors):
        cm = "#%02X%02X%02X" % (brl[0],brl[1],brl[2])
        Rectangle(cv,tmp[0],tmp[1],tmp[0]+dg,tmp[1]+4,
            fill=cm,outline="",tag="colorcube")
        tmp[0] = tmp[0] + dg
        brl[2] = (brl[2] + hr) % 0x100

def GreenYellow():
    global bll,cv
    brl = [0,0xFF,0]
    tmp = bll[:]
    for i in range(ncolors):
        cm = "#%02X%02X%02X" % (brl[0],brl[1],brl[2])
        Rectangle(cv,tmp[0],tmp[1],tmp[0]+4,tmp[1]-dg,
            fill=cm,outline="",tag="colorcube")
        tmp[1] = tmp[1] - dg
        brl[0] = (brl[0] + hr) % 0x100

def YellowWhite():
    global bul,cv
    brl = [0xFF,0xFF,0]
    tmp = bul[:]
    for i in range(ncolors):
        cm = "#%02X%02X%02X" % (brl[0],brl[1],brl[2])
        Rectangle(cv,tmp[0],tmp[1],tmp[0]+dg,tmp[1]+4,
            fill=cm,outline="",tag="colorcube")
        tmp[0] = tmp[0] + dg
        brl[2] = (brl[2] + hr) % 0x100

def WhiteCyan():
    global bur,cv
    brl = [0xFF,0xFF,0xFF]
    tmp = bur[:]
    for i in range(ncolors):
```

continues

LISTING 21.1 continued

```
        cm = "#%02X%02X%02X" % (brl[0],brl[1],brl[2])
        Rectangle(cv,tmp[0],tmp[1],tmp[0]+4,tmp[1]+dg,
            fill=cm,outline="",tag="colorcube")
        tmp[1] = tmp[1] + dg
        brl[0] = (brl[0] - hr) % 0x100

def BlackBlue():
    global fll,cv
    brl = [0,0,0]
    tmp = fll[:]
    for i in range(ncolors):
        cm = "#%02X%02X%02X" % (brl[0],brl[1],brl[2])
        Rectangle(cv,tmp[0],tmp[1],tmp[0]+dg,tmp[1]+4,
            fill=cm,outline="",tag="colorcube")
        tmp[0] = tmp[0] + dg
        brl[2] = (brl[2] + hr) % 0x100

def BlackRed():
    global fll,cv
    brl = [0,0,0]
    tmp = fll[:]
    for i in range(ncolors):
        cm = "#%02X%02X%02X" % (brl[0],brl[1],brl[2])
        Rectangle(cv,tmp[0],tmp[1],tmp[0]+4,tmp[1]-dg,
            fill=cm,outline="",tag="colorcube")
        tmp[1] = tmp[1] - dg
        brl[0] = (brl[0] + hr) % 0x100

def RedMagenta():
    global ful,cv
    brl = [0xFF,0,0]
    tmp = ful[:]
    for i in range(ncolors):
        cm = "#%02X%02X%02X" % (brl[0],brl[1],brl[2])
        Rectangle(cv,tmp[0],tmp[1],tmp[0]+dg,tmp[1]+4,
            fill=cm,outline="",tag="colorcube")
        tmp[0] = tmp[0] + dg
        brl[2] = (brl[2] + hr) % 0x100

def MagentaBlue():
    global fur,cv
    brl = [0xFF,0,0xFF]
    tmp = fur[:]
    for i in range(ncolors):
        cm = "#%02X%02X%02X" % (brl[0],brl[1],brl[2])
        Rectangle(cv,tmp[0],tmp[1],tmp[0]+4,tmp[1]+dg,
            fill=cm,outline="",tag="colorcube")
        tmp[1] = tmp[1] + dg
        brl[0] = (brl[0] - hr) % 0x100
```

```
def BlackGreen():
    global fll,cv
    brl = [0,0,0]
    tmp = fll[:]
    eg = dg / 2
    for i in range(ncolors):
        cm = "#%02X%02X%02X" % (brl[0],brl[1],brl[2])
        Polygon(cv,
            tmp[0],tmp[1],
            tmp[0]+eg,tmp[1]-eg,
            tmp[0]+eg+3,tmp[1]-eg+3,
            tmp[0]+3,tmp[1]+3,
            fill=cm,outline="",tag="colorcube")
        tmp[0] = tmp[0] + eg
        tmp[1] = tmp[1] - eg
        brl[1] = (brl[1] + hr) % 0x100

def BlueCyan():
    global flr,cv
    brl = [0,0,0xFF]
    eg = dg / 2
    tmp = flr[:]
    for i in range(ncolors):
        cm = "#%02X%02X%02X" % (brl[0],brl[1],brl[2])
        Polygon(cv,
            tmp[0],tmp[1],
            tmp[0]+eg,tmp[1]-eg,
            tmp[0]+eg+3,tmp[1]-eg+3,
            tmp[0]+3,tmp[1]+3,
            fill=cm,outline="",tag="colorcube")
        tmp[0] = tmp[0] + eg
        tmp[1] = tmp[1] - eg
        brl[1] = (brl[1] + hr) % 0x100

def RedYellow():
    global ful,cv
    tmp = ful[:]
    brl = [0xFF,0,0]
    eg = dg / 2
    for i in range(ncolors):
        cm = "#%02X%02X%02X" % (brl[0],brl[1],brl[2])
        Polygon(cv,
            tmp[0],tmp[1],
            tmp[0]+eg,tmp[1]-eg,
            tmp[0]+eg+3,tmp[1]-eg+3,
            tmp[0]+3,tmp[1]+3,
            fill=cm,outline="",tag="colorcube")
```

continues

LISTING 21.1 continued

```
        tmp[0] = tmp[0] + eg
        tmp[1] = tmp[1] - eg
        brl[1] = (brl[1] + hr) % 0x100

def MagentaWhite():
    global fur,cv
    tmp = fur[:]
    brl = [0xFF,0,0xFF]
    eg = dg / 2
    for i in range(ncolors):
        cm = "#%02X%02X%02X" % (brl[0],brl[1],brl[2])
        Polygon(cv,
            tmp[0],tmp[1],
            tmp[0]+eg,tmp[1]-eg,
            tmp[0]+eg+3,tmp[1]-eg+3,
            tmp[0]+3,tmp[1]+3,
            fill=cm,outline="",tag="colorcube")
        tmp[0] = tmp[0] + eg
        tmp[1] = tmp[1] - eg
        brl[1] = (brl[1] + hr) % 0x100

def LabelVertices():
    global cv,fll,flr,blr,bll,ful,fur,bul,bur
    CanvasText(cv,fll[0] - 17,fll[1],text="Black",tag="colorcube")
    CanvasText(cv,flr[0] + 25,flr[1],text="Blue",tag="colorcube")
    CanvasText(cv,blr[0] + 20,blr[1],text="Cyan",tag="colorcube")
    CanvasText(cv,bll[0] - 30,bll[1],text="Green",tag="colorcube")
    CanvasText(cv,ful[0] - 15,ful[1],text="Red",tag="colorcube")
    CanvasText(cv,fur[0] + 40,fur[1],text="Magenta",tag="colorcube")
    CanvasText(cv,bul[0] - 25,bul[1],text="Yellow",tag="colorcube")
    CanvasText(cv,bur[0] + 25,bur[1],text="White",tag="colorcube")

def ColorCube():
    # Back rectangle first:
    GreenCyan()
    GreenYellow()
    YellowWhite()
    WhiteCyan()
    # Diagonals:
    RedYellow()
    BlackGreen()
    MagentaWhite()
    BlueCyan()
    # Front rectangle:
    BlackBlue()
    BlackRed()
    RedMagenta()
    MagentaBlue()
```

```
189         LabelVertices()
190
191     if __name__ == "__main__":
192         # Vertices of the rgb cube
193         # fll = front lower left;
194         # bur = back upper right; etc.
195         # The various functions draw
196         # the necessary edges.
197         fll = [32,468]
198         flr = [286,468]
199         ful = [32,212]
200         fur = [286,212]
201         bll = [160,340]
202         blr = [412,340]
203         bul = [160,84]
204         bur = [412,84]
205
206         ncolors = 32
207         hw = 256
208
209         dg = hw/ncolors
210         hr = 0x100 / ncolors
211
212         def die(event=0):
213             sys.exit(0)
214
215         root = Tk()
216         root.title("RGB Color Cube")
217         cv = Canvas(root,width=512,height=512,borderwidth=0,
218             highlightthickness=0)
219         ColorCube()
220
221         button = Button(cv,text="Quit",background="black",
222             foreground="red",command=die)
223         Window(cv,468,32,window=button)
224
225         cv.pack()
226
227         root.mainloop()
228
```

(Note that if you are using a display with 256 or fewer colors, you should change the value of `ncolors` to 16; if you don't, you're likely to get slightly odd colors for your cube.) Most of this code should be very familiar from our previous discussions of the various Tk widgets, including the convenience functions that draw rectangles and polygons on the Canvas widget. Notice that in lines 221–223 we construct a Quit button and install it into the Canvas widget using the `Window()` convenience function. The only thing you haven't seen before occurs for the first time in line 11, where it says `cm = "#%02X%02X%02X" % (brl[0],brl[1],brl[2])`. This produces a string that looks like this: `"#000000"` for black and `"#FFFFFF"` for white. Tkinter requires all color specifications to be either names, such as `"red"`, `"white"`, or `"black"`, or RGB color strings that begin with the # sign (an octothorpe, remember). The following six hex digits specify coordinates in RGB space; the first two digits are the red location, the next two are the green location, and the final two are the blue location. A dark red would be specified by `"#800000"`, or precisely halfway along the red axis with no movement along the green or blue axes (axes being the plural of axis). In all the functions in Listing 21.1, we divide the length of a particular color axis into 32 parts (the number of colors we're using), and draw small rectangles or polygons of each resulting color until we've built the whole axis. Table 21.1 shows the color ranges for each axis, or edge, in the cube (given in the same order in which they're drawn).

TABLE 21.1 Color Ranges of the Color Axes

Axis	*Color Range*	*Function*
green-cyan (back lower left—back lower right)	#00FF00–#00FFFF	`GreenCyan()`
green-yellow (back lower left—back upper left)	#00FF00–#FFFF00	`GreenYellow()`
yellow-white(back upper left—back upper right)	#FFFF00–#FFFFFF	`YellowWhite()`
white-cyan (back upper right—back lower right)	#FFFFFF–#00FFFF	`WhiteCyan()`
black-blue (front lower left—front lower right)	#000000–#0000FF	`BlackBlue()`
black-red (front lower left—front upper left)	#000000–#FF0000	`BlackRed()`
red-magenta (front upper left—front upper right)	#FF0000–#FF00FF	`RedMagenta()`
magenta-blue (front upper right—front lower right)	#FF00FF–#0000FF	`MagentaBlue()`
black-green (front lower left—back lower left)	#000000–#00FF00	`BlackGreen()`
blue-cyan (front lower right—back lower right)	#0000FF–#00FFFF	`BlueCyan()`
red-yellow (front upper left—back upper left)	#FF0000–#FFFF00	`RedYellow()`
magenta-white (front upper right—back upper right)	#FF00FF–#FFFFFF	`MagentaWhite()`

I've only used a range of 0–32 on each axis, which gives a total of 32^3, or 32,768 colors; potentially, you can divide each edge into as many parts as you want, bounded only by the floating-point capabilities of Python. Think of the RGB color cube as Uncle Scrooge's money bin (which, as I remember it, is about the size of the Saturn Assembly Building), where each coin or bill is described by coordinates in three dimensions, and thus each item has a different color. The possibilities are limited only by the size of the coins or bills (Scrooge seemed to have a lot more coins than bills, though). Most computer color video cards allow for a limited range of colors, from 16 (low end) to 16,777,216 (high end). The latter is a color cube with 256 colors on each edge, and this is the maximum allowed by Tkinter's color specification strings.

The RGB color cube, although representing the corresponding colorspace accurately enough, doesn't really give you much of a feel for color relationships. For that, we turn to a color wheel, which you undoubtedly recall from your grade-school days. Figure 21.2 shows such a color wheel; it's simplified because the typical color wheel that used to be shown in dictionaries and encyclopedias was divided into segments, and this picture isn't.

FIGURE 21.2
A color wheel.

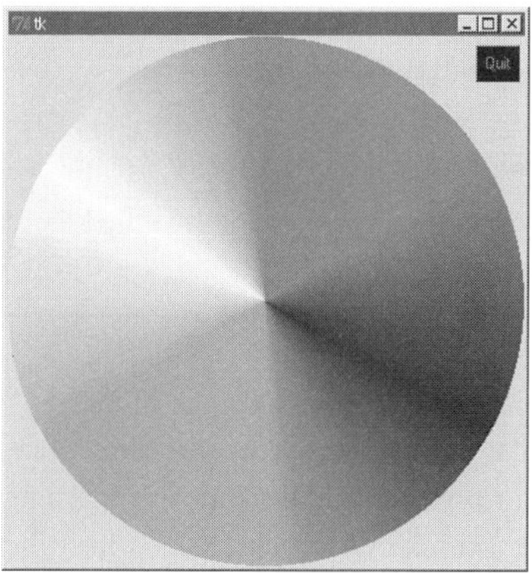

At the top, you see red; 120 degrees to the left is green, and 120 degrees to the right is blue. These are the primary colors, at least as far as computer circles (pun intended) are concerned. You see cyan 180 degrees from red; from green, magenta; and from blue, yellow. These are the complementary colors. Naturally, to really see the wheel in color, you must run the program given in Listing 21.2.

LISTING 21.2 tkwheel.py

```
 1 #!/usr/local/bin/python
 2
 3 from Tkinter import *
 4 from Canvas import Rectangle,Oval,Arc,Window
 5 from colormap import *
 6 import sys
 7
 8 cmap = SetupColormap0(360)
 9
10 root = Tk()
11 cv = Canvas(root,width=401,height=401,borderwidth=0,
12     highlightthickness=0)
13 ar = Oval(cv,0,0,400,400)
14 for i in range(360):
15     e = (i + 90) % 360
16     ps = Arc(cv,0,0,400,400,start=e,extent=1,fill=cmap[i],outline="")
17
18 def die(event=0):
19     sys.exit(0)
20
21 button=Button(cv,text="Quit",foreground="red",background="black",
22     command=die)
23 Window(cv,380,20,window=button)
24 cv.pack()
25
26 root.mainloop()
27
28
29
```

Very few new items are in this small program. One is in line 15, where we give the angle for the start of the pie slice (the default type, you will remember, for the `Arc()` convenience function). All the `Arc()` types define the 0 position or angle to be 90 degrees right instead of 90 degrees vertical. I think that's weird, so I adjust the starting angle to be where I think it ought to go. The other item you haven't seen before is the call to `SetupColormap0()` in line 8; `SetupColormap0()` comes from the `colormap` module (`from colormap import *`, line 5), which I don't show here. That's because this module, so that it can provide lists of colors (a colormap) in a particular order, builds the colormap in another colorspace, HLS (for hue-lightness-saturation). It's difficult to sort color specifications when they're in RGB, but very simple in HLS colorspace. The code for `colormap.py` is available on this book's Web page, `http://www.pauahtun.org/TYPython/`, but it is outside the scope of our discussion. You can use the various colormap functions without understanding how they work: Simply provide the number of colors you want, and all the `SetupColormapn()` functions will return a list containing the number of colors you asked for, and an additional entry at the end for black (the reason for this will become clear later when we discuss Mandelbrot sets).

RGB color specifications do lend themselves well to the construction of a list of gray levels; that's because any RGB spec where the red, green, and blue components are all identical is a gray level. Listing 21.3 shows the code for the `SetupColormap6()` function.

LISTING 21.3 `SetupColormap6()`

```
 1
 2  def SetupColormap6(ncolors):
 3      cmap = []
 4      xd = 1.0/ncolors
 5      for i in range(0,ncolors):
 6          r = g = b = 0xFF - ((i * xd)* 0xFF)
 7          cmap.append("#%02X%02X%02X" % (r,g,b))
 8      cmap.append("#000000")
 9      return cmap
10
```

You can see that this function is indeed very simple. By defining the length of our gray axis as 1.0, we can divide that by the number of colors, which will give us the amount by which to increment each gray level. You may be puzzled by my use of the term "gray axis," because there appears to be no such thing when you look at the color cube in Figure 21.1. If, however, you draw a diagonal line from the black vertex to the white vertex, you will see that each point on that line is described by identical coordinates in each `r`, `g`, or `b` dimension. In line 6, we multiply `xd`, our increment, times `i`, which gives us the location on the gray axis. We then multiply that times `0xFF` to convert the location into RGB dimensions. Figure 21.3 shows a gray colormap in a window.

FIGURE 21.3
Shades of gray.

Listing 21.4 shows the code to achieve this "fountain" of gray levels.

LISTING 21.4 `fountain.py`

```
#!/usr/local/bin/python

import sys, string
```

continues

LISTING 21.4 continued

```
 4
 5  from Tkinter import *
 6  from Canvas import Rectangle,Window
 7  from colormap import *
 8
 9  def die(event=0):
10      sys.exit(0)
11
12  w = 512
13  h = 64
14  root = Tk()
15  cv = Canvas(root,width=w,height=h,borderwidth=0,
16      highlightthickness=0)
17  cmap = Graymap(256)
18  wd = 2
19  x = y = 0
20  for i in range(256):
21      Rectangle(cv,x,y,x+wd,y+h,fill=cmap[i],width=0,outline="")
22      x = x+wd
23  qb=Button(root,text="Quit",command=die)
24  item=Window(cv,450,32,window=qb)
25  cv.pack()
26  root.mainloop()
27
```

If you wanted black on the left instead of on the right, it would be a simple matter to call `cmap.reverse()` on the returned colormap in line 17 because lists in Python have useful methods, such as `sort()` and `reverse()`. Line 17 shows a call to `Graymap()`, which is the same as a call to `SetupColormap6()`; it returns a list of Tkinter color strings, which is then indexed for each drawn rectangle to provide the fill color. In this case, the fill color is simply a shade of gray, and the rectangles are 2 pixels wide by 64 pixels high. Fountains like this can be used in many places; the now extinct *PostScript Journal* introduced graylevel fountains and how to draw them in one of its issues; it began using them on interior page layouts in the next issue (then the journal died).

With today's modern color displays, it's probably of more interest to do color fountains. That's not particularly hard, given the same set of colormap functions we used to draw the color wheel in Figure 21.2. (If you wanted to do a color fountain using only one face of the RGB color cube, how would you do it without using any of the colormap functions?) Figure 21.4 shows the result of substituting `SetupColormap0()` for the `Graymap()` call (and a few other small tweaks, too).

FIGURE 21.4
A color fountain.

Listing 21.5 provides the full code.

LISTING 21.5 `colorfountain.py`

```
#!/usr/local/bin/python

import sys, string

from Tkinter import *
from Canvas import Rectangle,Window
from colormap import *

def die(event=0):
    sys.exit(0)
ncolors = 256
w = 256
h = 256
root = Tk()
frame = Frame(root)
cv = Canvas(frame,width=w,height=h,borderwidth=0,
    highlightthickness=0)
cmap = SetupColormap0(ncolors)
wd = w/ncolors
x = y = 0
for i in range(ncolors):
    Rectangle(cv,x,y,x+wd,y+h,fill=cmap[i],width=0,outline="")
    x = x+wd
qb=Button(frame,text="Exit",command=die,
    foreground="red",background="black")
frame.pack()
cv.pack(side=TOP)
qb.pack(side=LEFT)
root.mainloop()

```

This is pretty much the same code, except for the width and height of the Canvas widget, as in Listing 21.4. Naturally, I expect you to run the program so that you can see what the color fountain really looks like. In the next hour, our color fountain provides an interesting background to our simple animations.

Animation

I was in college when Pong came out in 1972; I remember I went to Papa Charlie's (a pizza joint in Chicago's Greektown) with a bunch of friends after a long weekend spent digging around in quarries and along railroad tracks near Ottowa, Illinois, looking for fossils for a geology course. We sat down, looked over where the pinball machines were, and saw a monitor with a white bouncing ball on it. I've never been very interested in games, but I admit that I tried this one out. I lost interest after a while, but I was still kind of impressed with the computer. The last computers I'd dealt with had been room-filling monsters ("I helped create the Y2K bug," remember), and here was a machine about the size of a photo booth that could actually do graphics and play games. Looking back, I can see that this was the moment when my interest in computers was rekindled. The next quarter, I took a zooarchaeology course. The professor suggested that we identify some thousands of animal bone fragments, gathered from sites in Turkey, and tabulate our results on computer. He knew someone who had written a program to do statistical analyses, and he thought we could adapt our data format to this program. The project never panned out, but I've been involved with computers, one way or another, ever since.

So I thought that the best way to introduce you to animations would be to show you a Pong-style program; real Pong has one or two paddles, and you're supposed to stop the ball from speeding past you and off the screen, but to me this is just not interesting (not to mention beyond my hand-eye coordination). Because I have lots of Mayan glyphs lying around, it seemed natural to use glyphs instead of a ball and to allow several glyphs bouncing around instead of just one. Because I wanted a more interesting background, we'll use the color fountain we developed in the last section as the background for our jumping glyphs. Just what everyone needs, right?

We need to take a small digression first, however. We won't actually get to the jumping glyphs until the next hour; in the meantime, let's shoot some pool.

When you watch Pong, at first you think that it's just like shooting pool. That is, the ball hits an edge and bounces off at the same angle. If it hits at a 45-degree angle, it will fly off at a 45-degree angle. You can see this in action when you run the program shown in Listing 21.6.

Listing 21.6 tkpool.py

```
#!/usr/local/bin/python

import sys, string

from Tkinter import *
from Canvas import Rectangle,Line,ImageItem,CanvasText
from math import *


w = 128.0
h = 256.0
xp = 0
yp = h
xdelta = 2.0
ydelta = -2.0
wball = None
filename="white.gif"

img = None
txt = None

def Radians(x):
    return(x * (pi/180.0E0))

def Degrees(x):
    return(x * (180.0/pi))

def die(event=0):
    sys.exit(0)


def moveball(*args):
    global cv,img,h,w,wball,xp,yp,xdelta,ydelta
    cv.move(wball,xdelta,ydelta)
    if xp >= 0.0 and yp >=0.0:
        if xp >= w:
            xdelta = xdelta * -1.0
        xp = xp + xdelta
        yp = yp + ydelta
        cv.after(10,moveball)
    else:
        cv.delete(wball)

def chsize(event):
    global w,h,xp,yp,xdelta,ydelta
    w = event.width
```

continues

LISTING 21.6 continued

```
    h = event.height

def shoot(event):
    global cv,img,h,w,wball,xp,yp
    global xdelta,ydelta,filename,txt
    img = PhotoImage(file=filename)
    xp = event.x
    yp = event.y
    xdelta = 2.0
    if yp < h/2.0:
        if ydelta < 0:
            ydelta = ydelta * -1.0
    else:
        if ydelta > 0:
            ydelta = ydelta * -1.0
    a = yp - h/2.0
    bw = w - xp
    # A is the angle formed by hypotenuse
    # a is the height of the triangle, side a
    # b is the width of the triangle, side b
    # c is the length of hypotenuse, side c
    # All three trig routines _could_ return 0,
    # so these calls could be put inside a try:
    # except: block.
    A = atan2(a,bw)
    deg = Degrees(A)
    c = 2.0/sin(A)
    b = 2.0/tan(A)
    xdelta = abs(b)
    cv.delete(wball)
    cv.delete(txt)
    wball = ImageItem(cv,xp,yp,image=img)
    txt = CanvasText(cv,w-25,h-25,font="Helvetica 14",
        text="%02d" % int(deg))
    cv.after(10,moveball)

if __name__ == "__main__":
    root = Tk()
    cv = Canvas(root,width=w,height=h,borderwidth=0,
        background="#409040",
        highlightthickness=0)
    cv.bind("<Configure>", chsize)
    cv.bind("<Button-1>", shoot)
    root.bind("<Escape>", die)
    cv.pack(expand=1,fill=BOTH)
    root.mainloop()
```

Several new things are in this program; I'll discuss them after you look at Figure 21.5.

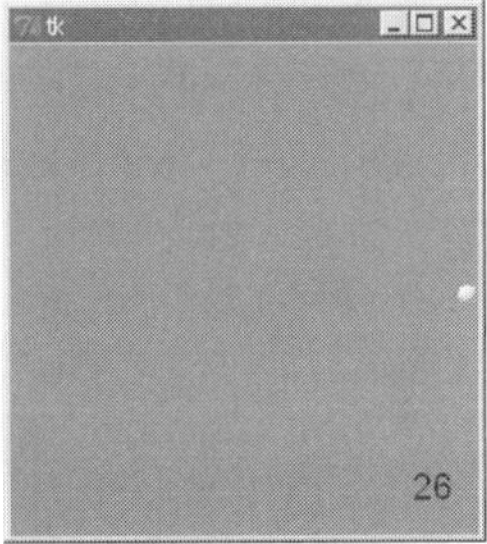

FIGURE 21.5
Shooting pool.

In lines 83–93, we build a typical Tk window, a Canvas widget inside that, and in line 91, we tell `pack()` that the Canvas should be expandable (allowed to change size) and that it should always fill up the whole of its containing widget, the root window. Not only does this make sure that the Canvas fills up the entire window, it also allows users to change the size of the root window by grabbing one of the standard resize areas on the window border and moving the edges or the corner to shape the window to whatever dimensions they like. Because we always need to know exactly how big the window is, we install a function that gets called whenever the window is resized. We use the `bind()` method in line 88, using `"<Configure>"` as the event we want to be called back on; in lines 44–47, we see that all the `chsize()` callback does is write down the dimensions of the Canvas widget for us.

In line 90, we're using the `bind()` method again, to call `die()` whenever the user hits the Esc key; that way, we don't have to provide a Quit or Exit button. We have to install this callback on the root window, however, because the root window always gloms on to all keystrokes and doesn't pass them on to the Canvas widget. In line 89, we add a callback for a mouse click anywhere in the Canvas widget, and this callback, `shoot()`, is what does the real work. It shoots a pool ball from wherever you click toward the center of the right edge of the Canvas, where it will bounce off at the same angle that it was sent. There are some gotchas, which I'll explain as we get to them as we go through the detailed discussion of `shoot()`.

The `shoot()` function, before anything else, grabs the ball image (line 52), using the `PhotoImage()` function that we saw in the previous hour. You can substitute any GIF image you want for this, but it should be relatively small and square. The next thing it does, in lines 53 and 54, is to write down the `x,y` coordinate of the mouse click in the `xp` and `yp` variables so that another function, `moveball()`, can see and use them. This function calls the `move()` method in the Canvas widget, using the `wball` variable; the Canvas widget knows where the ball image is and moves it by the amount specified. This amount is stored in the `xdelta` and `ydelta` variables; they're called `delta` variables because in mathematics, any quantity that represents a small change in a vector (direction and speed) is traditionally represented with the Greek letter delta, Δ. Lines 56 through 61 check to see in which direction the ball should move: toward the top of the window if the user has clicked in the bottom half, and toward the bottom if the user has clicked in the top half. Because we must know the angle at which the ball is going to bounce, we've got to use trigonometry; it really can't be avoided, but it's beyond the scope of this book to teach you trig (see the exercises for a good Web page that will help if you need it). You're just going to have to take my word that the trig functions are necessary—and that they work.

To use trig, we must know some numbers, such as the width and height of the right triangles we're working with. Whenever the mouse is clicked and we obtain the `x,y` coordinate, we have all we need to construct a triangle. The height of our triangle is calculated in line 62, `a = yp - h/2.0` (we always aim the ball at the same coordinate, the center of the right edge of the window), and the width in line 63, `bw = w - xp`. Figure 21.6 shows the traditional names for sides and angles of a right triangle.

FIGURE 21.6
Right-triangle nomenclature.

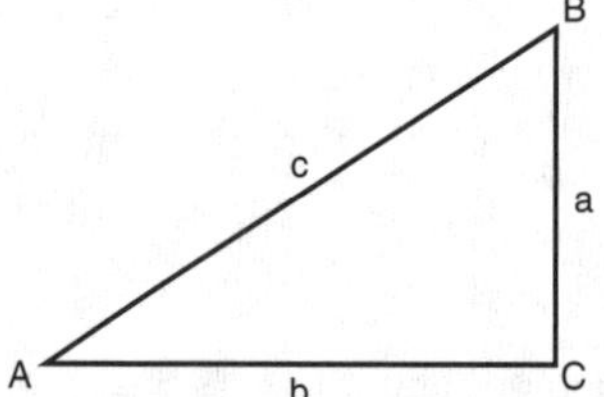

You can see that what I've called "width" corresponds to the length of side b, and height corresponds to the length of side a; side c is the hypotenuse (remember the Pythagorean Theorem? Here it is in action). Because we know the lengths of sides a and b, we can easily calculate angle A. We do that in line 71, `A = atan2(a,bw)`. You could use the `atan()` function instead of `atan2()` from the math module (`from math import *`), but then you would have to divide the length of side a by the length of side b first. The `atan2()` performs this division for us before calculating the arctangent of angle A. In the preceding picture, by the way, the points of the triangle labeled A and B correspond to the mouse click (A) and the center of the right edge of the window (B). C is some distance along the y axis from point B.

Because all the trig functions in the math module operate on and return values in radians, rather than in degrees, we need a function to calculate degrees from radians, and that is to be found in lines 25 and 26. Although all circles contain 360 degrees, only 6.28318530718… radians are in the same 360 degrees; that is, 2 * pi radians = 360 degrees. The trig functions prefer radians, but we're going to display the calculated angle on our Canvas widget, so we need the `Degrees()` function. I've also provided the corresponding `Radians()` function, which takes degrees and returns radians, even though we don't use it in this program. Line 72 calls the function and stores the result in the `deg` variable.

Line 74 (`b = 2.0/tan(A)`) calculates the length of side `b` for us by taking the tangent of angle `A` when the length of side a is set to 2.0 pixels. Side `a` represents our `ydelta` variable, and we set it small enough to give a reasonable sense of motion when the program is running. The answer to our equation here can come back either positive or negative, and because we want the ball to shoot off only in a rightward direction, we use the absolute value of the answer, as you can see in line 75 (`xdelta = abs(b)`). At this point, we've done all the math we'll need in this function.

Lines 76 and 77 delete the old ball image and the old text, if either one exists in the Canvas widget. In line 78, we add the ball image to the Canvas at the `x,y` coordinate determined by the mouse click. In lines 79 and 80, we create a text item for the Canvas widget, placed in the lower-left corner, that tells us the angle at which we've shot the ball.

The real function to move the ball is called in line 81, `cv.after(10,moveball)`. What the call to the Canvas's `after()` method does is install a timer that takes 10 milliseconds to go off, at which time the `moveball()` function will be called. Turning to the `moveball()` function in lines 32–42, we can see that its most important job is to call the Canvas's `move()` method on the `wball` object (built in the `shoot()` function, line 78) by our small deltas, `xdelta` and `ydelta`. However, the function must also detect whether the ball has reached the edge of the window, and that is done by checking the x coordinate only, in line 36, where we compare that `x` coordinate with the width of the window. If the ball is at the edge, we simply multiply the `xdelta` times `-1`, which has the effect of reversing the ball's direction. The angle is the same, only the direction has changed. This is the essence both of pool and Pong; reverse the sign of the delta, and you change the direction and reflect the angle. If, for example, the ball comes in at an exact 45-degree angle, when the sign of the delta is reversed, the ball bounces off the edge at a 135-degree angle. The edge forms a 180-degree angle; to calculate the angle of the bounce, simply subtract the input angle from 180 degrees.

Summary

In this hour, you've learned some details of RGB colorspace—how to draw fountains in gray levels and in color. You've learned how to use the Canvas widget to do simple animations, and you probably read more about trigonometry than you really wanted to know (although it hasn't been much).

Next hour, we'll move on to the bouncing glyphs program (which should seem easier to you after the tkpool program), and at last to Mandelbrot sets.

Workshop

Q&A

Q Is that really all there is to pool? Can I become a hustler with what I've learned here and my pocket calculator?

A Angles and trig are the easiest part of pool. You've also got to account for the spin (in whatever direction—horizontal, vertical, or something in between) of the ball, the friction of the ball against the felt of the tabletop, whether your finger twitched when you stroked the cue, and on and on. Chaos theory has a lot more to say about who wins pool games than trig. But hey, if you want to try it, don't let me stop you. (But you're not ready for chaos theory.)

Q I thought trig was hard; this stuff looks easy. Is it?

A It's much easier now than it was before calculators and computers. You used to have to look up all your angles in printed trig tables; for example, you would have had to look up in the table to find out which angle had a tangent of 0.488673541719. Now you can just use the `atan()` or `atan2()` functions (or the inverse trig buttons on your calculator) to find out that the right angle is 24.4439547804 degrees.

Quiz

1. What are the complementary colors if the primaries are red, green, and blue?
    a. Yellow, orange, and mauve
    b. Chartreuse, pink, and purple
    c. Yellow, magenta, and cyan
    d. Anti-red, anti-green, and anti-blue
2. What's the simplest way to reverse the orders of the colors in Figure 21.4, the color fountain?
    a. You have to change the hue angle inside the `colormap` module.
    b. Obtain the list of colors and call its `reverse()` method.
    c. Change the starting color index when you're accessing the list of colors.
    d. You have to use a different colorspace.

3. What do you think will happen if you change the sign of both `xdelta` and `ydelta` in the `moveball()` function in `tkpool.py`?
   a. The ball would fly through the edges of the window.
   b. The ball would hit the left edge and bounce off.
   c. The ball would disappear.
   d. The ball would backtrack its course and trace a path directly underneath its origin at the mouse click.

Answers

1. c, if the primary colors are red, green, and blue (as they are in RGB colorspace), the complementary colors are yellow, magenta, and cyan. Other colorspaces can have different primary colors. YMC colorspace, for instance, makes yellow, magenta, and cyan the primary colors. What does that make red, green, and blue?
2. b, because the colormap functions all return ordinary Python lists, all you have to do is call the `reverse()` method for the returned list. Choice three is also feasible, but not, I think, as simple.
3. d, changing the `ydelta` sign would flip the ball's trajectory to the other half of the window from where the sign-change for `xdelta` put it; it would zip right back under the mouse pointer.

Exercises

The best place on the Web to start learning about color, and the most accurate, by far, is Charles Poynton's Color Technology page, at `http://www.inforamp.net/~poynton/Poynton-color.html`.

For more information on Pong and its history, start by visiting `http://members.spree.com/sip/stompsearch/gamesite/cooljava/pong/default.htm`. An intriguing bit of history can be found here: `http://www.fas.org/cp/pong_fas.htm`.

For an excellent short refresher course in trigonometry, visit `http://aleph0.clarku.edu/~djoyce/java/trig/`.

Find out why radians are useful in trigonometric functions. Start at the same page.

Modify `tkpool.py` so that `xdelta` is always 2.0 pixels rather than `ydelta`.

Hour 22

Tk Graphics III

Willy was a rather unusual snake, for he was fond of reading. Snakes don't usually care much about books, probably because they haven't any hands to hold them with.

—Walter R. Brooks, in Freddy the Pilot

In the previous hour, we continued learning about Tk graphics, including color and some simple animation. This hour, we continue with more animation and finish up with the geometry managers. At the end of the hour, you will be able to

- Use the Canvas widget for more animations
- Use the three geometry managers, Place, Pack, and Grid.

More Animation

In the previous hour, I promised to show you how to make a Pong-like animation using Mayan glyphs instead of little white balls. Let's start by defining our playing field, so to speak. Figure 22.1 shows you what we're going to draw.

FIGURE 22.1
The playing field.

Pretty boring, right? Especially in grayscale. Run the code shown in Listing 22.1 to see what it looks like in color.

LISTING 22.1 tkfield.py

```
#!/usr/local/bin/python

import sys, string, random
from Tkinter import *
from Canvas import ImageItem,Rectangle,CanvasText
from colormap import *

class Glyphs(Frame):
    def die(self,event=0):
        sys.exit(0)

    def __init__(self,parent=None,nobj=0,wwidth=640,wheight=480):
        self.pause=0
        self.xdelta=[]
        self.ydelta=[]
        self.xmin = 16
        self.ymin = 16
        self.windowwidth = wwidth
        self.windowheight = wheight
        self.xlim=self.windowwidth - self.xmin
        self.ylim=self.windowheight - self.ymin
        self.xpos=[]
        self.ypos=[]
        self.img = []
        self.pictures = []
        self.deltav = 1
        self.parent=parent
    Frame.__init__(self, self.parent)
    Pack.config(self)

        self.nobj = nobj
    self.buildglyphs(nobj)
```

22

```
    def buildglyphs(self,n=1):
        self.ncolors = 128
        self.cmap = SetupColormap1(self.ncolors)

    self.draw = Canvas(self,
            width=self.windowwidth, height=self.windowheight)
        self.llabel=CanvasText(self.draw,self.windowwidth - 100,
            self.windowheight - 32, text="",font="Helvetica 20")
        self.parent.bind("<Escape>",self.die)
        sr = 1+(self.windowheight / self.ncolors)
        x = 0
        y = 0
        w = self.windowwidth
        for c in self.cmap:
            if c == "#000000":
                break
            item=Rectangle(self.draw,x,y,w,y+sr,fill=c,
                outline="",width=0)
            y = y + sr
    self.draw.pack()

if __name__ == "__main__":
    wwidth=-1
    wheight=-1
    if len(sys.argv) > 1:
        nobj=string.atoi(sys.argv[1])
        if len(sys.argv) > 3:
            wwidth=string.atoi(sys.argv[2])
            wheight=string.atoi(sys.argv[3])
    else:
        nobj=-1
    root=Tk()
    if wwidth == -1:
        wwidth=root.winfo_screenwidth()
        wheight=root.winfo_screenheight()
    if nobj == -1:
        suff=""
    else:
        suff=" Brothers"
    root.title("Flying Glyph" + suff)
    glyphs = Glyphs(root,nobj,wwidth,wheight)

    glyphs.mainloop()
```

Although this code doesn't do much but put up a window, it's really quite useful. That's because we're building a framework for a larger application rather than a small program that puts up one little window with a bunch of colors in it. The larger application is going to be somewhat complex, and that is why we are starting with a class, `Glyphs`, that starts in line 8. `Glyphs` inherits from the Frame widget, which means that it is itself a widget, giving access to the Frame widget's methods. When a class inherits from a parent, it has to call the parent's `__init__()` method manually, and this is done in line 28. In line 29, we call the `pack()` method, which must be done before the widget becomes visible. The way it's done here is so that when the class is instantiated, the returned class is ready for use. Lines 74 and 76 show how we create the instance and then call that instance's `mainloop()` method. This should point out to you that almost all Tk widgets inherit that `mainloop()` method and so can function as standalone applications. To prove it, take a look at Listing 22.2.

LISTING 22.2 tkm.py

```
#!/usr/local/bin/python
from Tkinter import *
import sys

def die(event=0):
    sys.exit(0)

x = Button(None,text="Hello, World!",command=die)
x.pack()
x.mainloop()

```

See? All we're doing is creating a button, without the usual call to `root=Tk()` that we've seen before. This runs fine, but you can't call the `title()` method, and several other features are missing, but it's perfectly serviceable, especially when you only need something like a warning box, or perhaps a (very) minimal entry box. Most of the time, you're going to need the features that only a Toplevel widget can provide.

In line 42 of Listing 22.1, we've bound the Esc key to the `die()` method so that we don't have to provide a Quit button. In lines 67 and 68, we obtain the width and height of the user's display; the default size of our window is the entire screen. You can change that easily, if you want; you could, for example, divide the screen width and height by two. Lines 47–52 draw many rectangles on the Canvas widget, in varying colors. Here, they start at the top and work down, unlike the fountain effect we used in the preceding chapter. For a different effect, you could use one of the other `SetupColormapn()` functions in the `colormap` module. Remember that the last element in the `cmap` list is always black, however, which is why there is a break if the element we're using in the loop is black. Notice also that the CanvasText item we're creating in lines 40 and 41 will not be visible because it has been set to the empty string; later on, we'll see what use it is. All the rest of the variables in class `Glyphs` are for future use, and we will proceed to use them in the next few steps.

The first thing we're going to do is add support for images; up to 20 images, as a matter of fact. We're also going to add random placement of the images into their starting positions. Listing 22.3 shows the complete code with the new additions.

LISTING 22.3 tkfield2.py

```
#!/usr/local/bin/python

import sys, string, random
from Tkinter import *
from Canvas import ImageItem,Rectangle,CanvasText
from colormap import *

class Glyphs(Frame):
    def die(self,event=0):
        sys.exit(0)

    def __init__(self,parent=None,nobj=0,wwidth=640,wheight=480):
        self.smallglyphlist = ["x_ahau.gif","x_imix.gif","x_ik.gif",
            "x_akbal.gif", "x_kan.gif", "x_chicchan.gif", "x_cimi.gif",
            "x_manik.gif", "x_lamat.gif", "x_muluk.gif", "x_oc.gif",
            "x_chuen.gif", "x_eb.gif", "x_ben.gif", "x_ix.gif",
            "x_men.gif", "x_cib.gif", "x_caban.gif", "x_etznab.gif",
            "x_cauac.gif",
        ]
        self.bigglyphlist = ["ahau_m.gif","imix_m.gif","ik_m.gif",
            "akbal_m.gif", "kan_m.gif", "chicchan_m.gif", "cimi_m.gif",
            "manik_m.gif", "lamat_m.gif", "muluk_m.gif", "oc_m.gif",
            "chuen_m.gif", "eb_m.gif", "ben_m.gif", "ix_m.gif",
            "men_m.gif", "cib_m.gif", "caban_m.gif", "etznab_m.gif",
            "cauac_m.gif",
        ]
        self.pause=0
        self.xdelta=[]
        self.ydelta=[]
        self.xmin = 16
        self.ymin = 16
        self.windowwidth = wwidth
        self.windowheight = wheight
        self.xlim=self.windowwidth - self.xmin
        self.ylim=self.windowheight - self.ymin
        if self.windowwidth < 800:
            self.glyphlist = self.smallglyphlist
        else:
```

continues

LISTING 22.3 continued

```
            self.glyphlist=self.bigglyphlist
        self.xpos=[]
        self.ypos=[]
        self.img = []
        self.pictures = []
        self.deltav = 1
        self.parent=parent
        Frame.__init__(self, self.parent)
        Pack.config(self)

        if nobj<0 or nobj>len(self.glyphlist):
            nobj=len(self.glyphlist)
        self.nobj = nobj
        self.buildglyphs(nobj)

    def buildglyphs(self,n=1):
        self.ncolors = 128
        self.cmap = SetupColormap0(self.ncolors)

        self.draw = Canvas(self,
            width=self.windowwidth, height=self.windowheight)
        self.llabel=CanvasText(self.draw,self.windowwidth - 100,
            self.windowheight - 32, text="",font="Helvetica 20")
        self.parent.bind("<Escape>",self.die)
        sr = 1+(self.windowheight / self.ncolors)
        x = 0
        y = 0
        w = self.windowwidth
        for c in self.cmap:
            if c == "#000000":
                break
            item=Rectangle(self.draw,x,y,w,y+sr,fill=c,
                outline="",width=0)
            y = y + sr

        self.deltav = self.windowwidth/128 + 1

        for i in range(n):
            self.img.append(PhotoImage(file=self.glyphlist[i]))
            if i == 0:
                self.xmin = self.img[i].width()/2
                self.ymin = self.img[i].height()/2
                self.xlim=self.windowwidth - self.xmin
                self.ylim=self.windowheight - self.ymin

            if i%2==0:
                self.xdelta.append(self.deltav)
                self.ydelta.append(self.deltav)
            else:
                self.xdelta.append(-self.deltav)
                self.ydelta.append(-self.deltav)

```

```
 91                 self.xpos.append(random.randint(self.xmin,self.xlim))
 92                 self.ypos.append(random.randint(self.ymin,self.ylim))
 93
 94                 self.pictures.append(ImageItem(self.draw,self.xpos[i],
 95                     self.ypos[i], image=self.img[i],
 96                     tags=self.glyphlist[i]))
 97
 98             self.draw.pack()
 99
100     if __name__ == "__main__":
101         wwidth=-1
102         wheight=-1
103         if len(sys.argv) > 1:
104             nobj=string.atoi(sys.argv[1])
105             if len(sys.argv) > 3:
106                 wwidth=string.atoi(sys.argv[2])
107                 wheight=string.atoi(sys.argv[3])
108         else:
109             nobj=-1
110         root=Tk()
111         if wwidth == -1:
112             wwidth=root.winfo_screenwidth()
113             wheight=root.winfo_screenheight()
114         if nobj == 1:
115             suff=""
116         else:
117             suff=" Brothers"
118         root.title("Flying Glyph" + suff)
119         glyphs = Glyphs(root,nobj,wwidth,wheight)
120
121         glyphs.mainloop()
```

The biggest change that you can immediately see is the addition of a couple of lists of very funny-looking names in lines 13–26. These are the names of the image files we're going to use in our flying glyph machine; these images, which can be found on the book's Web site (also see `http://www.pauahtun.org/days.html`) along with the program, should be located in the same directory from which you run the program. Despite my reservations about GIF files, you will notice that all the image files listed are just that. The reasons are twofold:

1. PNG files, the generally superior suggested replacement for GIFs, have transparency, but PNG transparency is not supported by the two major Internet browsers. While waiting for browsers to catch up, buy a commercial GIF transparency program, such as Alchemy Mindwork's Gif Construction Set Pro, that you know is legal. Gif Construction Set Pro is legal.
2. `PhotoImage()` supports only PPM and GIF files; PPM does not support transparency.

There are two lists: `smallglyphlist`, which contains a list of 32×32 glyphs, and `bigglyphlist`, which contains a list of 64×64 glyphs. In line 36, there's a check to see if the window width is less than 800; if so, small glyphs are used; otherwise, the big ones are. I determined the size at which to use small or large glyphs empirically. That means I tried it out until it looked OK to me. Modern software engineering terminology that means the same thing is iterative development, or stepwise refinement. With other programming languages, this sort of cut-and-try development is frowned upon, unless it has a fancy name. You're supposed to write specifications until your ears bleed, and finally you get to code. When you use Python, writing detailed specs for all but very large projects is kind of hopeless; by the time you write enough Python code to let you determine how to write the spec, you're done. And usually done before lunch, too.

Further comments on the code: When we create images in line 78, we append them to a list (`img`) where we can get at them later; we'll need to, if we want to move them. The next few lines, 79–83, grab the size of the first image in the list and calculate how close to the edges the flying glyphs can approach. By default, images are placed by the Canvas widget using their dead centers; to make it look as if the images are bouncing off the edges, we don't let them come closer than one-half their dimensions. In line 75, we calculate something called deltav; a term from rocket science (pronounced "delta vee," it's supposed to be written with the Greek delta) that indicates how fast a rocket's acceleration is increasing. Our glyphs don't increase their acceleration over time, but we'll use the term anyway, simply as a way to indicate whether the glyphs move in little steps (for little glyphs) or big steps (big glyphs). Lines 85–90 apply positive or negative deltav to the glyphs depending on whether their position in the creation order is odd or even. This means some glyphs will start bouncing to the right and some to the left. Lines 92 and 93 decide where the glyph is going to appear in the Canvas widget. The call to `random.randint()` chooses an integer value between the ranges we calculated earlier, which for a 256×256 window is going to be 32 and 224 for both the width and height of the window. We append those chosen values to the list of `x` positions (`xpos`) and the list of `y` positions (`ypos`). Lines 95–97 finally let us create the actual Canvas widget ImageItems, which we store in yet another list, `pictures`. After we create the pictures, they will show up on the Canvas after we call `mainloop()` (line 121). At this time, you should run this program by typing the command line `python tkfield2.py 1 256 256`. That should give an image that looks like Figure 22.2—a single glyph on a 256×256 window.

FIGURE 22.2
One (non) flying glyph.

The next time you run it, the glyph should be placed somewhere else. If you see the glyph, enter **`python tkfield2.py 20 256 256`** on the command line, and you should see something like Figure 22.3.

FIGURE 22.3
All the (non) flying glyphs.

If you run the program without any command-line arguments, your entire screen should be taken up and the glyphs should be the large-size ones. I'm not providing a screen shot of that here because it would be larger than this page (or I could shrink it, in which case the glyphs would be the same size as the ones you see here). Run the program.

Now we're ready to move the glyphs (imagine the glyphs in Figure 22.3 moving all over the place). The code for the next step is shown in Listing 22.4.

LISTING 22.4 tkfield3.py

```
#!/usr/local/bin/python

import sys, string, random
from Tkinter import *
from Canvas import ImageItem,Rectangle,CanvasText
from colormap import *

class Glyphs(Frame):
```

continues

LISTING 22.4 continued

```
    def die(self,event=0):
        sys.exit(0)

    def __init__(self,parent=None,nobj=0,wwidth=640,wheight=480):
        self.smallglyphlist = ["x_ahau.gif","x_imix.gif","x_ik.gif",
            "x_akbal.gif", "x_kan.gif", "x_chicchan.gif", "x_cimi.gif",
            "x_manik.gif", "x_lamat.gif", "x_muluk.gif", "x_oc.gif",
            "x_chuen.gif", "x_eb.gif", "x_ben.gif", "x_ix.gif",
            "x_men.gif", "x_cib.gif", "x_caban.gif", "x_etznab.gif",
            "x_cauac.gif",
        ]
        self.bigglyphlist = ["ahau_m.gif","imix_m.gif","ik_m.gif",
            "akbal_m.gif", "kan_m.gif", "chicchan_m.gif", "cimi_m.gif",
            "manik_m.gif", "lamat_m.gif", "muluk_m.gif", "oc_m.gif",
            "chuen_m.gif", "eb_m.gif", "ben_m.gif", "ix_m.gif",
            "men_m.gif", "cib_m.gif", "caban_m.gif", "etznab_m.gif",
            "cauac_m.gif",
        ]
        self.pause=0
        self.xdelta=[]
        self.ydelta=[]
        self.xmin = 16
        self.ymin = 16
        self.windowwidth = wwidth
        self.windowheight = wheight
        self.xlim=self.windowwidth - self.xmin
        self.ylim=self.windowheight - self.ymin
        if self.windowwidth < 800:
            self.glyphlist = self.smallglyphlist
        else:
            self.glyphlist=self.bigglyphlist
        self.xpos=[]
        self.ypos=[]
        self.img = []
        self.pictures = []
        self.deltav = 1
        self.parent=parent
        Frame.__init__(self, self.parent)
        Pack.config(self)

        if nobj<0 or nobj>len(self.glyphlist):
            nobj=len(self.glyphlist)
        self.nobj = nobj
        self.buildglyphs(nobj)

    def buildglyphs(self,n=1):
        self.ncolors = 128
        self.cmap = SetupColormap0(self.ncolors)

```

```
        self.draw = Canvas(self,
            width=self.windowwidth, height=self.windowheight)
        self.llabel=CanvasText(self.draw,self.windowwidth - 100,
            self.windowheight - 32, text="",font="Helvetica 20")
        self.parent.bind("<Escape>",self.die)
        sr = 1+(self.windowheight / self.ncolors)
        x = 0
        y = 0
        w = self.windowwidth
        for c in self.cmap:
            if c == "#000000":
                break
            item=Rectangle(self.draw,x,y,w,y+sr,fill=c,
                outline="",width=0)
            y = y + sr

        self.deltav = self.windowwidth/128 + 1

        for i in range(n):
            self.img.append(PhotoImage(file=self.glyphlist[i]))
            if i == 0:
                self.xmin = self.img[i].width()/2
                self.ymin = self.img[i].height()/2
                self.xlim=self.windowwidth - self.xmin
                self.ylim=self.windowheight - self.ymin

            if i%2==0:
                self.xdelta.append(self.deltav)
                self.ydelta.append(self.deltav)
            else:
                self.xdelta.append(-self.deltav)
                self.ydelta.append(-self.deltav)

            self.xpos.append(random.randint(self.xmin,self.xlim))
            self.ypos.append(random.randint(self.ymin,self.ylim))

            self.pictures.append(ImageItem(self.draw,self.xpos[i],
                self.ypos[i], image=self.img[i],
                tags=self.glyphlist[i]))

        self.draw.pack()
        self.after(10, self.moveglyphs)

    def moveglyphs(self, *args):
        if self.pause==1:
            self.after(10, self.moveglyphs)
            return

        for n in range(self.nobj):
```

continues

LISTING 22.4 continued

```
107             self.draw.move(self.glyphlist[n], self.xdelta[n],
108                 self.ydelta[n])
109             tmp = self.xpos[n] + self.xdelta[n]
110             if tmp > self.xlim or tmp < self.xmin:
111                 self.xdelta[n] = self.xdelta[n] * -1
112                 self.xdelta[n] = self.xdelta[n] + \
113                     random.choice((0,1)) - 2
114                 if self.xdelta[n] == 0:
115                     self.xdelta[n] = self.xdelta[n] + 1
116             self.xpos[n] = self.xpos[n] + self.xdelta[n]
117
118             tmp = self.ypos[n] + self.ydelta[n]
119             if tmp > self.ylim or tmp < self.ymin:
120                 self.ydelta[n] = self.ydelta[n] * -1
121                 self.ydelta[n] = self.ydelta[n] + \
122                     random.choice((0,1)) - 2
123                 if self.ydelta[n] == 0:
124                     self.ydelta[n] = self.ydelta[n] + 1
125             self.ypos[n] = self.ypos[n] + self.ydelta[n]
126
127         self.after(10, self.moveglyphs)
128
129 if __name__ == "__main__":
130     wwidth=-1
131     wheight=-1
132     if len(sys.argv) > 1:
133         nobj=string.atoi(sys.argv[1])
134         if len(sys.argv) > 3:
135             wwidth=string.atoi(sys.argv[2])
136             wheight=string.atoi(sys.argv[3])
137     else:
138         nobj=-1
139     root=Tk()
140     if wwidth == -1:
141         wwidth=root.winfo_screenwidth()
142         wheight=root.winfo_screenheight()
143     if nobj == 1:
144         suff=""
145     else:
146         suff=" Brothers"
147     root.title("Flying Glyph" + suff)
148     glyphs = Glyphs(root,nobj,wwidth,wheight)
149
150     glyphs.mainloop()
```

What's new here? A call to the `moveglyphs()` method in line 99, and the definition of the method in lines 101–127. You've already seen how to use the `after()` method in the preceding hour, so you already know that when your callback is called by `after()`, you must call `after()` again in the callback. Line 127 does this, as does line 103. The check in line 102 to see if the `pause` variable is set is so that we have a means of halting the motion of the glyphs; we'll hook this variable up later.

You may be wondering why I've only used a single callback for `after()`; why not have an individual callback for each and every glyph? The answer is fairly simple: In UNIX, the number of timers available to any given program is essentially unlimited; however, in Windows, the number of timers is severely limited and is therefore a scarce resource. Windows 95 supposedly removed the hard-coded limit, but if so, it did nothing to support the removal of that limit. Program performance suffers greatly when you go over about 10 timers, so having more is really not an option on Windows. Having just one timer that does a lot of work provides adequate performance.

The basic structure of `moveglyphs()` is fairly simple—even simpler, actually, than our previous program, `tkpool.py`, from the preceding hour. You might have noticed that I don't even `import math` here; there's a reason for that. In our little pool-shooting demo, we used trig to calculate the angles for us. Here, though, we are emulating Pong—and Pong doesn't bother with trig. Trigonometry can be pretty compute-intensive, and in 1972, I would bet they only had something like a 6502 CPU and 1 or 2 kilobytes of memory to play with. You don't do trig on machines like that, especially not to move a ball around a screen. Now, remember in the previous hour that I said that when you first watch Pong, you think it's just like shooting pool? Here's why it isn't: If you have a ball that bounces continually around the screen, and you do not vary either the angles or the bounce point, the ball will follow the same path for every bounce. We don't want that, and after you watch Pong for a few minutes, you realize that it's not at all like pool. No trig, no pool: What's going on here?

Let's go through the `for` loop in `moveglyphs()`. The loop is controlled by the number of objects we've created; we stuffed the images into the `img` list in line 77 and added the ImageItems to the Canvas in line 94, stuffing them into the `pictures` list. When we created the ImageItems, we also gave them `tags`, or strings by which we can refer to them so that we can move them around, in line 96. We just used the name of the file for the tags, which is the easiest way. So what we do in the body of the loop is to move the appropriate glyph by the glyph's own `xdelta` and `ydelta`, by calling the Canvas widget's `move()` method in line 107. We use the tag we gave the glyph when we created it.

After the glyph has been moved, we figure out what is going to happen to it the next time through the loop (which will be the next time `after()` is called). We need to write down the new position for the glyph, too. In line 109, we take the old `x` position, add `xdelta` to it, and put the result into a variable, `tmp` (which is temporary). If the position is inside the x limits (`xmin` and `xlim`), we just transfer the new x position to `xpos` (line 116). If the new position is at one of the edges, however, we need to take action, which is the function of lines 111–115. Line 111 flips the angle, just like we did in `tkpool.py`, in the previous hour. Then, we add the value of `xdelta` and the results of `random.choice()` minus two. (The `random` module, by the way, is the random number generator of choice for Python.) The `choice()` method selects one of the elements of the tuple it expects as an argument (0,1) and returns it. This will be either 0 or 1. We then subtract 2 from the result, giving -1 or -2, and add that to the new value of `xdelta`. In line 114, we check to see whether the new value is 0, and if so, add 1 to it. The effect of these lines (111–115) on the glyph's `xdelta` is simple: Every time the glyph hits the edge of the window, we just fiddle with the `xdelta` a little bit, which changes the length of the b side of the triangle. What triangle, you ask? Well, watch the glyphs move for a minute. You'll see that they never move straight up and down or straight right to left. They always move at an angle; in fact, they move along the hypotenuse of the right triangle formed by the b side (`xdelta`) and a side (`ydelta`). The delta values are always integers and are always fairly small values, so the triangles formed are never too large and take a limited range of values. Because we only change `xdelta` and `ydelta` at the edges of the window, the glyphs keep moving along straight lines between bounces. Sometimes you will see a glyph take a particularly sharp angle after a bounce, and then on the very next bounce travel off very slowly at a very different angle. The first case could be produced by an `xdelta` of 1 and a `ydelta` of 9, for example, whereas the second could be caused by an `xdelta` of 2 and a `ydelta` of 1.

Lines 119–124 do the same thing, only for the `ydelta`, or, more properly, the a side of the triangle. I believe that you can now see how we can get away with no trigonometric functions being called in either our flying glyph program or in Pong.

Listing 22.5 shows again the complete program, with just a few small changes.

LISTING 22.5 tkfield4.py

```
 1  #!/usr/local/bin/python
 2
 3  import sys, string, random
 4  from Tkinter import *
 5  from Canvas import ImageItem,Rectangle,CanvasText
 6  from colormap import *
 7
 8  class Glyphs(Frame):
 9      def die(self,event=0):
10          sys.exit(0)
11
12      def snap(self,event=0):
13          if self.pause == 0:
```

```
            self.pause=1
        else:
            self.pause=0

    def lifter(self,event=0):
        x = self.draw.gettags(CURRENT)
        if len(x)==1:
            return
        self.llabel["text"]=x[0]
        self.draw.lift(self.llabel)
        y = self.draw.find_withtag(x[0])
        if y:
            self.draw.lift(y[0])

    def __init__(self,parent=None,nobj=0,wwidth=640,wheight=480):
        self.smallglyphlist = ["x_ahau.gif","x_imix.gif","x_ik.gif",
            "x_akbal.gif", "x_kan.gif", "x_chicchan.gif", "x_cimi.gif",
            "x_manik.gif", "x_lamat.gif", "x_muluk.gif", "x_oc.gif",
            "x_chuen.gif", "x_eb.gif", "x_ben.gif", "x_ix.gif",
            "x_men.gif", "x_cib.gif", "x_caban.gif", "x_etznab.gif",
            "x_cauac.gif",
        ]
        self.bigglyphlist = ["ahau_m.gif","imix_m.gif","ik_m.gif",
            "akbal_m.gif", "kan_m.gif", "chicchan_m.gif", "cimi_m.gif",
            "manik_m.gif", "lamat_m.gif", "muluk_m.gif", "oc_m.gif",
            "chuen_m.gif", "eb_m.gif", "ben_m.gif", "ix_m.gif",
            "men_m.gif", "cib_m.gif", "caban_m.gif", "etznab_m.gif",
            "cauac_m.gif",
        ]
        self.pause=0
        self.xdelta=[]
        self.ydelta=[]
        self.xmin = 16
        self.ymin = 16
        self.windowwidth = wwidth
        self.windowheight = wheight
        self.xlim=self.windowwidth - self.xmin
        self.ylim=self.windowheight - self.ymin
        if self.windowwidth < 800:
            self.glyphlist = self.smallglyphlist
        else:
            self.glyphlist=self.bigglyphlist
        self.xpos=[]
        self.ypos=[]
        self.img = []
        self.pictures = []
        self.deltav = 1
        self.parent=parent
```

continues

LISTING 22.5 continued

```
        Frame.__init__(self, self.parent)
        Pack.config(self)

        if nobj<0 or nobj>len(self.glyphlist):
            nobj=len(self.glyphlist)
        self.nobj = nobj
        self.buildglyphs(nobj)

    def buildglyphs(self,n=1):
        self.ncolors = 128
        self.cmap = SetupColormap0(self.ncolors)

        self.draw = Canvas(self,
            width=self.windowwidth, height=self.windowheight)
        self.llabel=CanvasText(self.draw,self.windowwidth - 100,
            self.windowheight - 32, text="",font="Helvetica 20")
        self.parent.bind("<Escape>",self.die)
        self.parent.bind("<Button-1>",self.snap)
        self.parent.bind("<Button-3>",self.lifter)
        sr = 1+(self.windowheight / self.ncolors)
        x = 0
        y = 0
        w = self.windowwidth
        for c in self.cmap:
            if c == "#000000":
                break
            item=Rectangle(self.draw,x,y,w,y+sr,fill=c,
                outline="",width=0)
            y = y + sr

        self.deltav = self.windowwidth/128 + 1

        for i in range(n):
            self.img.append(PhotoImage(file=self.glyphlist[i]))
            if i == 0:
                self.xmin = self.img[i].width()/2
                self.ymin = self.img[i].height()/2
                self.xlim=self.windowwidth - self.xmin
                self.ylim=self.windowheight - self.ymin

            if i%2==0:
                self.xdelta.append(self.deltav)
                self.ydelta.append(self.deltav)
            else:
                self.xdelta.append(-self.deltav)
                self.ydelta.append(-self.deltav)

            self.xpos.append(random.randint(self.xmin,self.xlim))
            self.ypos.append(random.randint(self.ymin,self.ylim))
```

```

            self.pictures.append(ImageItem(self.draw,self.xpos[i],
                self.ypos[i], image=self.img[i],
                tags=self.glyphlist[i]))

        self.draw.pack()
        self.after(10, self.moveglyphs)

    def moveglyphs(self, *args):
        if self.pause==1:
            self.after(10, self.moveglyphs)
            return

        for n in range(self.nobj):
            self.draw.move(self.glyphlist[n], self.xdelta[n],
                self.ydelta[n])
            tmp = self.xpos[n] + self.xdelta[n]
            if tmp > self.xlim or tmp < self.xmin:
                self.xdelta[n] = self.xdelta[n] * -1
                self.xdelta[n] = self.xdelta[n] + \
                    random.choice((0,1)) - 2
                if self.xdelta[n] == 0:
                    self.xdelta[n] = self.xdelta[n] + 1
            self.xpos[n] = self.xpos[n] + self.xdelta[n]

            tmp = self.ypos[n] + self.ydelta[n]
            if tmp > self.ylim or tmp < self.ymin:
                self.ydelta[n] = self.ydelta[n] * -1
                self.ydelta[n] = self.ydelta[n] + \
                    random.choice((0,1)) - 2
                if self.ydelta[n] == 0:
                    self.ydelta[n] = self.ydelta[n] + 1
            self.ypos[n] = self.ypos[n] + self.ydelta[n]

        self.after(10, self.moveglyphs)

if __name__ == "__main__":
    wwidth=-1
    wheight=-1
    if len(sys.argv) > 1:
        nobj=string.atoi(sys.argv[1])
        if len(sys.argv) > 3:
            wwidth=string.atoi(sys.argv[2])
            wheight=string.atoi(sys.argv[3])
    else:
        nobj=-1
    root=Tk()
    if wwidth == -1:
        wwidth=root.winfo_screenwidth()
```

continues

LISTING 22.5 continued

```
160            wheight=root.winfo_screenheight()
161        if nobj == 1:
162            suff=""
163        else:
164            suff=" Brothers"
165        root.title("Flying Glyph" + suff)
166        glyphs = Glyphs(root,nobj,wwidth,wheight)
167
168        glyphs.mainloop()
```

All we've done here is add two new methods, `snap()` and `lifter()` (lines 12–26), and have bound those methods to events (lines 79 and 80). The first, `snap()`, is bound to the `"<Button-1>"` event on the mouse and makes all the glyphs stop. That's the function of the `pause` variable, which is checked by `moveglyphs()` every time it is called; if `pause` is set to 1, then `moveglyphs()` only calls `after()` and then returns. So even though `snap()` (for snapshot) is very simple, its effect is large.

The second new function, `lifter()`, does two things. It's bound to the `"<Button-3>"` event; when you click your right mouse button on the window, line 19 checks to see if there is a glyph underneath the mouse pointer. If there is one, the `x` variable will contain more than one element, and the first member of the tuple will contain the tag that we added when we created the ImageItem. If we've found a glyph, then lifter will use the tag as text for the CanvasText item created in line 76. Because it's kind of hard to right-click a moving glyph, use the `snap()` method (left-click) to freeze the display and right-click a stationary glyph. The result is shown in Figure 22.4.

FIGURE 22.4
Taking names.

There are several directions in which you could go with the flying glyph program; see the exercises for some suggestions.

The next section discusses geometry managers, but with very little code.

The Geometry Managers

Tkinter has three geometry managers, whose main job is to manage where widgets are placed inside another widget, how big widgets are, and where they all go in relation to each other. I'm not going to spend much time on these; for one thing, you've been using one of them ever since you began studying Tkinter in this part of the book. For another, they are fairly simple, and usually you will need only one of them at a time to perform fairly basic geometry management.

The three managers are listed in order of complexity:

- The Place geometry manager
- The Pack geometry manager
- The Grid geometry manager

Because Python is an OO language, and because all widgets inherit behavior from parent classes, the geometry managers are provided as class methods on every widget; you don't, as in other GUI toolkits, have to create a manager and tell it about the widgets it's going to control. The geometry managers come into existence only when you call their specific methods on any widget you create: `place()`, `pack()`, or `grid()`.

Place

The place manager, although it is the simplest, is also rather hard to use. You can do two things with it:

- Place widgets at specific `x,y` coordinates.
- Place widgets relative to their parent or relative to other widgets.

Ordinarily, you don't want to hard-code widget coordinates; it's just not a productive way to spend your time. Additionally, doing so makes it very hard to allow users to resize your applications. To do it, however, simply call the `place()` method on any widget, like this.

```
x = Button(root,text="Place")
x.place(x=10,y=10)
```

The preceding code will set `x,y` coordinates to 10, so that 10 pixels space will be between the left and top edges and the Button widget. More interesting, however, is the capability to place widgets relative to their parent. Listing 22.6 shows a class definition that uses the Place manager to stick widgets around the edges of a window.

LISTING 22.6 Placing Widgets Relatively

```
60
61  class Placer:
62      def __init__(self,w):
63          global death
64          opts=[(N,0.5,0),
65              (NE,1,0),
66              (E,1,0.5),
67              (SE,1,1),
68              (S,0.5,1),
69              (SW,0,1),
70              (W,0,0.5),
71              (NW,0,0),
72              (CENTER,0.5,0.5),
73              ]
74          for an,xx,yy in (opts):
75              item=Button(w,text=an)
76              item.place(relx=xx,rely=yy,anchor=an)
77              if an == CENTER:
78                  item["command"] = die
79                  item["image"] = death
80              else:
81                  item["command"] = lambda x=an : prn(x)
82
```

The line numbers indicate that this is a fragment of a larger file, `tkgeom.py`, which is downloadable from this book's Web site. Figure 22.5 shows the window constructed by the Placer class.

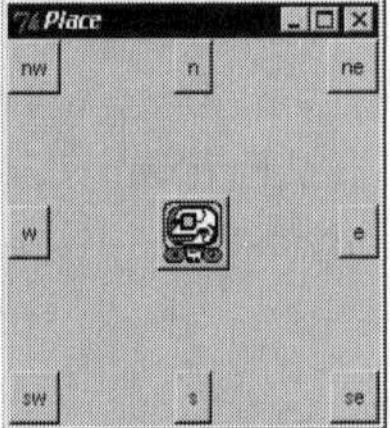

FIGURE 22.5
Place relative geometry management.

To explain how this is done, you must assume that each side of the window (in this case it's simply the root window) has a length of 1 (no matter how long it really is), and relative placement coordinates are specified with decimal fractions instead of pixels. The `opts` list contains, as tuples, the three arguments needed by the `place()` method call in line 76. For example, the first iteration through the `for` loop unpacks the first tuple in the list into the variables an, xx and yy, which are passed to the Place manager like this (with the variables replaced with their values).

```
item.place(relx=0.5,rely=0,an=N)
```

That is, center the widget at the top of the parent window, using the North side of the widget; if you look at the top of Figure 22.5, you'll see that indeed, the N button appears at top center. If the anchor variable (an) is CENTER, we make that the Quit button and stuff an image into it instead of the usual boring Quit or Exit text. That's the Mayan glyph for death, by the way. Appropriate enough for a Quit button, I should think. But this does illustrate a useful technique; you can build a button that has text on it, but if you decide to use an image instead of the text, you do not need to remove the text. Images override text in Label and Button widgets, so all you have to do to get a button with an image is to set the image property to whatever image you want (after you create the image using `PhotoImage()`, a step not shown in the preceding code). You should examine the `opts` list tuple items and figure out what each one is doing when called with the `place()` method. If you resize the window, the centered button will remain centered, and all the rest of the buttons will stick to the appropriate edges of the window.

Pack

This is the one you've been using all along, every time you've called the `pack()` method in previous chapters' programs. The Place geometry manager is good for static (hard-coded) placement and relative placement, but the Pack manager is extremely good for stacks and sticks (or columns and rows, if you prefer). That is, the best way to use it is to put widgets with a similar orientation inside a Frame widget and pack them. The code in Listing 22.7 does just that.

LISTING 22.7 Packing Them In

```

class Packer:
    def __init__(self,w):
        global death
        n = 0
        self.a = Frame(w)
        self.a.pack(side=TOP,expand=1,fill=BOTH)
        for i in range(3):
            item=Button(self.a,text=`n`)
            item.pack(side=LEFT,expand=1,fill=BOTH)
            item["command"] = lambda x=n : prn(x)
            n = n+1
```

continues

LISTING 22.7 continued

```
        self.b = Frame(w)
        self.b.pack(side=TOP,expand=1,fill=BOTH)
        for i in range(3):
            item=Button(self.b,text=`n`)
            item.pack(side=LEFT,expand=1,fill=BOTH)
            if i == 1:
                item["command"] = die
                item["image"] = death
            else:
                item["command"] = lambda x=n : prn(x)
            n = n+1
        self.c = Frame(w)
        self.c.pack(side=TOP,expand=1,fill=BOTH)
        for i in range(3):
            item=Button(self.c,text=`n`)
            item.pack(side=LEFT,expand=1,fill=BOTH)
            item["command"] = lambda x=n : prn(x)
            n = n+1

```

We're doing nine buttons, just as we did with the Place manager, but here we create three frames (`self.a`, `self.b`, and `self.c`) and create three buttons inside each Frame widget. In the center frame, we treat the center button the same way we did using the Place manager. Thus, we have a stack of three Frame widgets, each of which contains a stick of three buttons. Figure 22.6 shows how this looks in action.

FIGURE 22.6
Pack geometry management.

Buttons `0`, `1`, and `2` are in frame `self.a`; `3`, death and `5` are in `self.b`; and `6`, `7`, and `8` are in `self.c`. The whole window is resizable; grab one of the corners, stretch it, and see what happens. It works that way because we specified the `expand=1` option and the `fill=BOTH` option for all the frames and all the buttons in each frame. Play around with various combinations of fill options and see what happens; for example, change the fill option to None, X, or Y.

Grid

This is the most interesting and most versatile geometry manager. It recalls the table-drawing commands from the `troff` add-on, `tbl`. If you have no idea what that means, you're probably better off. Basically, the Grid manager divides a window into a grid with columns and rows. You don't have to tell it in advance how many rows and columns; it figures out what it needs from the `grid()` calls you make. Listing 22.8 shows code that should explain.

LISTING 22.8 Gridlock

```
11
12 class Gridder:
13     def __init__(self,w):
14         global death
15         names=["A","B","C",
16             "D","E","F",
17             "G","H","I",
18             ]
19         n = 0
20         for i in range(3):
21             for j in range(3):
22                 item=Button(w,text=names[n])
23                 if names[n] == "E":
24                     item["command"] = die
25                     item["image"] = death
26                 else:
27                     item["command"] = lambda x=names[n] : prn(x)
28                 item.grid(row=i,column=j,sticky=E+W+N+S)
29                 n = n+1
30
```

All we're doing here is creating nine buttons again, using two nested `for` loops. Notice the `grid()` call in line 28, which assigns the buttons to their row and column places. We also set the `sticky` option, which in this case tells the Grid manager that it's free to expand the widgets it is holding any way it wants. Figure 22.7 shows how the Grid manager looks with our nine buttons when running.

FIGURE 22.7
Grid geometry management.

You're probably thinking that the Grid doesn't look that different from the Pack, but wait until you start doing really complicated window layout. With just a few tiny changes, we can do something fairly tricky by using the Pack manager in an additional row of the Grid manager. The revised code is in Listing 22.9.

LISTING 22.9 Using Pack Inside Grid

```

class Gridder:
    def __init__(self,w):
        global death
        names=["A","B","C",
            "D","E","F",
            "G","H","I",
            ]
        n = 0
        for i in range(3):
            for j in range(3):
                item=Button(w,text=names[n])
                if names[n] == "E":
                    item["command"] = die
                    item["image"] = death
                else:
                    item["command"] = lambda x=names[n] : prn(x)
                item.grid(row=i,column=j,sticky=E+W+N+S)
                n = n+1
        f = Frame(w)
        b1=Button(w,text="Phobos")
        b1["command"] = lambda x="fear" : prn(x)
        b2=Button(f,text="Deimos")
        b2["command"] = lambda x="terror" : prn(x)
        b1.pack(side=LEFT)
        b2.pack(side=RIGHT)
        f.grid(row=3,column=0,columnspan=3)

```

Figure 22.8 shows how it looks when running.

FIGURE 22.8
Grid and Pack managers together.

It would be much harder to arrange the two bottom buttons the same way using only the Grid manager. Note that you must be careful; if you make a mistake and use the wrong parent for the two extra buttons `b1` and `b2`, the Grid and Pack managers will be trying to configure the same window (the root window), and they will get into a little war. You'll have to kill the program, because it will never appear on your screen. You can use one geometry manager inside another, but you cannot use different geometry managers in the same window with the same parent.

In the next chapter, we use the Grid manager, with a helping hand from the Pack manager, when we put together a GUI for viewing Mandelbrot set graphics.

Summary

In this hour, you learned how to build a Pong-like mechanism to make animation possible, and you learned a bit about the three geometry managers: Pack, Place, and Grid. Later, you learn about the math behind Mandelbrot sets and build a GUI viewer for the set.

Workshop

Q&A

Q Is Alchemy Workshop the only company that provides a legal product for making GIF files transparent or animated?

A No. CompuPic, from Photodex, provides transparency, if not animation; also, it supports more formats than most of Alchemy's programs. Some freeware programs are out there, but I would be very leery of using these; their legal status is problematic at best. You should research the question, however, and choose the program that will fit your needs. I'm not making recommendations, only telling you about a couple of programs that are legal according to the current understanding of the GIF situation. Naturally, I disclaim all responsibility for anything whatsoever.

Q Why is the layout in Figure 22.8 so hard? It doesn't look that tricky to me.

A If you divide the horizontal dimension into three equal parts, as is done in row 0 (`A`, `B`, and `C`), there is no way to tell the Grid manager to divide row 3 (Phobos and Deimos) into two parts. If you really want to use only the Grid manager, you have to tell it to divide row 0 into six parts and set the `columnspan` option on buttons `A`, `B`, and `C`. In row 3, you would set the `columnspan` option to `3` on each of the two buttons. It's really much simpler to just add a Frame and use the Pack manager in row 3.

Quiz

1. What do we use instead of trigonometric functions in `tkfield4.py`?
   a. A random number generator
   b. Pre-plotted `x,y` coordinates
   c. Log tables
   d. Calculus

2. Why don't we use a different timer for each flying glyph in `tkfield4.py`?
   a. It would mean we would have to provide 20 times the code.
   b. We do, it just looks like a single timer.
   c. Windows has draconian limits on the number of timers you can have running.
   d. We would in a production environment, but for pedagogical purposes, using only one is fine.
3. How do we stop the glyphs from moving in `tkfield4.py`?
   a. We remove the timer callback.
   b. We fake it by simply plugging the same values into `xdelta` and `ydelta` all the time.
   c. We set a flag that tells the timer callback to return without doing anything.
   d. We set a flag that tells the timer callback to set itself as the timer callback and to return before moving any glyphs.

Answers

1. a, judicious use of a random number generator from the `random` module allows us to dispense with the use of trig functions.
2. c, Windows 95 has supposedly dropped the limits on the number of timers you can have active, but seems to have done nothing to support many timers. Creating more than 10 timers brings a computer to its (metaphorical) knees. Whether limits are imposed by design or by accident, they are still limits; 10 timers is insufficient.
3. d, right-clicking anywhere in the window sets a flag; the timer callback sees the flag the next time it activates, and it sets itself as the timer callback, as usual, but it returns before moving any glyphs. A later right-click unsets the flag.

Exercises

To learn more about the glyphs I've used here, visit `http://www.pauahtun.org/days.html`. These are the glyphs for the 20 named days of the Mayan tzolk'in, a sacred calendar of 260 days.

Alchemy Mindworks can be found at `http://www.mindworkshop.com/alchemy/alchemy.html`. A statement regarding the legality of its product regarding GIFs can be found at `http://www.mindworkshop.com/alchemy/lzw.html`. Gif Construction Set Pro also does animated GIFs for you. CompuPic can be found at Photodex's Web site, `http://www.photodex.com`.

Investigate what it would take to make `tkfield4.py` resizable. Hint: Don't forget that many rectangle objects are available in that Canvas widget, in addition to the glyphs.

Change the glyphs to something else that pleases you—Mah Jongg tiles, for instance.

HOUR 23

The Mandelbrot Set

It is difficult to include trees and coyotes in a bibliography.

—Georgia Johnson

In the preceding hour, we finished our discussion of Tk graphics and covered the geometry managers available in Tkinter. In this hour, we apply everything we've learned in the previous six hours to build a complete application that allows the calculation and display of Mandelbrot sets and associated Julia sets.

The Mandelbrot Set

In 1985, the August *Scientific American* arrived; many of the engineers where I worked came in the next morning with some simple Mandelbrot programs, and by the end of the week nearly everyone had her own program. By Monday, there was a noticeable sluggishness when trying to get any real work done on any of the seven company computers (two Vaxen and five Goulds), caused by the number of Mandelbrot calculations running simultaneously.

This scenario was probably repeated all over the country, although I think our site had a larger proportion of engineers than most others. At the time, the best graphics machine I could get my hands on was an Intelecolor terminal, restricted to downloading at 9600 baud. Even though it took only five minutes to compute a Mandelbrot on our fastest machine (a now-extinct Gould NP1), it could take hours to download the resulting graphic to the display. It was agonizing, and the tube had only eight colors, anyway. I tried to get the company to spring for an Ethernet card for my terminal, but my boss said "No way! I know what you want it for!" And I could hardly argue with him.

I suspect that for the first few months after the appearance of that *Scientific American* issue, 90% to 95% of our national computing capability was dedicated to the production of Mandelbrot Set graphics. Now you, too, although belatedly, can contribute.

If you compute Mandelbrots in C nowadays, they get done really quickly. Chances are that the machine you're using to learn Python on is at least three times as fast as the Gould NP1 we were using. Several friends and I managed to reconstruct the clock speed of the NP1 as 33MHz; in 1985, this was a very fast machine, built with ECL logic and four processors. One of the machines I'm writing this book on is a 400MHz single-processor system, and another system is a dual-processor 266. In 1985, the only possible language to write Mandelbrot calculators in was C, because anything else would have been blindingly slow. The program you're going to see here, however, is written entirely in Python and Tkinter, so you should be prepared for slow execution times, at least by today's standards. Even though all the computation is done in Python and not a C extension, I can still compute and display a graphic from the set in five minutes or less. After you understand what's going on, you can search out faster implementations; at least one quite rapid Python version is out there, but it uses the Numeric extension (NumPy, available at `http://numpy.sourceforge.net/`) to Python, and the wxPython windowing GUI for Windows (available at `http://alldunn.com/wxPython/`), both of which are far beyond the scope of this book.

I'm sure you've all seen pictures of the Mandelbrot set, but just in case, see Figure 23.1.

This is an image of the whole set. Pixels colored black are members of the set; everything else is a nonmember. In a recent documentary on the Mandelbrot set, hosted by Arthur C. Clarke and featuring Benoit Mandelbrot (who discovered the set in 1980). Dr. Clarke explained that the Mandelbrot set was larger than the universe. Or at least, that was his conjecture. He checked with Stephen Hawking, just to make sure. Dr. Hawking agreed, citing the lower limit on the size of physical things, the Planck Length (1.616×10^{-33} cm). Smaller by far than a quark, this dimension is one of the fundamental constants of our universe. Nothing tinier can possibly exist. But there are no such limits when we are dealing with a mathematical model such as the Mandelbrot set; the only limits are the floating-point capabilities of your computer—which are severe, by the way. You really need unlimited precision to do really good 'brots, but then, who's got that? Not even Python, or at least not yet.

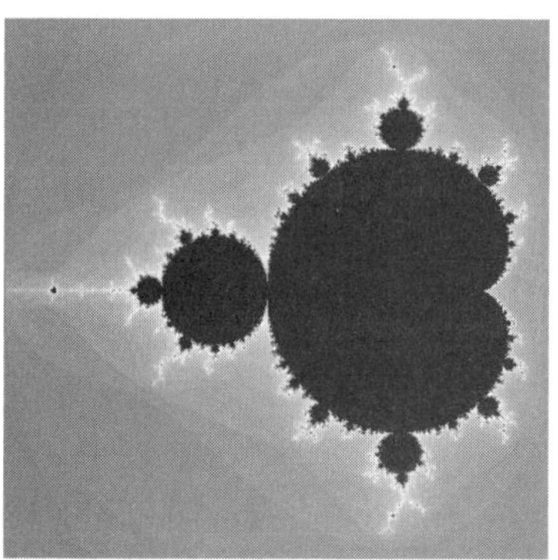

FIGURE 23.1
The Mandelbrot set.

Mathematics

The math for calculating the set is extremely simple. The basic formula is

$$z = z^2 + c$$

Certain assumptions are left out of the equation. Both `z` and `c` are complex numbers, and the formula neglects to mention that it is applied to every pixel in a field representing a portion of the complex plane. For the Mandelbrot set, the portion of that plane that is of interest stretches from `-2.0` to `2.0` in the `x` dimension, and from `-2.0` to `2.0` in the `y` dimension (`-2.0` is at the upper left). To clarify, remember from our earlier discussion of complex numbers that they are composed of a real and an imaginary part. The complex plane treats the `x` coordinate as the real part of a complex number, and the `y` coordinate as the imaginary part. Therefore, any single point on the complex plane expresses a complex number; this is `c` in the preceding formula. You can create the complex number `c` easily in Python by using `c=complex(x,y)`. In Figure 23.2, you see a diagram showing the important part of the complex plane.

As with any dimension, the `x` and `y` dimensions here contain an infinite number of points. Because we are going to display our results on a computer screen, we don't have to calculate the infinite number of points in the plane that is the result of multiplying infinity `x` times infinity `y`, but can confine our calculation to the number of visible pixels in any given section of the plane. For the program used in this chapter, the view port I've chosen is 400×400 pixels. Therefore, although an infinite number of points are on each dimension, we are looking at only 400 of those points in each dimension: this is known as the *resolution* of the axis we are looking at. For the program in this chapter, then, I'm using an x resolution of 400 and a y resolution also of 400. But that still means that the area we cover is 160,000 pixels—a not insubstantial number.

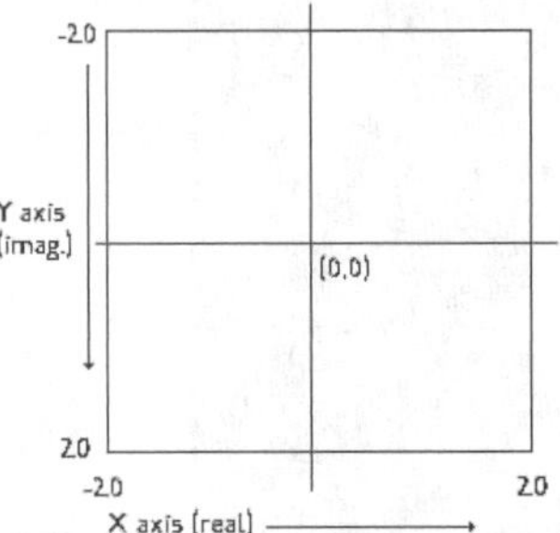

FIGURE 23.2
The complex plane.

That number increases when we know what we are calculating. We must apply the formula `z = z² + c` to each pixel. But we don't know what z is, do we? You can view it as a third dimension, if you will, a measure of the distance above the complex plane (as in dimensions x, y, and z). For each pixel, then, we need to decide whether the pixel is a member of the Mandelbrot set, in which case we color the pixel black. If the pixel is not a member of the set, we need to know how far above the complex plane the pixel is, and color it appropriately. How do we decide if a pixel, or point, is a member of the set? We apply our formula to a particular pixel and watch what happens to its distance from the origin of the plane at `(0,0j)`. Then, we can apply these extremely simple rules.

1. Points that never move far away from the plane are members of the set, and we color them black.
2. Points that move away from the plane toward infinity are not members of the set, and we color them according to the speed at which they move away from the plane.

As you know, it is not a good idea to try to compute "never" and "infinity," so we draw some arbitrary limits to enable us to label, or color, points. The first limit is the cutoff distance above the complex plane. The size of the x axis is `4.0`, the distance from `-2.0` to `2.0`, so the z axis, you might think, should be 4.0. Because we don't want to calculate negative distances, however, we confine ourselves to the range `0` to `2.0`. The distance above the plane itself is calculated by using our formula `z = z² + c`, and then by applying the `abs()` function. Note that `abs()` is a function that accepts numeric arguments of any type, so you don't need to import either the `math` or the `cmath` modules.

The abs() function for ordinary numbers simply removes all signs from the number; abs(-4) returns 4, and abs(3.14159) returns 3.14159. Calculating the absolute value of a complex number is a little more, well, complex. You calculate the squares of the parts and add them, and then take the square root of the result. That is, given a complex number, (-0.5,1j) for example, the absolute value is:

```
sqrt((-0.5 * -0.5) + (1 * 1))
sqrt((0.25) + (1))
sqrt(1.25)
1.11803398875
```

You can run the above lines of code in an interactive Python session; note that none of the numbers shown are actual complex numbers. To use complex numbers, run these lines of code, also in an interactive session:

```
c = -0.5+1j
abs(c)
```

You should get the same answer: 1.11803398875. (If you don't, either you're working on a system with out-of-the-ordinary features, such as very large floating-point numbers, or something is seriously wrong with your Python installation.) With conventional languages such as C, which do not have built-in complex numbers, we would have to jump through some hoops to calculate the absolute value, and this would complicate our code. Luckily, we are using Python, so we can apply our formula virtually unchanged, and I won't bother to explain the complications that would have to be used in other languages (I'm trying to get you to use Python, after all!). Here is the algorithm we will use (this is pseudocode, not real Python):

```
for every pixel in the x dimension:
    for every pixel in the y dimension:
        c = complex(x,y)
        for every pixel in the z dimension:
            if abs(z) > 2.0:
                break
            z = (z**2) + c
        color the z pixel black if abs(z) was never true
        else color the z pixel according to the number of iterations
         before it went above 2.0
```

Points on the edges of the plane are going to start off already above our 2.0 limit. Consider abs(-2.0+-2.0j), which is 2.82842712475, so the iteration count (how many loops it takes to go above 2.0) is going to be zero. The small program in Listing 23.1 lets you observe the behavior of any single point on the complex plane.

LISTING 23.1 ctest.py

```
 1  #!/usr/local/bin/python
 2
 3  import sys
 4  import string
 5
 6  c=-0.5+1j
 7  z=0j
 8
 9  if len(sys.argv)>2:
10      r=string.atof(sys.argv[1])
11      i=string.atof(sys.argv[2])
12      c=complex(r,i)
13
14  print "initial value of c", abs(c)
15  for i in range(64):
16      print "step",i,"value of z",z,"distance (abs()) of z",abs(z)
17      if abs(z)>2.0:
18          break
19      z = (z**2) + c
20  print "color z", i
```

The default values in lines 6 and 7 are what we've used for examples before. The default output is shown in Listing 23.2.

LISTING 23.2 Output of ctest.py

```
initial value of c 1.11803398875
step 0 value of z 0j distance (abs()) of z 0.0
step 1 value of z (-0.5+1j) distance (abs()) of z 1.11803398875
step 2 value of z (-1.25+0j) distance (abs()) of z 1.25
step 3 value of z (1.0625+1j) distance (abs()) of z 1.45907719124
step 4 value of z (-0.37109375+3.125j) distance (abs()) of z 3.14695655694
color z 4
```

Naturally, values close in to the center `(0,0j)` are going to be colored black, and values out at the edges are going to be colored with whatever color we start with. Thus, we can say that values far from the Mandelbrot set are going to escape to infinity rapidly, and the closer we get to the set the slower the values will escape. When they do not escape, they are members of the set. We can view the behavior of nonmember points on the plane as being attracted by infinity. The concept of attractors is part of chaos theory, but that shouldn't intimidate you; all it means is that, left to themselves, that's where they'll head. Because we have no infinite and infinitely capable computers, we don't know if these points that are not members of a set really travel to infinity, but for all practical purposes, we can treat them as if they do.

Choosing a color is based on the number of iterations it takes to determine if a pixel escapes to infinity. In Listing 23.2, the color is `4`, or because we will use the same colormap functions from the `colormap` module that we used for our animations in the last two chapters, the fourth color in whatever colormap we use. For the default colormap, this is the color `"#F2620C"`. Listing 23.3 shows `ctest.py`, modified to display the color chosen.

LISTING 23.3 `ctest2.py`

```
#!/usr/local/bin/python

import sys
import string
from colormap import *

from Tkinter import *

cmap = SetupColormap0(64)

c=-0.5+1j
z=0j

if len(sys.argv)>2:
    r=string.atof(sys.argv[1])
    i=string.atof(sys.argv[2])
    c=complex(r,i)

print "initial value of c", abs(c)
for i in range(64):
    print "step",i,"value of z",z,"distance (abs()) of z",abs(z)
    if abs(z)>2.0:
        break
    z = (z**2) + c
print "color z", i, cmap[i]

root=Tk()
root["background"]=cmap[i]
root.mainloop()
```

The Mandelbrot Program

The picture in Figure 23.1 was drawn with the program shown in Listing 23.4.

LISTING 23.4 mandelbrot2.py

```
#!/usr/local/bin/python

from Tkinter import *
from Canvas import Line,Rectangle
import sys
import string
from colormap import *
from tkFileDialog import *

class Msize:
    def __init__(self,xr=400,yr=400,xs=-2.0,ys=-1.25,xw=2.6,yw=2.6):
        self.xresolution = xr
        self.yresolution = yr
        self.cxsize = self.xresolution
        self.cysize = self.yresolution
        self.znought = 0j
        self.xstart = xs
        self.ystart = ys
        self.xwidth = xw
        self.ywidth = yw
        self.xend = self.xstart + self.xwidth
        self.yend = self.ystart + self.ywidth
        self.xdiv = self.xwidth / self.xresolution
        self.ydiv = self.ywidth / self.yresolution

    def __call__(self):
        return (self.xstart,
            self.ystart,
            self.xwidth,
            self.ywidth,
            self.xend,
            self.yend,
            self.xdiv,
            self.ydiv
        )
    def set(self,x0,y0,xw,yw):
        self.xstart = x0
        self.ystart = y0
        self.xwidth = xw
        self.ywidth = yw
        self.xend = self.xstart + self.xwidth
        self.yend = self.ystart + self.ywidth
        self.xdiv = self.xwidth / self.xresolution
        self.ydiv = self.ywidth / self.yresolution

    def __repr__(self):
        s = "xstart %s ystart %s xwidth %s ywidth %s xend %s yend %s" \
            " xdiv %s ydiv %s xresolution %s yresolution %s" % \
```

```
            (self.xstart,self.ystart,
            self.xwidth,self.ywidth,
            self.xend,self.yend,
            self.xdiv,self.ydiv,
            self.xresolution,self.yresolution)
        return s

class AboutDialog:
    def __init__(self,parent,s="Mandelbrot"):
        self.logotxt="""%s Cruiser
Copyright © 1999, 2000
by Ivan Van Laningham
Written for
Teach Yourself Python in 24 Hours""" %(s)
        top = self.top=Toplevel(parent)
        top["background"] = "white"
        self.i=PhotoImage(file="X_GodNLogo5.gif")
        self.lg = Label(top,text="",bd=0)
        self.lg["image"] = self.i
        self.lg.pack()
        self.l=Label(top,text=self.logotxt,bd=0,background="white")
        self.l.pack(side=LEFT)
        self.b = Button(top, text="OK", command=self.ok,
            background="#008000",foreground="white")
        self.b.pack(side=LEFT)

    def ok(self):
        self.top.destroy()

class Mandel:
    def __init__(self,ncolors,root,xs=-2.0,ys=-1.25,xw=2.6,yw=2.6,
        xr=400,yr=400,
        im=["64-mdb5.gif", "64-mdb5.600.gif", "64-mdb5.800.gif",],
        qn="Quit",qim=["x_cimi.gif","x_cimi.gif"]):
        self.root = root
        self.debug = 0
        self.useimages = 0
        self.origxstart = xs
        self.origystart = ys
        self.origxwidth = xw
        self.origywidth = yw
        self.origxresolution = xr
        self.origyresolution = yr
        self.xstart = xs
        self.ystart = ys
        self.xwidth = xw
        self.ywidth = yw
        self.xend = self.xstart + self.xwidth
        self.yend = self.ystart + self.ywidth
```

continues

Listing 23.4 continued

```
        self.mdb = None
        self.waitvar = 0
        self.xresolution = xr
        self.yresolution = xr
        self.cxsize = self.xresolution
        self.cysize = self.yresolution
        self.znought = 0j
        self.xdiv = self.xwidth / self.xresolution
        self.ydiv = self.ywidth / self.yresolution
        self.calculating=0
        self.ncolors = ncolors
        self.ncolorlist = ["2",
            "4",
            "8",
            "16",
            "32",
            "64",
            "128",
            "256",
            "512",
            "1024"
        ]
        self.colormaps = {"map 1":SetupColormap0,
            "map 2":SetupColormap1,
            "map 3":SetupColormap2,
            "map 4":SetupColormap3,
            "map 5":SetupColormap4,
            "map 6":SetupColormap5,
            "map 7":SetupColormap6,
        }
        self.imagelist=im
        self.cmapcommand=SetupColormap
        self.cmapname = "map 1"
        self.cmap = self.cmapcommand(self.ncolors - 1)
        self.stopnow = 0
        self.mdsize=None
        self.xdrawn=None
        self.ydrawn=None
        self.zdrawn=None
        self.uxl = 0
        self.uyl = 0
        self.uil = 0
        self.progress = None
        self.progressize = 10
        self.xlab = None
        self.ylab = None
        self._label = None
        self.cv = None
        self.scX = None
```

```
        self.scY = None
        self.scZ = None
        self.x0 = None
        self.x1 = None
        self.y0 = None
        self.y1 = None
        self.zlabel = None
        self.listbox = None
        self.listbox1 = None
        self.qbutton = None
        self.cbutton = None
        self.cabutton = None
        self.rbutton = None
        self.qimg = [None,None]
        self.cimg = None
        self.caimg = None
        self.rimg = None
        self.J = None
        self.qname = qn
        self.qimage = qim
        self.locked = 0
        self.qaction = None
        self.afterid = None

        self.buildMenu()
        self.buildAndSetButtons()

        self.buildNColorControl()
        self.buildCMapControl()

        self.buildXYLabels()
        self.setXYLabels()

        self.buildProgress()
        self.buildCanvas()

        self.waitvar = IntVar(0)
        self.root.title("Mandelbrot Cruiser")
        self.afterid = self.listbox.after(250,self.colorpoll)

    def setXYLabels(self,m=None):
        if not self.__dict__.has_key("center"):
            self.center=0j
        if m == None:
            xs = "X start %f width %f xdiv %f" % \
                (self.xstart, self.xwidth, self.xdiv)
            self.xlab["text"] = xs
            ys = "Y start %f width %f ydiv %f" % \
                (self.ystart, self.ywidth, self.ydiv)
```

continues

LISTING 23.4 continued

```
            self.ylab["text"] = ys
            self.zlabel["text"]="Zoom:%f\nC = %s" % \
                (self.xwidth/self.xwidth,self.center)
        else:
            xs = "X start %f width %f xdiv %f" % \
                (m.xstart, m.xwidth, m.xdiv)
            self.xlab["text"] = xs
            ys = "Y start %f width %f ydiv %f" % \
                (m.ystart, m.ywidth, m.ydiv)
            self.ylab["text"] = ys
            self.zlabel["text"]="Zoom:%f\nC = %s" % \
                (self.xwidth/m.xwidth, self.center)

    def resetter(self,event=0):
        if self.calculating:
            return
        self.xstart = self.origxstart
        self.ystart = self.origystart
        self.xwidth = self.origxwidth
        self.ywidth = self.origywidth
        self.xend = self.xstart + self.xwidth
        self.yend = self.ystart + self.ywidth
        self.xdiv = self.xwidth / self.xresolution
        self.ydiv = self.ywidth / self.yresolution
        self.mdsize=Msize(self.xresolution,self.yresolution,
            self.xstart,self.ystart,self.xwidth,self.ywidth)
        self.setXYLabels()
        self.cv.delete(ALL)
        self.progress.delete(ALL)
        self.xdrawn = None
        self.ydrawn = None
        self.zdrawn = None
        self.mdb = self.dithimage()
        self.img = self.cv.create_image(self.xresolution/2, \
            self.yresolution/2, anchor=CENTER, image=self.mdb)
        self.scX.set(self.xresolution/2)
        self.scY.set(self.yresolution/2)
        self.scZ.set(self.yresolution/2)

    def zoomer(self,event=0):
        if self.calculating:
            return
        if self.mdsize == None:
            self.mdsize=Msize(self.xresolution,self.yresolution,
                self.xstart,self.ystart,self.xwidth,self.ywidth)
        oldxw = self.xwidth
        oldyh = self.ywidth
        w = self.x1 - self.x0
```

```
        xp0 = self.x0 * self.xdiv
        xp1 = self.x1 * self.xdiv
        newxst = self.xstart + xp0
        newxe = self.xstart + xp1
        h = self.y1 - self.y0
        yp0 = self.y0 * self.ydiv
        yp1 = self.y1 * self.ydiv
        newyst = self.ystart + yp0
        newye = self.ystart + yp1

        self.mdsize.set(newxst,newyst,
            newxe - newxst,
            newye - newyst)
        self.setXYLabels(self.mdsize)

    def xliner(self,event=0):
        if self.calculating:
            return
        n=self.scX.get()
        y=self.scY.get()
        x1 = n * self.xdiv
        x1 = self.xstart + x1
        y1 = y * self.ydiv
        y1 = self.ystart + y1
        self.center=complex(x1,y1)
        if self.xdrawn==None:
            self.xdrawn = Line(self.cv,n,0,n,self.yresolution-1,
                fill="#ffffff")
        else:
            self.cv.coords(self.xdrawn,n,0,n,self.yresolution-1)
        self.setXYLabels(self.mdsize)

    def yliner(self,event=0):
        if self.calculating:
            return
        n=self.scY.get()
        x=self.scX.get()
        x1 = x * self.xdiv
        x1 = self.xstart + x1
        y1 = n * self.ydiv
        y1 = self.ystart + y1
        self.center=complex(x1,y1)
        if self.ydrawn==None:
            self.ydrawn = Line(self.cv,0,n,self.xresolution-1,n,
                fill="#ffffff")
        else:
            self.cv.coords(self.ydrawn,0,n,self.xresolution-1,n)
        self.setXYLabels(self.mdsize)
```

continues

LISTING 23.4 continued

```

    def zliner(self,event=0):
        if self.calculating:
            return
        self.xliner()
        self.yliner()
        n=self.scZ.get()
        x=self.scX.get()
        y=self.scY.get()
        x1 = x * self.xdiv
        x1 = self.xstart + x1
        y1 = y * self.ydiv
        y1 = self.ystart + y1
        self.center=complex(x1,y1)
        lima = min(x,y)
        limb = min(self.xresolution - x, self.yresolution - y)
        limc = min(lima,limb)
        # x and y are the coordinates of the center.
        # x0 and y0 are the upper-left coordinates:
        self.x0 = x - n
        if self.x0 < 0:
            self.x0 = 0
        self.y0 = y - n
        if self.y0 < 0:
            self.y0 = 0
        # x1 and y1 are the lower-right coordinates:
        w = x - self.x0
        if w > limc:
            w = limc
        self.x1 = x + w
        if self.x1 > self.xresolution-1:
            self.x1 = self.xresolution-1
        if self.x1 - self.x0 > (limc * 2):
            self.x0 = self.x1 - (limc * 2)
        h = y - self.y0
        if h > limc:
            h = limc
        self.y1 = y + h
        if self.y1 > self.yresolution - 1:
            self.y1 = self.yresolution - 1
        if self.y1 - self.y0 > (limc * 2):
            self.y0 = self.y1 - (limc * 2)
        if x == 0 or y == 0:
            self.x0 = self.y0 = 0
            self.x1 = self.y1 = self.xresolution-1
        if self.x1 - self.x0 == 0 or self.y1 - self.y0 == 0:
            self.x0 = self.y0 = 0
            self.x1 = self.y1 = self.xresolution-1
        if self.zdrawn==None:
```

```
            self.zdrawn = Rectangle(self.cv,self.x0,self.y0,
                self.x1,self.y1,outline="#ffffff")
        else:
            self.cv.coords(self.zdrawn,self.x0,self.y0,self.x1,self.y1)
        self.zoomer()

    def die(self,event=0):
        self.stopnow = 1
        self.root.quit()

    def cancel(self,event=0):
        self.stopnow = 1
        self.cv.delete(ALL)
        self.xdrawn=None
        self.ydrawn=None
        self.zdrawn=None
        self.progress.delete(ALL)
        self.mdb = self.dithimage()
        self.img = self.cv.create_image(self.xresolution/2,
            self.yresolution/2, anchor=CENTER, image=self.mdb)
        self.cv.update()

    def colorpoll(self):
        if self.calculating:
            pass
        else:
            now=self.listbox.curselection()
            nn = string.atoi(self.ncolorlist[string.atoi(now[0])])
            if nn != self.ncolors:
                self.ncolors = nn

            x = self.listbox1.curselection()
            s = x[0]
            tmname = self.listbox1.get(s)
            if tmname != self.cmapname:
                self.cmapname = tmname
                self.cmapcommand = self.colormaps[self.cmapname]
        self.afterid = self.listbox.after(250,self.colorpoll)

    def updateProgress(self):
        if self.stopnow:
            return
        Rectangle(self.progress,
            self.uxl,self.uyl,
            self.uxl+self.progressize - 2,self.uyl+16,
            fill=self.cmap[self.uil % self.ncolors],
            outline="",
            width=0)
        self.progress.update()
```

continues

LISTING 23.4 continued

```
        self.uxl = self.uxl + self.progressize
        self.uil = self.uil + 1

    def waitcalc(self):
        if self.calculating:
            return
        self.cv.after(1,self.calc)
        self.cv.wait_variable(self.waitvar)

    def calc(self):
        self.waitvar.set(1)
        self.cv.delete(ALL)
        self.xdrawn=None
        self.ydrawn=None
        self.zdrawn=None
        self.progress.delete(ALL)
        self.mdb = self.dithimage()
        self.img = self.cv.create_image(self.xresolution/2,
            self.yresolution/2, anchor=CENTER, image=self.mdb)
        oldcursor = self.cv["cursor"]
        self.cv["cursor"] = "watch"
        self.calculating=1

        if self.mdsize != None:
            self.xstart,self.ystart,self.xwidth,self.ywidth, \
                self.xend, self.yend,self.xdiv,self.ydiv = \
                self.mdsize()

        x = self.xstart
        self._label["text"] = \
            "Beginning calculation with %d colors %s..." % \
            (self.ncolors,self.cmapname)
        self.cmap = self.cmapcommand(self.ncolors - 1)
        if self.ncolors < 64:
            dwell = 64
        else:
            dwell = self.ncolors
        self.scX.set(self.xresolution/2)
        self.scY.set(self.yresolution/2)
        self.scZ.set(self.yresolution/2)
        if self.debug == 0:
            for xX in range(self.xresolution):
                y = self.ystart
                for yY in range(self.yresolution):
                    c = complex(x,y)
                    z = self.znought
                    i = 0
                    for i in range(dwell):
                        if abs(z)>2.0:
```

```
                            break
                        z=(z**2)+c
                    hcol = self.cmap[i % self.ncolors]
                    self.mdb.put((hcol,),(xX,yY,xX+1,yY+1))

                    y = y + self.ydiv

                    if self.stopnow:
                        self.updateProgress()
                        self.stopnow=0
                        self._label["text"] = "Finished calculation."
                        self.uil = self.uyl = self.uxl = 0
                        self.calculating=0
                        self.resetter()
                        self.cv["cursor"] = oldcursor
                        self.waitvar.set(0)
                        return
                    if xX != 0 and xX % self.progressize == 0 \
                        and yY == 0:
                        self.updateProgress()
                x = x + self.xdiv
            self.img = self.cv.create_image(self.xresolution/2,
                self.yresolution/2, anchor=CENTER, image=self.mdb)
        self.cv.update()
        self.updateProgress()
        self._label["text"] = "Finished calculation."
        self.mdsize=Msize(self.xresolution,self.yresolution,
            self.xstart,self.ystart,self.xwidth,self.ywidth)

        self.setXYLabels(self.mdsize)
        self.uil = self.uyl = self.uxl = 0
        self.stopnow = 0
        self.calculating=0
        self.cv["cursor"] = oldcursor
        self.waitvar.set(0)

    def changeImages(self,event=None):
        if event != None:
            self.useimages = event
        elif self.useimages:
            self.useimages=0
        else:
            self.useimages=1
        try:
            self.qbutton.grid_forget()
            self.cbutton.grid_forget()
            self.rbutton.grid_forget()
            self.cabutton.grid_forget()
            del self.qbutton
```

continues

LISTING 23.4 continued

```
            del self.cbutton
            del self.rbutton
            del self.cabutton
        except:
            pass
        self.buildAndSetButtons()

    def dithimage(self):
        if self.mdb != None:
            del self.mdb
        if self.xresolution == 600:
            f=self.imagelist[1]
        elif self.xresolution == 800:
            f=self.imagelist[2]
        else:
            f=self.imagelist[0]
        self.mdb = PhotoImage(file=f)
        return self.mdb

    def about(self,event=0):
        d = AboutDialog(self.root)
        self.root.wait_window(d.top)

    def saveit(self,event=0):
        sname = asksaveasfilename(initialfile="untitled.ppm",
            filetypes=[("PPM files", "*.ppm")])
        if sname and self.mdb:
            self.mdb.write(sname,format="ppm")

    def popJulia(self,event=0):
        if self.J == None:
            import julia2
            topl=Toplevel(self.root)
            topl.transient(self.root)
            self.J = julia2.Julia(self.ncolors,topl)
            n=self.scX.get()
            y=self.scY.get()
            x1 = n * self.xdiv
            x1 = self.xstart + x1
            y1 = y * self.ydiv
            y1 = self.ystart + y1
            self.J.center=complex(x1,y1)
            self.J.lock(1)
            self.J.setXYLabels()
            self.J.waitcalc()
        elif self.J.calculating:
                print "Sorry!" # This needs an error box.
        else:
            s=self.J.root.state()
```

```
            if s != "normal":
                self.J.root.deiconify()
            n=self.scX.get()
            y=self.scY.get()
            x1 = n * self.xdiv
            x1 = self.xstart + x1
            y1 = y * self.ydiv
            y1 = self.ystart + y1
            self.J.center=complex(x1,y1)
            self.J.lock(1)
            self.J.setXYLabels()
            self.J.waitcalc()


    def buildMenu(self):
        bar = Menu(self.root)
        filem = Menu(bar)
        filem.add_command(label="Save as...",command=self.saveit)
        filem.add_command(label="Use button images",
            command=self.changeImages)
        filem.add_separator()
        filem.add_command(label="Exit",command=self.die)
        bar.add_cascade(label="File", menu=filem)
        helpm=Menu(bar)
        helpm.add_command(label="About",command=self.about)
        bar.add_cascade(label="Help", menu=helpm)
        self.filem = filem
        self.root.config(menu=bar)

        self.pop=Menu(self.root)
        self.pop.add_command(label="Show Julia set...",
            command=self.popJulia)
        self.pop["tearoff"]=0

    def buildButtons(self):
        self.qbutton=Button(self.root,text=self.qname)
        if self.qaction != None:
            self.qbutton["command"] = self.qaction
        else:
            self.qbutton["command"] = self.die

        self.cbutton=Button(self.root,text="Cancel",
            command=self.cancel)
        self.rbutton = Button(self.root,text="Reset",
            command=self.resetter)
        self.cabutton=Button(self.root,text="Calculate",
            command=self.waitcalc)
        if self.useimages:
            self.qimg[0]=PhotoImage(file=self.qimage[0])
```

continues

LISTING 23.4 continued

```
            self.qimg[1]=PhotoImage(file=self.qimage[1])
            self.qbutton["image"] = self.qimg[self.locked]
            self.cimg=PhotoImage(file="x_akbal.gif")
            self.cbutton["image"] = self.cimg
            self.rimg=PhotoImage(file="G718.gif")
            self.rbutton["image"] = self.rimg
            self.caimg=PhotoImage(file="xoc_1.gif")
            self.cabutton["image"] = self.caimg

    def buildAndSetButtons(self):
        self.buildButtons()
        self.qbutton.grid(row=0,column=0)
        self.cbutton.grid(row=0,column=1)
        self.rbutton.grid(row=0,column=4)
        self.cabutton.grid(row=0,column=5)

    def buildNColorControl(self):
        f1 = Frame(self.root,width=60,height=32)
        scrollbar = Scrollbar(f1, orient=VERTICAL)
        self.listbox=Listbox(f1,exportselection=0,height=1,
            width=5,yscrollcommand=scrollbar.set,selectmode=SINGLE)
        n = 0
        ns = -1
        for i in self.ncolorlist:
            if i == str(self.ncolors):
               ns = n
            self.listbox.insert(END,i)
            n = n + 1
        if ns == -1:
            self.ncolorlist.append(str(self.ncolors))
            self.listbox.insert(END,str(self.ncolors))
            ns = n
        scrollbar.config(command=self.listbox.yview)
        self.listbox.pack(side=LEFT)
        scrollbar.pack(side=LEFT)
        self.listbox.select_set(ns)
        self.listbox.see(ns)
        f1.grid(row=0,column=2)
        self.root.columnconfigure(2,minsize=30)

    def buildCMapControl(self):
        f2 = Frame(self.root,width=70,height=32)
        scrollbar1 = Scrollbar(f2, orient=VERTICAL)
        self.listbox1=Listbox(f2,exportselection=0,height=1,
            width=6,yscrollcommand=scrollbar1.set,selectmode=SINGLE)
        k = self.colormaps.keys()
        k.sort()
        for i in k:
```

```
            self.listbox1.insert(END,i)
        scrollbar1.config(command=self.listbox1.yview)
        self.listbox1.pack(side=LEFT)
        scrollbar1.pack(side=LEFT)
        self.listbox1.select_set(0)
        f2.grid(row=0,column=3)
        self.root.columnconfigure(3,minsize=70)

    def buildXYLabels(self):
        self.xlab = Label(self.root,text="")
        self.ylab = Label(self.root,text="")
        self.xlab.grid(row=1,column=0,columnspan=3,sticky=W)
        self.ylab.grid(row=1,column=3,columnspan=3,sticky=E)
        self._label=Label(self.root,text="")
        self._label.grid(row=2,column=1,columnspan=5)
        self.zlabel=Label(self.root,text="Zoom:%f" % 1.0)
        self.zlabel.grid(row=2,column=0)

    def buildProgress(self):
        f=Frame(self.root)
        self.progress = Canvas(f,width=self.cxsize,height=16,
            borderwidth=0,highlightthickness=0,selectborderwidth=0)
        self.progress.pack(side=TOP)
        f.grid(row=3,column=0,columnspan=6)

    def buildCanvas(self):
        f = Frame(self.root,width=self.cxsize+54,height=self.cysize+54)

        self.cv = Canvas(f,width=self.cxsize, height=self.cysize,
            borderwidth=0,highlightthickness=0,selectborderwidth=0)
        self.mdb = self.dithimage()
        self.img = self.cv.create_image(self.xresolution/2,
            self.yresolution/2, anchor=CENTER, image=self.mdb)
        self.cv.place(relx=0.5,rely=0.5,anchor=CENTER)
        self.scX = Scale(f,orient=HORIZONTAL,from_=0,
            to=self.xresolution - 1,
            length=self.cxsize, showvalue=0,command=self.xliner)
        self.scX.set(self.xresolution/2)
        self.scX.place(relx=0.5,rely=0,anchor=N)

        self.scY = Scale(f,orient=VERTICAL,from_=0,
            to=self.yresolution - 1,
            length=self.cysize,command=self.yliner, showvalue=0)
        self.scY.set(self.yresolution/2)
        self.scY.place(relx=0,rely=0.5,anchor=W)

        self.scZ = Scale(f,orient=HORIZONTAL,to=0,
            from_=self.yresolution - 1,length=self.cxsize,
            showvalue=0,command=self.zliner)
```

continues

LISTING 23.4 continued

```
683             self.scZ.set(self.yresolution/2)
684             self.scZ.place(relx=0.5,rely=1,anchor=S)
685             f.grid(column=0,row=4,columnspan=6)
686             self.cv.bind("<Button-1>",self.clicker)
687             self.cv.bind("<Button-3>",self.clacker)
688
689         def clicker(self,event=0):
690             x,y=event.x,event.y
691             x1=self.xstart+(x*self.xdiv)
692             y1=self.ystart+(y*self.ydiv)
693             self.scY.set(y)
694             self.scX.set(x)
695
696         def clacker(self,event=0):
697             self.pop.post(event.x_root,event.y_root)
698
699     if __name__ == "__main__":
700         if len(sys.argv)>1:
701             ncolors=string.atoi(sys.argv[1])
702         else:
703             ncolors=32
704         root=Tk()
705         mandel=Mandel(ncolors,root)
706
707         mandel.root.mainloop()
708
```

There is obviously much too much code to give detailed explanations of every line, so I'll just give capsule descriptions of some of the more important parts. Figure 23.3 shows the default appearance of `mandelbrot2.py` when you start it up.

Figure 23.4 shows the alternate appearance (available on the File menu: `File->Use button images`; or, edit `mandelbrot2.py` and set `useimages=1`) on startup.

The class `Msize`, lines 10–55, provides a way to keep track of the size of the image we're viewing. We use it to precalculate where in the set we want to look and how small a division of the `x` and `y` dimensions each pixel in the `x` and `y` resolutions we need. This gives us a zoom ratio, which you can see in action when you run the program. Using the scrollbars, you can pick a square area of the larger image to zoom in on to examine in greater detail. Figure 23.5 shows a rectangle already picked out.

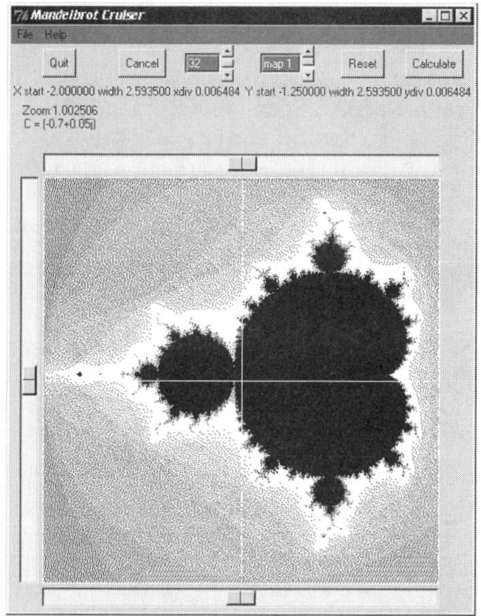

FIGURE 23.3
Running `mandelbrot2.py`.

FIGURE 23.4
Use button images.

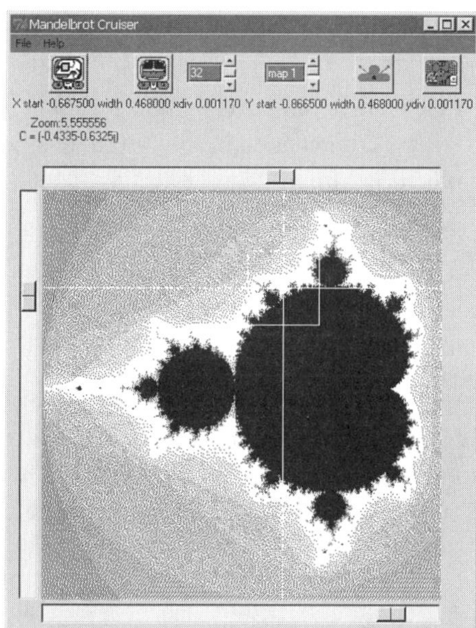

FIGURE 23.5
Preparing to zoom in, 5.55 to one.

And the next shot, Figure 23.6, shows the calculated section.

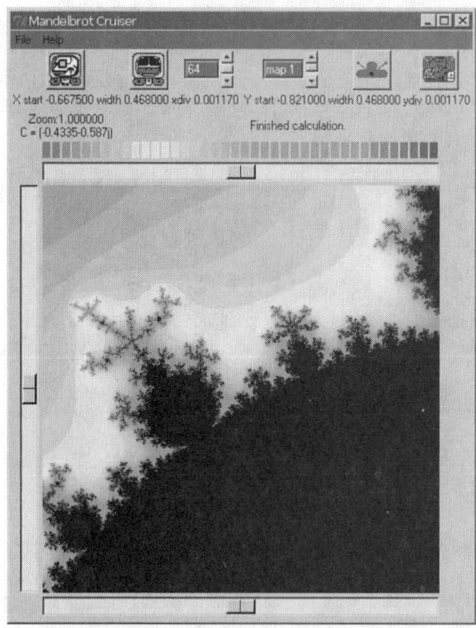

FIGURE 23.6
Zooming in.

We build the whole application as a class, `Mandel`; this makes it easy to modify, using inheritance, for the calculation of Julia sets, which we cover briefly later in this chapter. The list of images, `im` in the `__init__()` method in line 79, allows us to provide precomputed Mandelbrots when the application starts up; that's shown in Figures 23.3 and 23.5. That way, if we want to bypass computation of the full set and proceed directly to a zoom, it's easy to know where we are.

The `colorpoll()` method, lines 363–379, lets us avoid having to double-click the scrolled list boxes for the number of colors and for the colormap selector; every 250 milliseconds, the method is activated and checks whatever values have been set, and those values are transferred to the class items, `self.ncolor` and `self.cmap`.

The `xliner()`, `yliner()`, and `zliner()` methods allow us to pick the center of a square anywhere on the complex plane and zoom in to view it in greater detail. The `x` and `y` methods draw lines according to the position of the scrollbars, whereas the `zliner()` method adjusts the size of the zoomed square depending on the position of the bottom scrollbar.

The `calc()` method in lines 399–473 is where the grunt work is done. Because the resolution is 400 pixels, that means we have to choose the color for 160,000 pixels; some will have no more than one iteration, while all the pixels that are in the set will have whatever `dwell` is set to—at least `64`.

Most of the rest of the methods in class `Mandel` are self-explanatory; if you have questions, reread the code and watch the behavior onscreen. However, lines 517–549 require explanation.

Julia Sets

Gaston Maurice Julia, who served as a soldier in World War I, discovered the sets that bear his name sometime before 1918, when he published the details of their construction. Although he was somewhat famous among the mathematicians of his day, his work was forgotten until Benoit Mandelbrot discovered the Mandelbrot set, based at least partly on Julia's work. It may surprise you to learn that Julia sets were found first, but you need to remember that the real wonder is that Julia, without the aid of modern high-speed computers, was able to discover any fractal objects at all.

The main difference between Mandelbrot and Julia sets is that in the Mandelbrot, we cruise across all points in the set, transform the *x,y* coordinate into a complex number, and then determine whether the point escapes to infinity. In the Julia set, we do the same thing, except that we pick a single point out of the Mandelbrot set to provide the `x,y` coordinate. We still cruise across all points in the complex plane, and we still calculate whether `z` escapes to infinity, but we keep the value `c` constant throughout the entire calculation. We use the complex coordinate `x,y` to provide the starting value of `z`, instead of `(0,0j)` as we do for the Mandelbrot set. What this means is that we can use essentially the same calculation to display Julia sets, and that we can also use the Mandelbrot set from which to pick points. Figure 23.7 shows the Julia set calculated from the point `(-0.778, -0.1515j)` selected from the Mandelbrot set.

You can zoom into the Julia sets using the application provided here, just like you can with the Mandelbrot set. Figure 23.8 shows the selection of a square to zoom in on.

Figure 23.9 shows the zoomed square.

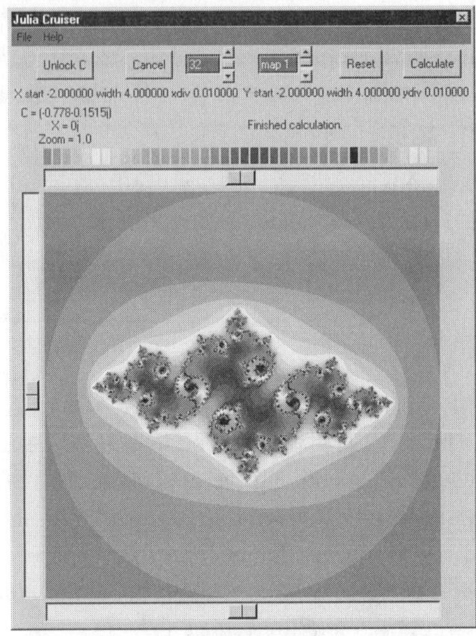

FIGURE 23.7
Julia set for (`-0.778, -0.1515j`).

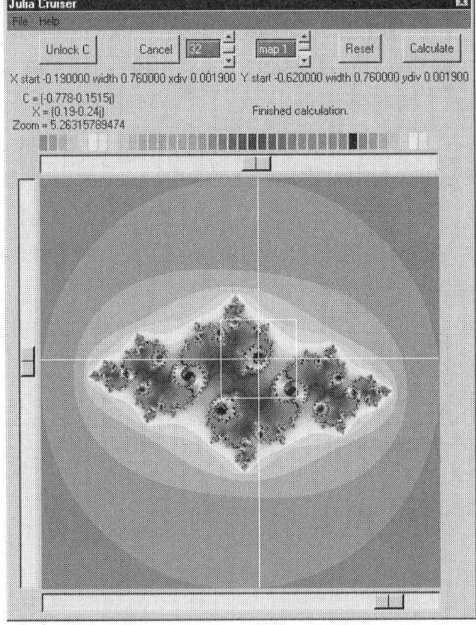

FIGURE 23.8
Preparing to zoom.

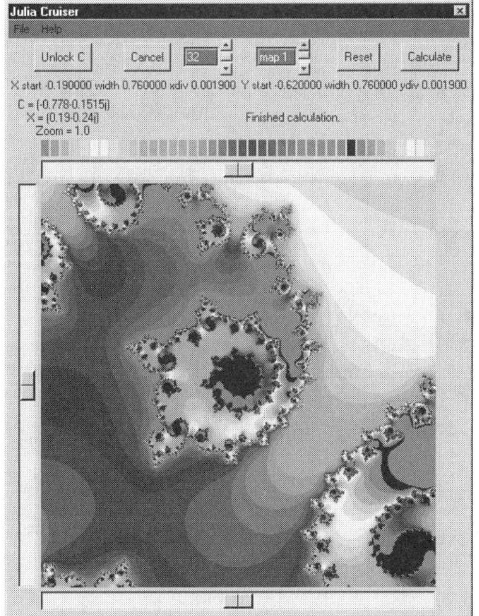

FIGURE 23.9
Zoomed.

Because we made Mandel a class, we can use it to inherit from when we build class Julia. Listing 23.5 shows the additional file required.

LISTING 23.5 julia2.py

```
#!/usr/local/bin/python

from Tkinter import *
from Canvas import Line,Rectangle
import sys
import string
from colormap import *
from tkFileDialog import *
from mandelbrot2 import *

class Julia(Mandel):
    def __init__(self,ncolors,root,xs=-2.0,ys=-2.0,xw=4.0,yw=4.0,
        xr=400,yr=400,
        im=["new-mdb.gif", "new-mdb.600.gif", "new-mdb.800.gif",],
        qn="Lock C",qim=["x_kankin_1.gif","x_pop_1.gif"]):
        Mandel.__init__(self,ncolors,root,xs,ys,xw,yw,xr,yr,im,qn,qim)
        self.calculating=0
        self.center=0j
        self.root.title("Julia Cruiser")
        self.qaction=self.lock
        self.qbutton["command"] = self.qaction
```

Listing 23.5 continued

```
        self.locked=0
        self.xhairs=0j
        self.filem.delete(4)
        self.filem.delete(3)
        self.root.protocol('WM_DELETE_WINDOW',self.killafter)

    def killafter(self):
        self.root.withdraw()

    def lock(self,locker=None):
        if locker != None:
            self.locked=locker
        elif self.locked==0:
            self.locked=1
        else:
            self.locked=0
        if self.locked:
            self.qbutton["text"]="Unlock C"
        else:
            self.qbutton["text"]="Lock C"
        if self.useimages:
            self.qbutton["image"] = self.qimg[self.locked]

    def popJulia(self,event=0):
        pass

    def setXYLabels(self,m=None):
        if not self.__dict__.has_key("center"):
            self.center=0j
            self.xhairs=0j
        if m == None:
            xs = "X start %f width %f xdiv %f" % \
                (self.xstart, self.xwidth, self.xdiv)
            self.xlab["text"] = xs
            ys = "Y start %f width %f ydiv %f" % \
                (self.ystart, self.ywidth, self.ydiv)
            self.ylab["text"] = ys
            self.zlabel["text"]="C = %s\nX = %s\nZoom = %s" % \
                (self.center, self.xhairs, self.xwidth/self.xwidth)
        else:
            xs = "X start %f width %f xdiv %f" % \
                (m.xstart, m.xwidth, m.xdiv)
            self.xlab["text"] = xs
            ys = "Y start %f width %f ydiv %f" % \
                (m.ystart, m.ywidth, m.ydiv)
            self.ylab["text"] = ys
            self.zlabel["text"]="C = %s\nX = %s\nZoom = %s" % \
                (self.center, self.xhairs, self.xwidth/m.xwidth)

```

```
    def xliner(self,event=0):
        if self.calculating:
            return
        n=self.scX.get()
        y=self.scY.get()
        x1 = n * self.xdiv
        x1 = self.xstart + x1
        y1 = y * self.ydiv
        y1 = self.ystart + y1
        if not self.locked:
            self.center=complex(x1,y1)
        self.xhairs=complex(x1,y1)
        if self.xdrawn==None:
            self.xdrawn = Line(self.cv,n,0,n,self.yresolution-1,
                fill="#ffffff")
        else:
            self.cv.coords(self.xdrawn,n,0,n,self.yresolution-1)
        self.setXYLabels(self.mdsize)

    def yliner(self,event=0):
        if self.calculating:
            return
        x=self.scX.get()
        n=self.scY.get()
        x1 = x * self.xdiv
        y1 = n * self.ydiv
        x1 = self.xstart + x1
        y1 = self.ystart + y1
        if not self.locked:
            self.center=complex(x1,y1)
        self.xhairs=complex(x1,y1)
        if self.ydrawn==None:
            self.ydrawn = Line(self.cv,0,n,self.xresolution-1,n,
                fill="#ffffff")
        else:
            self.cv.coords(self.ydrawn,0,n,self.xresolution-1,n)
        self.setXYLabels(self.mdsize)

    def zliner(self,event=0):
        if self.calculating:
            return
        self.xliner()
        self.yliner()
        n=self.scZ.get()
        x=self.scX.get()
        y=self.scY.get()
        x1 = x * self.xdiv
        y1 = y * self.ydiv
        x1 = self.xstart + x1
```

continues

LISTING 23.5 continued

```
        y1 = self.ystart + y1
        if not self.locked:
            self.center=complex(x1,y1)
        self.xhairs=complex(x1,y1)
        self.setXYLabels(self.mdsize)
        lima = min(x,y)
        limb = min(self.xresolution - x, self.yresolution - y)
        limc = min(lima,limb)
        # x and y are the coordinates of the center.
        # x0 and y0 are the upper left coordinates:
        self.x0 = x - n
        if self.x0 < 0:
            self.x0 = 0
        self.y0 = y - n
        if self.y0 < 0:
            self.y0 = 0
        # x1 and y1 are the lower right coordinates:
        w = x - self.x0
        if w > limc:
            w = limc
        self.x1 = x + w
        if self.x1 > self.xresolution-1:
            self.x1 = self.xresolution-1
        if self.x1 - self.x0 > (limc * 2):
            self.x0 = self.x1 - (limc * 2)
        h = y - self.y0
        if h > limc:
            h = limc
        self.y1 = y + h
        if self.y1 > self.yresolution - 1:
            self.y1 = self.yresolution - 1
        if self.y1 - self.y0 > (limc * 2):
            self.y0 = self.y1 - (limc * 2)
        if x == 0 or y == 0:
            self.x0 = self.y0 = 0
            self.x1 = self.y1 = self.xresolution-1
        if self.x1 - self.x0 == 0 or self.y1 - self.y0 == 0:
            self.x0 = self.y0 = 0
            self.x1 = self.y1 = self.xresolution-1
        if self.zdrawn==None:
            self.zdrawn = Rectangle(self.cv,self.x0,self.y0,
                self.x1,self.y1,outline="#ffffff")
        else:
            self.cv.coords(self.zdrawn,self.x0,self.y0,self.x1,self.y1)
        self.zoomer()

    def resetter(self):
        Mandel.resetter(self)
        self.locked=0
```

```
            self.qbutton["text"]="Lock C"
            self.center=0j
            self.xhairs=0j

        def calc(self):
            self.waitvar.set(1)
            self.cv.delete(ALL)
            self.xdrawn=None
            self.ydrawn=None
            self.zdrawn=None
            self.progress.delete(ALL)
            self.mdb = self.dithimage()
            self.img = self.cv.create_image(self.xresolution/2,
                self.yresolution/2, anchor=CENTER, image=self.mdb)
            oldcursor = self.cv["cursor"]
            self.cv["cursor"] = "watch"
            self.calculating=1

            if self.mdsize != None:
                self.xstart,self.ystart,self.xwidth,self.ywidth, \
                    self.xend, self.yend,self.xdiv,self.ydiv = \
                    self.mdsize()

            x = self.xstart
            self._label["text"] = \
                "Beginning calculation with %d colors %s..." % \
                (self.ncolors,self.cmapname)
            self.cmap = self.cmapcommand(self.ncolors - 1)
            if self.ncolors < 64:
                dwell = 64
            else:
                dwell = self.ncolors
            C = self.center
            self.scX.set(self.xresolution/2)
            self.scY.set(self.yresolution/2)
            self.scZ.set(self.yresolution/2)
            if self.debug == 0:
                for xX in range(self.xresolution):
                    y = self.ystart
                    for yY in range(self.yresolution):
                        z = complex(x,y)
                        i = 0
                        for i in range(dwell):
                            if abs(z)>2.0:
                                break
                            z=(z**2)+C
                        hcol = self.cmap[i % self.ncolors]
                        self.mdb.put((hcol,),(xX,yY,xX+1,yY+1))

```

continues

LISTING 23.5 continued

```
                    y = y + self.ydiv

                    if self.stopnow:
                        self.updateProgress()
                        self.stopnow=0
                        self._label["text"] = "Finished calculation."
                        self.uil = self.uyl = self.uxl = 0
                        self.calculating=0
                        self.resetter()
                        self.cv["cursor"] = oldcursor
                        self.waitvar.set(0)
                        return
                    if xX != 0 and xX % self.progressize == 0 \
                        and yY == 0:
                        self.updateProgress()
                x = x + self.xdiv
            self.img = self.cv.create_image(self.xresolution/2,
                self.yresolution/2, anchor=CENTER, image=self.mdb)
        self.cv.update()
        self.updateProgress()
        self._label["text"] = "Finished calculation."
        self.mdsize=Msize(self.xresolution,self.yresolution,
            self.xstart,self.ystart,self.xwidth,self.ywidth)

        self.setXYLabels(self.mdsize)
        self.uil = self.uyl = self.uxl = 0
        self.stopnow = 0
        self.calculating=0
        self.cv["cursor"] = oldcursor
        self.waitvar.set(0)

    def about(self,event=0):
        d = AboutDialog(self.root,"Julia")
        self.root.wait_window(d.top)

    def clicker(self,event=0):
        x,y=event.x,event.y
        x1=self.xstart+(x*self.xdiv)
        y1=self.ystart+(y*self.ydiv)
        self.scY.set(y)
        self.scX.set(x)

    def clacker(self,event=0):
        pass

if __name__ == "__main__":
    if len(sys.argv)>1:
        ncolors=string.atoi(sys.argv[1])
    else:
```

```
267         ncolors=32
268     root=Tk()
269     julia=Julia(ncolors,root)
270
271     julia.root.mainloop()
272
```


I have few comments for the Julia code. Mostly, what we need to do in this code is to modify existing behavior, so we provide our own methods, which will override corresponding ones in the Mandel code. These are methods such as `calc()`, `clicker()`, and `popJulia()`, which need either to do something different or to do nothing instead of something. The thing we do that is really different is to change the label and behavior of the Quit button; for the Julia displayer, we use what is now the Lock button to lock the selection of the value for `c` so that we can still use the scrollbars to select a center point and adjust the size of the zoom box. If we didn't do that, every time we moved the scrollbars we would move the Julia set to unknown territory. The `lock()` method in lines 32–43 is where most of this work is done. When we start up a Julia set exploration (in line 517 and so on), we also set the center point and lock that center. Then we automatically start the calculation; all this is done in lines 529–532 of Listing 23.4.

Summary

During this penultimate hour, we've learned about Mandelbrot and Julia sets, how to calculate them, and used Tkinter to provide a GUI for displaying them. In the next hour, we will talk about CGI Web programming and finish up with a few odds and ends and a bit of (horrors) philosophy.

Workshop

Q&A

Q Besides running computers to their maximum capacity, what good are Mandelbrots?

A If you are immune to the beauty of the sets as some people are (including my wife: "Yuck. Looks like paisley!" she says), you should realize that fractal geometry and chaos theory have useful applications in everything from weather prediction to image compression.

Q You didn't really mention fractal geometry in this chapter. What's that?

A This is a term and a branch of mathematics founded by Benoit Mandelbrot. It is his contention that fractal geometry is the geometry of nature; things small are similar to things large. Look at coastlines: start from space, zoom in (just like we do with the Mandelbrot or Julia sets), and notice that no matter how close you get, it looks in general just like it did from space. Search the Web for more information; there's a ton out there. See the book referenced in the exercises.

Quiz

1. What is the formula for the Mandelbrot set?
   a. $E = mc^2$
   b. $a = r^2$
   c. $z = z^2 + c$
   d. $F = G (m_1 m_2)/d^2$
2. About how many floating-point operations does it take to calculate a Mandelbrot 400 by 400 pixels in 32 colors?
   a. 160,000
   b. 1,000,000,000
   c. 5,120,000
   d. 2,560,000
3. How many Julia sets are in the Mandelbrot set?
   a. One
   b. 160,000
   c. One for each point
   d. An infinite number

Answers

1. c, the Mandelbrot formula (minus extraneous fluff) is $z = z^2 + c$.
2. d, the last answer, 2,560,000 is probably closest to the truth. It can't be 160,000, because we have to iterate over the points, and they are not all at the same distance from the complex plane. And if it were 5,120,000, all the pixels would be black, and we wouldn't be calculating it because it would be boring.
3. c, there is one Julia set for each point in the Mandelbrot, which has been called a catalog for the Julia sets. Because the number of points in the Mandelbrot set is infinite, the number of Julia sets is also infinite.

Exercises

A fun page combining the Planck constants and googolplexes can be found at `http://www.informatik.uni-frankfurt.de/~fp/Tools/GetAGoogol.html`.

For more information on Mandelbrot sets, see the following:

- A. K. Dewdney. "Computer Recreations" in *Scientific American* 253, no. 2 (August 1985): 16-24.
- Benoit B. Mandelbrot. *The Fractal Geometry of Nature.*. San Francisco: W. H. Freeman and Company, 1977, 1982. ISBN 0-7167-1186-9.
- `http://linas.org/art-gallery/escape/escape.html`
- *Colours of Infinity*: Documentary shown on PBS featuring Arthur C. Clarke, Benoit Mandelbrot, Michael Barnsley, and Ian Stewart. I can't track down more information than this; it was shown during pledge week here in Salt Lake, and they shrank the credits to an unreadable size. An Internet search turns up nothing.

For more information on computer graphics, the generally acknowledged bible is: *Computer Graphics: Principles and Practice, Second Edition in C* by James D. Foley, Andries van Dam, Steven K. Feiner and John F. Hughes. New York, NY: Addison-Wesley, 1990.

HOUR 24

Miscellany

This dog just ran a thousand miles.

—Lynda Plettner, musher, talking about her lead dog RG, at the end of the 1999 Iditarod.

In the preceding hour, we talked about Mandelbrot and Julia sets and their mathematics, and we discussed a program to calculate and display them. This hour, which is mostly miscellany, starts off with a brief introduction to Web CGI programming. Then we talk about right practice, right attitude, and right understanding.

CGI

As you know from previous chapters, CGI stands for common gateway interface. The programming paradigm for Web CGI programming is a little different from normal, interactive programs. With CGI, you put your Python programs into a specific location and then access the program with your Web browser; the program emits output in a language called HTML, or Hypertext Markup Language. Various embellishments exist to HTML, such as those that allow users to fill out forms and submit the information back to the same, or to a different, program. A full explanation of Web servers, Web browsers, HTML, and CGI programming is far beyond the scope of this book; see the exercises for a few resources to find out more.

My own setup includes a rather slow server, running the Windows NT 4.0 OS, with SP5 and the Apache 1.3.9 Web server for Win32. A more stable combination is to run Linux instead of NT, with the same version of the Apache server for Linux. NT is more convenient for me at work right now. I assume that you have access to a Web server and that you have it set up properly. Many ISPs provide some form of free Web-page hosting as a fringe benefit when you buy monthly internet service, although few of these free services provide Python. Perl is much more common, but call the ISP and ask for Python. After Python is installed and running, you usually need to know where it lives on the Web server machine; this is the case with the Apache Web server, at any rate. Because I installed and maintain my own Web server, I know where Apache lives and I know where Python lives. The cgi-bin (the common location for CGI programs) is where I put the completed Python programs, and on my system, that is in `c:\inetpub\cgi-bin`; Apache lives in `c:\Apache` and Python in `c:\Python`. All Python programs placed in the cgi-bin directory must, for Apache, begin with the "hash-bang" line, `#!c:\Python\python.exe` or they will not run. In Hour 15, we discussed the `fixhash.py` program for automatically tracking down errors in this first line of Python programs and fixing those errors, also automatically, and you may find it useful if you end up maintaining your own Web server.

If you are not running your own Web server and you have been able to persuade your ISP to install Python, you will need to verify that they have installed Python correctly. All the standard modules must be installed where Python can find them, and most especially the `cgi.py` module is required for useful Python CGI programs. If your ISP is running NT, then all the ISP has to do is run the install program for Python and inform whatever Web server they are running where Python lives on their system. It's a little more complicated on Linux, but if the ISP administrator follows the installation instructions included with the Python distribution, everything should work correctly. If it does not, you will have to work with the ISP administrator to attempt to solve the problem. The Python mailing list may be able to help if you get into this situation.

Listing 24.1 shows the traditional "Hello, World!" program modified to run on the Web.

LISTING 24.1 `hellocgi.py`

```
#!c:\Python\python.exe

def print_content():
    print "Content-type: text/html"
    print
```

```
def print_header():
    print "<html><title>Pythonic Hello World</title><body>"

def print_footer():
    print "</body></html>"

print_content()
print_header()
print "Hello, World!"
print_footer()
```


`/usr/bin/python` is where Python lives on my home Linux machine. I mirror my actual Web site here at home and make sure that as far as is possible, the Python CGI programs work the same way under both NT and Linux. This setup allows me to develop Web applications without using the actual server for testing and development; after programs are debugged on the home server, I can upload them to the real server, and 99% of the time they just drop in and run. Figure 24.1 shows what happens when we drop `hellocgi.py` into the cgi-bin directory and access the Web page with Netscape.

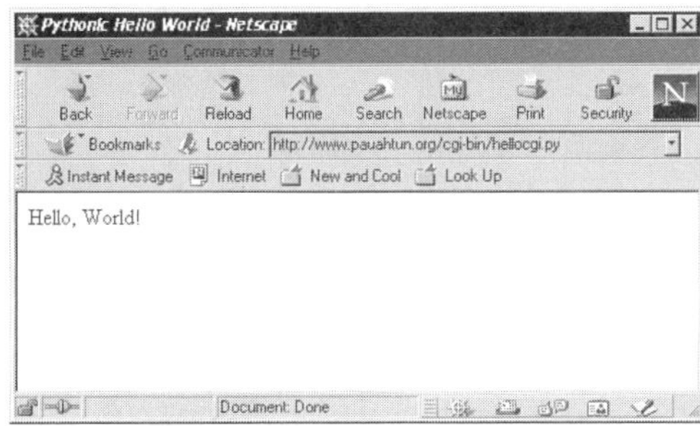

FIGURE 24.1
Hello, Web world.

The URL you can see in the Location field includes not only the Web server address (`http://www.pauahtun.org`) and the name of the script (`hellocgi.py`), but also the CGI bin directory between the two: `cgi-bin`. That's the name of whatever directory is designated as the CGI binary location on your system; although you can name it anything you want, it is traditionally called "cgi-bin." As you can see, this test program doesn't do much. The most important thing to observe in the listing of the code is the `print_content()` function; no matter how complicated your CGI programs get, you always need to begin by running this function. It prints the line `Content-type: text/html` to the Web server; this tells the server that the information it is receiving is to be displayed to the user.

Let's do something slightly more complicated; we will build a form that users can fill out from their Web browsers to register for software. When the Submit button is pushed, the program shown in Listing 24.2 sends email to you and to the person who submitted the form.

LISTING 24.2 register.py

```
#!c:\Python\python.exe
import os
import sys
import cgi
import SMTP

thisscript=os.environ["SCRIPT_NAME"]

mailhost="mail.callware.com"
mailfrom="ivanlan@callware.com"
mailto="ivanlan@callware.com"
ccto="ivanlan@callware.com"

def print_content():
    print "Content-type: text/html"
    print

def print_header():
    print """<html><title>Pythonic Registration Form</title>
    <body bgcolor=white text=black>"""

def print_footer():
    print "</body></html>"

def print_form():
    print """<h1 align=center>Please Register!</h1>
<p>Please register software before downloading it.  Thank you,
%s
<hr>
<p>
<form name=form action=%s method=post>
  Enter your name:
  <input type="edit" name="name"><br>
  Enter your email address:
  <input type="edit" name="email"><br>
  Enter the name of the software you are downloading:
  <input type="edit" name="software"><br>
  Enter the amount you are willing to pay in dollars for the software:
  <input type="edit" name="pay"><br>
  <hr>
  <input type="submit">
  <input type="reset">
```

```
</form>
""" % (os.environ["SERVER_NAME"],thisscript)

print_content()
print_header()

form = cgi.FieldStorage()
if form.has_key("name") and form.has_key("email"):
    nm = form["name"].value
    em = form["email"].value
    sw = form["software"].value
    mn = form["pay"].value
    print """<p align=center><font size=7>Thank you!
    </font><font size=3><br>
    <hr>
    """
    print """<p align=left>Thank you %s.  Your email address, %s,
    will shortly receive an invoice for %s dollars, for downloading
    the %s package. If you do not pay up within 5 business days,
    all your files will be erased.<br>
    <hr>
    <p align=right>Have a nice day<img src="../Gif/smiley.gif">
    """ % (nm,em,mn,sw)
    msg="""Hello, %s (%s):
You recently downloaded %s from %s.
Please send %s dollars immediately to:

Ransom
PO Box 6969
Washington DC 55512

If you do not send money, we have a catapult.
Thank you for your attention to this matter.

Anonymous
""" %(nm, em, sw, os.environ["SERVER_NAME"],mn)

    s=SMTP.SMTP(mailhost)
    s.send_message(mailfrom, em,
        "Software Registration", msg)
    s.send_message(mailfrom, ccto,
        "Software Registration", msg)
    s.close()
else:
    print_form()
print_footer()
```

This version is set up for my official Web site; for your own version, just edit lines 7–11, substituting your Web server's name and cgi-bin directory, where appropriate, and also changing the email address to your own. When you enter the correct URL into the Location field of your Web browser, you should see something like Figure 24.2.

FIGURE 24.2
Accessing `register.py`.

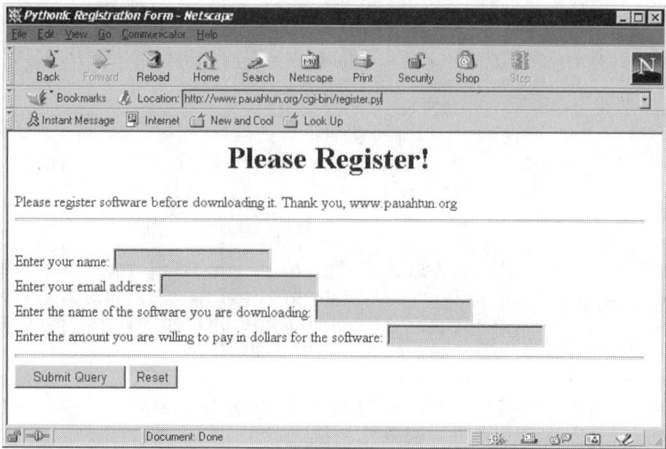

Fill in the form with your name and correct email address, press the Submit button, and you should see a Web page similar to Figure 24.3.

FIGURE 24.3
Submitting `register.py`.

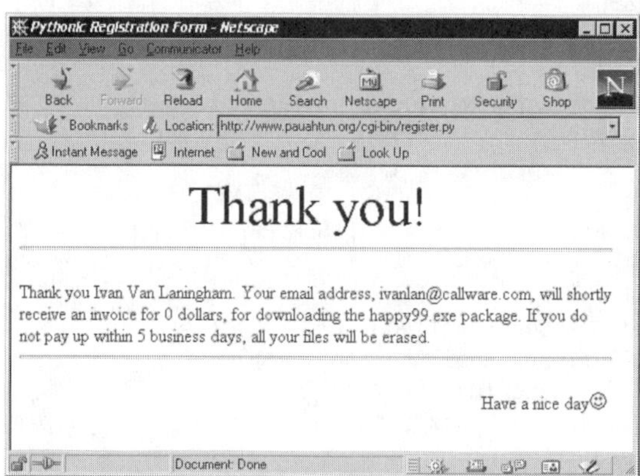

Before you can run this program, you need to obtain Vladimir Ulogov's SMTP module, which can be found at `http://starship.python.net/crew/gandalf/SMTP.py`. This module wraps up the standard `smtplib` module to make it extremely easy to use. Lines 79–84 show just how easy it is to use. As long as you know what your proper mail host is, this form works just fine on Linux, Windows 95/98, and NT. It will probably work on Macintoshes, too, but I have no way of testing this.

To analyze what is happening in the registration program, look at lines 44 onward in Listing 24.2. The main part of the program starts by printing the content-type, and then printing the header. This is always the same (check the title bars in the two previous illustrations), but in line 48 we instantiate an object of class `FieldStorage` from the `cgi` module (imported in line 4). In CGI programs, it is easy to build forms, but hard to read them after users fill them out. The `cgi` module makes it relatively painless to read them. Line 49 checks to see whether the `form` object has been filled out; if calls to the `has_key()` method fail, the user has not entered any text into the associated form element. If line 49 is `false`, we drop down to line 86 and call the `print_form()` function, which is what displays the blank form shown in Figure 24.2 (`print_form()` goes from line 24 to line 44). If, however, line 49 evaluates to `true`, beginning in line 50 we process the information the user has provided, defining the message to be sent in lines 65–77 and displaying the Web page shown in Figure 24.3 to let users know their information was received correctly. After we have defined the message to be emailed, lines 79–84 create an SMTP object, which connects to your mail server and sends copies of the message to the appropriate parties (lines 80 and 82). We close the email connection in line 84 after sending our messages.

To recap, here is the basic outline for any Python CGI program you write:

- Import modules, define variables and functions (lines 2–44).
- Define a function to print a form that has a Submit button (see line 40) and that uses the `post` method (line 30).
- Make sure that you submit the form to the script itself (lines 7 and 43).
- Create an instance of the form (line 48).
- Test to see whether the form has been filled out (line 49).
- If no, print the form (line 86) to the Web browser.
- If yes, read the information using `cgi.FieldStorage` and act on it (lines 50–84).
- Print the end of the HTML page (`print_footer()` in line 87).

Armed with this outline, perseverance, and Python, no CGI programming task should be beyond you.

Debugging

On top of my monitor, I have several large plastic insects. When people ask why I have them there, I tell them that those bugs are my totems. Usually, they then ask what totems are, and I tell them that totems are the heads of animal clans; some Native American tribes have worked out covenants with, for example, the buffalo totem. What the totem grants to the tribes is permission to kill and use individual members of the animal clan, and thus increase the tribe's chances of survival; what the totem asks in return is ritual observance, usually in the form of parts of the animal that are not eaten or used and a ceremony begging forgiveness for taking a life that is sacred to the totem. If these observances are not followed, the hunters of the tribe risk offending the totem, who would retaliate by refusing to send any more individuals of the clan to offer themselves for the gain of the tribe. (And if you think totemism is not part of the American way of life, you should start looking around you. Consider all those ads on TV that feature happy cows, dancing pigs, singing chickens, and the like—all anthropomorphized and sending the clear message, "It's okay to eat us.")

Debugging conventional languages is a task that can occupy a significant portion of the development time for almost any sort of project. In fact, if it weren't for bugs, the number of software engineers employed today would be a lot smaller than it is now. Which is why I have my totems out, visible to everyone; I don't want the totems of the various bug clans to stop sending me individuals to find and fix. You might think this is pretty silly, but you never know. It doesn't hurt, and it serves as a constant reminder that everything is connected to everything else. Especially in software, where "a weed is a treasure."

At the same time, Python is so easy to debug that it's scary; whenever a problem occurs with a program, the Python interpreter will almost always tell you exactly which line is at fault. And most of the exception messages are fairly clear, after you catch on to the basics of the language and have encountered some of the more common errors a few times. But a couple of techniques do help that are transferable from more conventional languages to Python.

Perhaps the most basic technique is inserting `print` statements into your code so that you can observe what's happening to one or more variables during execution of the program. Don't underestimate the power of this technique, especially in Python; it is perhaps the quickest way to find out if your design has been accurately translated into your implementation. Using C or some compiled language, inserting `printf()` calls into the source is not nearly as efficient, because after modifying the source, you must recompile the program before you run it. In Python, you change the program and immediately run it. The overhead for putting in and taking out `print` statements is usually pretty small in Python.

The next major technique is stepping through the code. That is, instead of running the program as any user normally would, you run it under another program called a debugger. For command-line Python programs, the debugger is named `pdb`. The documentation for it can be found at `http://www.python.org/doc/current/lib/module-pdb.html`, and it is quite clear. My own experience with `pdb` has shown me that the best use of it, by far, is to proceed step-by-step through a function or method to see if what I think is happening in the code really is happening. You can use `assert()` to do some of the same work without using the debugger, however; it tells Python, "Here's what I think is happening; if I'm wrong, throw an exception." But sometimes there is no substitute whatsoever for using `pdb` to stop after it encounters a certain function, and then to step through the code in that function line-by-line, inspecting variables to make sure that they contain the values you think they do and that the function is doing what you think it should depending on those values.

But I think reading the code is still the most important debugging technique. Whenever something goes wrong, inspect your code. Pretend you are a computer (and really, when you come down to it, that's what a programmer is supposed to do best) and step, in your mind, through each line of your code; fill in variables and try to determine what you are really telling Python to do here. It may not be what you think is going on, and reading and rereading your code may sometimes be the only way to convince yourself that you told Python to do the opposite of what you meant. If you can't figure out the answer to your problem this way, add a `print` statement or two; don't go overboard here, or soon you will render your code unreadable and you will lose track of what you were trying to accomplish in the first place. If that technique fails, it is time to fire up the debugger and observe in excruciating detail exactly what is happening. Detailed coverage of this process is, however, beyond the scope of this book.

Right Practice

Zazen practice is the direct expression of our true nature. Strictly speaking, for a human being, there is no other practice than this practice; there is no other way of life than this way of life.

—*Shunryu Suzuki,* Zen Mind, Beginner's Mind

Far too much of modern programming relies on ugly tools and ugly code to produce ugly results. Plenty of people say, "Who cares if it's ugly, as long as it works?" Other programmers say, "We don't know what ugly is; we don't know what beautiful is." They are all right. Gregory Bateson once said to Margaret Mead, "I don't know what art is." Said Mead, "That's all right, Gregory. I do."

No one ever knows what beautiful is, or what art is, until she does it. The only way to know whether you're doing art is to do it. This is what is meant by "right practice." Practice first, analyze later. In other words, you can't afford to question the validity of what you are doing when you are doing it; and in Zen terms, when you eat a strawberry, eat the strawberry. That is, eat the strawberry and do not examine or discuss or analyze the eating utensils, the plates, the whole chain of cause and effect from strawberry seed to harvesting to table and your plate. The strawberry is there; it is a fact, and it is to be enjoyed for exactly what it is.

And of course, the strawberry, like Python, is connected to everything else, so sometimes you do have to consider the eating utensils. But most of the time, you don't have to. This is because Python, unlike so many programming languages, doesn't force you to pay attention to the wrong things and the wrong ideas. If you have gone through this book and paid attention and have practiced regularly, you have learned enough about Python to let the tools become you. This is the aim of right practice—to stop thinking about the tools with which you work.

Right Attitude

When you become you, Zen becomes Zen. When you are you, you see things as they are, and you become one with your surroundings.

—*Shunryu Suzuki,* Zen Mind, Beginner's Mind

To put it another way: When Python becomes Python, you become you. Many times during the early stages of practice, you will become fed up and won't have any idea why you started trying to learn this language in the first place. You should be prepared for this. Some schools of Zen hit students with sticks at crucial points, attempting to awaken them from complacency and jar their attention back to what they should be doing—practicing. Other schools of Zen simply tell the student that at some point they will hate Zen, and that they should be prepared to renew their efforts at these times.

At the annual Maya Meetings in Austin, Texas, the major conference and workshop for Mayanists in the world, such an attitude has become institutionalized. The last six days of the conference are given over to hands-on workshops. I describe the long workshops as "being locked in a room, handed untranslated inscriptions, and being told, 'Translate this.'" First-time participants in these workshops are told, on their first day, how they will feel during the week. The first couple of days, nothing will make any sense whatsoever. You will be lost, but you will see that everyone else is lost and confused, too. By Wednesday afternoon or Thursday morning, you will be angry. You will want to chuck the whole thing, climb on a plane, and go home. Ride this out, because by Thursday afternoon or Friday morning, you will experience an "Aha!" moment; you will think you understand what you are doing. This is the breakthrough moment, not because you really understand what's going on (you don't), not because you suddenly, magically know how to translate glyphs, but because you attain the right attitude toward what you are doing.

I think that this is an extremely important process, because for one thing, by warning beginners up front that their attitudes and feelings throughout the week are going to follow a pattern similar to what hundreds of other students have gone through, beginners' attention is focused right away on practicing and on being prepared for the inevitable course of the practice. Focus is drawn from the student to the practice; students move from "Oh, poor me," to "If I just keep slogging away, they said I'd get it." And they do. As will you.

Another important consequence of this process is that the field of Mayan studies has grown considerably, and considerably stronger, in the 25 years that the Maya Meetings have been running, due largely to the simple assumption by their founder, Linda Schele, that everyone has something to contribute. Although not every beginner has gone on to become a famous Mayanist, some few have. Many other students have made important contributions to the field; some glyphs would never have been translated without beginners' insights. Linda assumed from the very beginning that anyone could come to the workshops; everyone was welcome. Attendance was not limited to an academic elite. The only prerequisite was that you had to care about epigraphy and Mayan studies. Passion, bordering on obsession, was not only expected but helpful.

In programming, too, passion—bordering on obsession—is expected. To put it another way: when you have a conversation with someone, it is best to pay attention to her. Your attitude should not be, "I wish she would shut up so I can talk about myself," but rather, "If I listen to her instead of talking about myself, I might learn something interesting. I might be surprised. My mind might stretch."

Think of programming as a conversation or, if you will, a dialectic, between you and the machine. Your mind might stretch.

Right Understanding

Zen is not some kind of excitement, but concentration on our usual everyday routine.

Our understanding of Buddhism is not just an intellectual understanding. True understanding is actual practice itself.

—*Shunryu Suzuki,* Zen Mind, Beginner's Mind

I said a few lines ago that the breakthrough moment at the Maya Meetings was when students thought they knew what was going on, when they experienced an "Aha!" moment. This moment is not true understanding, only the awakening of right attitude. Right understanding comes much later. It comes when you understand that the practice and the attitude are one, and that programming as a process comprises hundreds—if not thousands—of "Aha!" moments. Not a single moment, but a never-ending stream of them.

Years ago, when I was trying to write science fiction, I used to wonder where the "real" authors got their ideas. I struggled with ideas; every time I thought of something that I could possibly work into a story, I would write it down on an index card (there were no personal computers then, and especially, there were no PDAs) and file it carefully away. Nothing ever came of these because I was so busy searching for and writing down these ideas that I never wrote the stories. This is a good thing, because the "ideas" were tired clichés, and the stories that would have been written would not have been worth reading.

"Real" science fiction authors are constantly asked, "Where do you get your ideas?" In fact, this is the most asked question. One author used to reply "I steal them." And this is far more profound than you might think, because it's what we all do. No idea is new; no idea occurs in a vacuum, like hydrogen atoms in the steady-state cosmology; no idea is original. All ideas grow out of the things that influence us, and the things that influence us are ideas. "New" ideas are simply little twists of concepts that already exist. By being aware of what is going on around you, by focusing on your everyday routine, you come to realize, in a non-intellectual way, that there are needs to be filled, and indeed, a never-ending stream of needs. Some of these needs may be yours, which you can fulfill by writing a small program in Python to take care of, as we did earlier with the `fixhash.py` program; some of these needs may be others', in which case you can analyze the problem and build tools in Python to provide a solution. Some needs may be a company's needs, in which case Python might provide the perfect prototyping language, or the perfect glue language, or sometimes even the perfect production language. But in all cases, when you write programs, you soon come to understand that every line in your programs has been written, at one time or another, by someone else, albeit to serve different needs. You steal every line and change every line.

In a sense, all the lines and words and ideas that make up programs are reused, recycled, and reinvigorated constantly. It is a process that has been going on for years and that promises to continue into the foreseeable future. Carl Sagan said, "We are all made of star-stuff." The atoms that make us up originated in the incandescent furnaces of novae—exploded stars that fling these atoms outward to the universe. Eventually, planetary systems form from the stellar detritus; eventually, life; eventually, us.

Where does this get you? First you practice without understanding; then, you practice with the attitude, the knowledge, that if you persevere, you will "get it"; finally, you understand that practice itself is understanding enough. I mean, here is the point: you learn so much through your practice, and you practice so much that you gain the kind of attitude and understanding that sinks below your intellectual mind. Eat the strawberry without thinking about exactly what you are going to do with the fork, the plate, the left-over leaves. Ride the bicycle without wondering how you stay upright. As shown in

Figure 24.4, write the program without thinking about your tools; simply write the program. Be the program.

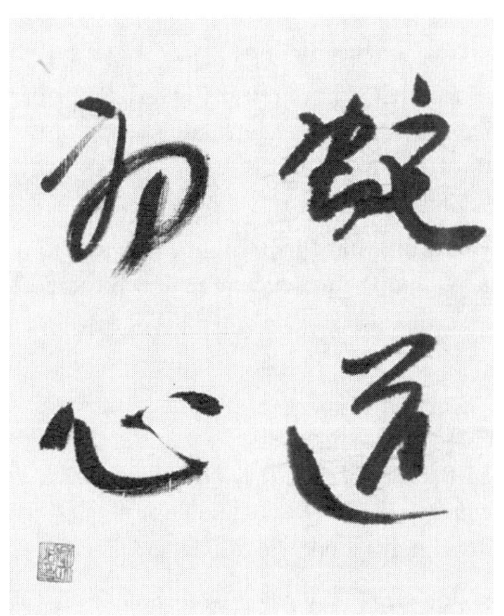

FIGURE 24.4
Xuhua Lin drew this calligraphy especially for this book. It means, loosely translated, "Python Mind, Beginner's Mind."

Summary

The practice of Zen mind is beginner's mind. The innocence of the first inquiry—what am I?—is needed throughout Zen practice. The mind of the beginner is empty, free of the habits of the expert, ready to accept, to doubt, and open to all the possibilities. It is the kind of mind which can see things as they are, which step by step and in a flash can realize the original nature of everything. This practice of Zen mind is found throughout the book. Directly or sometimes by inference, every section of the book concerns the question of how to maintain this attitude through your meditation and in your life. This is an ancient way of teaching, using the simplest language and the situations of everyday life. This means the student should teach himself.

—Richard Baker, Introduction to Zen Mind, Beginner's Mind

Workshop

Q&A

Q Did you ever sell any science fiction?

A Nope. But I sure acquired a lot of rejection slips. Some of them I still have; my favorite is the one that says "No," scrawled in pencil on a two-inch square of paper. This was from the Ted White *Amazing Stories*, by the way, for those of you who care about such things.

Q It sounds like you think that the point of programming is not the programs at all, but the process and the practice of programming. Is that the case?

A That is the nature of the Buddha.

Exercises

To learn more about HTML, see *HTML: The Definitive Guide, 3rd Edition*, by Chuck Musciano and Bill Kennedy, from O'Reilly. Also useful is *Dynamic HTML: The Definitive Reference*, by Danny Goodman, also from O'Reilly.

A massive compendium of excellent debugging techniques is *Code Complete: A Practical Handbook of Software Construction* by Steve C McConnell. Microsoft Press; ISBN: 1556154844.

For some more of my views on eating strawberries (if you're not completely sick of them), visit `http://www.pauahtun.org/vietnam/abacus.html`. Actually, I don't care for strawberries, but it sounds better to say "strawberry" than "tuna steak."

PART IV
Appendixes

Hour

APPENDIX A

Selected Bibliography

Not all of the following books were used directly in the writing of this book, but all have proved invaluable over the years in developing my programming knowledge, style, and philosophy. One way or another, they might very well become powerful allies for you, too.

- Bateson, Gregory. *Steps to an Ecology of Mind*. New York, NY: Ballantine, 1973. Classic papers, witty and charming style; what more could you ask? Includes an astonishing paper on dolphins learning how to learn.
- Bateson, Gregory. *Mind and Nature: A Necessary Unity*. New York, NY: Dutton, 1979. Simple, but not easy.
- Beckmann, Peter. *A History of Pi*. New York, NY: St. Martin's Press, 1976. More than fascinating—spellbinding.
- Bergin, Thomas J., and Richard G. Gibson, eds. *History of Programming Languages*. Reading, MA: Addison-Wesley, 1995. Covers later programming languages such as Ada, Algol 68, C, C++, CLU, Discrete Simulation Languages, FORMAC, Forth, Icon, Lisp, Concurrent Pascal, Pascal, and Smalltalk. Not nearly as fascinating as the 1981 Wexelblat volume, but worthwhile nonetheless.

- Hall, Edward T. *The Silent Language*. New York, NY: Doubleday, 1959.
- Kernighan, Brian, and Dennis Ritchie. *The C Programming Language*. 2nd edition. New York, NY: Prentice-Hall, 1988. I prefer the first edition, but the second is somewhat more up-to-date. It's all here; everything you need to know about C is in this book, along with excellent general programming advice.
- Knuth, Donald E. *The Art of Computer Programming.* Volume 1: *Fundamental Algorithms.* 3rd edition. Reading, MA: Addison-Wesley, 1997. Profound and indispensable. `http://Sunburn.Stanford.EDU/~knuth/`.
- Knuth, Donald E. *The Art of Computer Programming.* Volume 2: *Seminumerical Algorithms.* 3rd edition. Reading, MA: Addison-Wesley, 1997. Profound and indispensable. `http://Sunburn.Stanford.EDU/~knuth/`.
- Knuth, Donald E. *The Art of Computer Programming.* Volume 3: *Sorting and Searching.* 2nd edition. Reading, MA: Addison-Wesley, 1998. Profound and indispensable. `http://Sunburn.Stanford.EDU/~knuth/`.
- Lutz, Mark. *Programming Python.* Sebastopol, CA: O'Reilly, 1996. Fat, packed with information and technique. Pythonistas who are already programmers will find this most useful.
- Lutz, Mark. *Python Pocket Reference*. Sebastopol, CA: O'Reilly, 1998. Absolutely indispensable until you memorize it all.
- Lutz, Mark, and David Ascher. *Learning Python*. Sebastopol, CA: O'Reilly, 1999. Informal, chatty, light style; for Pythonistas with some programming experience.
- Nahin, Paul J. *An Imaginary Tale: The Story of the Square Root of Minus One.* Princeton, MA: Princeton University Press, 1998. Delightful and fascinating.
- Niven, Larry. *Rainbow Mars*. New York, NY: St. Martin's Press, 1999. Time travel.
- Philip, Alexander. *The Calendar: Its History, Structure and Improvement.* Cambridge, MA: Cambridge University Press, 1921. Delightful, earnest, and useful, this little book contains the only *readable* and understandable explanation of epacts that I know of.
- Pirsig, Robert M. *Zen and the Art of Motorcycle Maintenance: An Inquiry into Values*. New York, NY: William Morrow & Company, 1974. Read the section on being stuck. Read the section on handlebar shims. Check out Steele and Disanto's *Guidebook*.

- Press, William H., Saul A. Teukolsky, William T. Vetterling, and Brian P. Flannery. *Numerical Recipes in C: The Art of Scientific Computing*. Cambridge, MA: Cambridge University Press, 1993. Good stuff and useful, but watch out. A whole Web site (`http://math.jpl.nasa.gov/nr/nr.html`) is dedicated to errors and inefficiencies in this book. But it's a good collection of starting points, anyway.
- Steele, Thomas J., and Ronald L. Disanto. *Guidebook to Zen and the Art of Motorcycle Maintenance*. New York, NY: William Morrow & Company/Quill, 1990. Worthwhile road map.
- Suzuki, Shunryu. *Zen Mind, Beginner's Mind*. New York, NY: Weatherhill, 1972. Well, what did you expect?
- Thompson, J. Eric S., *Maya Hieroglyphic Writing: An Introduction.* 3rd edition. Norman, OK: University of Oklahoma Press, 1971. Dated (the first edition came out in 1950) and not particularly helpful as far as glyph translations go, but important and useful from a mathematical standpoint. Learned, turgid style to which some have objected violently.
- Watters, Aaron, Guido van Rossum, and James C. Ahlstrom. *Internet Programming with Python*. Foster City, CA: IDG Books Worldwide, 1996. Nice emphasis on CGI programming from Guido himself, among others.
- Wexelblat, Richard L., ed. *History of Programming Languages*. Chestnut Hill, MA: Academic Press, 1981. Fascinating, entertaining history of many of the earlier programming languages; C, C++, and so on are not covered, but all the fundamental and original languages are, such as FORTRAN, APL (one of the ancestors of Python), Simula, COBOL, and so on. You can spend weeks on just the endpapers.

APPENDIX B

Editors for Python

Many fine editors are available on the Internet; these are just a few.

vi and vim

The vi (pronounced vee-aye) editor is the classic UNIX editor, which has been ported to many other platforms, including Windows. Originally written for Berkeley UNIX by Bill Joy (now with Sun Microsystems), the basic command set has remained unchanged for two decades. It has been extended and improved, but all the commands, tricks, and shortcuts that I learned in the early '80s still work, and work well, on all the platforms I work on.

The vim editor (vi improved) is the best extended version of vi available. This version has a vastly extended command set, can do syntax coloring, and even has a special Python mode to ensure correct indentation and coloring. Figure B.1 shows vim, with my personal preferences enabled, editing a Python program.

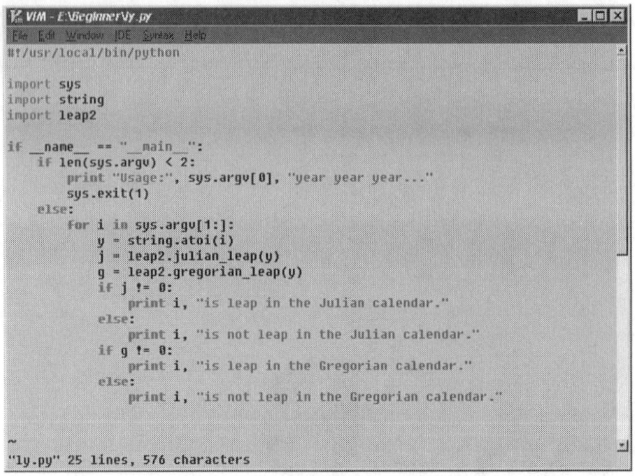

FIGURE B.1
vim editing a Python program.

```
#!/usr/local/bin/python

import sys
import string
import leap2

if __name__ == "__main__":
    if len(sys.argv) < 2:
        print "Usage:", sys.argv[0], "year year year..."
        sys.exit(1)
    else:
        for i in sys.argv[1:]:
            y = string.atoi(i)
            j = leap2.julian_leap(y)
            g = leap2.gregorian_leap(y)
            if j != 0:
                print i, "is leap in the Julian calendar."
            else:
                print i, "is not leap in the Julian calendar."
            if g != 0:
                print i, "is leap in the Gregorian calendar."
            else:
                print i, "is not leap in the Gregorian calendar."

~
"ly.py" 25 lines, 576 characters
```

You can find out everything you need to know about downloading, installing, running, and customizing vim at

`http://www.vim.org/`

vim is freeware.

Emacs

Emacs is undoubtedly the most customizable editor for anything that has ever existed. The following is a short quote from the online FAQ on Emacs (`http://www.emacs.org/FAQ/faq_4.html#SEC27`) regarding the history of the program:

> Emacs originally was an acronym for Editor MACroS. RMS [Richard M. Stallman, founder of the Free Software Foundation] says he "picked the name Emacs because 'E' was not in use as an abbreviation on ITS at the time." The first Emacs was a set of macros written in 1976 at MIT by RMS for the editor TECO (Text Editor and COrrector, originally Tape Editor and COrrector) under ITS on a PDP-10. RMS had already extended TECO with a real-time full screen mode with reprogrammable keys. Emacs was started by Guy Steele as a project to unify the many divergent TECO command sets and key bindings at MIT, and completed by RMS.

In the popular mythology, however, Emacs has come to stand for escape-meta-alt-control-shift, referring to the complex key combinations to perform frequent commands shipped as the default. I like Emacs and once spent six weeks learning Emacs Lisp (the dialect of Lisp created specifically for the construction of Emacs) and customizing

Emacs expressly to suit my style of work. I actually prefer it to vi, but now that I must work on Windows machines as well as UNIX and Linux ones, I find that to use my custom keybindings, I need to invest substantial sums in keyboards, and it's just easier, and quite portable, to use vi.

To give you a view of what the default version looks like, however, Figure B.2 shows the version I occasionally run on my Windows machines.

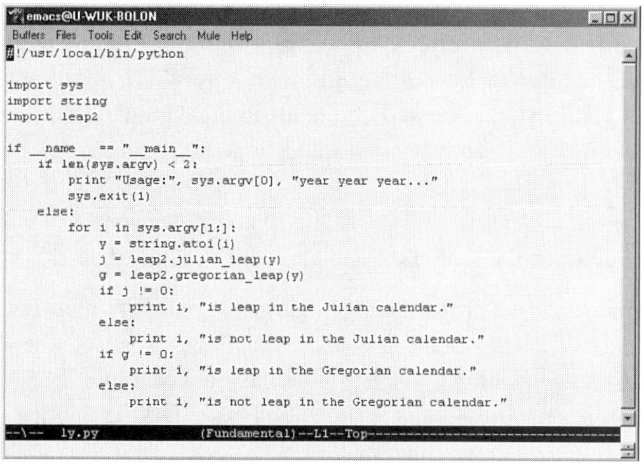

FIGURE B.2

Emacs editing a Python program.

```
emacs@U-WUK-BOLON
Buffers Files Tools Edit Search Mule Help
#!/usr/local/bin/python

import sys
import string
import leap2

if __name__ == "__main__":
    if len(sys.argv) < 2:
        print "Usage:", sys.argv[0], "year year year..."
        sys.exit(1)
    else:
        for i in sys.argv[1:]:
            y = string.atoi(i)
            j = leap2.julian_leap(y)
            g = leap2.gregorian_leap(y)
            if j != 0:
                print i, "is leap in the Julian calendar."
            else:
                print i, "is not leap in the Julian calendar."
            if g != 0:
                print i, "is leap in the Gregorian calendar."
            else:
                print i, "is not leap in the Gregorian calendar."
--\--  ly.py          (Fundamental)--L1--Top-----------------------------
```

Emacs, too, is also freeware. The best place to go for information on all aspects of Emacs care, feeding, and mythology is

`http://www.emacs.org/`

Xemacs

This editor, Xemacs, which is also freeware, is based on Emacs, initially on version 19 from the FSF. It purports to be "EMACS: The Next Generation." I don't run this myself, so no figures are included here, but many on the Python mailing list speak highly of it. The best place to go for downloading information is the home page at

`http://www.xemacs.org/`

Alpha

Alpha is a shareware editor for Macintosh; the shareware fee is quite reasonable, however, and again, many people speak very highly of it on the Python mailing list. Go to

`http://alpha.olm.net/`

for information. I don't have a Macintosh, so no figures are included here.

IDLE

IDLE comes with your Python distribution, but it may not be preinstalled for you on many Linux distributions. Even on the Red Hat distribution, which uses Python extensively in its configuration programs, IDLE is not installed by default. The reason is that IDLE became available beginning with Python 1.5.2, and Red Hat 5.2 distributes 1.5.1 (certainly a stable version, and all the examples and code in this book should work without change). Red Hat 6.0 and 6.1 come with 1.5.2, including IDLE, installed in /usr/bin.

I think that IDLE is worth the trouble of installing it, but many may not feel that way. On certain Linux distributions, for example, it is very difficult to get running. On Red Hat, you can build Python yourself, but to avoid breaking the Red Hat scripts, you need to install it into `/usr/bin` instead of the default `/usr/local/bin`; this is easily accomplished by specifying `./configure —prefix /usr/bin` when you run the configure script before compiling Python. If you have no idea what I'm talking about, it's probably best if you leave the Red Hat 5.2 Python 1.5.1 installed version in place.

The Windows installer for Python 1.5.2 gives you everything Python, plus IDLE, except that it doesn't make a desktop shortcut for IDLE. Refer to Hour 2 for instructions on how to make one yourself. Although you've seen lots of figures of IDLE in action in this book, IDLE's editor window is shown in Figure B.3, editing the same Python program previously shown in the other editors.

FIGURE B.3

IDLE editing a Python program.

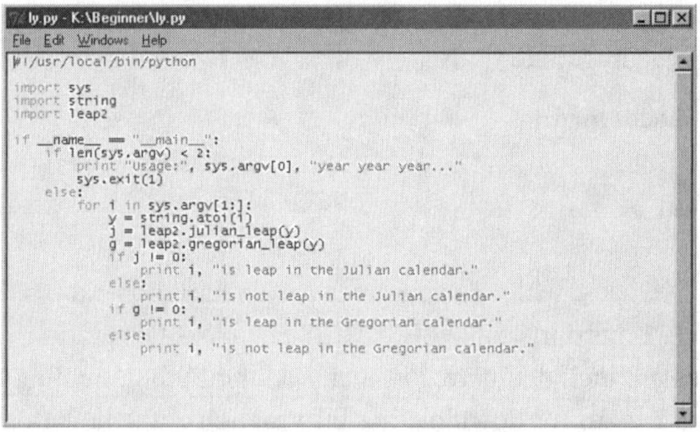

The usual place for Python information, including IDLE, is

`http://www.python.org/`

An extremely nice tutorial on IDLE, written by Daryl Harms, is available at

`http://www.python.org/doc/howto/idle/`

It combines color pictures with detailed explanations.

Appendix C

Reserved Words and Identifiers in Python

Reserved Words

Python won't allow you to use any of its reserved words as variable or function names. The following is the full list, with very brief explanations:

`and`

Logical `and`.

`assert`

Assert that some condition exists or is true.

`break`

Break out of a `while` or `for` loop.

`class`

Begin a class definition.

continue

Immediately go to top of `while` or `for` loop.

def

Begin a function definition.

del

Delete (destroy) following object.

elif

`if` clause.

else

`if` clause; also used with `for`, `while`, and `try`.

except

Execute following statements if `try` failed.

exec

Run Python code.

finally

Execute following statements if `try` succeeded.

for

Begin a `for` loop.

from

Begin a qualified `import` statement.

global

Look in global namespace ("module global") for following variable names.

if

`if` clause.

`import`

Find, read, and execute a module, allowing you access to the variables, functions, and classes within.

`in`

Membership in sequence.

`is`

Identity query.

`lambda`

Begin unnamed function definition.

`not`

Logical `not`.

`or`

Logical `or`.

`pass`

Do nothing.

`print`

Output.

`raise`

Notify of exceptional condition.

`return`

Exit function.

`try`

Try the following statements and see if they work.

`while`

Begin `while` loop.

Reserved Identifiers

Certain classes of identifiers (variable or function names) have special meanings. These are

`_`

This variable is used in the interactive interpreter mode *only*. When it exists, it stores the result of the last evaluation; the variable lives in the `__builtin__` module. If it does not exist, it has no special meaning and is not defined. Leave this one to Python.

`_*`

Any variable beginning with an underscore is not imported by `from module import *`. It's OK to create your own variables that begin with one underscore, but you should, by convention, use it only in the module where you created it.

`__*__`

Any name beginning and ending with two underscores is defined by Python: includes `__main__`, `__import__`, `__add__`, and so on. You can implement some of the functions yourself (see Appendix D), but never create variables with a name like this.

`__*`

Used in class-private name mangling; you won't really need this because it's a fairly advanced concept, but you can find out more about it at `http://www.python.org/`.

Built-in Names

The `__builtin__` module contains a minimum set of function names that you should never try to use, either as function names or variable names. You *can* redefine them, but you won't like the results. Redefining these names falls under the category of "things that ought not to be done." The following is the full list. Find out more at the usual place, `http://www.python.org/`.

`__import__()`

`abs()`

`apply()`

`buffer()`

`callable()`

`chr()`

`cmp()`

`coerce()`

`compile()`

`complex()`

`delattr()`

`dir()`

`divmod()`

`eval()`

`execfile()`

`filter()`

`float()`

`getattr()`

`globals()`

`hasattr()`

`hash()`

`hex()`

`id()`

`input()`

`intern()`

`int()`

`isinstance()`

`issubclass()`

`len()`

`list()`

`locals()`

`long()`

`map()`

`max()`

`min()`

`oct()`

`open()`

`ord()`

pow()

range()

raw_input()

reduce()

reload()

repr()

round()

setattr()

slice()

str()

tuple()

type()

vars()

xrange()

APPENDIX D

Special Class Methods in Python

Special class methods are an important feature of Python, making it an extremely flexible language. All user-defined classes may provide implementations of these methods, which are called or invoked whenever the appropriate action is called for by the Python interpreter. You'll find detailed discussion of all these methods in Chapter 13, "Special Class Methods in Python." What is listed here is intended only to jog your memory, not to provide a detailed explanation. Therefore, the methods are listed here in alphabetical order. A listing by use can be found at the official Python Reference Manual: `http://www.python.org/doc/current/ref/index.html`, Section 3.3. Each explanation is preceded by the general use of the method.

Note that in the following methods, when it says "return the result" or something like that, you need to create a new object to return. For instance, `x = x + y` uses *x* and *y* as inputs but creates a whole new object to return, which is assigned to *x* after the calculation is performed.

__abs__(*self*)

Numeric; return the absolute value of *self* (no sign).

__add__(*self*,*other*)

Numeric and sequence; add *self* to *other* or concatenate *self* and *other*, and return the result.

__and__(*self*,*other*)

Numeric; return the result of bitwise `and'ing (&)` *self* with *other*.

__call__(*self*[,*args*])

Class; if it makes sense to treat your class as a function, implement this method; *args* are optional.

__cmp__(*self*,*other*)

Class, others; called by all comparison operations. Return `-1` if *self* is < *other*, `0` if *self* and *other* are equal, and `1` if *self* is > than *other*.

__coerce__(*self*,*other*)

Numeric; called whenever *self* and *other* must be converted to a common type for some sort of arithmetic operation. Usually, you convert *other* to an instance of your class, although you could convert your class to whatever type *other* is. Return a tuple: (*self*,*other*).

__complex__(*self*)

Numeric; if your class can be converted to a complex number, return that complex equivalent.

__del__(*self*)

Class; called when an instance of your class is about to be destroyed. Lots of gotchas; see Chapter 13 for details.

__delattr__(*self*,*name*)

Access; called when `del object.`*name* is called.

__delitem__(*self*,*key*)

Sequence and mapping; called when `del object[`*key*`]` is called.

__delslice__(*self*,*i*,*j*)

Sequence and mapping; called when `del object[`*i*:*j*`]` is called.

__div__(*self*,*other*)

Numeric; divide *self* by *other* and return the result.

__divmod__(*self*,*other*)

Numeric; divide *self* by *other* and return a tuple of the result and the remainder.

__float__(*self*)

Numeric; if your class can be converted to a floating point number, return that floating point equivalent.

__getattr__(*self*,*name*)

Access; called only if `object.`*`attribute`* lookup fails. Return the value of *attribute* or raise `AttributeError`.

__getitem__(*self*,*key*)

Sequence and mapping; called when a call to `object[`*`key`*`]` is made. Keys are usually integers; negative index implementation must be done in this method if your class supports it.

__getslice__(*self*,*i*,*j*)

Sequence and mapping; called when a call to `object[`*`i:j`*`]` is made. Both *i* and *j* are integers; negative index implementation is up to this method.

__hash__(*self*)

Class; return a 32-bit value that can be used as a hash index. Called by using your class object as a key for a dictionary and by the built-in *hash()* function. If your class is mutable, do not implement the `__hash__` method.

__hex__(*self*)

Numeric; return a string representing the hexadecimal equivalent of your class.

__init__(*self*[,*args*])

Class; called when an instance of your class is created. The *args* optional.

__int__(*self*)

Numeric; if your class can be converted to an integer, return that integer equivalent.

__invert__(*self*)

Numeric; return the result of a bitwise `invert` operation `(~)`.

D

`__len__(self)`

Sequence and mapping; called by built-in function `len()`. Return the length of your class, however you want to define it.

`__long__(self)`

Numeric; if your class can be converted to a long integer, return that long integer equivalent.

`__lshift__(self,other)`

Numeric; return the result of performing a left-shift (`<<`) by *`other`* bits or units on your class, but only if it makes sense.

`__mod__(self,other)`

Numeric; divide *`self`* by *`other`* and return the remainder.

`__mul__(self,other)`

Numeric; multiply *`self`* times *`other`* and return the result.

`__neg__(self)`

Numeric; perform the equivalent of multiplying your class times -1 and return the result.

`__nonzero__(self)`

Class; return `0` or `1` for truth testing. `if` *`your instance`*`:` expressions, and so on.

`__oct__(self)`

Numeric; return a string containing an octal representation of your class.

`__or__(self,other)`

Numeric; perform the equivalent of a bitwise `or` operation (`|`) on your class and return the result.

`__pos__(self)`

Numeric; perform the equivalent of multiplying your class times `1`. This is the *`identity`* operation.

`__pow__(self,other[,modulo])`

Numeric; perform the equivalent of exponentiating *`self`* to the *`other`* power. If the *`modulo`* argument is provided, perform `(`*`self`*` ** `*`other`*`) % `*`modulo`*.

`__radd__(self,other)`

Numeric; add `self` and `other` and return result. Called for, for example, `1 + class` instead of `class + 1`.

`__rand__(self,other)`

Numeric; return the result of bitwise `and'ing (&) self` with `other`. Called when left operand is not an instance of your class.

`__rdiv__(self,other)`

Numeric; divide `self` by `other` and return the result. Called when left operand is not an instance of your class.

`__rdivmod__(self,other)`

Numeric; divide `self` by `other` and return a tuple of the result and the remainder. Called when left operand is not an instance of your class.

`__repr__(self)`

Class; called by the `repr()` built-in function and string conversions (backquotes). By convention, this is supposed to return a string that can be used later to re-create the class instance.

`__rlshift__(self,other)`

Numeric; return the result of performing a left-shift `(<<)` by `other` bits or units on your class, but only if it makes sense. Called when left operand is not an instance of your class.

`__rmod__(self,other)`

Numeric; divide `self` by `other` and return the remainder. Called when left operand is not an instance of your class.

`__rmul__(self,other)`

Numeric; multiply `self` times `other` and return the result. Called when left operand is not an instance of your class.

`__ror__(self,other)`

Numeric; perform the equivalent of a bitwise `or` operation (`|`) on your class and return the result. Called when left operand is not an instance of your class.

__rpow__(*self*,*other*)

Numeric; perform the equivalent of exponentiating `self` to the *other* power. No r-equivalent to `pow_(self,other[,modulo])`. Called when left operand is not an instance of your class.

__rrshift__(*self*,*other*)

Numeric; return the result of performing a right-shift (>>) by *other* bits or units on your class, but only if it makes sense. Called when left operand is not an instance of your class.

__rshift__(*self*,*other*)

Numeric; return the result of performing a right-shift (>>) by *other* bits or units on your class, but only if it makes sense.

__rsub__(*self*,*other*)

Numeric; subtract *other* from `self` and return the result. Called when left operand is not an instance of your class.

__rxor__(*self*,*other*)

Numeric; perform the equivalent of a bitwise `xor` operation (^) on your class and return the result. Called when left operand is not an instance of your class.

__setattr__(*self*,*name*,*value*)

Access; called when an attempt to assign `object.attribute = value` is made. When implementing this, insert the value in the dictionary of instance attributes: `self.__dict__[name] = value`.

__setitem__(*self*,*key*,*value*)

Sequence and mapping; called when an attempt to assign `object[key] = value` is made. Keys are usually integers.

__setslice__(*self*,*i*,*j*,*sequence*)

Sequence and mapping; called when an attempt to assign `object[i:j] = sequence` is made. Keys are usually integers.

__str__(*self*)

Class; called by the *str()* built-in function and by the *print* statement (also the % formatting expression); should return a string, but it's not required to be an actual Python expression in the same way that the return value of `__repr__` is supposed to be.

`__sub__(self,other)`

Numeric; subtract `other` from `self` and return the result.

`__xor__(self,other)`

Numeric; perform the equivalent of a bitwise `xor` operation (^) on your class and return the result.

APPENDIX E

Other Python Resources

Almost everything you want to know about Python can be found at the following Web site:

`http://www.python.org/`

If you are searching for Python code, extension modules and importable modules, the best place to start your search is The Vaults of Parnassus at `http://www.vex.net/parnassus/`. In addition to an excellent search engine, modules and packages are indexed by topic.

However, a few other sites are also interesting, and a few pages at `www.python.org` deserve special mention.

Python for the Atari:

`http://www.qnx.com/~chrish/Atari/MiNT/python.html`

Macintosh Python Resources:

`http://www.cwi.nl/~jack/macpython.html`

The Macintosh page describes features of the Python distribution that are available only on Macintosh, including Just van Rossum's Integrated Development Environment, which includes an editor, a debugger, and a class browser.

Python implemented in Java:

`http://www.jpython.org//`

A Python tutorial by Aaron Watters:

`http://www.networkcomputing.com/unixworld/tutorial/005/005.html`

Starship Python:

`http://starship.python.net/`

Starship Python is the place where members of the PSA (Python Software Activity) can get free Web space and can post their modules and extensions for Python for free download. The site contains lots of interesting and useful modules.

Join the PSA at

`http://www.python.org/psa/`

Numerical Python and Python at the Lawrence Livermore National Laboratories:

`http://xfiles.llnl.gov/python.htm`

Python and the sciences:

`http://www.python.org/topics/scicomp/`

All the Python mailing lists can be found at the following site:

`http://www.python.org/psa/MailingLists.html`

A commercial site, but very interesting projects, nonetheless:

`http://www.pythonware.com/`

Non-English resources for the Pythonista:

`http://www.python.org/doc/NonEnglish.html`

Finally, the most up-to-date, official documentation should always be available at

`http://www.python.org/doc/`

In addition, Appendix A, "Selected Bibliography," in this book provides a listing of Python and related books to which you can refer.

INDEX

Symbols

A

B

E

F

G

H

M

N

O

Q

R

S

T

U

V

W

X-Y-Z